Discourses of Endangerment

D1334436

Discourses of Endangerment

Ideology and Interest in the Defence of Languages

Edited by Alexandre Duchêne and Monica Heller

continuum

Continuum
The Tower Building
11 York Road
London SE1 7NX

80 Maiden Lane
Suite 704
New York, NY 10038

British Library Cataloguing-in-Publication Data
A catalogue record for this book is available from the British Library.

ISBN: HB: 0–8264–8745–9

Typeset by Fakenham Photosetting Limited, Fakenham, Norfolk
Printed and bound in Great Britain by Biddles Ltd, King's Lynn, Norfolk

Contents

Notes on Contributors   vii

⟩ Chapter 1: Discourses of endangerment: Sociolinguistics, globalization and social order   1
Monica Heller and Alexandre Duchêne

✗ Chapter 2: Defending diversity: Staking out a common global interest?   14
Shaylih Muehlmann

⟨ Chapter 3: Indigenous language endangerment and the unfinished business of nation states   35
Donna Patrick

Chapter 4: Discourses of endangerment: Contexts and consequences of essentializing discourses   57
Alexandra Jaffe

Chapter 5: Who wants to save 'le patois d'Évolène'?   76
Raphaël Maître and Marinette Matthey

Chapter 6: *Français, acadien, acadjonne*: Competing discourses on language preservation along the shores of the Baie Sainte-Marie   99
Annette Boudreau and Lise Dubois

Chapter 7: The future of Catalan: Language endangerment and nationalist discourses in Catalonia   121
Joan Pujolar

Chapter 8: Language endangerment, war and peace in Ireland and Northern Ireland   149
Tony Crowley

Chapter 9: Voices of endangerment: A language ideological debate on the Swedish language   169
Tommaso M. Milani

Chapter 10: Defending English in an English-dominant world: The Ideology of the 'Official English' movement in the United States   197
Ronald Schmidt, Sr.

Chapter 11: Protecting French: The view from France   216
  Claudine Moïse

Chapter 12: Embracing diversity for the sake of unity:
Linguistic hegemony and the pursuit of total Spanish   242
  José del Valle

Chapter 13: Language endangerment and verbal hygiene:
History, morality and politics   268
  Deborah Cameron

Index   286

Notes on Contributors

Annette Boudreau
Département d'études françaises
Université de Moncton
Moncton, NB
Canada E1A 3E9
boudrean@umoncton.ca

Deborah Cameron
Rupert Murdoch Chair of Language and Communication
Oxford University
Worcester College
Oxford OX1 2HB
UK
deborah.cameron@worc.ox.ac.uk

Tony Crowley
Harley Burr Alexander Chair in the Humanities
Scripps College
Claremont
CA91711
USA
tcrowley@scrippscollege.edu

José del Valle
Ph.D. Program in Hispanic and Luso-Brazilian Literatures and
Languages
Ph.D. Program in Linguistics
The Graduate Center – The City University of New York
365 Fifth Avenue
New York, NY 10016
USA
jdelvalle@gc.cuny.edu

Alexandre Duchêne
Allgemeine Sprachwissenschaft
Universität Basel
Totengässlein 3
4051 Basel
Switzerland
alexandre.duchene@unibas.ch

Lise Dubois
Département de traduction et des langues
Université de Moncton
Moncton, NB
Canada E1A 3E9
duboisl@umoncton.ca

Alexandra Jaffe
Department of Linguistics
California State University, Long Beach
1250 Bellflower Blvd, Long Beach, CA 90840
USA
ajaffe@csulb.edu

Monica Heller
CREFO/OISE
University of Toronto
252 Bloor Street West
Toronto, Ontario
Canada M5S 1V6
mheller@oise.utoronto.ca

Raphaël Maître
Centre de dialectologie et d'étude du fançais regional
Université de Neuchâtel
Avenue du Peyrou
2000 Neuchâtel
Switzerland
raphael.maitre@unine.ch

Marinette Matthey
Laboratoire LIDILEM
Université de Stendhal Grenoble 3
BP 25
38040 Grenoble CEDEX 9
France
marinette.matthey@u-grenoble3.fr

Tommaso M. Milani
Centre for Research on Bilingualism
Stockholm University
106 91 Stockholm
Sweden
tommaso.milani@biling.su.se

Claudine Moïse
Centre d'études canadiennes d'Avignon et du Vaucluse (CECAV)
Université d'Avignon et des Pays de Vaucluse
74, rue Louis Pasteur
84029 Avignon cedex 01
France
claudine.moise@univ-avignon.fr

Shaylih Muehlmann
Department of Anthropology
University of Toronto
100 St. George Street
Toronto, Ontario
Canada M5S 3G3
shaylih.muehlmann@utoronto.ca

Donna Patrick
School of Canadian Studies/Sociology and Anthropology
Carleton University
1125 Colonel By Drive
Ottawa, Ontario
Canada K1S 5B6
dpatrick@connect.carleton.ca

Joan Pujolar
Estudis d'Humanitas i Filologia
Universitat Oberta de Catalunya
Av. Tibidabo 39–43
08035 Barcelona
Spain
jpujolar@uoc.edu

Ronald Schmidt, Sr.
Political Science Department
California State University, Long Beach
1250 Bellflower Blvd, Long Beach
CA 90840-4605
USA
rschmidt@csulb.edu

1 Discourses of endangerment: Sociolinguistics, globalization and social order

Monica Heller and Alexandre Duchêne

Discourses of endangerment

The text below appeared on UNESCO's website in 2006 :

> International Mother Language Day (21 February 2006)
> The world's nearly 6,000 languages will be celebrated on International Mother Language Day, an event aimed at promoting linguistic diversity and multilingual education.
> Ensuring that these languages can continue in use alongside the major international languages of communication is a genuine challenge to countries worldwide.
> Today, about half of the 6,000 or so languages spoken in the world are under threat.
> (http://portal.unesco.org/education/en/ev.php-URL_ID=27387&URL_DO=DO_TOPIC&URL_SECTION=-279.html [accessed 1 February 2006])

This is but one of many examples of similar texts which appear frequently in this early twenty-first century period, citing the number of languages in the world today (figures vary, but at the time of writing texts seem to have settled on a figure somewhere between 5,000 and 6,000) and the proportion which are deemed likely to disappear (here half, elsewhere somewhat more), sometimes with an estimate of the amount of time it will take for them to do so (20, 50, 100 years). Many of these texts are indeed produced by UNESCO and agencies it funds; others are produced by academics, non-governmental organizations (NGOs), state agencies and journalists. They can be found circulating in a number of spaces, from academic conferences and publications, to state-sponsored events, to the public intellectual press (the *New Yorker* devoted an article to the question in 2005) to your daily newspaper. Generally speaking, when they have a focus at all, they concern so-called 'small' languages, that is, languages with a small number of speakers, frequently indigenous.

Many of these texts go on to explain why this phenomenon should be considered of concern. There are several main tropes (cf. the focus issue of the *Journal of Linguistic Anthropology* 2002). The first is that languages each contain unique features, and if we are to arrive at an adequate understanding of what language is and how it works, we must be careful to preserve the range of forms and features present in our current array, and seek to reconstruct the nature of languages already lost, to the best of our ability. (In many ways, this argument can be seen as lying in continuity with the Boasian North American tradition of descriptive linguistics – cf. Darnell (2001) – insofar as it takes a position against hierarchical and evolutionary theories of language, and for theories which place all languages on an equal footing in terms of their contribution to universal understandings of human linguistic and cultural capacities.) A broader version of this argument, which parallels the ties between Boasian and Sapirian approaches to linguistics, is that each language represents a unique worldview and unique forms of knowledge, such that the loss of a language is equivalent to a collective loss of knowledge about the world (and in this respect, this argument resonates with various versions of the Sapir–Whorf hypothesis, which can be glossed as proposing that cultural knowledge is 'encoded' in some way in linguistic form).

Both these forms of argumentation legitimate their position by appealing to one or both of two overarching ways of understanding linguistic diversity. One links linguistic diversity to biodiversity, arguing that preserving the diversity of the world's languages is as good for the cultural environment as biodiversity is for the material one (cf. Mühlhäusler 1996; stronger versions of this argument hold that linguistic and biological diversity are actually organically linked, since knowledge about the environment is encoded in language; cf. Maffi 2001). The other constructs linguistic diversity as part of the world's cultural heritage. Finally, all these arguments are mustered in a political version of this position, which holds that speakers have the right to protect their language against the incursion of more powerful ones (Skutnabb-Kangas 2000).

Our purpose here is to take some critical distance from this explosion of discursive material, and ask : why this? why now? Partly, this seems to us to be an important thing to remember to do any time there are mass waves of enthusiasm for any particular discourse, whether it concerns language or anything else. In addition, as socio-linguists, we want to ask why language in particular seems to have a hold not only on the imaginations of linguists (from whom you'd

2

expect such a degree of interest), but on those of other kinds of actors, ranging from the King of Spain to local ecologists to pharmaceutical companies.

This is, then, most definitely not a book which takes UNESCO's (and others') affirmations at face value. We aren't sure there are 6,000 languages in the world; we aren't even sure how you can count languages. We are curious about what it means to say a language 'dies' or 'disappears': what happened to change? We wonder, instead, why these formulations are so common; why people are comfortable with the basic premises of the arguments (that there are x number of languages and that y% of them will disappear in z years); why explanations of why this 'fact' should be of public concern take the form they do. We ask, in the end, what this is really all about, and why it matters to so many people. We also ask what the consequences are, and for whom, of formulating things in this way.

This necessarily also means asking questions about our own roles as producers of discourse in this field. While this is always a relevant question to ask, it becomes even more salient when language issues are prominent in public debate, and academics are called upon to provide expert discourses, to take positions, and, frequently, to take action. At the same time, the issue arises of where the discourse of language endangerment in fact originated; certainly the discipline of linguistics has been centrally implicated in its production and circulation. Linguists and anthropologists not only use the field of language endangerment as a place to affirm expertise and professional, technical knowledge but also to legitimize their disciplines in terms of the social relevance of their fields. The book therefore also aims to interrogate current practices of linguistic expertise, in order to gain some purchase on understanding the consequences of our own actions. This does require a certain amount of deconstruction of what have become naturalized assumptions about language endangerment and about what we as sociolinguists ought to be doing about it, bearing in mind of course that there are many different kinds of stakeholders (see Jaffe, Matthey and Maître, Milani and Muehlmann, this volume).

In order to try to address our questions, we have taken a multipronged approach, with the involvement of a number of scholars (and scholar-activists) who are familiar with different parts of the territory. Our central means of approach centre around the organizing concepts of *ideology* and *interest*. We understand this discursive space to centrally involve specific ideologies of language. For example, for any of this to make sense, minimally, languages have to be understood as things we can count, and as bounded (if internally variable) spaces independent in some way of other forms of social practice. So we ask

3

what the ideological dimensions of this discourse are: What ideologies of language are involved? Are there struggles over them ? What other ideologies (of nation state, of indigeneity, of evolution, of social justice, of gender, of class, and so on) are involved? Next, we ask what is at stake in these discursive practices? Who stands to gain or lose what by the production or reproduction of ideological complexes around language endangerment? In whose interest is it to promote or contest such discourses?

Most importantly we have attended to the idea of *endangerment*. Inspired by Cameron's work on verbal hygiene (Cameron 1995 and this volume), we have taken the position that discourses of language endangerment are fundamentally discourses about other kinds of threats which take place, for specific reasons, on the terrain of language. The linguistic order is a space which is partly constitutive of the social order, and the moral order which regulates it. Often, the linguistic moral panic involves the quality of language (no one knows how to spell anymore, no one respects grammar, teenage girls use 'like' too much, people use too much 'uptalk', that is, question intonation for declarative utterances, and so on); while such elements certainly feature in the discourses we examine here, two other concerns loom larger, that is, the lexical purity of languages and their boundaries. The threat is to the very existence of languages (from 6,000 we go to 5,999 to 5,998 and ever lower), and requires attention to signs of incursions, understood as virus-like attacks on the essence of the languages in question which necessarily undermine their health and potentially lead to their demise.

There is, then, an investment in a social order in which a specific form of diversity remains stable. We argue that discourses of language endangerment are discourses about some broader sense of endangerment, about some threat from outside (from some Other) to the social order; at the same time, that threat discourse, for reasons that we need to discover, is produced and managed on the terrain of language. The particular form that this discourse takes revolves around the maintenance of a stable set of relations among units which are at once formally similar (all languages attached to a set of speakers, a set of values, an encyclopedia of knowledge), and radically different from each other (each set of values and of forms of knowledge being unique). The moral dimensions involved concern claims to universal ideas about social justice based on the contribution of diversity to all humanity, as long as diversity takes one particular (universal) shape. Nonetheless, the availability of the discourse can allow for forms of contestation that create new grounds of struggle, especially where ideologies of language cast it in a central role in the construction of meaning and of social organization.

4

Having said that, casting a cursory glance around where discourses of endangerment appear allows us to note that, while much of the discourse indeed focuses on 'small' languages, we can find similar (and sometimes identical) arguments appearing regarding most of the world's 'large' languages, indeed the very 'glottophagic' languages (to use Calvet's term; Calvet 1979) most language endangerment discourse targets as the bulldozer languages of the world. In this volume, we have assembled texts about four of them: Swedish, Spanish, French and, Public Enemy No. 1, US English. This fact alone gives us pause: there must be something else going on than linguistic McDonaldization if exactly the same discourse is used in the defence of English, and say, Ladino, Peul or Cree.

We conclude from this that this particular moral panic is at least in part about the management of diversity. Now, this is not a new problem for social organization; minorities have long been a problem for nation states, as nation states have been for the minorities they construct, whether through internal or extra-boundary colonialism. For many years, however, that tension took the form of struggles over political rights and political structures (Hobsbawm 1990). Indeed in academic discourse we find a long history of studies of language policy and language planning, and of language maintenance and shift which reflect that essentially political and national understanding of linguistic diversity (Rubin and Jernudd 1971; Fishman 1991; Spolsky 2004). In the 1990s, Skutnabb-Kangas and others began to reformulate this struggle in universal terms of human rights (Skutnabb-Kangas 2000), and shortly afterwards there began to appear arguments casting concerns in different terms altogether. On the political front, discourse has turned away from human rights, and towards the technical means for the establishment of consensual spaces (see Schmidt, this volume). Discourse of minority (and notably indigenous) rights is increasingly accompanied by an equally universalizing discourse framed in terms of the contributions of linguistic diversity to ecological balance and to a collective scientific and cultural heritage (see Muehlmann, this volume). Finally, an entirely new framework has appeared, one which casts language as a neutral space assuring access to global markets (see del Valle, this volume).

That the new discursive orientations should have appeared in the mid-1990s makes sense if we understand that period as being one of consolidation of a globalized new economy based on services and information (in which, of course, language is central), but in which nation states continue to play an important role. Existing nation states, and existing minority and indigenous movements, have a stake in reproducing their boundaries, as a central means of controlling access

5

to the production and circulation of resources with which they seek to maintain privileged relationships. At the same time, there is room for new actors, notably supranational agencies (such as UNESCO, which has been particularly active in the production of the language endangerment discourse) and paragovernmental agencies they fund (such as Mercator, EBLUL, Linguapax), and NGOs, which may or may not be linked to other interests, such as religious or commercial ones. The current panic seems therefore to be a version of the old problem of how to divide up the world's resources among constituted groups, but with two new issues to be faced: 1) what is the basis of collective constitution of the groups in question? In the past states went to war and signed treaties, carving up desired territory and populations among themselves. While that practice has not entirely disappeared, it is contested by the claims of the carved and by those of new carvers, less interested in the mediation of the state than they formerly were; and (2) what discursive regimes render such activities legitimate? The *mission civilisatrice* no longer convinces.

Language ideology and (national) interest

In the next section we will outline some of the ways the chapters in this volume approach the question we are asking. We suggest that we first need to understand the discursive construction of 'language endangerment': how is it described, how is it legitimized, and by whom? That is, in whose interest is it to mobilize resources around the defence of languages, and why?

We then go on to argue that when we look at the ways in which such discourses actually construct the image of threat and develop protective strategies, we see a degree of spread and complexity greater than we usually tend to imagine. It looks like it is possible to set up a discourse of endangerment under multiple conditions of relations of power: we hear it as much about so-called majority languages as we do about so-called minority or indigenous languages and often at the same time; in addition, sometimes we fail to hear it under conditions where one would think it would be available. It is not therefore in any straightforward sense about specific forms of inequality. Instead, in our last section, we suggest that it may have more to do with the management of diversity within the framework of the opportunities and dangers presented by the globalized new economy.

As we suggested above, the central element of the construction of the problem is the concept of danger. Here the source and target of danger is language constructed as an organic, systematic whole, which has a life of its own outside of social practice. Indeed a frequent critique of language endangerment discourse is that it displaces concerns with speakers on to a concern with languages (Blommaert 2001; Heller 2004). For us this point flags the importance of exploring the reason why this displacement occurs: it is the beginning of understanding the ways in which an ideology of language as organic is tied to ideologies of culture and nation. That is, part of what is going on here has to do with attempts to maintain the language–culture–nation ideological nexus. In this frame, talking about language rather than speakers makes perfect sense, especially since speakers can change language (but languages need speakers). This puts us on the path of understanding the importance of an ideological complex in which language figures centrally but is not the only element. This is about more than essentializing languages, it is about the reproduction of the central legitimating ideology of the nation state.

The chapters in this volume show that the effort to maintain this discursive complex is widespread. It is adopted in a number of different spaces. Nonetheless it is clear that the agents of these discourses are for the most part the same kind of agent that has long been active in the production and reproduction of nationalist or quasi-nationalist language ideologies: lexicographers, grammarians, linguists, journalists, anthropologists, educators and government functionaries. For example, Pujolar discusses the circulation of this discourse in the Catalan media; Jaffe and Crowley talk about the mobilization of schooling as a site of protection of endangered languages; Boudreau and Dubois discuss the role of both media and schooling in a francophone community in eastern Canada; Milani, Jaffe, Muehlmann and Maître and Matthey describe the sometimes uncomfortable involvement of linguists and anthropologists in the language advocacy movement, while Crowley and Pujolar evoke the role of historians and grammarians outside the academy; finally, Patrick analyses state discourses with respect to indigenous languages in Canada. Having said that, modernist producers of discourses of language rights and of linguistic autonomy and homogeneity were generally in the service of the state and its agencies; while this is sometimes still the case, Muehlmann points out that contemporary discourses of language endangerment are increasingly produced by international or transnational agencies. The most important international agency is clearly UNESCO and other agencies to whose funding it contributes (Unesco Chair for Research on Language Endangerment, Linguapax). At the same time, a number of largely university-driven NGOs have also appeared since the mid-1990s. Finally, we find the discourse of endangerment among transnational indigenous mobilization movements, as Patrick points out.

And while none of the contributors to this volume addresses the question directly, we also note the historical continuity in the role of transnational religious organizations in the kind of descriptive linguistics which has played an important, if complex, role in colonialism (Fabian 1986; Bitterli 1989; Meeuwis 1999; Patrick 2003), and which now is often part of activism in the endangered languages movement. One central example is the Summer Institute of Linguistics (SIL), founded in 1934; the SIL is currently a member of the language endangerment NGO Terralingua and hosts the NGO's language archive on its website.[1]

Taken together, these examples demonstrate that what we are seeing is in part a reshaping of old discourses by the same actors, but also in part the emergence of new international and transnational discursive spaces where these discourses are being produced (Muehlmann and Duchêne, in press). The political economy which produced the institutions of linguistics and anthropology is shifting, but not metamorphizing beyond recognition. Rather, existing discourses and their institutional bases (and major proponents) lay the basis for reorientation under contemporary conditions.

In a similar vein, while we tend to think of language endangerment discourses as being about marginalized languages, we can see a number of threads of historical continuity that allow us to understand why this discourse appears as often with respect to so-called dominant languages as with respect to marginalized ones. Although work on language maintenance and language shift has clearly focused on minorization, it nonetheless took up the same ideas of boundedness and purity that have long characterized nationalist ideologies of language. The question remains as to how to explain the appropriation of language endangerment discourses by supposedly dominant languages. We return to this question below.

First let us look at what the articles show us: many articles do deal with language endangerment discourses where you would expect to find them. Pujolar, Jaffe and Crowley, in examining Catalan, Corsican and Gaelic respectively, show the emergence (and occasional non-emergence) of language endangerment discourses with respect to quasi-nation language minorities, in which the danger is located in perceived pressure from a centralizing nation state (Spain, France, Britain). Matthey and Maître discuss the *patois d'Evolène*, a remnant of linguistic variability under homogenizing pressure from a standardizing language (in this case French); this case has parallels in the situation of Nova Scotia *acadjonne* described by Boudreau and Dubois, although here there is double threat from both French and English. Patrick and Muehlmann discuss the position of the indigenous languages of the Americas.

On the other hand, other contributors point out the multiple ways in which a discourse of language endangerment is used in defence of precisely the same languages constructed as a source of danger in the previous cases. All these cases allow us to recognize the complex positioning involved. This is perhaps most fully described in Milani's chapter on Sweden, which shows how politicians and linguists together construct Swedish in opposition to both indigenous and immigrant minorities, on the one hand, and English on the other. Swedish as a national language is thus held to be in need of protection from the outside, that is, from the threat of English as an international language, and from the inside, from its own minorities. Moïse and Schmidt both take up the problem of the national language under threat from inside with respect to France's construction of its immigrant minorities, and discourses of protection of US English with respect to the incursion of Spanish. Del Valle takes up another dimension with respect to Spanish which could be equally applied to French and to English as international languages. He discusses the continuity between Spain's need to construct Spanish as unitary and hegemonic on the territory of Spain (as opposed to Basque, Catalan or Galician resistance), and Spain's attempts to position itself as hegemon in a transnational and globalized space in which its authority could be attacked both by English and by other claimants to the position of Spanish hegemon, notably from Latin America.

What this volume shows is, first, that the discourse of language endangerment is not simply about any obvious criteria of inequality: it is used as much in cases in which languages are constructed through a powerful centralized state and its agencies (e.g. the legal system), as in cases where weak institutional structures are involved; it is used in cases where it is possible to claim huge numbers of speakers as much as in cases where there are very few. Second, it becomes clear that language endangerment discourses are not in any straightforward sense about the actual disappearance of languages: English, French and Spanish are scarcely likely to disappear off the planet anytime soon. Third, in the face of these cases, it is difficult to maintain arguments about the inherent coding of knowledge in languages and of humanity's heritage when we are dealing with languages for which we have ample evidence of institutionalization and change. So what is it all about? In our final section we will lay out some lines of thought emerging out of the chapters in this volume and which afford us some purchase on alternative understandings of discourses of language endangerment.

The spectre of globalization

Del Valle points out that a discourse of language endangerment emerges in Spain precisely at the moment when Spain must compete on a world market. This first requires a consolidation of the national market, already a long-standing problem. At the same time, while Spain can no longer mobilize the structures of empire, it *can* mobilize the legacy of empire, and attempt to construct an international Spanish-speaking market in which Spain can manoeuvre for a dominant position. This market has the potential to place Spanish (and in particular Spain as a source of Spanish) advantageously both with respect to English and with respect to other sources of Spanish speakers. But because the globalized new economy has no place for a legitimizing discourse of political coercion, Spain aligns itself with what *does* form the new bases of discursive legitimacy: Spanish as a neutral language of communication, of harmonious transnational encounter, of anything but ethno-national affiliation. This case provides us with two keys. First it reminds us that we are still within the discursive regime of the nation state. Nation states themselves remain actors concerned to retain their privileges on an increasingly globalizing, mobile and diversified stage. Nation states retain their central role in the construction and protection of markets for their own bourgeoisie; however, whereas in the past those markets were primarily national, they now increasingly require a focus on positioning national markets on the international scene.

The threat for the nation state is therefore double: it must protect its internal coherence (increasingly under threat from both local and immigrant sources of diversity), and they must protect themselves with respect to other strong actors on the world stage. At the same time, resistance movements which have long existed within this discursive regime remain equally tied to a certain dimension of it, notably the construction of homogeneity. However, as in the case of nation states, it is no longer adequate to appeal to political legitimizing discourses; in order to preserve the gains of the mobilization movement which created them, it is now necessary to situate themselves within new legitimizing discourses which make sense in the context of globalization: among these we find tropes of biodiversity and of contributions to the world's collective heritage.

One way, then, to understand the emergence of discourses of language endangerment in the 1990s is to situate them in the context of the problems and opportunities presented to nation states, and to the minorities they created, by the globalized new economy (in much the same way as Romanticism can be understood as both resisting and contributing to the construction of modernist nation states). In some cases we may be dealing with modernist reactions against globalization, that is, desperate attempts to save nationalism (whether of majority or minority variety) in the face of processes which may threaten the ability of national structures to reproduce themselves or to achieve their traditional goals. At the same time, we may also be witnessing attempts on the part of structures inherited from modernist nationalism and the minority resistance movements it engendered to position themselves advantageously with respect to the opportunities the globalized new economy affords. If we return to the case of Spain, as Del Valle points out, recasting Spanish as a neutral language of communication and encounter both allows Spain to retain a privileged position under new conditions and also allows it to move away from responsibility for problems caused by its colonial and postcolonial adventures.

Let us close with a consideration of the implications of this argument for our work as linguists and anthropologists. We understand our disciplines as emerging from the development of the nation state, as centrally implicated in the construction and propagation of national languages, and in the quasi-nationalist movements of resistance which appropriated the dominant discourse and turned it against the centralizing and colonizing nation state (Bauman and Briggs 2003). Linguistics and anthropology have contributed both to hierarchizing regimes which construct inequality, among them Nazism (Hutton 1999), and to universalizing counter-discourses aiming at equality. The discourse of language endangerment situates itself in the latter tradition, while adopting many of the features of theories of language and culture (essentialism, organicism, homogeneism) which are available for the construction of inequality based on difference. If we understand this discourse as fundamentally being about concerns to retain collective identity (based on modernist ideologies of identity) and to advance collective interest under conditions which make competition more salient and more available, this requires us to rethink the reasons why we hold onto the ideas about language and identity which emerged from modernity. Rather than assuming we must save languages, perhaps we should be asking instead who benefits and who loses from understanding languages the way we do, what is at stake for whom, and how and why language serves as a terrain for competition.

References

Bauman, R. and Briggs, C. (2003), *Voices of Modernity: Language Ideologies and the Politics of Inequality*, Cambridge: Cambridge University Press.

11

Bitterli, U. (1989), *Cultures in Conflict: Contact Between European and Non-European Cultures, 1492–1800*. Stanford: Stanford University Press.

Blommaert, J. (2001), 'The Asmara Declaration as sociolinguistic problem: reflections on scholarship and linguistic rights'. *Journal of Sociolinguistics* 5, (1), 131–42.

Calvet, L. J. (1979), *Linguistique et Colonialisme: Petit Traité de Glottophagie*. Paris: Payot.

Cameron, D. (1995), *Verbal Hygiene*. London: Routledge.

Darnell, R. (2001), *Invisible Genealogies: A History of Americanist Anthropology*. Lincoln, NB: University of Nebraska Press.

Fabian, J. (1986), *Language and Colonial Power*. Cambridge: Cambridge University Press.

Fishman, J. (1991), Reversing Language Shift. Clevedon, UK: Multilingual Matters.

Heller, M. (2004), 'Analysis and stance regarding language and social justice', in: D. Patrick and J. Freeland (eds), *Language Rights and Language Survival: Sociolinguistic and Sociocultural Perspectives*. Manchester, UK: St. Jerome, pp. 283–6.

Hobsbawm, E. (1990), *Nations and Nationalism since 1760*. Cambridge: Cambridge University Press.

Hutton, C. (1999), *Linguistics and the Third Reich: Mother-Tongue Fascism, Race and the Science of Language*. London: Routledge.

Journal of Linguistic Anthropology, 2002, 12, 2.

Maffi, L. (ed.) (2001), *On Biocultural Diversity: Linking Language, Knowledge and the Environment*. Washington, DC: Smithsonian Institution Press.

Meeuwis, M. (1999), 'Flemish nationalism in the Belgian Congo versus Zairean anti-imperialism: continuity and discontinuity in language ideological debates', in J. Blommaert (ed.), *Language Ideological Debates*. Berlin: Mouton de Gruyter, pp. 381–424

Muehlmann, S. and Duchêne, A. (in press). 'Beyond the nation-State: international agencies as new sites of discourses on bilingualism', in M. Heller (ed.), *Bilingualism: A Social Approach*. London: Palgrave Macmillan.

Mühlhäusler, P. (1996), *Linguistic Ecology: Language Change and Linguistic Imperialism in the Pacific Region*. London: Routledge.

Patrick, D. (2003), *Language, Politics and Social Interaction in an Inuit Community*. Berlin: Mouton de Gruyter.

Rubin, J. and Jernudd, B. (ed.) (1971), *Can Language be Planned? Sociolinguistic Theory and Practice for Developing Nations*. Manoa: University Press of Hawaii.

Skutnabb-Kangas, T. (2000), *Linguistic Genocide in Education or Worldwide Diversity and Human Rights?* London: Lawrence Erlbaum.

Spolsky, B. (2004), *Language Policy*. Cambridge: Cambridge University Press.

Notes

1 SIL's current mandate includes such statements as: 'Founded over 70 years ago, SIL International is a faith-based organization that studies, documents, and assists in developing the world's lesser-known languages. SIL's staff shares a Christian commitment to service, academic excellence, and professional engagement through literacy, linguistics, translation, and other academic disciplines. SIL makes its services available to all without regard to religious belief, political ideology, gender, race, or ethnic background' (www.sil.org/sil/).

2 Defending diversity: Staking out a common global interest?[1]

Shaylih Muehlmann

Over the past two decades the word *biodiversity* has figured centrally in environmental and political debates, and has become a key signifier of social and environmental crisis. Once understood to apply exclusively to biological and ecological variability within and between species and ecosystems, the term has recently undergone significant metaphorical expansion into other domains. This chapter charts the trajectory of the incorporation of this concept within the movement to save 'endangered languages', a movement in which linguistic or biolinguistic diversity is increasingly portrayed as most crucially at risk of extinction.

Recent work in anthropology has examined the current fascination with biodiversity in both academic and popular environmental discourses (Conklin and Graham 1995; Escobar 1996, 1999; Brosius 1997, 1999; Braun 2000; Bamford 2002). These critiques have argued that, far from simply describing an objective reality, the concept of biodiversity also constructs the threat to the environment in a particular way, prescribing the role that certain actors should play. In this chapter I argue that when the concept of biodiversity is extended to the language advocacy movement, the threat to linguistic diversity is constructed in a similar manner, prescribing the same roles for the actors involved, particularly indigenous people. I consider the ambiguities and contradictions that arise as environmental discourses are appropriated and transformed in the literature on language endangerment.

In examining the ideological effects of current discourses on biolinguistic diversity, I do not mean to deny the existence of the threats to either the environment or minority languages. Instead I aim to understand why bio- or biolinguistic diversity has become the relevant conceptual frame for understanding and responding to these threats. I examine the consequences of understanding these issues through the framework of biodiversity by analysing how this discourse portrays nature, indigeneity and language, and by asking whose interests are served and overlooked by this particular construction. I argue that discourses taken up by language endangerment campaigns construe the threat to languages and the environment in a way that essentializes language, nature and indigenous people. These essentializing discourses, rather than highlighting the interrelationships between biodiversity and linguistic diversity, have concealed the complex ways that social marginalization intersects with linguistic and environmental processes.

I will carry out this analysis by examining how environmental and linguistic discourses in the promotional materials of certain conservation programmes have converged through a keyword: 'diversity'. Following Williams (1976), I trace the trajectory of the keyword 'diversity' as an index of the development of an emerging discourse on bio-linguistic endangerment. In his analysis of keywords, Williams interrogates accepted meanings and reveals variation and contestation behind the appearance of continuity. Focusing on a keyword provides a window into the workings of a larger discourse and tracing its trajectory offers a means of making sense of situated interests within shifting relations of power, as political economic conditions change.

Converging crises: from biodiversity to biocultural diversity

Since the 1980s there has been a rapid growth of local, national and transnational environmental non-governmental organizations (NGOs) and bureaucracies concerned both with environmental management and with implementing various forms of global environmental governance (Brosius 1999). Within this expanding regime of environmentalism, biodiversity has emerged as a central object of regulation.

According to Bamford (2002), the term *biodiversity* was rarely encountered in popular discourse even ten years ago, but has now become ubiquitous in scientific and non-academic writing. Bamford suggests that this fascination is partially attributable to the range of potent meanings the term expresses. She argues that:

> encapsulated within its use are an array of meanings including late twentieth century efforts to stave off species extinction; the growth and proliferation of the conservation movement; a thorough-going critique of the destructive tendencies of industrial society, and a growing recognition of the pervasiveness of global interdependencies. (2002: 36)

It is this very range of meanings that has facilitated a parallel increase of interest in the concept of diversity in linguistics, especially in

15

the context of discussions of language obsolescence. Linguists have argued that, just as biological diversity is in a state of crisis, so too is cultural diversity, and the impending decline in the overall linguistic diversity on the earth has been widely cited as evidence of this paralleled crisis. Terralingua, an NGO founded in the mid-1990s to protect the biological, linguistic and cultural diversity of the earth, succinctly expresses these converging crises in the following passage from the organization's website:

> It is apparent that many of the same socioeconomic and political factors, such as economic globalization, overexploitation of natural resources, and growing worldwide sociocultural homogenization, are negatively impacting on all forms of diversity. The current biodiversity extinction crisis is well known. But a comparable, and converging, crisis is affecting the world's cultures, and particularly the diversity and richness of languages. (Terralingua 2005)

The notion of bio-diversity is indeed so encompassing in its semantic grasp that a series of more specific variations have developed emphasizing the term's various connotations, including *biocultural* diversity and *biolinguistic* diversity. In a review of the recent literature on biolinguistic diversity, Maffi (2005) points out that while the 1980s was the decade of *biodiversity* – the term describing 'the massive, human-made extinction crisis threatening the diversity of life in nature' – then the 1990s might be called the decade of *biocultural diversity*, 'when the concept of an intimate link between biological, cultural and linguistic diversity was put forth' (Maffi 2005: 600).

Linguistic and cultural diversity have become topics of debate in a myriad of different political, academic and cultural arenas. Setting migration quotas, controlling illegal immigration, protecting minority rights and affirmative action programmes are only a few of the topics that fuel these ongoing debates. In their ethnography of debates on diversity in the context of migrant policies in Belgium, Blommaert and Verschueren (1998) argue that despite the various political positions taken on diversity, an orienting feature of mainstream debates is that diversity is rhetorically turned into a problem, and a problem that needs to be 'managed'. While this chapter will examine a very specific path the discourse of diversity has taken, connecting environmental and linguistic conservation efforts to a common agenda, the discourse I examine shares the assumption Blommaert and Verschueren describe. Specifically, it assumes that the problem with biolinguistic diversity is its impending extinction and it construes this problem in a manner that radically constrains the options for solutions.

The relationship between linguistic and biological diversity has been characterized in a variety of different ways in the emerging literature on the subject (Harmon 1996, 2002; Posey 1999; Nettle and Romaine 2000; Skutnabb-Kangas 2000; Maffi 2001; Mufwene 2001; Skutnabb-Kangas *et al.*, 2003). For example, the geographical correlations between areas of high linguistic and biological diversity have prompted examination into the empirical links responsible for this correspondence (Nettle and Romaine 2000; Maffi 2001). In addition, the metaphor of language as a biological species has been extended to the concept of a 'language ecology', which has been elaborated as an analytical tool (Haugen 1972; Mühlhäusler 1996; Mufwene 2001), as well as critiqued for the inaccuracies in the analogy (Crawford 1998; England 2002). The complex ways that the field of biocultural diversity has developed is not the focus of this chapter, however (see Maffi 2005 for a comprehensive review of this literature). Instead, my concern here is a very specific manifestation of the current interest in linguistic diversity. In particular, I will explore how the concept of linguistic diversity has been taken up by endangered language movements, NGOs and certain academic programmes as a rhetorical strategy in campaign materials. I focus on the promotional texts produced by such institutions, including websites, pamphlets, campaign materials and publications.

The last decade has witnessed a rapid proliferation of NGOs that have emerged to protect the biocultural or biolinguistic diversity of the earth. Some examples of these new NGOs include: Linguapax (1987), the Foundation for Endangered Languages (1994) and Terralingua (1996). In their efforts to protect the biocultural or biolinguistic diversity of the planet, these organizations all borrow elements from contemporary environmental rhetorics of biodiversity. They have appealed to the legitimacy of ecological discourses by drawing on the paradigm of biodiversity conservation that had gained such success in the environmental movement (see Conklin and Graham 1995). Maffi describes how parallels were established between the ideas of biocultural or biolinguistic diversity and the better known phenomenon of biodiversity loss in order to rally linguists and others around the issue of language endangerment (2005: 602).

In what follows I will examine how the notion of biocultural or biolinguistic diversity has emerged across these multiple contexts and why it emerged at a particular historical juncture when language ideologies appear to disconnect from nation state ideologies. The various institutions and NGOs that have used this discourse in the environmental and language endangerment movements have done so to promote very different interests. For some it has provided a new way of legitimating late capitalist expansion and the corporate exploitation of symbolic and environmental resources. For others, it has provided a framework for expressing an anti-globalizing stance concerned with protecting these resources and their perceived indigenous 'stewards'. Despite the different interests involved, all these positions share the assumption that the crisis facing biocultural or bilinguistic diversity needs to be ameliorated in a way that implicates and constrains the involvement of indigenous people by essentializing their relationship to both language and nature. I will examine the role of the word 'diversity' in this essentializing process by analysing how it displays the properties of a keyword: it connects areas that are generally kept separate, masks radical semantic variation by its continuous verbal identity and often expresses a contradiction (McKeon 1977). I will argue that, as with environmental discourses on biodiversity, linguistic discourses on biolinguistic diversity forge tenuous connections between capitalism and conservation, efforts to revitalize and efforts to archive, and the simultaneous valorization and dehumanization of indigenous people.

Precarious connections: capitalism, conservation and custodians of diversity

Critics of contemporary environmentalism have identified some of the contradictions inherent in the concept of biodiversity. Escobar (1996) has argued that rather than challenging the basic premises of modern industrial society, campaigns to conserve biological diversity represent a deepening of capitalist interests in the Third World. In her research on Conservation International (CI), Bamford (2002) notes that one of the organization's most aggressive campaigns to date has been centred on the field of 'bioprospecting', or the search for biological resources and accompanying indigenous knowledge primarily for the purpose of commercial exploitation. Bamford points out that the mandate of CI's 'Shaman's Apprentice Program' is to 'encourage local tribes to record their knowledge, to be proud of their culture, and profit from it economically' (quoted in Bamford 2002: 40).

CI cites an array of statistics in support of their mandate: approximately 40 billion dollars is spent annually on plant derived drugs and another 10 billion is generated each year through the sale of rainforest products. CI advertises that its 'sustainable development' programme does more than simply generate cash income for communities; it also impresses upon local people the importance of their ongoing participation in the cash economy. Bamford goes on to describe the prevalent use of business metaphors in CI's published literature, which regularly refers to 'biological wealth' and 'ecological riches', all the while maintaining: 'resource protection is good business for everyone' (quoted in Bamford 2002). Bamford argues that this rhetoric is fairly representative of contemporary campaigns to save biodiversity. She points out that while these rhetorics claim to take a stand against the excesses of corporate industry and colonial history, the discourses produced by CI and other biodiversity advocates 'often read more like a manual on saving late twentieth century capitalist society' (2002: 40).

A similar tension between an emancipatory agenda, which resists the exploitation of indigenous people and resources, and an imperialist, capitalist rhetoric is evident in the discourses produced by advocates of linguistic diversity. Michael Silverstein argues[2] that there is a parallel between how linguists are perceived by many local communities – as 'extractors' of cultural wealth – and pharmaceutical companies who find local remedies and the expert knowledge of shamans and develop this knowledge in the for-profit global industrial sector. In the Amazon basin alone, Western pharmacologists have extracted hundreds of local plant remedies whose properties have been synthesized in laboratories across the globe (Moran *et al.* 2001). Silverstein claims that arguments by the 'endangered language Greens' among linguists for rescuing local linguistic–conceptual 'wealth' have as much of a hollow ring as the statements that ethnopharmacologists make to local peoples. Hill (2002) makes a similar point, suggesting that both expressions of universal ownership and commodifying metaphors describing humanity's linguistic 'treasures', 'wealth' and 'riches' may be alienating to speakers of endangered languages and may potentially undermine advocacy efforts. Hill argues that these arguments may be interpreted as a threat to expropriate a resource, rather than as an expression of universal human value (2002: 122).

Ethno-biological research has had a significant ideological impact on both environmental and linguistic preservation discourses. Conklin and Graham (1995) argue that 'bioprospecting' largely legitimized the goal of preserving biodiversity because it became attached to the idea of preserving indigenous knowledge and, by extension, preserving indigenous peoples. The language endangerment discourses have extended this programme to preserving indigenous languages. In fact, recent interest in the links between language and environment has arisen in part from the work carried out over the past few decades by ethnobiologists studying the indigenous knowledge of local flora, fauna and ecosystems (Maffi 2005: 601). In the endangered language movement the parallel between 'bioprospecting' and linguistic documentation is not just discursive. The extension of concern over the linguistic

19

dimension of ethno-pharmocological knowledge has also resulted in linguists actively engaging in the same kinds of activities by archiving endangered languages often with the very aim of saving 'ethno-pharmocological taxonomies'.

Recent efforts to archive biocultural diversity have produced a second tension between the aims to preserve or 'save' diversity and an intention to document or archive diversity. The efforts to document and archive biological and linguistic diversity have been critiqued for blurring the distinction between documenting diversity as opposed to advocating for its continued survival. Bamford (2002) describes how members of the Human Genome Diversity Project have collected samples of DNA to be stored in a permanent database of human genetic variation: the project will study the cells of indigenous people, even if the people themselves disappear. An important corollary of contemporary conservation rhetoric, Bamford argues, is that it serves to naturalize Third World peoples by presenting them as an endangered 'sub-species' and construing their genetic material as more valuable than their lives.

In much the same way that the genome project construes genetic material, the campaign material of endangered language programmes also appears to prioritize languages over their speakers. This privileging of language is particularly evident in campaigns that focus on archiving languages as opposed to revitalizing them. For example, the Hans Rausing Project[3] is specifically geared towards the archiving of linguistic diversity, justifying their mandate by arguing: 'a handful of civilizations left us the ideas that form the basis of today's world. Countless others left behind nothing. No thoughts, insights or culture. Because they left us no language' (SOAS 2002). The argument continues: 'Without a language record a civilization is dead. With no hope of resurrection. And with 3,000 of the planet's 6,000 language cultures now facing threat of extinction in your lifetime, that's something humanity can't afford to let happen'. The suggestion that a 'civilization' is not really dead if it has been documented echoes the Genome project's apparent de-prioritization of the lives in question.

While endangered language projects consistently present themselves as being unproblematically aligned with speakers of endangered languages, it is important to recognize that archiving languages does not necessarily contribute to their continued survival. The Hans Rausing Project's promotional literature challenges its audience with the slogan 'can your voice help support the voices of millions?' while simultaneously claiming that their goal lies in 'creating an invaluable resource – and a basis for all future action'. The project sits precariously between these two goals.

There have been some attempts to explicitly align the goals of revitalization and documentation in the rhetoric on language loss. For example, McLaughlin argues that creating a written form of oral languages contributes to efforts to teach the language in schools and thus to revitalization efforts more broadly (1992). However, maintenance strategies that ossify the text form of language often fail to recognize the way that oral traditions shape language transmission (Darnell 2003). Derrida (1996) has written extensively on the disparate implications of archiving, which he suggests represent both an attempt to preserve something to be remembered and to leave out something to be forgotten.

A third tension that is present in both environmentalists' and linguists' appeals to the discourse of biological and linguistic diversity is the simultaneous valorization and dehumanization of indigenous people. Brosius points out that biodiversity discourses create certain kinds of subjects. He argues that the notion of biodiversity not only constructs the threat to the environment in a certain way, but also constructs how that threat should be handled and lays the groundwork for prescribing the role that certain kinds of actors should play (1999: 282). He uses the example of how increasing concern over the destruction of the tropical rainforest has resulted in the valorization of particular categories of subjects who we feel should live in them, specifically, indigenous peoples. People who are excluded from this category – those who should not live in the rainforest – are peasants and migrants from urban areas. He argues that this particular construction of the category of indigeneity often coincides with an effort to valorize communities that have previously been denied standing. This process depends on the deployment of images to a broad audience that assert a natural connection between indigenous peoples and the environment (Brosius 1999).

The endangered language communities that are foregrounded in the literature on language loss are also often identified as 'indigenous'. This is equally misleading, as many communities of endangered language speakers are left out by this identification, particularly, minority languages of the European Union (such as Breton, Occitan or Sami) as well as languages endangered in diaspora communities (for example, Gaelic in Cape Breton). As in the environmental movement, indigenous communities are valorized in endangered language campaign literature. This valorization is also often accomplished through the use of essentializing images.

A poignant example of this essentializing imagery can be found in a poster for the Hans Rausing Project, which was displayed at my own institution, in the department of anthropology at the University of Toronto. The photograph on this poster is of a Jiga Muguga tribesman, shrouded by greenery and decorated in white clay, charcoal and paint (note, however, that the specifics of the tribe and place were not indicated on the poster; I emailed the School of Oriental and African Studies (SOAS) for this information). The caption beside his head reads, 'What's on his mind? You may never know'. Below the logo for the project in the right lower corner of the poster it reads, 'because every lost word means a lost world'. The slogan 'What's on his mind? You may never know' implies that when the people of Papua New Guinea's languages are lost, their thoughts will be as well. While this phrase is probably intended as a Whorfian appeal to worldview, it has the effect of making the relevant people icons rather than agents. This is exacerbated by the exotic portrayal of the speaker, who is shown in 'tribal' dress and surrounded by nature.

The tensions in these portrayals of indigenous people have also had the effect of rendering their roles ambiguous. As Bamford points out, 'if the rhetoric on biodiversity is fairly uniform in treating "nature" as one big shopping mall, it evinces a certain amount of confusion in knowing exactly how to situate indigenous people in the dialogue' (2002: 41). In some ways it appears that indigenous people are assigned a privileged position in the emerging rhetoric: they are given the role of 'steward', in charge of preserving the last remaining vestiges of biodiversity on the planet. However, Bamford emphasizes that while the position of 'steward' may appear to place people in a position of empowerment, it is a position which is nonetheless replete with contradictions. She claims that contemporary rhetoric not only constructs the 'native' as 'super hero'; it also has the effect of naturalizing those very people upon whom the survival of the planet supposedly depends by framing cultural difference as genetic difference (2002: 41).

The position that local people occupy in the diversity discourse as it extends to the issue of endangered languages is analogous to what Bamford describes. A common tactic in the literature on endangered languages is to present speakers of threatened languages as 'natural allies' of language preservationists. This is particularly striking in the repeated use of the terms 'guardians of diversity' (Nettle and Romaine 2000) or 'custodians of endangered languages' (Hill 2002) to refer to both their speakers and communities. These terms act to shift responsibility of language preservation solely onto the speakers of endangered languages. It also glosses the fact that while some language preservation efforts are community generated (see Nettle and Romaine 2000), this is not always and certainly not necessarily the case.

In sum, the discourses on diversity, in both environmental conservation and campaigns for endangered languages, make precarious connections between capitalism and conservation, efforts to revitalize and efforts to archive, and the valorization and dehumanization of indigenous people. The idea that a keyword tends to connect areas that are normally kept separate (McKeon 1977) is particularly salient in arguments for the conservation of diversity. In fact, the merging of biological and linguistic appeals to diversity has resulted in a keyword whose powerful persuasive effect prescribes a common agenda for all of humanity. This argument is clearly articulated on Terralingua's website:

> Everybody should care about the loss of our life-support systems, in nature and culture. And everybody should care about the abuses and the human rights (including linguistic human rights) violations that are at the root of much of this loss. Join Terralingua in working for biocultural diversity worldwide! (Terralingua 2005).

This is a powerful rhetoric which leaves little room to ask questions about whose interests might be served by these preservation efforts, or whose interests might be overlooked.

Williams contends that keywords are sites at which the meaning of social experience is negotiated and contested (1976: 20). What is particularly salient in this case, however, is how the continuous verbal identity of the keyword 'diversity' neutralizes the contradictions it encompasses. Contestations and negotiations are erased, highlighting the hegemonic mechanism of keywords. The notion of 'diversity' provides a new terrain on which the representation of an apparently globalized, common interest is staked out. The contestations at work here, and the question of what difference diversity makes to whom, are subsumed under the guise of this common agenda.

Tracing the trajectory: from the nation state to the global world

The keyword *diversity* has unlocked a discursive space through which a common interest is articulated. This is achieved partially through the semantic variation it encompasses and the contradictions that it conceals. In the previous section I attempted to denaturalize this discourse by examining its underlying assumptions and the internal tensions it conceals. Another important task in interrogating this discourse is to examine why it arose at a particular historical moment. Why did contemporary diversity rhetorics proliferate specifically in the 1980s and 1990s in both the environmental movement and the language endangerment movement? Following Williams' assertion that variations and changes of word use are not mere confusions of meaning but 'historical and contemporary substance' (1976: 21), I will

23

trace this particular use of the word 'diversity' to a particular historical juncture under shifting political and economic conditions.

Since the rise of European nation states in the nineteenth century, issues of bilingualism were debated in the context of nation states and their institutions. Discourses on multilingualism emphasized constitutional rights for linguistic minorities, perpetuating the ideology of languages as homogeneous, bounded units, an ideology which was also a product of the rise of nationalism (Hobsbawm 1990; Billig 1995; Hill 2002). As socio-linguists have documented, this discourse focusing on minority languages adopted the very discourse of the centralized homogenous nation states which marginalized them, and created them as a category in the first place (Heller 1999, 2002; Jaffe 1999; Heller & Martin Jones 2001).

The surge of interest in linguistic diversity emerged at the moment when these ideologies of minority languages began to disconnect from nation state ideologies. As nation states began to expand their economic networks, they became increasingly integrated into an international capitalist system that ostensibly undermines the control of any given state. It is through this apparent erosion of state control that a new, 'globalizing' economy has called into question the role of nation states. It is also this perception of expanding global interconnection that has interrupted a discourse on multilingualism that appealed to the legitimacy of the nation state to argue for minority language rights (Heller 2002).

This political and economic shift has had several effects on discourses of language endangerment. It has made language endangerment NGOs more visible because supranational organizations such as the United Nations and UNESCO, and international NGOs such as Linguapax, Terralingua and the Foundation for Endangered Languages, become newly legitimate voices on issues of multilingualism rather than state institutions such as schools and administrations. This political and economic shift has also influenced the discourses produced on language endangerment which now appeal to the legitimacy of ecological discourses by drawing on the paradigm of biodiversity conservation. This has shifted language policy debates from an emphasis on linguistic rights to what is now more often formulated as linguistic human rights, and from linguistic diversity to biolinguistic, or biocultural, diversity. The appeal to diversity therefore incorporates the discourse of linguistic rights (understood in relation to the nation state) but emerges in a way that takes a slightly different shape. While languages are still represented as homogeneous units, it is the diversity between languages and their vulnerability to global expansion that is emphasized.

24

Through this shift in emphasis, the discourse on biolinguistic diversity also functions to sustain nation state ideologies at precisely the moment when the idea of the homogeneous nation state is losing credibility (see also Cameron, this volume; Heller 2002; Muehlmann & Duchêne, in press). The notion of biolinguistic diversity appears to highlight the interconnectedness of the 'global world', and specifically the connections between culture, nature and language, while maintaining an ideology of languages as distinct wholes. Just as the concept of minority language and linguistic human rights only makes sense in relation to the discursive formation of the nation state, the discourse of 'diversity' is framed by the threat of capitalist economic expansion and globalization. But as we have seen in the various and contradictory stances in the discourse, the notion of biocultural diversity also expresses an ambivalence towards the threat of global expansion (see also Cameron, this volume). While it provides a discourse that resists the homogenizing forces of global capitalism it also legitimates the expansion of corporate interests through programmes of sustainable diversity management.

In either form, the discourse of biocultural diversity has depended heavily on the appropriation of a particular ideology of the 'indigenous'. Gupta (1998) traces a similar political and economic path of origin for the notion of indigeneity, claiming that it gained its salience at the same historical moment during transitions in the global economy. He points to the geographic expansion and restructuring of capitalist production in the last decades of the twentieth century in which cultures in remote regions, previously on the margins of the global economy, were increasingly drawn into its circuits of production and consumption. By this view, indigeneity emerges at exactly the moment that these sites and cultures come under threat of disruption or displacement by global economic forces.

Instead of simply existing as a political identity framed in terms of a prior occupation of land, the category of indigeneity obtains its full political potency in the context of other discourses. In Gupta's account, the power of the notion of indigeneity arises from a dual meaning; it can be articulated as a political identity in response to the displacements of global capitalism, but it also becomes another means of commodifying and thus incorporating 'remote' people into a global capitalist system. Gupta argues that this precarious category of 'the indigenous', thus becomes an 'alternative, eco-friendly, sustainable space outside or resistant to modernity' (1998: 179).

Braun (2002) has critiqued Gupta's account, arguing that a purely political economic explanation for the emergence of the new semantic and political power of the notion of indigeneity fails to account for the full dynamics of semantic change. Braun points out that the concept of indigeneity carries multiple meanings and is deployed in different ways. On one level, 'indigenous' refers to a political identity pitted against colonial ambitions and settler states as Gupta describes. However, Braun argues that it is also, crucially, a relational term that takes its significance amidst a group of meanings more directly relevant to ecopolitics. He contends that indigeneity emerged not solely as a result of capitalist modernity's spatial extension into remote places (since this is a constant element of modernization); rather, it arose in a more 'conjunctural' mode, where these displacements occurred simultaneously with a negative re-evaluation of modernity (which began to gather force in the 1960s), and a new meta-narrative of sustainability (that emerged in the 1980s). Braun argues that it was the combination of these two discursive developments, coinciding with late twentieth-century capitalist extensions, that resulted in the view of contemporary global expansions through a negative discourse of modernization-as-disruption (2002: 92).

Tracing the explosion of interest in biocultural diversity to the crisis of the nation state and the expansion of global capitalism would also tell only part of the story. In order to understand biocultural diversity's full semantic effect, it needs to be contextualized as a term that, while emerging at a specific political and historical juncture, obtained its full potency as a signifier within a wider discourse, in which narratives of sustainability, modernity and indigeneity play a central role.

A cluster of keywords: biodiversity, sustainability and indigeneity

Williams draws attention to 'clusters', or particular sets of interrelated words, and shows how they can have systematic interconnections (1977: see also Williams 1983). While he argues that it is useful to pick out words of an especially problematic nature, and consider their own internal development and structure, he also admits that 'most active problems of meaning' are embedded in actual relationships, which are diverse and variable within the structures and processes of social and historical change (1977: 23). 'No word stands on its own', but is rather always an element in the social and semantic processes on which its uses depend. Following Williams, the concept of diversity, in many of its current manifestations (biocultural-linguistic diversity) can be shown to stand in a complex relation to a set of other concepts, such as modernity, sustainability and in particular, the concept of indigeneity. The relationships between these concepts, as well as the political and economic processes in which they are embedded, must be untangled in order to understand the full implications of the contemporary fascination with diversity, in all its forms.

Conklin and Graham (1995) have begun to trace some of the connections between these concepts as they relate to environmental discourses on biological diversity. They argue that the emergence of the concept of indigeneity in Brazilian environmentalist planning coincided with arguments for the protection of cultural and biological diversity. Until recently environmental advocacy focused solely on protecting flora and fauna; the presence of people tended to be seen as an obstacle to environmental preservation (Hecht and Cockburn 1989: 27). As environmental philosophy shifted to emphasize 'sustainable development', rather than strict preservation, an ecological rationale for defending indigenous people emerged. The authors describe how during the 1980s environmentalist NGOs began to promote development models that made the promotion of local equity and the preservation of local cultures a central component of development planning. It was at this time that 'Indians – formerly seen as irrelevant to economic development – now were championed as the holders of important keys to rational development' (1989: 698).

Braun (2002) has also analysed how a discourse of indigeneity dovetailed with environmental politics on Canada's west coast in the 1980s and 1990s. He describes how environmental rhetoric in the campaign to save the rainforest on Clayoquot Sound made First Nations people visible, but only by incorporating them within the terms of anti-modern preservationist politics. This left the First Nations in British Columbia with limited options, since participating in the region's resource economies means they risk losing what many non-natives consider authentic indigenous culture and as a result, their right to speak as indigenous peoples for their lands.

By these accounts, environmentalist arguments for the protection of biodiversity which conflate indigenous people with the nature being saved, are one expression of concern over the extension of capitalist modernities. Of course this conflation has a longer historical reach: the idea of the 'noble savage' extends back to Rousseau and romanticist thought more broadly. But in this particular invocation the image of the noble savage has been 'refracted through a romantic primitivist lens that conflates the preservation of cultural diversity with the preservation of biodiversity' (Braun 2002: 81). In this incarnation, the noble savage has particular contemporary political appeal as it allows for the assumption that native peoples' views of nature, and ways of using natural resources, are consistent with the goals of Western conservationists.

This is an assumption that has been enthusiastically embraced in discourses on language endangerment. The idea that indigenous people are 'natural conservationists' has not only been expressed through use of the essentializing images (as we saw in the poster from SOAS above). The connection between sustainable ecological practices and indigenous languages has also been explicitly invoked in language endangerment discourses. The following statement from Terralingua is representative of how this argument has been made:

> People who lose their linguistic and cultural identity may lose an essential element in a social process that commonly teaches respect for nature and understanding of the natural environment and its processes. Forcing this cultural and linguistic conversion on indigenous and other traditional peoples not only violates their human rights, but also undermines the health of the world's ecosystems and the goals of nature conservation. (Terralingua 2005)

The connection this statement makes between indigenous knowledge, indigenous languages and the survival of the planet is constructed as more than merely sufficient; indeed, in these discourses the relationship between good environmental management and indigenous languages is consistently represented as a necessary one. If a language is lost, so is knowledge about the environment and respect for nature and its health. The immense advantage of the discourse of indigeneity for both environmental and linguistic conservationists is also clear from the quotation above; the discourse takes on a humanitarian stance of defending human rights and oppressed, disempowered people, not just protecting plants and animals or linguistic taxonomies (Hecht and Cockburn 1989: 698).

The emergence of the discourse of biocultural diversity in the language endangerment and environmental conservation movements indicates that preservationist campaigns are most persuasive when they work through a discourse of indigeneity rather than one that relies solely on linguistic or ecological arguments. This discourse moves beyond the ecologizing discourse that Cameron describes (this volume) of diversity as a good in itself by recognizing that without the connection to indigenous struggles, foreigners' protests against deforestation or language endangerment can be construed as yet another instance of self-interested first world interference in Third World affairs. This is, in fact, how the environmental movement has been widely portrayed in the Brazilian media, where indigenous activists have been depicted as pawns of foreign economic imperialists seeking to interfere with national affairs and control the country's resources (Conklin and Graham 1995: 698).

Therefore, the current prominence of the notion of biocultural diversity arose through the conjunction of a cluster of meanings that developed under the specific political and economic circumstances of the late twentieth century. As nation states were drawn into more international market systems, a discourse of environmental sustainability emphasizing the threat to biocultural diversity developed. In the negative re-evaluation of modernity that had already gained momentum, indigenous people emerged as the focal point, a symbol with an inherent capacity to resist modernity, participate 'sustainably' in a market economy and thus, ameliorate the threat to biocultural diversity. The relationships among these concepts also paralleled and constrained a set of social relationships, in which new alliances between environmentalists, linguists and indigenous people have formed.

It is clear that in some contexts these alliances have benefited both environmentalist and indigenous interests. Recent events suggest, however, that the international alliance between environmental and indigenous rights movements may prove fragile and collide with indigenous people's own goals. This is becoming evident from the increasing number of complaints against NGOs that have recently been reported from the field. In Chiapas, CI has been accused by the local press of trying to enlist the Mexican military to expel peasant families from the Lacondon Forest, and bioprospecting for corporations in the Mayan forest region (Chapin 2004). In another project, in the Laguna del Tigre area of Guatemala, a CI project developed into a bitter fight over resources with a local NGO, ending with angry villagers setting the CI research station on fire (*ibid.*). These instances suggest that while environmentalists' primary goal is to promote natural resource management, indigenous peoples often seek self-determination and control over their own resources, a goal which does not necessarily align with the goals of conservation NGOs.

Brazilian indigenous leaders, for instance, have consistently defined self-determination to include control over their lands and the right to use them as they choose. Conklin and Graham (1995) describe several instances in Amazonia in which indigenous communities have asserted control over economically valuable natural resources and chosen to use them in environmentally destructive or 'unsustainable' ways. They cite the case in 1989 of Guajajara Indians taking hostages to force FUNAI (the Brazilian Indian foundation) to allow them to sell lumber from their land, as well as the case of Kayapo leaders in Brazil granting timber companies concessions to log large tracts of virgin mahogany and other tropical hardwoods (1995: 703). Conklin and Graham argue that the Brazilian case suggests that the stereotype of indigenous people as natural conservationists forms a precarious foundation for indigenous rights advocacy because it misrepresents the realities of many indigenous peoples' lives and priorities (1995: 697).

29

There is an equal danger in assuming that speakers of endangered languages necessarily choose to preserve their native languages. As Mufwene argues (2004), the vitality of languages cannot be dissociated from the socioeconomic interests and activities of its speakers who are often adapting to changing socioeconomic conditions. Mufwene critiques the arguments of endangered language advocates for overshadowing the agency with which people select and give up particular languages, and he urges linguists concerned with rights of languages to ask themselves whether these rights prevail over the right of speakers to adapt competitively to their new socioeconomic conditions (2004: 219).

Ultimately, both environmental and linguistic conservationists use the interconnectedness highlighted by a discourse of diversity to champion their own goals, whether expressed in a desire to expropriate or rescue symbolic and environmental resources. In the process, these discourses alternately hold the endangerment of languages or nature as the necessary cause of social marginalization. The endangered language movement builds its discourse on the assumption that safeguarding indigenous languages helps protect nature because indigenous people have a natural interest in sustaining ecological relations. The environmental conservation movement assumes that the preservation of nature necessarily preserves indigenous cultures and languages because indigenous people are seen to have an essential relation to nature.

Some will argue that these essentialisms, despite the complex relationships they obscure, are strategic. Indeed, the texts on which I've focused this analysis are marketing texts, specifically designed to generate funding and support. Thus these discourses are not only tailored for their persuasive effect, but the strong causal argument they make for the connections between language, indigenous people and the environment is a particularly simplified form of the discourse on biolinguistic diversity that has emerged. Nonetheless, it is an extremely important form of this discourse, not only working its way into mainstream representations, but showing up in university departments and shaping the priorities of NGOs and international agencies programme initiatives. What is at stake in the perpetuation of this rhetoric in language endangerment programmes? One final parallel with environmental discourses may serve as a foreboding indication.

In a recent and controversial article published in *World Watch*, Chapin argues (2004) that in the last several years discussion of 'natural' alliances between conservationists and indigenous peoples, or the need to work closely with local communities in the major conservation organizations, has largely disappeared. He documents how conservationist NGOs (Chapin focuses on the three largest: World Wildlife Fund, Conservation International and The Nature Conservancy, notably, the latter two have funded Terralingua's Projects) have begun to distance themselves from indigenous peoples because these organizations are increasingly dominated by the view that indigenous people are the 'enemies of nature, rather than political actors who can form an environmental constituency' (2004: 27).

Chapin attributes the recent unravelling of alliances between indigenous groups and biodiversity conservation efforts to several specific fissures. He argues that the failure of many community-based conservation projects has led conservationists to suspect that after indigenous peoples are given tenure to their lands, there is no assurance they will work to conserve its biodiversity. Chapin also chronicles how NGOs have been unwilling to side with indigenous groups in instances where they have come up head-to-head with the private companies, governments and multilateral agencies that make up their funding base. This has resulted in an increasing and mutual suspicion on the part of conservation NGOs and indigenous groups.

The fact that these organizations are increasingly insisting that what they do is conservation and not 'poverty alleviation' (Chapin 2004: 27), is a clear indication of the potential effects of an essentializing discourse that assumes that saving plants, animals and languages will necessarily alleviate the social problems experienced by indigenous peoples. When the discourse begins to unravel, it loses its strategic potency for everyone involved. The reduction of indigenous identity to a natural instinct of preservation also occludes other kinds of potential eco-political alliances. The links between indigenous people, and otherwise marginalized, poor and disempowered populations has been made irrelevant by this discourse, despite the fact that these populations often suffer similar forms of linguistic and environmental discrimination.

Ironically, these reductionist arguments defy the very insight that a focus on biocultural diversity might otherwise afford: that social, linguistic and ecological processes are mutually constitutive and can only be isolated in their most reified of forms. There is no doubt that language obsolescence and environmental degradation are processes deeply implicated in the organization of social inequality. It is the disempowered whose languages 'die' and the marginalized and poor who suffer the effects of environmental degradation most immediately. But from this fact alone we cannot conclude that saving languages or rainforests will reverse the social processes that marginalize some groups in the first place.

31

Through its appearance of continuity and wide semantic grasp, the keyword *diversity* has articulated numerous and sometimes contradictory interests, all prescribing their agenda as a universal solution to the crisis of biolinguistic diversity. In the process, languages, indigenous people and the environment have been reified, and their interconnections have been simplified. While the potency of the concept of biolinguistic diversity has drawn public attention to a connection between linguistic and environmental and social processes, we cannot let its power as a keyword also allow us to take for granted a simple relationship between environmental and linguistic conservation and social justice. Ultimately, we need to more carefully examine how linguistic, environmental and economic processes intersect in order to know how to account for the varied interests involved in cases of language endangerment.

References

Bamford, S. (2002), 'On being 'natural' in the Rainforest marketplace: Science, Capitalism and the commodification of biodiversity'. *Social Analysis*, 46, (1), 35–50.

Billig, M. (1995), *Banal Nationalism*. London: Sage.

Blommaert, J. and Verschueren, J. (1998), *Debating Diversity: Analysing the Discourse of Tolerance*. London: Routledge.

Braun, B. (2002), *The Intemperate Rainforest: Nature, Culture, and Power on Canada's West Coast*. Minneapolis: University of Minnesota Press.

Brosius, P. (1997), ' "Endangered forest, endangered people". Environmentalist Representations of indigenous knowledge'. *Human Ecology*, 25, (1), 47–69.

Brosius, P. (1999), 'Analyses and interventions: anthropological engagements with environmentalism'. *Current Anthropology*, 40, (3), 277–310.

Cameron, D. (this volume), 'Language endangerment and verbal hygiene: history, morality and politics', in A. Duchêne and M. Heller (eds), *Discourses of Endangerment: Interest and Ideology in the Defense of Languages*. London/ New York: Continuum International.

Chapin, M. (2004), 'A challenge to conservationists'. *World Watch*, 17, (6), 17–31.

Conklin, B., and Graham, L. (1995), 'The shifting middle ground: Amazonian Indians and eco-politics'. *American Anthropologist*, 97, (4), 695–710.

Crawford, J. (1998), 'Endangered native American languages: what is to be done and why?'. Available at www.ncela.gwu.edu/miscpubs/crawford/endangered.htm, accessed 18 July 2003.

Darnell, R. (2003), 'Indigenous language stability and change among the Plains Cree of Northern Alberta and the Ojibwe of Southwestern Ontario'. Paper presented at the *8th International Pragmatics Association Meeting*, Toronto, ON, July 2003.

Derrida, J. (1996), *Archive Fever*. Chicago: University of Chicago Press.

England, N. (2002), 'Commentary: further rhetorical concerns. *Journal of Linguistic Anthropology*, 12, (2), 141–3.

Escobar, A. (1996), 'Constructing nature: elements for a post structural political Ecology', in R. Peet and M. Wats (eds), *Liberation Ecologies: Environment, Development, Social Movements*. London: Routledge.

Escobar, A. (1999), 'After nature: steps to an antiessentialist political ecology'. *Current Anthropology*, 40, (1), 1–30.

Gupta, A. (1998), *Postcolonial Developments: Agricultural in the Making of Modern India*. Durham, NC: Duke University Press.

Harmon, D. (1996), 'Losing species, losing languages: connections between biological and linguistic diversity'. *Southwest Journal of Linginguistic*, 15, 18–108.

Harmon, D. (2002), *In Light of Our Differences: How Diversity in Nature and Culture Makes Us Human*. Washington, DC: Smithsonian Institution Press.

Haugen, E. (1972), 'The ecology of language', in S. Anwar (ed.), *The Ecology of Language, Essays by E. Haugen*, Stanford: Stanford University Press. pp. 324–39.

Hecht. S. and Cockburn, A. (1989), *The Fate of the Forest: Developers, Destroyers and Defenders of the Amazon*. New York: Verso.

Heller, M. (1999), *Linguistic Minorities and Modernity: a Sociolinguistic Ethnography*. New York: Longman.

Heller, M. (2002), 'Language, education and citizenship in the post-national era: notes from the front'. *The School Field*, XIII, 6, 15–31.

Heller, M. and Jones, M. (eds) (2001), *Voices of Authority: Education and Linguistic Difference*. Westport, CT: Ablex Publishing.

Hill, J. (2002), ' "Expert Rhetorics" in advocacy for endangered languages: Who is listening, and what do they hear?' *Journal of Linguistic Anthropology*, 12, (2), 119–33.

Hobsbawm, E. (1990), *Nations and Nationalism since 1760*. Cambridge: Cambridge University Press.

Jaffe, A. (1999), *Ideologies in Action: Language Politics on Corsica*. Berlin: Mouton de Gruyter.

Maffi, L. (ed.) (2001), *On Biocultural Diversity: Linking Language, Knowledge, and the Environment*. Washington, DC: Smithsonian Institution Press.

Maffi, L. (2005), 'Linguistic, cultural and biological diversity. *Annual Review of Anthropology* 29, 599–617.

McKeon, M. (1977), 'Review of "Keywords" '. *Studies in Romanticism*, 16, 128–39.

McLaughlin, D. (1992), *When Literacy Empowers: Navajo Language in Print*. Albuquerque: University of Mexico Press.

Moran, K., King, S. and Carlson, T. (2001), 'Biodiversity and prospecting: Lessons and prospects'. *Annual Review of Anthropology*, 30, 505–26.

Muehlmann, S. and Duchêne, A. (in press). 'Beyond the nation-State: international agencies as new sites of discourses on bilingualism', in M. Heller (ed.), *Bilingualism: A Social Approach*. New York: Palgrave Macmillan.

Mufwene, S. (2001), *The Ecology of Language Evolution*. Cambridge, UK: Cambridge University Press.

Mufwene, S. (2004), 'Language birth and death', *Annual Review of Anthropology*, 33, 201–22.

Mühlhäusler, P. (1996), *Language Change and Linguistic Imperialism in the Pacific Region*. London: Routledge.

Nettle, D. and Romaine, S. (2000), *Vanishing Voices*. Oxford, England: Oxford University Press.

Posey, D. (ed.) (1999), *Cultural and Spiritual Values of Biodiversiy*. London/ Nairobi: Intermed. Technol. Publ., UNEP.

School of Oriental and African Studies (SOAS) (2002). Hans Rausing Language Project. 2003–2004 Course Handbook for MA in language documentation and Description, Ph.D in Field Linguistics.

Skutnabb-Kangas, T. (2000), *Linguistic Genocide in Education – Or Worldwide Diversity and Human Rights?* Mahwah, NJ: Lawrence Erlbaum Associates.

Skutnabb-Kangas, T., Maffi, L. and Harmon, D. (2003), *Sharing A World of Difference. The Earth's Linguistic, Cultural, and Biological Diversity*. Paris: UNESCO Publishing. UNESCO, Terralingua and World Wide Fund for Nature.

Terralingua, 2005. Available at //www.terralingua.org/AboutTL.htm, accessed 13 May 2005.

Williams, R. (1976), Keywords: *A Vocabulary of Culture and Society*. Oxford: Oxford University Press.

Williams, R. (1983), *Culture and Society*. New York: Columbia University Press.

Notes

1 I thank the editors of this volume, Monica Heller and Alexandre Duchêne, for encouraging me to develop this chapter and for their comments along the way. I would also like to thank Joshua Barker and Abigail Sone for comments on various drafts. An earlier version of this chapter was presented in 2003 at SALSA XII (Texas Linguistic Forum), Austin, TX: University of Texas Department of Linguistics.

2 Personal correspondence, 31 October, 2002

3 Some of the examples I draw on from the Hans Rausing Endangered Language Project were taken from a website which has been significantly revised since this chapter was written. The project's current website (www.hrelp.org) features far less of the essentializing discourses of its predecessor.

3 Indigenous language endangerment and the unfinished business of nation states

Donna Patrick

> We believe that protecting First Nation, Inuit and Métis languages is another step in the continual process of Canada's nation building. As the Supreme Court of Canada and others, including the Royal Commission on Aboriginal Peoples, have noted, Canada has unfinished business with the First Nations, Inuit and Métis peoples of this country.
> *Report of the Task force on Aboriginal Languages and Cultures* (2005: 74)

Indigenous mobilization in the late twentieth and early twenty-first centuries has been conceived largely as part of a continuous struggle against colonization, land appropriation, broken treaty promises, assimilation, marginalization and genocide. At the international level, concerns over language in particular have given rise to a supranational discourse, which has made language endangerment and language rights issues part of international agendas in both governmental and non-governmental arenas, and brought the plight of Indigenous languages to the attention of a growing public. The international prominence of these issues can be traced to the 1953 UNESCO document *The Use of Vernacular Languages in Education*, and can be seen today not only in the work of such non-governmental organizations (NGOs) as Terralingua, Linguapax and the Foundation for Endangered Languages, but also in the considerable amount of academic research devoted to them (see e.g. Grenoble and Whaley 1998; Henze and Davis 1999; Crystal 2000; Nettle and Romaine 2000; Fishman 2001; Hinton and Hale 2001; Maffi 2001; Stuknabb-Kangas *et al.* 2003; Freeland and Patrick 2004; May 2005; Muehlmann and Duchene, in press).

Yet, despite this supranational turn, endangered language issues remain largely a matter for nation states. This is because these issues remain, to a large degree, shaped by national concerns and constructed through national spaces, which provide openings for mobilization and for the legitimization of Indigenous claims. Accordingly, many of these concerns have been taken up at national and local levels. As Smith notes, 'some communities [have] focused primarily on cultural revitalization', while 'others, either as separate organizations or as small groups of individuals, [have become] much more intent on engaging in reorganizing political relations with the state' (1999: 111). While a description of activist work in terms of this division of labour might well reflect how such work has been conceived, it overlooks the extent to which Indigenous political and cultural activism, and the discourses associated with them, have overlapped in practice. Moreover, it overlooks the importance of language and language rights as a mobilizing force that is both political and cultural, uniting Indigenous activists and their communities in the twin goals of achieving 'nationhood' and cultural 'survival', and allowing them to tap into international discourses, including a number of conventions and covenants on language endangerment and protection, which provide further support for their goals.

In what follows, I shall be trying to spell out how language rights, and the discourses surrounding them, have acted as just such a 'mobilizing force' in the struggle of Indigenous groups for greater autonomy. My focus will be language endangerment discourse in Canada, a country in which the politics of language, land claims, and Aboriginal[1] mobilization is well established, and where language endangerment discourse echoes that found elsewhere.

While the Indigenous language discourse to be examined here is, to some extent, unique to the political, economic and historical conditions of Canada, there are, nevertheless a number of points that pertain to language endangerment discourse in general. In other words, the Canadian Indigenous language discourse has similarities with both Indigenous language and minority language movements found elsewhere, including language movements of national minorities, such as French in Canada, Welsh in the United Kingdom or Corsican in France. In both Indigenous and national minority language mobilization, smaller political collectivities are vying for a social, cultural and economic space and some form of territorial integrity within the nation state. While each collectivity might aim for a particular kind of minority or Indigenous relationship with the state – from outright separation, to retaining some kind of nation-like status (i.e. remaining within the jurisdiction of the larger nation state), or holding some form of regional or local control over institutions and municipalities – the common underlying drive to gain 'territory' or a land base is at the root of the language mobilization.

In addition to this underlying link to land, language endangerment discourse also tends to highlight particular facts about language in order to build a case for language promotion (and thereby promotion for the group itself). Some of these facts include the high rates of language attrition and the concomitant loss of (1) local knowledge and culture associated with the language; (2) cultural diversity that enriches the nation; and (3) crucial tangible and intangible cultural heritage that defines the nation. Also key to this discourse are the appeals at times to linguistic essentialism, which ties particular language varieties to 'authentic' cultural practices and socio-cultural groups, inhabiting particular social places and localities.

Despite these similarities found in language endangerment discourses, there are some important differences between Indigenous groups and national minorities. For one thing, Indigenous groups tend to form a more fragmented social category, often more marginalized and with smaller numbers than national minorities. In large part, this marginalization is rooted in the oppositional nature of Indigenous economies and notions (or lack of notions) of land 'ownership' – economies which have largely been at odds with the economic and material beliefs and practices of the colonizers. In other words, non-Western, non-capitalist Indigenous economies have often been subjugated by the aggressive, expanding, market-oriented colonial settlers. Harvesting practices have not only been grounded in different forms of land tenure, but also in different cosmologies governing social and cultural meanings and human relationships to the natural world. For many Indigenous groups, the idea of unifying around a cohesive, unifying nationalistic discourse and using state apparatuses to gain control, 'ownership' or 'rights' to land is in direct opposition and conflict with the Indigenous values and beliefs that the groups want to protect. This paradox and complexity can lead to greater fragmentation in the group, but it also means that the way that language and land become discursively linked in language endangerment discourse can vary among groups as well.

Despite the variation, however, there are also common links in Indigenous language discourse. In order to gain clout and support for Indigenous languages and Indigenous movements within and beyond the nation state, the discourses have relied on moral appeals to human and Indigenous rights, social justice and protecting biodiversity. As we shall see, certain discursive strategies emphasizing such appeals also draw on the importance of protecting 'traditional knowledge' (as opposed to other forms of 'cultural knowledge') and linking linguistic diversity to biodiversity.

That being said, what is arguably distinctive about language endangerment discourse in Canada, particularly as constructed by

Aboriginal groups themselves, is the specific highlighting of the 'unfinished business' of land negotiations and the reconciliation between Aboriginal groups and the Canadian state. This need for reconciliation stems from decades of assimilationist paternalistic policies and the need for the federal government to recognize (1) past mistakes in the colonization process; (2) rights to land and territories that include rights to resources and economic development on these lands; and (3) the need to renegotiate new relationships between First Nations, Inuit and Métis and the Canadian state – relationships that are rooted in the nation-to-nation relationships established in the treaty-making of the past.

Language becomes important in this discourse, since language was lost through colonial practices, which included residential schooling, the banning of particular rituals and cultural practices, land appropriation and economic degradation. Language has thus gained importance in cultural and spiritual revitalization movements, and these in turn are linked to the need for greater autonomy and control over lands within the Canadian state.

In the discussion to follow, we shall examine a recent instance of such language endangerment discourse, exemplified in the June 2005 *Report to the Minister of Canadian Heritage*, prepared by the *Task Force on Aboriginal Languages and Cultures*, a group of ten First Nation, Inuit and Métis representatives that was formed in 2003. As we shall see, this report has provided a space for the Aboriginal language survival movement in Canada to promote itself at the national level in the context of official bilingualism and heritage language promotion. However, while the Aboriginal language movement broadly echoes that of the French language movement in Canada for increased rights and recognition, there are differences. For one thing, the way that language and land are linked in the Aboriginal discourse is somewhat different from the French language debates that have characterized the country, including the Quebec movement for increased linguistic and territorial autonomy within Canada. The Aboriginal discourse is different not only because of the hundreds of outstanding land claims cases waiting to be legally settled between Aboriginal groups and the Crown, but also because of the diversity among Aboriginal populations and groups. This fragmentation among Aboriginal groups is based on different social and geographical realities and means that there is a more complex language movement at play with particular consequences for different groups of speakers.

Significantly, the essentializing of a link between Aboriginal language and Aboriginal land, though of great strategic value in the struggle for language preservation, risks excluding certain Aboriginal groups from the language endangerment discourse. Among these are members of urbanized Aboriginal communities, created as the result of significant levels of migration of Aboriginal peoples to cities. While such migration has tended not to involve a complete de-territorialization of people from their Aboriginal homeland 'territories', given considerable movement back and forth between these territories and cities, it has nevertheless sparked the construction of new identities and new cultural and linguistic practices that are shaping new forms of community. Thus, new forms of place-making – not necessarily linked to dominant interests in traditional, territorialized 'nationhood' – are creating new forms of 'locality' and 'community' in which First Nations, Inuit and Métis in Canada can thrive. This makes the question of what Aboriginal language is being saved for whom a pressing one, which indicates the need to create a more inclusive and radicalized discourse of language endangerment, consistent not only with the need for political reconciliation and restitution, but with increasing diversity within Aboriginal groups.

The rest of this chapter is organized as follows. The next section will review some of the historical forces that led to the current state of Aboriginal languages and of Aboriginal communities more generally. The third section will offer an analysis of language endangerment discourse, as it is exemplified in the *Task Force Report on Aboriginal Languages and Cultures* (hereafter the *Task Force Report*). The fourth section will provide a discussion of this discourse, drawing particular attention both to its social effects and to its limits, and briefly address the question 'What languages are being saved, and for whom?'. The final section will offer some concluding remarks, including the need for sociolinguistics to widen the scope of what is seen as 'language revitalization'.

The historical roots of Indigenous language endangerment in Canada

A useful place to start an investigation of the discourse of language endangerment in Canada is to consider the current situation of Aboriginal languages. Of the 50 or so Aboriginal languages still spoken in Canada, all but a handful have been classified as 'endangered', indicating that their chances of survival beyond this century are limited (Kincade 1991; Kirkness 1998; Cook 1998; *Task Force Report* 2005). One response to this situation, which has come from Aboriginal groups in particular, has been to make appeals for institutional support for language revitalization and protection. These appeals and the discourse constructed around them can thus be seen as integral parts of the revitalization movement. Before considering them in more detail, however, it is important to recognize the historical context that has led to language shift and language endangerment in the first place.

Prior to the arrival of Europeans, North America was populated by hundreds of distinct Indigenous groups, differing greatly not only in the languages that they spoke, but in their political, economic and social organization, which ranged from autonomous, rather isolated groups to vast confederacies. The cultural, political and economic knowledge of these groups was conveyed by means of oral traditions; this knowledge permitted these groups, 'as distinct as they were' with respect to language and culture, to develop 'shared diplomatic protocols which allowed for a free flow of trade on a continental scale' (Office of the Treaty Commissioner 1998: 14). In fact, when Europeans arrived in North America, they were able to adopt the east–west trade routes already established by the people living there.

During this period of initial European contact, alliances were forged between Europeans and Indigenous groups, primarily to ensure trade routes for the competing colonial trade companies. French and English interests in the fur trade resulted in particular trade patterns which sustained a more-or-less equal trade partnership between Europeans and Indigenous groups. This balanced relation, however, 'soon gave way to imbalance' when the lessening of hostilities between French and English resulted in a decline in the 'politically motivated flow of goods from European authorities to native American allies' (Wolf 1982: 194). Indigenous trappers became more dependent on the trading post, not only for guns and ammunition, but also for foodstuffs such as tea, flour and sugar, and other common trade items, such as cloth and tobacco. In the nineteenth century, as wildlife became depleted and contagious diseases decimated Aboriginal populations, economic conditions worsened for Aboriginal peoples. This was exacerbated by increased settlement, expansionist threats by the United States and the declining importance of the fur trade. In addition, pressure to settle Western Canada, which increased after the signing of the *British North America Act* (*BNA Act*) and the establishment of Canadian confederation in 1867, led in turn to an increase in treaty negotiations between First Nations and the Crown (see Morris 1991; Office of the Treaty Commissioner 1998; Ray *et al.* 2000;).

Since the signing of the *BNA Act*, the federal government has held responsibility for 'Indians and lands reserved for Indians', as prescribed in section 91(24) of the Act. This section was the legislative basis for the *Indian Act* of 1876 and the repressive Aboriginal policies that followed, which restricted movement, property rights, political rights, cultural practices, and the items that Aboriginal peoples were permitted to possess (McCarthy and Patrick 2005).[2] The *Indian Act* has had a profound effect on Aboriginal political, cultural and economic life, not least because it was the basis for the federal government's grouping of all Aboriginal peoples in Canada into a single legal–racial category – a grouping that ignores the tremendous heterogeneity of Aboriginal groups, with their distinct histories, languages and cultures.

The *Indian Act* and its revisions throughout the late nineteenth and early twentieth centuries set up the framework that governed Indians on the reserves created through the treaty process.[3] The provisions of the Act had the effect of: (1) formalizing the residential school system;[4] (2) stifling cultural and economic activity on reserves; (3) inhibiting the movement of Aboriginal peoples; and (4) depriving them both of recourse to legal action and of the ability to organize politically (McCarthy and Patrick 2005). These consequences of the Act are now widely recognized to have been dire, and political and legal action in recent years has sought to expose and redress the abuses and injustices for which it was directly or indirectly responsible. The brutality of the residential school system has been a particular target of legal action,[5] not only because this system required children to be separated from their families, and permitted them to be subjected to physical and psychological abuse, including punishment for speaking Aboriginal languages, but also because such abuses meant that the federal government had failed to provide adequate education to Aboriginal peoples, one of their fiduciary duties under the *BNA Act*.

After the Second World War, the international mobilization of Indigenous peoples (Smith 1999; Feldman 2001) and the rise of other social movements set in motion efforts to restore to Aboriginal peoples in Canada the material and symbolic resources, including land, languages and cultural heritage, that they had lost through assimilationist government policy. Efforts also were taken to foster respect for and to promote forms of Aboriginal 'nationhood' and to heal the relations between Aboriginal groups and the state. A milestone here was the entrenchment of Aboriginal rights in the 1982 *Constitution Act*,[6] the nature and extent of the land, hunting, fishing and other rights granted there being clarified through a series of court cases, such as *R v. Van der Peet* (1996), with significant implications for the conceptualization of Aboriginal culture and language in Canadian law (see Vallance 2003; Patrick 2005). Another milestone was the establishment of the Royal Commission on Aboriginal Peoples (RCAP) (1991–1996),[7] set up to examine Aboriginal state relations and Aboriginal relations with Canadian society as a whole, during a period of intense politicization of Aboriginal groups in Canada (see Dickason 2002: 393–431

41

for an overview). This commission produced a five volume report, which included recommendations concerning language. Specifically, it called for community-driven, community-managed initiatives, leading ideally to a Canadian Aboriginal Languages Foundation (RCAP vol. 3, ch. 6 sec. 2.5, recommendation 3.6.10). Although this foundation has still not been established, the concept seems to have re-emerged in the form of the Aboriginal Languages and Cultures Centre proposed in the *Task Force Report* (2005: 13, to be described in more detail below).

The growing prominence of Aboriginal rights as a national issue can also be traced to efforts begun in 1987 to establish a Canadian Heritage Languages Institute, to promote languages other than French and English.[8] This heritage language initiative coincided with the *Canadian Multiculturalism Act* (1988), intended to reflect and promote Canadian cultural and racial diversity.[9] One key failing of the Canadian Heritage Languages Institute initiative was its high degree of 'centralization' (as voiced by grassroots community representatives in consultations), as well as its exclusion of Aboriginal organizations (Paron 2005). Bill C-37 (1989), the heritage language legislation that finally resulted from this initiative, did include Aboriginal groups, but this inclusion was achieved without consultation with these groups, which was unacceptable to them.

This problem was rectified, to some extent, by the recent establishment by the Ministry of Canadian Heritage of an Aboriginal Language Task Force, consisting of ten Aboriginal representatives from First Nations, Inuit and Métis communities, which was set up in 2003 with a mandate to 'propose a national strategy to preserve, revitalize and promote First Nation, Inuit and Métis languages and cultures' (*Task Force Report* 2005: i). Despite this greater accommodation of Aboriginal concerns within the Department of Canadian Heritage, Aboriginal language issues nevertheless remain distinct from those of French and heritage languages in at least one important respect: namely, in how efforts to preserve and promote them can be justified. More specifically, the justification for promoting French and heritage languages has rested primarily on the link between language and culture and the unquestioned assumption that 'if the language is lost, then the culture is lost' – such a loss being highly undesirable in an officially pluralistic and multicultural society. However, such justifications are inadequate in the context of Aboriginal claims to language and cultural rights. This is, in particular, because these claims are rooted in the historical, political and economic relations of the First Peoples with Europeans and the way in which Canada has developed as a nation, which has meant that cultural and linguistic revitalization remains bound up with the continuing political and social struggles

42

reflected in the hundreds of still unsettled land claims and other kinds of 'unfinished Constitutional business' in the country. However, problems also arise because of the unique difficulties associated with defining and securing Aboriginal rights. As far as the Supreme Court of Canada is concerned, Aboriginal 'culture' is preserved only through the continuation of specific traditional practices such as hunting or fishing, and is not tied in any direct way to language use (see Patrick 2005). Since Aboriginal languages are facing 'extinction' even though many cultural practices have persisted, one needs to find arguments in addition to those that invoke links between language and culture in order to justify Aboriginal language promotion and revitalization. As it happens, such arguments have been advanced in the *Task Force Report*, which we shall be turning to in the next section.

The construction of language endangerment discourse in Canada

As just noted, the goal of promoting Aboriginal languages in Canada requires a language endangerment discourse that goes beyond the assumption that cultures die when languages die. This does not mean, however, that this discourse has eschewed a link between language and culture, which still figures prominently in the construction of Aboriginal identity and in the discourse on Aboriginal language endangerment in Canada. This can be seen in examples of this discourse that appear in the media as well as in 'official' discourse produced by political organizations, language activists and political leaders. In what follows, we shall be examining two examples of this discourse, both of which offer an Aboriginal perspective on how language revitalization and protection can be achieved in a linguistically politicized Canada; one text focuses more narrowly on the link between language and culture, while the other offers a broader and more complex treatment of language endangerment.

1. Language endangerment and the media

We can gather some sense of the role that the link between Aboriginal languages and cultures continues to play in language endangerment discourse in Canada from recent media coverage of language issues, which have arisen in the context of legislated French and English language use. For example, a 2004 article in Montreal's *Le Devoir*[10] describes how at the Second Conference on Aboriginal Languages, held in St. Sauveur, north of Montreal, in October of that year, the regional chief of the Assembly of First Nations of Quebec and Labrador asserted that Indigenous groups in Quebec need a law similar to Bill 101, the Quebec provincial legislation aimed at protecting the French language. What we see here is a parallel, made by an Aboriginal leader and affirmed in the newspaper article, between Aboriginal languages and French, which has benefited from provincial 'official language' laws, including those that aim to support its use in education, the workplace, and other institutional spheres. What we also find in this article is (the reporting of) an attempt to derive support for local efforts to protect linguistic diversity by invoking commonly held assumptions about the desirability of cultural diversity, by making a 'natural' link of language to culture. At the same time, there are appeals to existing language rights initiatives, already in place in Quebec, Canada and internationally. The former point is echoed in the assertion of a spokesperson for the Canadian Commission for UNESCO that 'la source de la diversité culturelle se trouve dans les langues. C'est à travers elles qu'on peut explorer d'autres façons de voir le monde. En les perdant, on perd des connaissances et des compétences'. ['the source of cultural diversity is in languages. It is through languages that we are able to explore other ways of seeing the world. When we lose languages, we lose knowledge and abilities'.] (Doyon 2004). The latter point is echoed in the assertion of the director of the conference that it is now necessary to see 'les initiatives nationales et internationales existantes' ['existing national and international initiatives'] and to put forward 'un plan d'action pour que le gouvernement reconnaisse la nécessité de preserver les langues autochtones' ['a plan of action so that the government recognizes the need to preserve Aboriginal languages']. The 'plan of action' suggested here, encompassing both federal and international levels, alludes to the existence of international covenants and conventions pertaining to language rights, promotion and revitalization.

Even this brief consideration of Aboriginal language endangerment discourse as reported in the popular media reveals how this discourse serves to naturalize the links between language, culture, ethnicity and nationhood, through references to the specific historical, social and political context of Canada and to the international sphere. Yet, those aspects of language endangerment discourse just reviewed hardly do justice to the complexity of this discourse, with its layering of elements related to national and international issues, including constitutional issues, the federal government's fiduciary duties and land rights, in the former case, and the covenants and conventions concerning traditional knowledge, biodiversity and indigenous rights in the latter.[11]

2. The 2005 Task Force Report *and strategic uses of essentialism*

The 2005 *Task Force Report*, already mentioned in the previous section, offers a clearer picture of the complexity of language endangerment discourse in Canada. The report provides a comprehensive treatment of Aboriginal language issues and exemplifies a systematic use of strategic essentialism, linking spiritual and healing aspects of language revitalization to cultural revitalization, legal and political reconciliation to Aboriginal and constitutional rights and language to 'the land'. The following sections will examine these linkages more closely, in order to see how language endangerment is broadly conceived as political and cannot be factored out of the larger concerns of restitution of land, resources and autonomy of First Nations, Inuit and Métis within Canada.

2.1 Language, land and spirituality

Arguably, the key link made in the *Task Force Report*, as in Aboriginal language endangerment discourse in Canada more generally, is between 'the people, their languages and the land' (2005: 20). While this, in itself, is not unique from other language struggles, such as the nationalistic movement in Quebec, which discursively connects people, language and a territory, the Aboriginal discourse is different in some key respects.

In the report, this particular linkage is made by emphasizing how Aboriginal groups' spirituality, cultural relationships and connection to the land (and thus, in turn, their legal and political struggles over land rights) are all tied to 'sacred and traditional knowledge', and particularly oral traditions, transmitted through Aboriginal languages. As such, these languages are constructed as a crucial part of Aboriginal existence – and also crucial for understanding the 'historic continuity' of Aboriginal peoples with the land and for interpreting treaties and other historical events related to the land (2005: 20).

The *Task Force Report* begins with an assertion of the central role of spirituality in Aboriginal cultural practices and the importance of language to spirituality. Language revitalization in this context is seen as part of a process of individual and community healing, both of which involve spiritual reconnection with the past and the land. Thus land, spirituality, healing and language are all interconnected: the land serves as a spiritual link between languages and those who speak them; and languages, as 'gifts from the Creator' and carriers of 'unique, irreplaceable values and spiritual beliefs', 'allow speakers to relate with their ancestors and to take part in sacred ceremonies'.[12] In

45

short, language is constructed as the key to fostering certain 'principles and values' and 'spiritual beliefs', and as a dynamic element in healing rituals and other practices that have become part of community-based First Nations, Inuit and Métis rehabilitation and other social service programmes.

The importance of language in this spiritual conception of the world is further emphasized by the claim that language encodes relationships and maintains the 'web of identities' that connect people – for example, through the use of particular words for introducing speakers (*Task Force Report* 2005: 22) – and by the claim that the meanings of particular words in a language are easily lost in translation. Thus, the word for 'land' in Aboriginal languages, which may have a holistic sense that includes its flora and fauna and 'the people's spiritual and historical relationship with it' (*ibid.*: 23), does not find a close parallel in its English translation equivalent.

The importance of Aboriginal languages in cultural practices also emerges from a consideration of the importance of oral traditions and oral history for Aboriginal groups. This importance is related not only to the recognition by the courts 'that oral history must have a role in Aboriginal rights and treaty cases' (*ibid.*: 24), but also to the fact that 'oral tradition has survived as a separate way of describing the human experience of this world' (*ibid.*: 25) and 'to its role in establish[ing] and maintain[ing] important relationships and pass[ing] them on intact to future generations' (*ibid.*: 24–25). The report notes, in particular, that oral history is used to 'educate the listener for a moral purpose, pass on aspects of culture through stories or sacred songs, or perhaps establish the claim of a family or clan to a territory or to social authority or prestige' (*ibid.*: 24). It thus describes unique experiences and stories of the world, which further justifies the preservation of the Aboriginal languages that have served these functions.

In a similar vein, the report asserts that languages harbour 'different philosophies' that 'are key to forming Aboriginal identities and [...] tied to distinctive languages and cultures' (*ibid.*: 24). Not only is language thus seen as the 'primary vehicle for culture' (*ibid.*: 7), but language and culture are viewed as 'inseparable concepts for First Nations, Inuit and Métis peoples' (*ibid.*: 25). This is because for 'many First Nation, Inuit and Métis languages are largely languages of relationship' (*ibid.*: 7) – reinforcing their tight connection to the land and their identities as the First Peoples of Canada, and enabling them to participate in sacred ceremonies. Moreover, since these languages are integral to 'the history of First Nation, Inuit and Métis peoples', they are also an integral part of Canadian identity and heritage, and thus should be revitalized and protected 'for all Canadians' (*ibid.*: 71).

46

Stepping back from the particular assertions about language and culture contained in the *Task Force Report*, we can see them not merely as articulating a particular cultural perspective but – given their appearance in a government task force report – also serving to justify and promote, first, the salience of 'land' in the preservation of language and culture and, second, the use of Aboriginal languages in practices that are part of individual and community decolonization and healing processes, through revitalized spiritualism. Strategic uses of linguistic essentialism, binding language to culture, and culture to land, are thus prevalent in the discourse in order to promote the idea that only certain worldviews connect human beings so closely to the land. Not only land, but also these worldviews need to be protected – something that is possible only if the languages encoding these worldviews are themselves protected.

That these assertions about language and culture have considerable strategic importance can also be seen in the *Task Force Report's* seeking of further support for them in national and international discourses, including those that promote the preservation of traditional ecological knowledge, biodiversity, cultural and linguistic diversity and Indigenous rights. For example, the report cites the finding of the *Red Book on Endangered Languages*, produced by the United Nations Educational, Scientific and Cultural Organization (UNESCO), 'that at least half of the world's languages are in danger of extinction by the end of this century', the 'vast majority [of which] are Indigenous' (*Task Force Report* 2005: 71). In addition, the report builds its case that Aboriginal languages should be revitalized because of their intimate connection to traditional Aboriginal knowledge, 'each people and their language represent[ing] a unique way of organizing information and knowledge about the ecosystem', by appealing to national and international discourses on biodiversity and to the need for Canada to fulfil its 'international obligations to protect cultural heritage' (*ibid.*: 82). These appeals to protecting 'intangible heritage' resonate with the previously mentioned links between language and culture and of culture to the land.

Also of strategic importance in the *Task Force Report* are national and international appeals to environmental protection and biological diversity. These appeals are tied to the protection of Aboriginal languages by emphasizing how these languages serve as repositories of traditional ecological knowledge. For example, the report cites Environment Canada and UNESCO statements about the importance of 'Aboriginal traditional knowledge', which 'encompasses all aspects of the environment — biophysical, economic, social, cultural and spiritual — and sees humans as an intimate part of it' (2005: 72). It also invokes Canada's status 'as a signatory to the international Convention on Biological Diversity', which requires the Canadian government to '[p]rotect and encourage customary use of biological resources in accordance with traditional cultural practices that are compatible with conservation or sustainable use requirements' (*ibid.*: 73). The report further emphasizes the need for Canada to also 'preserve and maintain knowledge, innovations and practices of indigenous and local communities embodying traditional lifestyles relevant for the conservation and sustainable use of biological diversity ... with the approval and involvement of the holders of such knowledge (Article 8(j) of the *Convention on Biodiversity* cited in the *Task Force Report* 2005: 73).

International conventions provide necessary clout to national pleas to provide resources to 'protect' languages; as the *Task Force Report* notes, Canada is falling behind 'international standards, such as UNESCO's yardstick on explicit and implicit government and institutional policy and attitudes to language' (2005: 75). To remedy this, action must be taken, such as fulfilling Canada's commitment to 'The Action Plan for the Implementation of the Declaration on Cultural Diversity ... [which] calls on member states to support and promote linguistic diversity and protect traditional knowledge' (*ibid.*: 82). This is in line with UNESCO's 'action plan for endangered languages'. What is arguably at the heart of this discourse is the idea that linguistic diversity is a desirable human 'good', with the richness of forms both within and across languages suggesting the richness of the natural world, just as biological diversity does.

The point in making these international appeals is that Canadian national identity has in part been constructed around its international commitments to human rights and to its national, liberal cultural policies that promote cultural diversity. That said, the *Task Force Report* makes it clear that if these international commitments are not upheld, as a nation 'Canada could well be characterized as continuing to promote, either actively or passively, assimilation of First Nation, Inuit, and Métis peoples' (2005: 75). Crucially tied to these appeals is the argument that the national discourse of Canada, through the entrenchment of First Nations, Inuit and Métis rights in the 1982 *Constitution Act*, affirms that 'government support of language revitalization is to be grounded in the principle that all First Nation, Inuit and Métis languages must be protected and promoted' (2005: 71). This issue will be explored in the next section.

2.2 Language and legal–political restitution

In addition to the link that the *Task Force Report* makes between language, land and spiritual values is the link that it makes between the revitalization of Aboriginal languages and the achievement of legal and political goals, such as the restitution of Aboriginal rights and Aboriginal 'nationhood'. The idea here, seen in strategic terms, is that Aboriginal language revitalization is a natural part of broader political goals of Aboriginal groups, which are achievable within the established Canadian political–legal framework. This means that 'enduring institutional support for First Nation, Inuit and Métis languages' and for the 'principles and values' embedded in these goes hand in hand with support for other Aboriginal rights and aspirations and with languages (consistent with the Canadian *Charter of Rights and Freedoms*), and with the Canadian federation.

Two intertwined ideas have a prominent place in this discussion. One is that treaties and the Canadian constitutional structure have provided the political space for Aboriginal nationhood, and for undertaking the task of resolving the 'unfinished business' between Aboriginal peoples and the Canadian government over land and other resources as well as over wrongs done to the language, culture and well-being of Aboriginal communities through assimilationist policies. The other, closely related, is that the First Nations, Inuit and Métis were founding peoples alongside the French and the English and that the Canadian government, with the settlement of the county, has a fiduciary duty to Aboriginal peoples to look after their interests, including support for their languages. Together, these ideas lead the report to conclude that the government should recognize Aboriginal linguistic rights and place Aboriginal languages on an equal footing with English and French, particularly as regards funding for language programmes.

The *Task Force Report* emphasizes that First Nations, Inuit and Métis each legitimize their status as distinct 'nations' through 'common bonds of language, culture, ethnicity and a collective will to maintain their distinctiveness' (2005: 26). This idea of Aboriginal nationhood, the report points out, is hardly a new one, but instead 'has been a key element of the relationship between First Nation, Inuit and Métis people and the Crown since the beginning', which has been 'expressed in the form of political autonomy and [...] reflected in the treaty process' (*ibid.*: 25). That is, the idea of Aboriginal nationhood is one with real legal force, and is consistent with the need for nation-to-nation agreements between Canadian Aboriginal groups and the federal government (and for government-to-government agreements between Aboriginal governments and the federal, provincial and territorial governments of Canada) to resolve ongoing disputes. However, Canada has in the past 'failed to honour the nation-nation relationship reflected in the Royal Proclamation[13] and the treaties' and adopted

49

assimilationist policies (*ibid.*: 26), which had the result of 'suppressing [Aboriginal] languages and cultures' (*ibid.*: v).[14] Accordingly, it is now Canada's duty to resolve the 'unfinished business' related to its commitments to the Aboriginal nations.

Indeed, the Canadian government's 'duty of loyalty and protection to the First Peoples of Canada' (*ibid.*: 27) looms large in the report, where this duty is understood to include not only the recognition of Aboriginal rights, as expressed in the *Constitution Act* (1982), s. 35(1), but also the recognition and protection of 'the equality of languages' (*Task Force Report* 2005: 71). Canada has yet to grant 'federal legislative recognition to promote and protect' Aboriginal languages (*ibid.*: v), spoken well before the arrival of the French and the English. What is required, then, is the treatment of these languages on an equal footing with French and English, to 'reverse the perception that First Nation, Inuit and Métis languages have less value than French or English'. This means rectifying the disparity 'between the national funding provided for French and English and that provided for First Nation, Inuit and Métis languages' (p. v), with funding for the latter languages to be brought, 'at a minimum, [to] the same level as that provided for the French and English languages' (*ibid.*: 75), as required to implement Aboriginal language immersion programmes (*ibid.*: 88).

Canada's 'duty of loyalty and protection' impinges on another key concern of Aboriginal nations, also closely tied to Aboriginal language and culture. This is the need for restitution for assimilative state policies and practices, such as those of the residential school system, which bear a large responsibility for ruptures in the transmission of knowledge about Aboriginal language, culture and traditional harvesting practices. As the *Task Force Report* points out, Indian Residential School and Indian Day School policies were 'meant to assimilate Indian children into Canadian society' by having 'them "un-learn" their indigenous language, culture, heritage and beliefs and to re-learn a foreign language, religion and way of life' (2005: 44). Such policies and practices instilled low self-esteem in Aboriginal children, severed their 'connection to their people', thus having an intergenerational impact, and led them to accept an inferior status for the Aboriginal languages (*ibid.*: v). Accordingly, compensation claims serving to redress these past injustices, the report asserts, must include claims for resources to restore the Aboriginal linguistic and cultural knowledge of which residential school students and their communities were deprived.

Implications of Aboriginal language endangerment discourse

As the discussion above has made clear, language endangerment issues in Canada are embedded in a highly political discourse centred on land and the role that land plays in Aboriginal cultures, including their spiritual values and languages. What also emerges from an examination of this discourse is the large number of outstanding court cases related to land claims and treaty rights in Canada and to compensation sought for abuse in the residential school system and for 100 years of assimilative policy. While the report makes clear that any legal compensation should be separate from funding for language protection and revitalization, the reasons why compensation has been sought in the first place figure prominently in language endangerment discourse. With the decline in trade and the weakening of political alliances, the Aboriginal – state relationship became, throughout the nineteenth and twentieth centuries, one that was dominated by assimilationist state policies and practices. Current efforts to heal the wounds created by this relationship involve efforts to make the government acknowledge the harm done and compensate for it. In this political context, Aboriginal language revitalization is clearly distinct from French, English and heritage language issues in Canada; that is, it is clearly not limited to retaining, revitalizing and promoting culture. Even with regards to the mobilization for the protection of French language, which also arose in response to economic English-language colonization and assimilation, the substance of the language discourse is different. For Aboriginal groups, language revitalization is linked to individual and community healing practices, the reclaiming of ties to land and place and constitutionally entrenched Aboriginal rights.

Although the above discussion of Indigenous language endangerment discourse in Canada has attempted to lay out the key elements, the complexities surrounding this discourse have still left us with at least one very basic question: namely, what kinds of language will be revitalized, and for whom? Given the highly 'territorialized' nature of the discourse, and the fact that language revitalization is largely justified through its connections to land, history and place, it is reasonable to ask where such a discourse leaves 'de-territorialized' Aboriginal individuals and communities, who risk being left out of the language survival/endangerment equation. The individuals and communities in question include, in particular, urban dwellers who have no close connection to those Aboriginal groups with claims to 'land', and who might speak highly urbanized versions of Aboriginal languages or engage in cultural practices that reflect strong urban

51

Aboriginal identities, but at the same time might lead to exclusion from more 'authentic' cultural and linguistic practices, associated more closely with land-based spiritual and community relationships. In other words, would one be seen as less 'Aboriginal' if one engaged in non-traditional, urban cultural and linguistic practices? If language is so connected to spirituality, can one be as 'authentically' spiritual without speaking the traditional language? To a large extent, these questions can find answers only through an investigation of lived local experiences and of the nature of this locality with respect to larger state and global processes, such investigation of a 'living' language making crucial use of fluid notions of language, including less 'standard', newer and culturally inventive ways of speaking. Such investigation would, therefore, be the next step in understanding the nature and broader implications of current Aboriginal language endangerment discourse in Canada.

Conclusion

The aim of this chapter has been to explore the discourse of language endangerment in Canada, the specific historical, political and economic conditions that have given rise to it, and the ideologies, practices and language issues associated with it. What we have found is that this discourse is part of a political strategy of Aboriginal groups in Canada to redress the wrongs created, in particular, from years of assimilationist federal government policy and practice and the government's failure to honour its treaty and other legal obligations to Aboriginal peoples; and that its basic goal is the resolution of 'unfinished business' related to these failures, which includes the revitalization of endangered Aboriginal languages. Finally, we have found that the discourse designed to promote these goals makes strategic use of certain assertions about the relation between Aboriginal languages and Aboriginal spirituality, culture and land.

What, I believe, we can hope to gain from such an investigation is some insight not only into this specific discourse and language revitalization movement, but also into similar language movements in other locales. However, as suggested in the introduction to this volume, there are many other questions which must be answered before we can achieve a serious understanding of this discourse. Among these are how the legitimacy of particular Indigenous languages is tied to other forms of legitimacy; who is engaged, and how, in the discourses and actions to 'save' these languages and who is not, and what is at stake for each group; and finally, what the consequences of these discourses are for the distribution of material and symbolic resources, including the maintenance of an Indigenous language in a community. Satisfying answers to these questions will depend on a fluid concept of language and a broadening of our conception of what counts as 'authentic' language revitalization in the twenty-first century.

References

Cook, E.-D. (1998), 'Aboriginal languages: History', in J. Edwards (ed.), *Language in Canada*. Cambridge: Cambridge University Press.

Crystal, D. (2000), *Language Death*. Cambridge: Cambridge University Press.

Dickason, O. P. (2002), *Canada's First Nations: A History of Founding Peoples from Earliest Times* (3rd edn). Oxford: Oxford University Press.

Doerr, A. (2000), 'Aboriginal Peoples, Royal Commission on', in *The Canadian Encyclopedia: Year 2000 Edition*. Toronto: McClelland & Stewart, pp. 3–4.

Doyon, F. (2004), 'S.O.S. langues autochtones – vers une loi 101 des Premières Nations?', *Le Devoir*, 18 October.

Feldman, A. (2001), 'Transforming peoples and subverting states', *Ethnicities* 1, 147–78.

Fishman, J. (ed.) (2001), *Can Threatened Languages Be Saved? Reversing Language Shift, Revisited: A 21st Century Perspective*. Clevedon, UK: Multilingual Matters.

Freeland, J. and Patrick, D. (eds) (2004), *Language Rights and Language Survival*. Manchester, UK: St. Jerome Publishing.

Grenoble, L. and Whaley, L. (eds) (1998), *Endangered Languages: Language Loss and Community Response*. Cambridge: Cambridge University Press.

Hall, A. J. (2000), 'Royal Proclamation of 1763', in *The Canadian Encyclopedia: Year 2000 Edition*. Toronto: McClelland & Stewart, pp. 2047–48.

Henze, R. M. and Davis, K. A. (1999), 'Authenticity and identity: lessons from Indigenous language education'. *Anthropology and Education Quarterly*, 30, 3–21.

Hinton, L. and Hale, K. (eds) (2001), *The Green Book of Language Revitalization in Practice*. San Diego: Academic Press.

Kincade, D. M. (1991), 'The decline of native languages in Canada', in R. H. Robins and E. M. Uhlenbeck (eds), *Endangered Languages*. Oxford: Berg, pp. 157–76.

Kirkness, V. J. (1998), 'The critical state of Aboriginal languages in Canada'. *Canadian Journal of Native Education*, 22, (1), 93–105.

Mackey, E. (2002), *The House of Difference: Cultural Politics and National Identity in Canada*. Toronto: University of Toronto Press.

Maffi, L. (ed.) (2001), *On Biocultural Diversity: Linking Language, Knowledge, and the Environment*. Washington, DC: Smithsonian Institution Press.

May, S. (ed.) (2005), 'Debating Language Rights'. Theme issue of *Journal of Sociolinguistics*, 9, (3).

McCarthy, A. and Patrick, D. (2005), 'Urban aboriginality and the changing political landscape in Canada'. Paper presented to the British Association of Canadian Studies, Canterbury, UK, April 2005.

Morris, A. (1991), *The Treaties of Canada with the Indians of Manitoba and the North-West Territories Including the Negotiations on Which They Were Based.* Saskatoon: Fifth House Publishers.

Muehlmann, S. and Duchêne, A. (in press), 'Beyond the Nation-States:: International agencies as new sites of discourses on bilingualism', in M. Heller (ed.), *Bilingualism: A Social Approach.* London: Palgrave.

Nettle, D. and Romaine, S. (2000) *Vanishing Voices: The Extinction of the World's Languages.* Oxford: Oxford University Press.

Office of the Treaty Commissioner (1998), *Statement of Treaty Issues: Treaties as a Bridge to the Future.* Saskatoon, Saskatchewan.

Paron, M. (2005), 'Managing Language, maintaining authenticity: Mapping approaches to language conservation initiatives in Canada, from the Canadian Heritage Language Institute to the Language and Cultures Council'. (MA Research Essay, School of Canadian Studies, Carleton University).

Patrick, D. (2005), 'Language rights in Indigenous communities: The case of the Inuit of Arctic Quebec'. *Journal of Sociolinguistics*, 9, (3), 369–89.

R. v. Van der Peet (1996), Supreme Court of Canada ruling, volume 2, 507 Available at www.lexum.umontreal.ca.

Ray, A. J., Miller, J. and Tough, F. J. (2000), *Bounty and Benevolence: A History of Saskatchewan Treaties.* Montreal: McGill-Queen's University Press.

Royal Commission on Aboriginal Peoples (1996), 5 volumes. Ottawa: Minister of Supply and Services.

Skutnabb-Kanga, T. Maffi, L. and Harmon, D. (2003), 'Sharing a World of Difference: The Earth's Linguistic and Cultural and Biological Diversity'. UNESCO. Terralingua, and World Wide Fund for Nature. Available (19 September 2005) at (www.terralingua.org).

Smith, L. T. (1999), *Decolonizing Methodologies: Research and Indigenous Peoples.* London, New York: Zed Books.

Task Force on Aboriginal Languages and Cultures (2005), *Towards a New Beginning: A Foundational Report for a Strategy to Revitalize First Nation, Inuit and Métis Languages and Cultures.* Report to the Minister of Canadian Heritage, June 2005.

UNESCO (1953) document on *The Use of Vernacular Languages in Education.* Paris: UNESCO.

Vallance, N. (2003). 'A comparison of the use of 'culture' by the Supreme Court of Canada in the recognition of Aboriginal rights and the protection of minority language education rights'. Paper presented to the Symposium on *Diversity and Equality: Understanding and Resolving the Conflicts Between Minorities and the Protection of Fundamental Freedoms in Canada*, University of Victoria, British Columbia.

Wolf, E. (1982) *Europe and the People Without History.* Berkeley: University of California Press.

Notes

1 In Canadian usage, the term *Aboriginal* refers to First Nations, Inuit and Métis people, who are recognized in the Canadian *Constitution Act* (1982), s. 35.

2 Since its establishment, the *Indian Act* has been continually revised through a series of amendments. However, the most comprehensive and significant revisions occurred in 1951, 1961 and 1985. These revisions included the removal of most discriminatory provisions, permitting the free movement off reserves, the right to organize politically, and the right to vote (which was legislated in 1962).

3 One issue in treaty negotiations was the use and occupancy of certain parcels of land and access to the resources that they contained. Although it remains an open question whether this included a ceding of territory, what is clear is that negotiations determined that specific portions of lands would be 'reserved' for the exclusive use of Aboriginal peoples.

4 According to the Ministry of Indian and Northern Affairs, '[t]he term "residential schools" generally refers to a variety of institutions which have existed over time, including: industrial schools, boarding schools, student residences, hostels, billets and residential schools' (www. inac.gc.ca, specifically, *Backgrounder: The Residential School System*, www.ainc-inac.gc.ca/gs/schl_e.html accessed September 2005). The residential school system predates Confederation, having grown out of Canada's experience with various missionary organizations. The Federal Government became significantly involved in developing and administering this school system as early as 1874, mainly to meet its obligation, under the *Indian Act*, to provide an education to Aboriginal people. A second goal was integration and assimilation into the dominant English-speaking, capitalist society.

5 Documentation of legal compensation and reconciliation claims can be found on the Assembly of First Nations website (www.afn.ca).

6 The three groups that constitute Aboriginal peoples in Canada (see n. 1) — namely, the First Nations, Inuit and Métis — have, as a result of their categorization as distinct groups in Canadian political-legal discourse, officially become distinct political entities, represented by the Assembly of First Nations (AFN), Inuit Tapiriit Kanatami (ITK) and the Métis National Council (MNC), respectively. Three other national organizations, the Native Women's Association of Canada (NWAC), Pauktutiit (the Inuit Women's organization) and the Congress of Aboriginal People (CAP), are also prominent in Aboriginal national politics. CAP is mandated to represent Aboriginal people regardless of their status or residency, one of its goals being the inclusion of non-status and urban Aboriginal people in the political process.

7 The five-volume report issued in November 1996 is commonly referred to as RCAP and is regarded as one of the most extensive Aboriginal perspectives on 'Canadian history and the role that aboriginal peoples should play in modern society' (Doerr 2000: 3).

8 The role of French and English was dealt with in the Royal Commission on Bilingualism and Biculturalism (B&B Commission), initiated in 1963 (which led to the *Official Languages Act* of 1969). Book 4 of the Royal Commission, published in 1969 under the title *The Cultural Contribution of other Ethnic Groups*, led to the establishment of official multiculturalism

policy in 1971, which later became entrenched in the *Multiculturalism Act* (1988).

9   Since then, there have been critiques concerning the contradictory nature of Canadian multiculturalism, which can be seen primarily as a homogenizing policy with the effect of transforming cultural diversity into a manageable entity (Mackey 2002).

10 The article, written by Frédérique Doyon and entitled 'S.O.S. langues autochtones — vers une loi 101 des Premières Nations?' ['SOS Aboriginal languages: Towards a Bill 101 for First Nations?'], appeared in the 18 October 2004 edition of *Le Devoir*, a French-language daily.

11 There are numerous international conventions relating to indigenous rights, culture and language. These include the *Universal Declaration of Human Rights* (1948), the *International Covenant on Civil and Political Rights* (1976), the International Labour Organization (ILO) *Convention 169 concerning Indigenous and Tribal Peoples in Independent Countries*, the *Convention of the Rights of the Child* (1989), the *Convention on Biological Diversity* (1992), the *Draft Declaration on the Rights of Indigenous Peoples* (1994), the *Universal Declaration of Cultural Diversity* (2001) and the UNESCO *Convention for the Safeguarding of the Intangible Cultural Heritage* (2003), (See *Task Force Report* 2005: 131).

12 All of these excerpts are taken from the Executive Summary of the Report, pp. i–xiv.

13 The Royal Proclamation of 1763 essentially ensured that lands held by 'several nations or tribes of Indians' were 'protected' as the 'hunting grounds' of these said groups by King George III of England. The Indian groups could sell their land to the British Crown but not to any private person. This established the constitutional basis for future treaty negotiations (Hall 2000: 2047).

14 The importance of treaties for Aboriginal peoples in Canada is a recurrent theme in the report, which figures both in various claims that it makes and even in its language. Most notable here is the use of phrases that echo those uttered at the conclusion of treaty negotiations, where they 'support[ed] the notion that the treaty relationship forged between parties was forever' (Morris 1991: 202; Office of the Treaty Commissioner 1998). We find such language in the assertion that restoring languages and cultures would ensure that Aboriginal nations remain strong for 'as long as the sun shines, the grass grows and the river flows' (Morris 1991: viii).

4 Discourses of endangerment: Contexts and consequences of essentializing discourses

Alexandra Jaffe

Introduction

This chapter takes a critical look at discourses of endangerment in a particular ethnographic context (Corsica). Its focus on both the causes and consequences of essentializing discourses about language endangerment in social and political context is used as a concrete case with which to discuss the implications of essentializing discourses in the public and academic sphere. The intent is to highlight the social and political processes that shape discourse in both endangered/minority language movements and within the worlds of academic research and among grant and policy-makers. This approach views both language activists and linguists as situated, interested social actors, and thus takes all discourses about language (including the trope of 'endangerment') as fundamentally political.

The Corsican case serves two illustrative functions. First of all, it identifies some of the unintended consequences of the promotion of minority or 'endangered' languages using essentializing discourses of language and identity which misrecognize some key aspects of social and linguistic practice and process. At the same time, an examination of Corsican sociolinguistic history cautions against an interpretation of these discourses as detachable from meaningful practice, and points to the ways and moments in which essentializing discourses become constitutive frames for the lived experience of identity through language. Second, the Corsican case also offers a suggestive alternative to essentializing discourses. Since the early nineties, Corsican language advocates have been promoting a 'polynomic' model of linguistic identity that makes variation and variability the centerpiece of practices of identification. This raises interesting questions about the conditions in which non-essentializing discourses can develop and take hold.

Essentialist discourses about language in Corsican language planning

In an essentialist perspective, the content of both 'language' and 'identity' and their iconic relationships are seen as fixed, ascribed/ natural and unproblematic. This ideological position is the cornerstone of many nationalist ideologies. In European nationalist discourse, described recently by Blommaert and Verschueren, it is taken for granted that language is a 'marker of essential identity, by association with a cluster of descent, history, culture, religion, economic status' (1998: 207). Within a nationalist discourse, therefore, language is a tool used to naturalize and legitimate political boundaries. Because language is being used in the service of a model of a bounded and homogenous nation, that boundedness and homogeneity is projected back onto language.

These ideological formations have had a profound effect on minority language revitalization movements like the Corsican one, because these movements' struggles for material and symbolic power and legitimacy have taken place in discursive fields dominated by essentialist ideologies of language and identity. Because these discourses only legitimate particular kinds of identity and particular kinds of difference, they inevitably shape the nature of minority language activists' claims to identity, rights or resources.

On the one hand, this influence is exercised from the 'outside': from centres of government power that control language policy. In the French context that influenced Corsican language activism, essential-izing ideologies had a long history in national-level discourses about French language, identity and citizenship in which regional/local languages and identities were targeted by policies of linguistic and cultural assimilation. But, as Ottavi (2004) points out, these ideol-ogies also structured more progressive discourses about the 'right to difference' that emerged in French public life after the Second World War and as a result of the post-colonial critique. In recog-nizing 'the region' as an administrative, economic and cultural entity, these discourses paved the way both for French regional nationalist movements like the Corsican one as well as for some political decen-tralization (the establishment of a Corsican Regional Assembly in 1982) and for educational policies that, over time, have opened the door of the French school to progressively greater teaching of the Corsican language.

These conditions affected Corsican language activism in several ways. First of all, dominant French ideologies that devalued languages other than French permeated Corsican experiences of schooling through the mid-seventies (and beyond). As they learned that French was a superior language, and the sole language of moral and civic virtue, Corsicans also learned that what they spoke was a 'patois': a non-language. Even after 1951, when (minimal) teaching of other French 'regional' languages in the public schools was authorized by the Loi Deixonne, Corsican was excluded on the basis that it was a dialect of Italian. At the same time, language activists were aware that many Corsicans had internalized linguistic stigma, and did not believe that Corsican was a legitimate language. Thus Corsican language activists who believed that it was important to teach Corsican in the school and to change diglossic language attitudes in order to protect the language were heavily constrained by dominant models of linguistic legitimacy. Representations of Corsican in this phase of language activism thus tended to essentialize language boundaries, by defining 'authentic' Corsican as a bounded code, located in a pre-contact past, maximally different from both French and Italian. I have labelled this position a 'purist' one, following the terms used in Corsican public discourse in the late 1980s to distinguish language activists working within this framework from their sociolinguistic colleagues.

Second, essentializing models of language and identity also entered into Corsican language activism via the Corsican nationalist movement. Under the influence of post-colonial social critiques, language shift – and minority language attrition – emerged in this and in other French ethnonationalist discourses as key elements of processes of linguistic and cultural alienation. The nationalist agenda thus took for granted a natural, essential link between the 'Corsican language' and the 'Corsican people', and sought to redress the 'unnatural' disruption of this link by processes of domination.

Contemporary discourses of endangerment in public discourse

Contemporary public discourses of endangerment, articulated in academic discourses and policy documents and proposals associated with language rights advocacy, have much in common with the essentializing dimensions of Corsican discourses about language in activist discourse through the mid-eighties. An exhaustive inventory of these texts goes beyond the scope of this chapter. Below, I offer seven illustrative examples from a set of documents published on the world wide web. Four of these documents are statements of philosophy by organizations funding endangered language research. These include two major American granting agencies (the National Science Foundation (NSF) and the National Endowment for the Humanities (NEH)), a granting programme housed in the University of London School for Oriental and African Studies (The Hans Rausing Endangered Languages Project HRELP)) and the Foundation for Endangered Languages (FEL). One document cited comes from the United Nations Educational, Scientific and Cultural Organization (UNESCO) website and establishes the philosophy of this international body's commitment to language diversity as an element of cultural diversity and human rights. The final document, a position statement by the Linguistic Society of America, represents one of the only professional academic organizations to take an official stand on endangered languages. These documents were chosen because they both represent the public face of their organizations and because they have a persuasive vocation, oriented towards a general public, rather than an academic audience:

1. Language is the DNA of a culture, and it is the vehicle for the traditions, customs, stories, history, and beliefs of a people. A lost language is a lost culture (NEH/NSF 2005).
   [NEH Chairman Bruce Cole, in a press release about joint NSF-NEH grants for the documentation of endangered languages]

2. Each language reflects a unique world-view and culture complex, mirroring the manner in which a speech community has resolved its problems in dealing with the world, and has formulated its thinking, its system of philosophy and understanding of the world around it ... with the death and disappearance of such a language, an irreplaceable unit in our knowledge and understanding of human thought and world-view is lost forever (UNESCO 2005).
   [Text under the heading, 'Why preserve linguistic diversity?' in the UNESCO webpage describing the on-line version of its 'Atlas of languages in danger of disappearing.']

3. Language diversity is essential to the human heritage. Each and every language embodies the unique cultural wisdom of a people (UNESCO 2003).
   [Beginning of a section titled 'Language Diversity in Danger' in a UNESCO document 'Language Vitality and Endangerment,' written by linguistic specialists on language endangerment.]

4. Today, there are about 6,500 languages and half of those are under threat of extinction within 50 to 100 years. This is a social, cultural and scientific disaster because languages express the unique knowledge, history and worldview of their communities (HRELP 2004).

[Web page of the Hans Rausing Endangered Languages Project, School of Oriental and African Studies]

5. Each endangered language embodies unique local knowledge of the cultures and natural systems in the region in which it is spoken (NSF 2005).

   [Introduction to the National Science Foundation's guidelines for Endangered Languages grants]

6. When a community loses its language, it often loses a great deal of its cultural identity at the same time[1] (Woodbury, no date)

   [Linguistic Society of America pamphlet, 'What does it mean to say a language is endangered?']

7. ...when language transmission itself breaks down...there is always a large loss of inherited knowledge...Along with it may go a large part of the pride and self-identity of the community of former speakers (FEL 2004).

   [Foundation for Endangered Languages: Manifesto]

As in the Corsican case, the implicit emphasis in these statements is on the properties of language-as-code (that can be documented) and its iconic relationship with the identity of bounded cultural groups. The discursive emphasis is on the connections between language and culture, which implicitly casts the content of both language and communities as fixed and unproblematic. In these and many other public (and academic) documents, we can also note the essentializing entailments of the biological metaphor (death, extinction), which fuses the linguistic and the biological in the image of language as species. The emphasis on language-as-code is also connected to arguments that are not about cultural specificity, but endorse the preservation of endangered languages as 'irreplaceable source[s] of linguistic and cognitive information'.

The second noticeable aspect of public discourses of endangerment is the focus on enumeration (England 2002; Hill 2002). All of these public documents cite either data from the Ethnologue database, or Crystal's book *Language Death* (2000) on the number of languages of the world (between 5,000–7,000) and the percentage of those languages that are at risk of extinction (50 per cent or more). I will have more to say about the implications of enumeration below, but here we can simply note that enumeration critically depends on the presence of clearly-bounded entities (languages) that can be counted, lost, described and saved.

I would argue that these public documents (all available on the Internet) have to be viewed in the same way as early Corsican activists' claims about the language. That is, they are efforts to influence public opinion and shape policy within existing discursive and ideological fields that only recognize particular kinds of linguistic and cultural identity and difference. In this respect, it is possible to view these documents as efforts to capitalize on public awareness and recognition of 'cultures' as belonging to discrete communities, and of languages as embodying those cultures in their vocabulary and structure (resulting from the widespread popularization of the Sapir-Whorf hypothesis). On this basis, organizations like the NSF, UNESCO, FEL, LSA and HRELP can attempt to mobilize progressive ideals of multiculturalism and the tolerance/celebration of diversity in the support of endangered languages. Essentializing discourses of language and culture (and their connection) have currency within 'rights' discourses, as they are legitimate notions of both collective rights (of ethnolinguistic groups to have their language) and individual rights (to choose a language). The essentialization of linguistic and cultural identity is also a bridge to the powerful trope of *ecology*; in particular its emphasis on the interdependence of all living organisms and societies and its characterization of protection of diversity as a global human imperative. In sum, the actions of Corsican language planners and the authors of these documents can be considered forms of 'strategic essentialism' (Spivak 1996 [1985]).

Intended and unintended consequences of essentializing discourses on Corsica

In my discussion so far, I have emphasized the structuring properties of dominant discourses about language and identity in the political and public fields of action in which both Corsican language activists and organizations defending endangered languages attempt to influence policy and practice. Here, I turn to the ways in which essentializing discourses created by language planners and advocates also structure experience and practice related to 'endangered' languages. In doing so, I take up the theme of a recent focus section of an issue of *The Journal of Linguistic Anthropology* (vol. 12, no. 2) devoted to the language of language endangerment: namely, that there is no neutral language to talk about language and the social processes in which it is embedded. The language we choose to talk about 'endangerment' and 'revitalization' always has entailments, and those entailments have social, cultural and political implications.

To explore some of these intended and unintended consequences, I turn again to the Corsican context, and the evolution of both language attitudes and language planning strategies and philosophies since the mid-seventies. In the first 15 years of language activism, Corsican activists worked hard to legitimate Corsican on both linguistic and social/political grounds. They devoted themselves to the codification and documentation of Corsican, producing an orthography, grammars, dictionaries and language-learning materials. They conducted a successful campaign on the regional and national level to get Corsican included in the Loi Deixonne so that it could be taught in the schools; in this period it would become a tested school-leaving subject and an integral part of University degree courses (through the Ph.D) in Corsican studies. In other areas of the public domain, activists pushed (albeit unsuccessfully) for the officialization of Corsican (and for compulsory Corsican language education) in the Regional Assembly, and (successfully) for the use of Corsican place names on public signage and in the media. The 'seventies' generation of activists were also prolific writers (poets, novelists, playwrights, lyricists) whose work constituted both corpus and status planning (that is, work on both the status of a language in a community and on linguistic form).

It is fair to say that much of this work either implicitly or explicitly represented Corsican as a bounded, historical linguistic code with an essential connection to Corsican identity. Over time, I have seen the ways in which these acts of linguistic legitimation have helped to change language attitudes and public discourse in the direction envisioned by language planners. Twenty years ago, many Corsicans refused to recognize Corsican as a legitimate language: I can remember being told I couldn't learn it because 'it didn't have a grammar'. Today, however, there is broad popular consensus that Corsican is a language and that it is a language worth speaking.

At the same time, these strategies of linguistic legitimation had a number of unintended consequences. Specifically, the making over of Corsican in the authoritative image of French in order to combat diglossia led to minority language purism and homogeneism. Corsican language purism, while good for the status of Corsican, stigmatized many habitual language practices, including codeswitching between Corsican and French and the use of contact-induced forms. In a purist framework, such forms were negatively evaluated as 'interference' from French. Here, we see the risks for the speakers of 'endangered' languages of essentializing discourses in which cultural identity is exclusively identified with language as a bounded, formal code. In this framework, language shift and other forms of contact-induced linguistic change become, by definition, forms of cultural deficiency at both the collective and the individual levels. The fact that not all Corsicans speak Corsican undermines claims to have a unique cultural identity and any other rights attached to that (including political self-determination). At the individual level, not speaking Corsican (or speaking it 'badly' or using mixed codes) can give rise to linguistic insecurity and, lurking in the background, a sense of cultural inauthenticity. For example, I still hear occasional disparaging comments about Corsican nationalists who don't speak Corsican, as though such a person couldn't possibly be culturally or politically credible.

There were other unintended consequences of the popular embrace of the notion that Corsican was a language. In effect, the legitimation of Corsican brought standard language ideologies into play in popular discourse; specifically, the conviction that a language had to have a single, unified norm. This, however, failed to disrupt long-standing cultural associations of authentic Corsican linguistic identity with particular regional varieties of the language. These competing ideologies of linguistic identity led to some of the impasses in Corsican language planning policy efforts, including failures to pass legislation officializing Corsican,[2] and resistance to making it a mandatory school subject. Corsican language planners confronted a public discourse in which the regional dialectal diversity of Corsican was often presented as an obstacle to the normalization and standardization that were seen as prerequisites for Corsican to take its place in formal, official institutions and domains. 'How can we teach Corsican in school,' people asked, 'if we can't agree on what Corsican to teach?' In short, the Corsican situation illustrates that language planning – and the discourses that sustain it – can disrupt the relationships with a language experienced by speakers as critical elements of that language's cultural value. These relationships are shaped both by local conditions and histories of practice (in which speaking Corsican was linked with speaking a specific variety of Corsican), as well as by histories of domination (in which speaking Corsican became exclusively associated with intimacy rather than authority). Overall, it is clear that discourses of language identity and endangerment in situations like the Corsican one affect (in sometimes unpredictable ways) the way that those languages are valued and used.

Alternative Corsican discourses of language and identity

It is also crucial to point out that within Corsican society, the purist/ essentialist discourse of language and identity was not hegemonic. By the early eighties, sociolinguistically trained Corsican language activists were taking stock of the side effects of the purism/essentialism I've outlined above. The mid-to-late eighties saw a public debate between leading figures identified with either the 'purist' or 'sociolinguistic' camps about how the Corsican language should be defined. Where the purists tended to locate 'authentic' Corsican in a pre-contact past, the sociolinguists defined Corsican as the usage of the contemporary speech community, and did not necessarily exclude contact-induced forms and practices as inauthentic. For the purists, a single norm was a desirable goal of language planning, and should be based on the expertise of 'authentic' (read, elderly) speakers and expert linguists. The sociolinguists, with their descriptive approach, located language norms and authority in the entire community of speakers. By the late eighties, the sociolinguistic position took a new turn, with the introduction of the concept of *polynomie* by the sociolinguist Jean-Baptiste Marcellesi. He defined a polynomic language as:

> une langue à l'unité abstraite, à laquelle les utilisateurs reconnaissent plusieurs modalités d'existence, toutes également tolérées sans qu'il y ait entre elles hiérarchisation ou spécialisation de fonction. Elle s'accompagne de l'intertolérance entre utilisateurs de variétés différentes sur les plans phonologiques et morphologiques, de même que la multiplicité lexicale est conçue ailleurs comme un élément de richesse (1989: 170).

> *a language with an abstract unity, which users recognize in multiple modes of existence, all of which are equally tolerated and are not distinguished hierarchically or by functional specialization. It is accompanied by tolerance of phonological and morphological variation by users, who also view lexical diversity as a form of richness.*

The polynomic perspective does not take the relationship of linguistic form and practice to community and identity for granted, but rather views it as an emergent property of social and political life. That is, the 'abstract unity' of a polynomic language is not primarily formal and linguistic, but social: it is the community that applies the label of 'language' to a set of linguistic practices. As an ideology of language, polynomie explicitly promoted a pluralistic perspective, endorsing the notion of language 'unity in diversity' that framed Corsicans' attachment to their local varieties of language as the foundation of their recognition of other varieties as legitimate language.

Over the last seven to ten years, the polynomic perspective has come to dominate some sectors of Corsican metalinguistic discourse. In particular, it has become the foundation of the curriculum at the Corsican IUFM (Institut Universitaire de Formation des Maîtres – or Teacher Training Institute) on Corsican language teaching methods.

Public and academic discourses: the repercussions of essentialism

In this section, I want to draw attention to some of the problematic entailments of essentializing discourses about language endangerment in the public and academic spheres, with reference to the following key elements: (1) the emphasis on language-as-code rather than language-as-practice; (2) the representation of language and community as fixed and unproblematic and how these lay the groundwork; for (3) discourses of enumeration and documentation; and (4) ecological/biological metaphors of language diversity. All of these things, I argue, misrecognize the fact that language practices and discourses about language are inherently political, social and ideological, and under-represent the role of those discourses about language in processes of language endangerment and revitalization/preservation.

1. Language-as-code

There is no doubt that languages are systematic codes. But there is also no doubt that that systematicity is also an artefact of selective and inherently ideological processes of codification. The Corsican case is only one of many around the world in which the codification process (what gets included) is the subject of social debate and contestation.

If we turn back to the public policy and advocacy documents introduced earlier, we find that they participate in the same ideological formation as early Corsican language planning. All of the organizations concerned use these documents as calls for academic action (and offers of funding) oriented towards the 'documentation' of endangered languages. This documentation includes the use of sophisticated recording technologies, and the collection of 'natural speech'; sometimes it includes the collection of culturally significant speech genres. But at its heart, the documentation envisioned is primarily formal: the orientation is towards the production of grammars, dictionaries and orthographies. Speech is recorded to 'preserve' it as a record of the language-as-system. As a consequence, the linguistic interventions endorsed by such a discourse inevitably result in texts that represent the language as a single, unified code. That code may not be intended by the linguists doing the documentation as a 'purist' one, and it may reflect a sophisticated distillation of everyday usage, but once written down it is inevitably read from within dominant language ideologies, and thus acquires the status of an authoritative standard.

Such documents thus have the potential to validate one form of a language over another, and thereby, to ascribe linguistic authority or legitimacy to some speakers over other speakers. In some cases, linguistic documents over-represent and thus privilege existing categories of speakers (for example, from a particular dialect area, generation or social stratum); in other cases, they contribute to the social validation of new forms of linguistic expertise (for example, academic knowledge). In the Corsican context, one of the reasons for popular resistance to language planning measures has been a reluctance to either bolster or undermine any one group of speakers' claims to superior endangered language competence and legitimacy. The polynomic approach is also clearly an effort to neutralize the creation of intra-Corsican language hierarchies.

The discourse of documentation has other implications associated in the embedded assumption that there is an empirical object (a language) ready to be captured on tape and written down. It is this that allows documentation to be represented as a straightforward task waiting to be accomplished by any capable linguist or member of the society. The presumed discrete unity of the object of study also allows the NSF to express the conviction that the language of inquiry can be satisfactorily standardized and that linguists will be able to come to an agreement about a shared object of study: 'Computerization will drive the development of a unified ontology for linguistics, eventually rationalizing inconsistent descriptive terminologies and analyses' (NSF 2005). In fact, as I explore below, there may not be an object of study that is completely independent of the language of description.

There are two crucial things missing from these accounts of the documentation process. First is the fact that, in contexts of language shift and revitalization, there are fundamental social debates about exactly what the linguistic features of language 'X' are, and who defines and embodies 'good' or 'authentic' language practice. Second, the linguistic anthropological literature has a by now well-established current of reflection on the situated, non-neutral and ideological nature of all processes of selection and transcription (see for example Ochs 1979; Bucholtz 2000, Jaffe 2000). In short, all documents created by insider or outsider linguists are, by definition, written from an ideological vantage point; the documents create the object as much as they reflect it.

The focus on language-as-code almost inevitably draws boundaries that tend to exclude and delegitimize the mixed codes and practices resulting from language domination, shift and revitalization. This has certainly been the case in Corsica, where despite 'sociolinguistic' and 'polynomic' incursions into public, discursive space, codeswitching and mixed forms tend to be evaluated as deficient with reference to purist models of both French and Corsican proficiency.

Finally, the objectification of language as a code is what makes possible discourses of enumeration, and the biological metaphors of 'species' and 'ecologies' often invoked in public discourses of endangerment. While the ecological metaphor has the advantage of highlighting the complex interrelationships between linguistic, social and material conditions that affect language choice, it tends to construct languages as separable from the environments that are viewed as either sustaining or weakening them. Mühlhäusler's formulation provides a partial remedy to this tendency: he emphasizes the effect of particular ecologies on the maintenance of linguistic *diversity* rather than on the maintenance of named codes (1996: 322). I would take this a step further, to emphasize the constitutive role of both language practices and discourses about language on the 'environment' or 'ecology'. Following the argument made above, the definition of what 'counts as' language 'X' or a 'good' version of language 'X' is both negotiated in and influences the social ecology.

We can make many of the same points about enumeration, drawing in particular on Urla's critical argument that statistical representations of non-dominant language practices constitute their objects (languages, speakers, communities) in ways that can both fragment and homogenize (1993). Because language is so intimately tied up with the politics of identity, enumeration is also always 'read' in relation to politically charged models and evaluative criteria. I am reminded here of a powerful lesson about the politics of representation that I got during my own dissertation research in 1988. I had enlisted the aid of students in a Corsican studies graduate class in distributing questionnaires about language practices to people that they knew. One student refused to give me her completed questionnaires back, because she said that her respondents had overrepresented how much they used Corsican, and thus underrepresented the extent to which Corsican was endangered and thus merited intervention. Others, however, were equally concerned about surveys that, in their view, underrepresented Corsican language use, because these called into question the legitimacy of Corsican as a cultural marker. Enumeration also, of course, raises crucial definitional questions about what can be counted (in survey data, it is always representations of practice) and the criteria used by either survey-makers or respondents to define what is meant by 'being a speaker' of a language.

2. Communities as homogenous and static

The social debates over language I have sketched draw our attention to the consequences of representing linguistic communities as

tities. This can be seen in the
in this chapter. It can also be
tive academic discourses that
measures elaborated through
and organizations with 'the
who the community is and who
some places, there is significant
vocacy path to be taken. But in
other cases (like the Corsican one), processes of both language shift and
revitalization have called all of these things into question, and people
are not unified around what will count as authentic communicative
practice, or who belongs to the 'speech community'. A homogenous
view of the endangered speech community is also unable to contend
with the local politics of such debates, which are always conducted
by situated social actors with particular interests and agendas (social,
political, economic and so forth). Just as there is no such thing as an
apolitical language planning programme, there is also no such thing as
an apolitical discourse of endangerment, since such discourses inevitably endorse some ideologies, agendas and interests over others.

Homogenous views of community can also be accompanied by
static views of culture and tradition. Consider the following extract
from the LSA pamphlet, 'What does it mean to say a language is
endangered?':

> Moreover, the loss [of language] is not only a matter of perceived
> identity. Much of the cultural, spiritual, and intellectual life of a
> people is experienced through language. This ranges from prayers,
> myths, ceremonies, poetry, oratory, and technical vocabulary, to
> everyday greetings, leave-takings, conversational styles, humor,
> ways of speaking to children, and unique terms for habits, behavior,
> and emotions. When a language is lost, all this must be refash-
> ioned in the new language ... for the most part such refashioning,
> even when social identity is maintained, involves abrupt loss of
> tradition. More often, the cultural forms of the colonial power take
> over, transmitted often by television. (Woodbury: no date)

This passage is, overall, a rich representation of the cultural salience
of language. But it represents the 'traditional' and the 'modern' or
'colonial' as opposed and mutually exclusive ways of being, and
implicitly identifies a culture's 'true' identity with a traditional past
and a single language. This account only represents one kind of
cultural identity and one kind of cultural conflict. In fact, processes of
cultural change in endangered language contexts, and their effects on
individuals and collectivities, are often more complex than this, and
the linguistic practices through which people live their cultural lives

69

are more heterogenous than such a model imagines. In the Corsican case, for example, people engage in (and transform) both 'traditional' linguistic and cultural practices at the same time as they express dominant language ideologies that have become defining elements of their cultural and linguistic experiences. In contexts of complex change and practice, there is no *a priori* way to know what kinds of shifts will be perceived as cultural 'loss' or 'rupture'.

Alternative models of language and identity

In the preceding critique, I have implicitly endorsed alternative models of language and identity that are practice rather than form-based, that acknowledge the political and social character of all identity claims, and that leave room for the multiple forms of language practice as well as heterogeneous and competing language ideologies among people who identify with endangered languages.

Such an approach (such as the one we find for example in the polynomic perspective promoted by a new generation of Corsican sociolinguists (Di Meglio 1991; Comiti 1992, 2004) would view language as a tool and a medium of the expression of identity without positing any necessary relationship, in endangered language contexts, between particular linguistic forms and 'authentic' communities. Rather, it would take into account the multiple ways in which particular linguistic forms acquire social and political meanings in particular historical and cultural contexts. In this view, processes of identification take place through practice, which is not limited to the use of a language, but includes representations of language (like discourses of endangerment). This acknowledges the conventional ways in which we understand a culture to be expressed through language, but it also allows us to understand the way that discourses structure lived experiences, and to recognize the conditions in which people come to experience the link between language-as-code and culture as an essential one. I take the defence of the subjective reality of this experience to be the link between language and culture that merits organizational and academic defence on humanistic and moral grounds associated with rights to dignity, and can involve the kinds of documentation supported by the various public organizations I have cited.

In fact, this kind of perspective validates a whole spectrum of possible local revitalization efforts (and hence, their support by academics and public instances). These include movements that take a hard line on the link between language use and cultural membership, and make certain levels of endangered language competence a prerequisite for various forms of social, cultural or economic benefits or forms of inclusion. But they also include efforts that have no discernible measurable outcomes on language competence, that will never produce anything more than 'semi-speakers' of various kinds, or may support the use of the language only in limited or ritual contexts. These kinds of results might never qualify as sustaining an endangered language conceived of as a 'full' linguistic code, but they can nevertheless be very meaningful for participants. The language in these cases is a focal element in cultural activity, but that activity is not oriented towards its full communicative use. Rather, select or partial uses of an endangered language become one of the ways that people signal their shared participation and shared cultural orientations in activities or events that invoke and may strengthen cultural identification. For example, I have observed and taken part in Corsican language classes for adults that fit into this category: participants don't and can't achieve significant levels of linguistic competence from these forums, but the time that they spend in the class is a positive experience of cultural identity. In short, this perspective shifts a language rights discourse away from individual or group rights to 'have' or 'own' a particular language, towards their rights to claim linguistic identities and to associate them with (or 'recognize' them in) any kind of linguistic form or practice.

We can take this a step further. Marcellesi's most recent account of *polynomie* (2003) does not just recognize *variation*, but takes *variability* as a central element of communicative practice, from the individual to the collective level. In other words, there is no assumption that individuals or groups will or should be linguistically consistent. Rather, they are seen as drawing selectively on a repertoire of forms. These forms may be systematically or stereotypically associated with particular social categories or stances, but even this systematicity does not completely predict the ends to which these linguistic resources may be used. With respect to discourses of endangerment, a defence of variability could shift the focus away from the survival of named linguistic codes towards the preservation of individual and collective access to the fullest possible repertoire of language practices. This would situate advocacy for endangered languages within a wider notion of language rights that would include: the rights of speakers of languages that are contextually 'endangered' even if they are globally strong; the rights of people who speak nonstandard forms of dominant languages, including ethnic and regional dialects, as well as nonnative varieties or even accents; the use of mixed codes; rights to institutional recognition of a diversity of oral and written norms and standards of style, performance, etc.; and rights of access to competence in standard/dominant languages, codes and styles.

What might be the conditions in which such a discourse could flourish? We can draw some inferences from the Corsican context, where a polynomic perspective has emerged and has been widely embraced by academics and educators over the last ten years. First of all, the concept of *polynomie* was introduced during a period in which the language was not fully standardized and in which standardization was socially contentious. While many Corsicans were heavily influenced by standard language ideologies, associating standardization with legitimacy, almost all Corsicans were resistant to anticipated outcomes of processes of standardization, in particular, to the potential erasure of regional or local linguistic particularities, and to the potential for new language hierarchies to benefit some speakers at the expense of others. In other words, they had an acute sensibility to both the meaningfulness of local particularity and to the political dimension of any kind of language planning. In public discourse about language through the eighties, the internal diversity of Corsican was often represented as an obstacle to its officialization and institutionalization; the idea of *polynomie* recast diversity as a fundamental element of Corsican speakers' mutual recognition of what it means to speak Corsican. It seems possible, therefore, to divert and recast ecological discourses of linguistic diversity in this fashion. At the same time, the fact that polynomie was advanced in public discourse at a time when the language was not highly institutionalized on Corsica suggests that it might be more difficult to recast the meaning of diversity in conditions of more advanced standardization/normalization of the 'endangered' language – whether undertaken from within, or from without (as in linguistic 'documentation' programmes). In fact, as Corsican has gained in institutional status, it has entered into domains that are structured by dominant language ideologies in ways that it is sometimes difficult to challenge, even by those with a commitment to a polynomic perspective. For instance, in Corsican bilingual schools, students whose teachers routinely expose them to different varieties of Corsican as legitimate tend to view the variety used by their teacher as the 'most correct' (Jaffe 2005).

It also has to be said that the polynomic principle has received the most traction on Corsica with respect to recognition of traditional, named regional varieties of Corsican. In this, it builds on previously underemphasized histories of inter-dialectal contact and accommodation between Corsican speakers. Marcellesi's endorsement of the notion of *variability*, however, has found a much more muted and tentative place in contemporary Corsican discourses about language, as variable linguistic practices in a context of language shift and revitalization still violate deeply-held convictions about the sanctity of language boundaries. Perhaps more importantly, they are difficult to embrace at a time when there is still insecurity about the robustness of the Corsican part of individual repertoires. Thus the emergence and persistence of new, non-essentializing discourses of language and identity depends on a delicate balance of political sensibility, attachment to local particularity, openness to the suspension of a traditional standardization agenda and linguistic security.

Conclusions

The complexities of Corsican language revitalization do not just illustrate that there are no neutral forms of endangered language advocacy, but also show that there are multiple and sometimes unpredictable consequences associated with any strategy or discourse. This applies to both essentializing and non-essentializing discourses. Here, I want to acknowledge the difficulty of putting non-essentializing discourses into practice in social fields that are profoundly structured by dominant, essentializing ideologies, from the macro level to the level of social psychology. My research and experience in Corsica has shown me that it can be difficult to put polynomie into practice in a context of language shift and revitalization. This is because institutions in which language revitalization take place (like schools) are not set up to recognize multiple norms and mixed codes, because it is difficult for speakers with lesser levels of Corsican competence to participate as equal partners in a collective norm-setting agenda, and because social and linguistic hierarchies are remarkably persistent. The polynomic perspective, with its emphasis on acts of collective *recognition* as the basis for linguistic identity, is just as silent as essentialist approaches on how we are to define or know the collectivity through its actions. Among the crucial questions it raises are: What constitutes recognition? How do we know when it has taken place? How is it manifested? In evaluating it, do we give differential weight to linguistic practices and metalinguistic discourses? Is recognition either present or absent, or can it manifest itself in a continuum of positions?

I would argue that these are the same kinds of questions about social and political process that I have raised with respect to essentializing discourses, and that they can only be studied empirically and ethnographically. This kind of research is also the only way to discover the strategic value of essentializing and non-essentializing discourses measured against goals of endangered language advocacy that are fundamentally moral and political rather than linguistic. In short, recognition of the social and the political dimensions of discourses of endangerment is critical even within a moral and ideological framework in which an essential relationship between language, culture and identity is posited as a given that must be defended. That defence can never just 'restore' a language; it will always inevitably create new linguistic, social and political realities.

References

Blommaert, J. and Verschueren, J. (1998), *Debating Diversity. Analysing the Discourse of Tolerance*. London: Routledge

Bucholtz, M. (2000), 'The politics of transcription'. *Journal of Pragmatics*, 32, 1439–65.

Comiti, J. M. (1992), *Les corses face à leur langue*. Ajaccio: Edizione Squadra di u Finusellu.

Comiti, J. M. (2004), 'Langue corse: une normalisation originale'. Available at www.interromania.com/studii/sunta/comiti/normalisation.htm – accessed 15 September 2005.

Crystal, D. (2000), *Language Death*. London: Verso.

Di Meglio, A. (1991), 'Polynomie et l'enseignement de la langue corse', in J. Chiorboli (ed.), *Actes du Colloque Internationale des langues Polynomiques*. Corte: Université de Corse, pp. 115–17. Available at www.interromania.com/media/pdf/ chiorboli/langues_polynomiques.pdf – accessed 15 September 2005.

England, N. (2002), 'Commentary: Further rhetorical concerns'. *Journal of Linguistic Anthropology*, 12, (2), 141–43.

Foundation for Endangered Languages (2004), *Manifesto*. Available at www. ogmios.org/manifesto.htm – accessed 5 June 2005.

Hans Rausing Endangered Languages Project (2004), *Endangered languages*. Available at www.hrelp.org/languages/ – accessed 5 June 2005.

Hill, J. (2002), '"Expert rhetorics" in advocacy for endangered languages: who is listening and what do they hear?'. *Journal of Linguistic Anthropology*, 12, (2), 119–33.

Jaffe, A. (2000), 'Introduction: Nonstandard orthography and nonstandard speech'. *Journal of Sociolinguistics*, 4, (4), 497–512.

Jaffe, A. (2005), 'La polynomie dans une école bilingue corse: bilan et défis'. *Marges Linguistiques*, 10. Available at www.marges-linguistiques.com – accessed 10 March 2005.

Journal of Linguistic Anthropology, volume 12, number 2, December 2002.

Marcellesi, J. B. (1989), 'Corse et théorie sociolinguistique: reflets croisés', in G. Ravis-Giordani (ed.), *L'île Miroir*. Ajaccio: La Marge, pp. 165–74.

Marcellesi, J. B. (2003), *Sociolinguistique: Epistémologie, langues régionales, Polynomie* (with T. Bulot and P. Blanchet). Paris: L'Harmattan.

Mühlhäusler, P. (1996), *Linguistic Ecology: Language Change and Linguistic Imperialism in the Pacific Region*. New York: Routledge.

National Science Foundation (2005), *Documenting endangered languages*. Available at www.nsf.gov/pubs/2004/nsf04605/nsf04605.htm – accessed 5 June 2005.

NEH/NSF (2005). *Federal agencies partner to document endangered languages.* Available at www.eukalert.org/pub_releases/2005-05/nsf-fap050505.php – accessed 5 June 2005.

Ochs, E. (1979), 'Transcription as theory', in E. Ochs and B. Schieffelin (eds), *Developmental Pragmatics.* New York: Academic Press, pp. 43–72.

Ottavi, P. (2004), 'Bilinguisme dans l'école de la République: le cas de la Corse' – (unpublished doctoral thesis, Paris: INRP).

Spivak, G. C. (1996) [1985], Subaltern studies. Deconstructing historiography', in D. Landry and G. MacLean (eds), *The Spivak Reader.* London: Routledge, pp. 203–36.

UNESCO (2003), *Intangible Cultural Heritage Unit Ad Hoc Expert Group on Endangered Languages.* Available at http://titus.fkidg1.uni-frankfurt.de/curric/dobes/UNESCOLgVit03Apr03.pdf – accessed 5 June 2005.

UNESCO (2005), *Atlas on Endangered Languages.* Available at http://portal. unesco.org/ci/en/ev.php-URL_ID=16548&URL_DO=DO_TOPIC&URL_SECTION=201.html – accessed 5 June 2005.

Urla, J. (1993), 'Cultural politics in an age of statistics: Numbers, nations and the making of Basque Identity', *American Ethnologist,* 20, (4), 818–43.

Woodbury, A. (no date), 'What does it mean to say a language is endangered?'. Linguistic Society of America pamphlet. Available at www.lsadc.org/faq/index.php?aaa=endangered.htm – accessed 5 June 2005.

Notes

1 With respect to the argument developed later in this chapter, the qualifier 'often' is important, and reflects the care taken by the authors of this document not to identify language as the sole vehicle for the experience or expression of cultural identity, and to relate that identity to language practices and not just language form.

2 A recent online poll by *Corsica Magazine* shows an almost dead heat between proponents and opponents of the officialization of Corsican.

5 Who wants to save 'le patois d'Évolène'?[1]

Raphaël Maître
Marinette Matthey

Introduction

The commune of Évolène, located at 1,500 metres above sea level in the Romand[2] part of the Swiss canton of Valais, is one of the last micro-regions (along with the Alpine valleys of the autonomous Italian region of Val d'Aosta) where the Francoprovençal vernacular is still spoken. Its 1,500 inhabitants live in five villages of 100 to 800 souls each. Évolène is one of the last places in French-speaking Europe in which the local vernacular, called 'patois d'Évolène'[3] by the residents, is still being learned as a first language alongside French by children in some (fewer and fewer) families. This form of language contact used to prevail in all of nowadays French-speaking Europe, but has disappeared almost everywhere; in the rest of Romand Switzerland this disappearance occurred over a long period, mainly between the seventeenth and the twentieth centuries. On the level of the community, this language contact presents a particular type of diglossia, characterized by a dynamic relationship between an official language, which is becoming more and more prevalent, and increasingly, the first language of the population, and a local vernacular which is more and more marginalized. This type of diglossia is known as *dilalia*.[4]

Over a period of three years (2001–2003) that included four fieldwork periods of six weeks in all, we conducted a sociolinguistic and dialectological research project in Évolène.[5] We carried out all the interviews together, as a team composed of a researcher in dialectology originating from this micro-region (R.M.) and a sociolinguist from a different region of Romand Switzerland (M.M.).

We completed around 80 interviews of an average duration of 90 minutes, of people with very diverse linguistic biographies. These sessions were taped and transcribed according to traditional conventions of conversational analysis. The main purpose of our project was to understand the place of Patois within the linguistic repertoire of the local population, the modalities of its use, its modes of acquisition

76

and the social representations attached to it (Maître and Matthey 2003, 2004; Matthey and Maître 2006; Elmiger and Matthey 2006), as well as to study the impact of the contact situation on the structures of the languages in contact (Maître, in preparation). Moreover, at the same time, we wanted to sound out potential expectations of the population concerning language policy with a view to sharing the results of our research with social actors interested in promoting the linguistic heritage of this touristic Alpine region, for example in the context of the school (from which the local language has always been excluded). This last objective became particularly salient for us when we looked back in a reflexive and critical perspective on the original grant proposal we submitted to the Swiss National Science Foundation (FNS) in 2001 to obtain financial support,[6] on the provisional results that we drew from our first year of research, and, above all, on the transcription of interviews taken from our first fieldwork period.

The aim of this chapter is to link an account of the ideological frameworks of the disciplines in which we work and in which we were trained (dialectology and the sociolinguistics of language contact) with a critical analysis of sections taken from our interviews. We will examine how our scientific presuppositions, but also our personal trajectories, contribute to shaping our exchanges with participants, and therefore also the data that we collect and analyse. Our chapter is divided into five parts: first, we will identify some of the ideological features characterizing the two research traditions to which we belong; then we will list the points where our approaches converged and on the basis of which we constructed our own project. Next, we will describe our provisional interpretation of the first data we collected in 2001. Finally, we will examine three fragments of conversation taken from our first 26 research interviews, in which one can observe discursive traces of the ideological standpoint informed by our disciplines and our trajectories, and that the very act of writing this chapter brought to light.[7] One will be able to see, through the correlation between two linked contexts, the disciplinary macrocontext and the interactional microcontext, how our positioning plays a role in the constitution of our interactional data, as well as in the provisional conclusions that we initially drew. In our view, all these considerations lead to the conclusion that the historical and ideological context cannot be dissociated from the construction of scientific knowledge.

1. What do we mean by ideology?

Since it is embedded in dominant discourse, the construction and interpretation of scientific data – as with any other scientific action

– partially eludes the researcher's awareness, and therefore his or her control. What we call the underlying *ideology* of the scientific act is this imprint, which in the end constitutes the social relevance of science, and which is, following Althusser, unconscious at the moment of the scientific action: 'une idéologie est un système (possédant sa logique et sa rigueur propres) de représentations (images, mythes, idées ou concepts selon le cas) doué d'une existence et d'un rôle historiques au sein d'une société donnée.' (1965: 238) ['An ideology is a system (with its own logic and rigour) of representations (images, myths, ideas or concepts depending on the case) endowed with a historical existence and role within a given society']. Althusser argues that 'l'idéologie comme système de représentations se distingue de la science en ce que la fonction pratico-sociale l'emporte sur la fonction théorique (ou fonction de connaissance).' (1965: 238) ['ideology as a system of representations is distinct from science in that the practico-social function prevails over the theoretical function (or function of knowledge)'].

We wish to emphasize, in the following lines, that this practico-social function – a function that we understand not only as the more or less explicit political aims of a scientific process, but also as the specifically social dimensions of the process of knowledge production (the researcher's personal history and education; work in teams; publications; fund raising ...) – fully belongs to the process of constructing knowledge. Ideology underlies the cultural definition of any scientific discipline; it is present in the researchers' personal motivations; it is called upon in the construction of a research project; it is necessarily taken into account, we assume, in the criteria necessary to obtain funds from granting agencies; it leaves traces in interactional data; it can be detected in the interpretation of these data; it justifies potential projects of political action; and it is amplified by the vulgarization and media coverage of research – for example, the markets of media and other forms of vulgarization are more attracted by subjects like ours, understood as 'language death', or subjects like the search for original languages than others more traditional within the field of linguistics (Israel 2001). In the end, if human sciences cannot be reduced to ideological actions, their ideological dimension motivates them and penetrates them through and through. That is why we can follow Heller (2002: 175) in saying that 'tout champ "scientifique" est foncièrement idéologique' ['any "scientific" field is fundamentally ideological'].

According to Althusser, ideology is not conscious; this is why a retrospective glance is relevant when, in response to Heller's call, one seeks to '[se] reconceptualiser comme productrices et producteurs de formes de savoir qui sont autant historiquement situées, sociologiquement ancrées et idéologiquement orientées que n'importe quel autre discours ou pratique' (2002: 187) ['to reconceptu-alize himself/herself as producer of forms of knowledge which are as much historically situated, as sociologically anchored and as ideologi-cally orientated than any other discourse or practice']. Looking back to the process of collecting and interpreting data allows the researcher to understand that she or he is not positioned outside the situation of the investigation, and to discover that it is difficult, in the heat of action, to raise certain kinds of questions (Heller 2002: 187), such as, for example, the question of knowing who wants to save the language which is one's very research topic. In our case, three years after our first research, a 'maturation of the results by second fermentation' seemed to us possible and that is what we submit here.[8]

The political and scientific context and the motivations of our project

In this chapter we wish to highlight a few of the ideological character-istics (in the sense defined above) of Romand dialectology and Swiss sociolinguistics of language contact. We do not intend here to provide a complete ideological history of the two disciplines; instead, we focus on the points that seem to us both constant in the disciplines throughout the twentieth century and relevant to our own thinking.

1. Romand dialectology: yesterday and today

In Switzerland, centuries-long contact with French led to the slow disappearance of the vernaculars. A direct result of this has been an ideological emphasis in dialectology since its early beginnings on the idea that language is tied to *heritage*. The sense of loss occasioned by the disappearance of regional languages, and that of urgency in the duty to react by an *acte de mémoire*, are not recent. The founding father of the *Glossaire des patois de la Suisse romande*,[9] Louis Gauchat, noted the following at the beginning of the twentieth century:

> On peut dire qu'à l'exclusion du Jura bernois, qui se rattache au groupe des patois franc-comtois, la Suisse romande a eu une fois une langue à elle, telle qu'elle n'existe nulle part ailleurs. Cette langue, qui était vraiment de chez nous, la Suisse est en train de la perdre. Le français de Paris a envahi nos vallons et la supplante partout. Nous n'aurons garde de nous répandre à ce sujet en plaintes vaines, car c'est là une nécessité économique imposée par les circonstances, et il serait puéril de nier les avantages de cette transformation. Mais la Suisse, qui fait tant de sacrifices pour la conservation d'espèces végétales ou animales menacées

de disparition, ne ferait-elle rien pour sauver d'un oubli total
l'instrument si original de la pensée de nos pères, la langue
qui pendant des siècles a servi à exprimer leurs joies et leurs
souffrances? (Gauchat 1914: 4–5)

*On can say that, with the exception of the Bernese Jura which
can be attached to the dialect of the Franche-Comté, Romand
Switzerland once possessed a language of its own, as it does not
exist anywhere else. Switzerland is currently losing this language,
which was really from our land. Parisian French invaded our
valleys and overwhelms it everywhere. We will not express vain
complaints on this subject, because it is an economic necessity
imposed by the circumstances and it would be childish to deny the
advantages of this transformation. But will not Switzerland, which
made so many sacrifices for the conservation of endangered plant
and animal species, do anything to save from complete oblivion
this original instrument of our fathers' thoughts, a language which
for centuries allowed them to express their joys and sufferings?*

Enunciative traces of Gauchat's affect emerge beneath his scientific knowledge. He mentions a language 'from our land', which,
lacking socioeconomic prestige, gave way to French; a situation that
he seems to experience as a glottocide, even though he recognizes the
advantages of the transition to French. One can notice that the question
of scientific action is also addressed: how could (Romand) Switzerland
not do something to save 'its' language from oblivion? Gauchat and
the philologists of the other linguistic regions of Switzerland at
the end of the nineteenth century appear to be developing a new
trend in philology centred around national heritage, thus positioning
themselves as social actors (cf. Heller 2002: 187).

Such are the ideological foundations on which this pioneer
institute of Romand Switzerland dialectology rapidly gained durable
respectability as a key actor in Gallo-Roman philology. Still today, its
expertise on the Romand dialectal space remains relevant within the
terms of the wider domain of European philology, based on the same
ideological foundations and operating by 'national' (or 'supranational',
or 'subnational') specialization.

The second major institution devoted to Romand dialectology
is the *Centre de dialectologie et d'étude du français régional* of the
University of Neuchâtel (abridged hereafter as the Centre de dialectologie), which for three decades now has been developing a research
tradition on French and the vernaculars in synchrony. The study of the
relations between the two represents one of its major focuses (cf. for
example Kristol 1998).

2. The 'Swiss model' of language contact

Between 1980 and 2000, the *Centre de linguistique appliquée* (CLA) of the University of Neuchâtel conducted qualitative sociolinguistic research on bilingualism and language contact. The epistemological foundations of what one may call 'the Swiss ideology of language contact' are to be found in (a) *comprehensive sociology* (Berger and Luckman 1986; Schutz 1987), which considers reality as a subjective construction by actors; (b) *methodological individualism*, which claims that 'selon l'individualisme méthodologique (quelle que soit la façon précise dont on l'interprète), on peut expliquer de façon satisfaisante les phénomènes sociaux en montrant qu'ils sont la conséquence des comportements individuels' (Sperber 1997: 123) ['(in whatever way one can interpret it), one can explain social phenomena in a satisfactory way by showing that they are the consequence of individual behaviours']; and (c) a *multilingual conception* of language and languages, in opposition to the monolingualism of nation states (Boyer 1999, 2001) and advocating a functional and non-purist vision of bilingualism (Lüdi and Py 2002).

These three epistemological pillars are at the basis of a non-conflictual approach to understanding bilingualism and language use in exolingual situations,[10] as opposed to the conflictual conception of Occitanists and Catalan sociolinguists (cf. Boyer 1999). This approach does not consider linguistic conflict as an external precondition to the diglossic situation and to the experience of the individuals living it. Quite the opposite, it constructs a methodological and interpretative framework which gives greater importance to actors' rationality and to the consensual values highly esteemed in Switzerland, while finely analysing concrete interactions in situations of language conflict. It does not rule out the possibility of a conflict in the field of languages, but the possible conflict is not understood as existing *a priori*, nor is it studied for itself. What is first considered are actors or communities of actors, who exploit different verbal repertoires in their daily language use. The CLA sometimes works alongside public groups, as for example in its recent project *biel.bienne – bilinguisme à bienne • kommunikation in biel*, financed by a private foundation of public interest. This project sought 'to put forward in its conclusions principles for a language policy specially adapted to multilingual regions'.[11] This approach has been labelled the 'Swiss interactionist and microlinguistic model' by Boyer (1999).

3. A few common points

One can say that both these disciplines in Switzerland, dialectology and contact sociolinguistics, are characterized by an ethnographic approach to their object (language for the first and linguistic use for the second), in the sense that they grant priority to fieldwork and to data collected from 'informants' or 'witnesses'.[12]

Behind their common ideological characteristics (acknowledging the centrality of identity in the first language, valorizing linguistic diversity, a non-conflictual approach to language contact, putting forward the concept of bilingual or multilingual language repertoire, interest in diglossia), appears a concern for relevance to the society to which the researchers belong. In a way, we can say that these scientific discourses endeavour to encourage social peace in the field of languages.

Interdisciplinary construction of the object of study

1. A typically Romand project

We met at the intersection of the two conceptual fields described above to co-develop our research project. The non-conflictual approach that we shared on the subject of language contact and linguistic usage became part of the 'scientific beliefs' that we brought with us, along with the view that Patois holds a value as a form of heritage. We embarked on our project with the idea that it was possible, and maybe desirable in the eyes of the concerned population, that our research could contribute to the promotion of Patois, within a peaceful relationship with French and in the context of the valorization of regional heritage. Among the main motivations that we emphasized for the SNF, under the heading 'Why is the planned research important?' ('En quoi réside l'importance des travaux projetés?'), we declared that we were willing to explore possibilities to extend the scientific aspects of our research into political action centered on schooling or tourism. This can be seen in the following quotation from our proposal to the FNS:

> Les résultats de la recherche devraient intéresser les instances communales et cantonales, dans la perspective de valorisation du patrimoine à usage interne et externe. On peut imaginer par ailleurs qu'un module *d'Eveil au langage* consacré au parler local soit intégré dans les programmes de connaissances de l'environnement en Valais, par exemple. On peut imaginer également que les résultats puissent faire l'objet d'une exposition durant la saison touristique. Ces démarches de valorisation devraient s'effectuer en partenariat avec les instances communales et cantonales

> *The results of the research should be of interest to the institu-*
> *tions of both the commune and the canton in the perspective of a*
> *valorization of the heritage for an external or internal usage. One*
> *can moreover imagine that an educational module on 'Language*
> *awareness' could be added to the curriculum of Connaissances*
> *de l'environnement in canton Valais, for example. One can also*
> *imagine that the results could be the basis of an exhibition set up*
> *during the tourist season. These measures of valorization should*
> *be accomplished with the partnership of the commune and the*
> *canton.*

We did not consider ourselves rescuers of the vernacular. Adopting a militant position was out of the question, as was the attitude of taking up arms to 'save Patois' from its predictable disappearance. We intended to *understand* the existing social representations, and *corollarily*, to explore potential social expectations on the subject of the implementation of a language policy promoting Patois. Beyond our role as describers of linguistic realities, we were willing to be available to serve as potential facilitators of heritage projects, if they responded to the expectations of the concerned population. Just as philologists at the end of the nineteenth century had developed the patrimonial trend of philology without losing their scientists' soul, we were ready to develop the patrimonial trend of Romand sociolinguistics.

2. A project seeking synergy between disciplines

Our project was in agreement both with dialectology and the sociolinguistics of language contact, disciplines from which it came and of which it represented a crossroads. It was also complementary at different levels. First, by choosing a research field where local Francoprovençal kept a function as a vernacular, the project greatly contributed to complete the too often partial image that mainstream sociolinguistics has of Romand Switzerland, reminding us that the vitality of Patois is still a relevant sociolinguistic fact on the local scale (cf. Maître 2003). Second, while exploring a research field usually favoured by dialectology from a sociolinguistic point of view, and while focusing on contact phenomena, the project put an emphasis on twentieth-century dialectal data, material which is usually studied for itself, and where this kind of consideration is mostly considered of a lesser importance. From an institutional point of view, we showed through this project that dialectology and the Swiss trend in sociolinguistics of language contact can be considered as complementary rather than parallel, as they are most often seen today in Romand Switzerland. Bringing together the resources of two centres from the same university, the CLA and the Centre de dialectologie, created an innovative synergy, a notion itself in accord with the new economic strategies of today's universities.

3. A personal project

Finally, our personal motivations converged with current trends in Swiss sociolinguistics. Before taking up this project, both the researchers had close non-professional ties with the region of Évolène. R.M. is personally involved with Patois, a language linked to his familial origins. M.M., who has been visiting the commune on holidays since childhood, is also sensitive to the notion of heritage, and above all to issues of first-language identity. During the interviews, she mentioned several times, as a parallel to Évolène, La Brévine and Le Locle, her region of origin, which presented a similar situation in the nineteenth century. This common involvement with Évolène greatly contributed to the birth of this project, and it crystallized our positive attitude towards Patois. Since in most regions of Romand Switzerland the diglossic relations between Patois and French disappeared in the course of the nineteenth century (cf. our quotation of Gauchat, above), we both considered it a privilege to have the opportunity to study Patois as a language which still had a role in the daily life of Évolène (albeit to varying extents, cf. Maître and Matthey 2003), rather than as a museum object. Thus, when we went to our fieldwork site, we were not neutral about our object of study. We will identify discursive traces of our involvement below.

Lastly, as we had chosen linguistic research as a profession, we were also financially concerned to convince the SNF that our project was of interest. When our project was funded, we set out to meet the people of Évolène, wanting to learn about their linguistic biographies and their linguistic representations.

First results of the research

After having analysed the first interviews that we had conducted, we concluded our first year of research with optimism regarding the relevance and the chances of success of acting in the direction of implementing a language policy, particularly the introduction in the school of a course on Patois for interested students (cf. Maître and Matthey 2004). Our interim report for the SNF also foresaw the possibility of such a politico-educational action, based on the grounds of our research interviews: we legitimated this procedure by the generally favourable attitudes that we had perceived in the discourse of the 27 people we had met up to that point. Following from this, we questioned a traditional belief of dialectology (see, among others, Knecht 1985) stating that Patois has no place in schools:

> Dans une vision fergusionnienne de la diglossie, le patois, variété basse, n'a pas sa place à l'école, lieu institutionnel impliquant l'utilisation de la variété haute (Ferguson 1959, Lüdi 1990). Knecht (1985) semble partager cette vision en partie. Pourtant, la plupart aujourd'hui se disent favorables à 'ce que l'école fasse quelque chose pour le patois'. Le mouvement séculaire de scolarisation a investi la vie quotidienne au point de rendre caduque la dichotomie *école et variété haute vs vie quotidienne et variété basse*. L'école peut aujourd'hui jouer un rôle dans la prise en compte de la réalité sociolinguistique de la commune. (Py *et al.* 2002: 2; our emphasis)

> *In Ferguson's view of diglossia, Patois, the low variety, has no place in school, an institutional space which implies the use of the high variety (Ferguson 1959, Lüdi 1990). Knecht (1985) seems to partly share this vision. However, most of the persons that we heard declared themselves favourable to the fact that 'school should do something for Patois'. The secular movement of schooling has positioned the school at the heart of daily life, thus invalidating the* **dichotomy school and high variety vs daily life and low variety**. *Today, school could be asked to play a role in taking into account the commune's sociolinguistic context.*

Looking back on the data

After we reread our transcription, keeping in mind the signs of contextualization that we could have given as elicitors of a discourse, we will show how an interactional framework is being constructed during the interviews, even when we did not seek it consciously; this framework oriented the discourse towards the provisional results that we have just described.

Before presenting the extracts, we want to point out that our research epistemology brought us to conceive of our interviews as conversations on themes, thus allowing the informants to talk about themselves (linguistic biography). As we consider language to be 'non-transparent', we do not think that we reach across it like a mirror to 'discover' the already formed linguistic representations of our interlocutors. We share the idea that the discourse that is addressed to us is also a product of the situation of utterance, that it partly emerges from this situation, and that we are involved both as researchers and as individuals in order to encourage the people that we meet to talk, and in our active listening. Furthermore, we use a dynamic and

85

intersubjective approach to the interview: we occasionally integrate our personal experiences as well as our first interpretations of previous interviews, in order to stress or elaborate on our interlocutors' statements. We will see that through this practice we create signs of affectivity, which grant Patois a strong symbolic capital and which bring to light, bit by bit, the ideological ingredients that we presented above.

1. Making explicit the motivations of I2

This extract[13] is from the beginning of an interview. I1 and I2 (Maître and Matthey) are led, following B's questions, to explain the reason for their study:

4   **B**   *mais le le&le total de toute cette étude / c'est pour quoi /*

5   I2   alors bon nous / on est au début hein \

6   I1   on est au début / on a commencé le premier octobre / là / . en fait / on a obtenu un crédit du : du Fonds National de La Recherche / . pour faire une étude de deux ans sur le . sur le patois d'Évolène mais d'aujourd'hui / comment il est parlé / comment il est utilisé . euh : \ est-ce que les enfants le parlent encore / c'est pour ça qu'on : on fait des entretiens . avec trois générations / . et puis euh : \ bien ça va donner lieu euh : à des articles / . peut-être un bouquin / peut-être que si on-on aura peut-être l'occasion de faire un *livre* / mais surtout I2

7   **B**   *hmhm*

8   I1   euh : \ il fait sa thèse là-dessus \

9   **B**   hmhm

10   I1   voilà donc lui / c'est :

11   **I2**   **moi j'ai toujours voulu faire un : . faire quelque chose sur le patois **

12   **B**   *hmhm*

13   **I2**   **j'ai toujours regretté de pas parler patois \ moi **

14   I1   (en riant :) ouais c'est ça

15   **B**   et et alors pour*quoi* \

16   I1   *il a* un compte à régler avec ses ancêtres \

17   [...]

18   **B**   et pourquoi / vous parlez pas \ vous le comprenez /\

19   I2   mais nous / on a jamais habité ici \

20   B   oui / moi non plus \ mais vous le comprenez /

21   I2   je comprends euh : \ le gros je comprends / .. et un petit peu je peux faire semblant de parler /

22   B   FÉLICITATIONS \

4.   **B**   **but the the&the whole of this study/what is it for/**

5.   I2   so well we/we're at the beginning eh/

6. I1 we're at the beginning/we started the first of October/
    (emphasis)/. In fact/ we got funds from : from the
    National Research Foundation/ . to conduct a two-year
    study on the. on Évolène Patois but nowadays/ how
    it is spoken/ how it is used. Uh:/ do the children still
    speak it/ that's why we : we are doing interviews. With
    three generations/ and so uh:/ well it will produce uh :
    articles/. Maybe a book/ maybe if we we maybe have the
    opportunity to write a *book*/ but mainly Raphaël

7. B   *hmhm*

8. I1 uh:/ he's writing his thesis on it\

9. B   hmhm

10. I1 so there it is so he/ it's :

11. **I2 I always wanted to do a : do something on Patois **

12. B   hmhm

13. **I2 I always regretted not speaking it\ myself **

14. I1 (laughing:) yes that's it

15. B   and and so why_\

16. I1 *he has things to settle with his ancestors *

23 [...]

24 B   and why / don't you speak \ you understand it /\

25 I2 but we / we never lived here \

26 B   yes / me neither \ but you understand it /

27 I2 I understand uh : \ I understand most of it / . and I can
    pretend to speak a little bit

28 B   CONGRATULATIONS \

Commentary

The sequence opens with B's question ('*the whole of this study, what is it for?*') and it gives I1 the opportunity to present the project: the elements which are mentioned are, first, the support of the SNF, then that the study is anchored in the everyday usage of Patois, and finally the answer to B's question ('*it will be the subject of articles, maybe a book or a PhD thesis*'). One can notice that this presentation mentions the importance of the embeddedness of Patois in the daily life of the informants, which justifies the interview. The declaration about the thesis triggers a side section in which I2 is led to say that he wishes he spoke Patois. In this sequence, I2 uncovers the affective ties linking him to his research topic; he introduces a context favourable to Patois, even if his joking with I1 (cf. turn 16) somewhat mitigates his regret about not speaking Patois. In these first minutes, which are particularly important for the construction of the interview structure, this sequence establishes an interpersonal relationship, in the guise, even if only symbolically, of a *we-code* (we are/would have liked to be Patois speakers), just as it makes explicit the positive value that we conferred on Patois, as individuals and as university researchers. Thus, this explicit manifestation of our attitudes produced an enthusiastic response ('congratulations!'). Moreover, B stayed until the end of the meeting, even when we had to interview her husband.

2. The researchers are pleased about the existence of a L2 speaker of Patois

In the following quotation,[14] I1 and I2 cannot hide their exultation when they learn about a speaker of Patois who learned it as a second language:

465	A	moi / je con*nais* . je connaiss-bon maintenant il il est parti l'année passée autrement je
466	I1	*hm*
467	A	**connaissais un-un Portugais **
468	I1	ah ouais /
469	A	**et il parlait le patois /**
470	I1	ah ouais
471	I2	c'est pas J par hasard il s'appelle quelque chose comme ça
472	A	euh : . il ba-il travaille avec K à Évolène \ . il a travaillé *douze ans* douze ans avec lui je crois
473	I2	*ah bon*
474	I1	il faisait quoi /
475	A	eux ils travaillaient à la ferme /\
476	I1	à la ferme /
477	A	ouais . eux ils parlaient patois / ...
478	I1	**heinhein c'est extra ça (rire I2)**
479	I2	ça c'est bien
480	I1	**ça c'est extra**
481	A	le (un?) portugais
482	I1	ouais
483	A	il avait il avait (pouffe) un accent / ça clair / ouais \
484	I2	puis puis le français / il parlait aussi / bien sûr \
485	A	oui .
486	I2	**chapeau**
487	I1	**ouais chapeau alors **

465	A	I/I kne. I knew-well now he's left last year otherwise I
466	I1	hm
467	A	**I knew a-a Portuguese man**
468	I1	oh yeah
469	A	**he spoke Patois /**
470	I1	oh yeah

471	I2	it wasn't J by any chance his name is something like that
472	A	uh : . he ba- he works with K in Évolène \ . he worked for twelve years twelve years with him I think
473	I2	*oh really*
474	I1	what did he do /
475	A	they worked on the farm /\
476	I1	on the farm /
477	A	yeah . They spoke Patois / ...
478	**I1**	**hey hey that's amazing (I2 laughs)**
479	I2	that's great
480	**I1**	**that's amazing**
481	A	(a?) Portuguese (man?)
482	I1	yeah
483	A	he had he had (laughs) an accent / of course / yeah \
484	I2	and and French / he spoke French too / of course \
485	A	yes .
486	**I2**	**hats off to him**
487	**I1**	**yeah hats off to him okay **

Commentary

I1 and I2's positive feedback ('that's amazing, that's great, hats off') shows again the emotional involvement of the researchers. After analysis, we can explain this enthusiasm by our noticing that diglossia is still showing some vitality, because Patois can be learned as a second language in an informal way through a process of socialization typical of the experience of migrants. In this sequence, this show of enthusiasm displayed the position we held with respect to our object of study: it could only be interpreted by our interlocutor as a sign of a favourable attitude towards Patois.

3. The researchers want to convince the interviewed of the value of Patois

This third quotation[15] shows how the researchers react quite sharply to the discourse of their interlocutor when she expresses her doubts about the relevance of integrating Patois in the school programme:

583	I2	**vous pensez que ce serait bien / de faire quelque chose sur le patois \ à l'école/**
584	A	je me demande / s'ils font pas / déjà ici à évolène
585	I2	ah
586	A	je me demande / s'ils font pas /
587	I1	ça on devrait demander /\ hein /

588   I2   hmhm .
589   A   **ouais . à l'école je sais pas / . je sais pas / comme vous-je vous dis c'est joli c'est folklorique MAIS . la valeur n'y est pas / hein **
590   I2   hm
591   I1   **bon la valeur marchande / mais la valeur identitaire et&et le le fait c'est quand même /**
592   A   *c'est joli /*
593   I1   **bien oui /** *avoir une langue* **que pour-qui est : .** *c'est votre langue /* **euh : ** *sur un très petit*
594   A   *c'est joli / mais*   oui ouais ouais
595   I1   **territoire /**
596   A   ouais / c'est notre langue / ouais&ouais ouais&ouais ouais
597   I1   **ça c'est quand même euh une richesse euh : (rire A)**
598   I2   **c'est une grande richesse /**
599   I1   **c'est quand même quelque chose / quoi \ ouais**
600   A   *c'est* vrai oui
601   I1   ouais
602   A   ça / c'est vrai oui

583   I2   do you think it would be good / to do something on Patois \ at school/\
584   A   I wonder / if they don't do it / even here in Évolène
585   I2   ah
586   A   I wonder / if they don't do it /
587   I1   we should ask that /\ eh /
588   I2   hmhm .
589   A   **yeah . at school I don't know / . I don't know / as you-I tell you it's pretty it's folkloric BUT . the value isn't there / eh **
590   I2   hm
591   I1   **well the exchange value / but the identity value and&and the the fact just the same it's /**
592   A   *it's pretty /*
593   I1   **well yes /** *to have a language that for-which is: .* **it's** *your language /* **uh : ** *on a very small*
594   A   it's pretty / but   yes yeah yeah
595   I1   **territory /**
596   A   yeah / it's our language / yeah&yeah yeah&yeah yeah
597   I1   **that's a treasure just the same uh : (A laughs)**
598   I2   **it's a huge treasure /**
599   I1   **that's something just the same / right \ yeah**
600   A   *that's true yes*
601   I1   yeah
602   A   that / that's true yes

Commentary

When she answers I2's question in the opening sequence ('do you think it would be good to do something on Patois in school?'), A appears skeptical: she thinks that Patois is 'folkloric' and 'nice' (with a slightly ironic implication). Her assertion 'there is no value in it' triggers a sharp reaction from the researchers: I1 suggests distinguishing between *market* and *identity value* and the two researchers agree on stressing the value of identity, arguing that Patois is 'a great treasure'. And A finally agrees ...

One can notice at the beginning of the sequence an example of unshared categorization between the informant and the researchers. For A, a speaker of the vernacular, a language which is in fact dominant in her linguistic usage, Patois is *nice*, but the fact that it has no value seems more important for her. The researchers, however, share scientific presuppositions favouring the dimension of identity in languages, and especially in first languages, inasmuch as linguistic practices and socialization are understood as intrinsically linked.[16] The processes of influence operating in any exchange are visible here: the pursuit of an agreement to end the exchange prompts A to finally admit the researchers' arguments, valorizing the identity function of Patois. This sequence clearly exemplifies the ideological gap between interviewer and interviewed, and the way that the statements uttered by the former are used as a frame for the latter's discourse.

Drawing on these three quotations taken from our corpus, we illustrated how a retrospective analysis of our transcriptions displays the co-constructed character of research data, taking into account the interventions of researchers (eliciting a discourse) in the constitution of field data.

One first sees that the informants' statements cannot be considered as a mechanical process that puts into discourse 'pure' representations, but as discourses that they co-construct *with the researchers who display a positive attitude towards the vernaculars and their speakers.*

One then notices that the former produces within these few conversational turns a significant number of the ideological characteristics found above, in the guise of attitudes and behaviours: the demonstration of enthusiasm for the vitality of Patois and its diglossic relationship with French; the pursuit of complicity with the people that we met regarding the feeling of loss; the legitimation of a research project through its scientific status; the legitimation of Patois alongside French; optimism on the subject of the relevance of a language policy to valorize the local language; a sensitivity for the function of identity in Patois as well as the patrimonial value of this language.

The conversational transcriptions of research interviews are, in this respect, an excellent tool to check who said what, after whom, who started such and such a theme, who suggested what to whom and who validated whose categorization. Without this tool, we would have believed for a long time, as we highlighted in our intermediary report, that the majority of Évolène's inhabitants had expectations regarding actions for the defence of Patois. However, thanks to these transcriptions, we discovered that the expression of a favourable attitude towards such actions was, in many ways, induced by the unfolding of the interview.

Two considerations

We would like to extend this reflexive exercise by emphasizing two points. First, the constitution of data in interview situations can be considered as a meeting space between academic knowledge drawn on by the researchers and experiential knowledge drawn on by all. In the situation of an interview, no clear boundary can be drawn between these two modes of knowledge, interconnecting to produce the data. We consider that a totally 'neutral' or 'depersonalized' interview is not relevant for the production of an interactive corpus of this kind. Moreover, we share Favret-Saada's point of view (1990), that it is impossible not to be *affected* by the field, by the people we work with. What needs to be done *then* is to *readjust* oneself (but not to *detach* oneself from the moments of these interviews)[17] in order to engage in the interpretation of data, in the constitution of scientific knowledge. This is what we did here when we shared this reflexive analysis. At the moment of theoretical reflection, the investigating subject becomes a part of the object of its own analysis.

Second, as we noticed at the conclusion of this reflexive analysis, the non-militancy of our scientific discourse (our goal is not to *defend* Patois d'Évolène against French), corresponds well to what we have called the 'Swiss ideology of language contact' (cf. above), which is linked to the basic premises of most Swiss sociolinguists (a group to which we belong, of course): language contact does not *de facto* entail *linguistic conflict* between locutors, and we can add: even when a process of change is under way.

Possibly prompted by this non-conflictualist ideology of language contact, we were able, through the analysis of our interview data, to formulate and consider as scientific knowledge (as 'truth') the following thesis: the progressive decline in the usages of the vernaculars is often associated with a feeling of *loss*, more or less painful depending on the person. This condition is linked to the fact that Patois operates as a vehicle for social identity, a symbol of the tie to tradition and old times; it is the means of expression and affirmation of loyalty to the community, the land and its history (cf. Maître and Matthey 2003, 2004; Matthey and Maître, in press). It is because they echo this feeling of loss that attitudes are generally positive towards potential projects to promote Patois (actions in the field of museography, or even distributing knowledge *about* Patois, at school or somewhere else). However, few speakers feel any desire to oppose by concrete actions what can be understood as a process of substitution (or in any case, change). The vitality of Patois is almost always considered the result of parents' choices, that is to say as a private matter *de facto* excluding any public interference; those families who indeed consciously (even militantly) speak the vernacular and apply a 'Patois-only family language policy' are part of a minority locally known by the nickname 'les enragés du patois', that is to say 'the Patois-crazed'. Finally, a last thing seemed significant: in the totality of our 80 interviews, we did not record any *spontaneous* speech advocating a glottopolitical action aiming at resisting current processes of changes in linguistic practice (that is, no one appealed to any notion aimed at 'saving Patois'). Following from this, an action seeking to promote the use of the vernacular, which would require substantial financial means, eventually appears to the eyes of the population as a superfluous luxury.[18]

The inhabitants' attitudes towards foreign language acquisition are similarly non-conflictualist: foreign languages are not seen as a threat to Patois or to French, but on the contrary as a form of capital that children gain in school and that can yield a profit while ensuring better socio-professional prospects.

In conclusion, the population does not consider itself as a spectator, or as a victim, of the process that gradually imposes French in everyday life and thus leads to the restriction in use of Patois. It is, however, an actor – and even a beneficiary in this process, if we are to believe our statistical study (Matthey and Maître, in press) showing that there is a significant correlation between social mobility and a strengthening of French in linguistic practice. Thus, the results of the interviews seem to confirm sociolinguistic theories about language change linked to social mobility: a speaker who can and/or wishes to break with traditional activities and structures, adapts his/her linguistic resources to this trajectory, and school merely materializes this intention as it allocates more and more time to second languages, in accordance with the parents' expectations regarding the professional integration of their children.

But in the end who wants to save *le Patois d'Évolène?*

Now that we brought to light some facets of the ideological under-pinnings of our project on Évolène, we are going to try to answer the following question: which of the actors mentioned in this text can be identified as militants for the survival of the linguistic usage of the vernacular at the dawn of the twenty-first century?

One of the objectives of our research project was to evaluate the expectations of Évolène's inhabitants regarding political support for Patois: we have no choice but to take note that such expectations are scarce. On the contrary, what is striking is the similarity in the attitudes of Gauchat in 1914 (who considered it 'childish' to lament over a bygone age) and that of the speakers of Patois in Évolène in 2005: even when the progressive disappearance of the vernaculars is visible and when one feels concerned by it, one does not see the necessity to counter it.

When we left in search of the identity and heritage dimensions of Patois d'Évolène, its speakers reminded us of something else: the vernacular in Évolène represents one of the elements of the linguistic repertoire; as such, it is a tool which is used depending on social relevance, situated in history and particular economic circumstances. Even if the local vernacular benefits from an identity and emotional attachment, this does not guarantee it much weight in real practice, faced with the reality of the francophone linguistic market: as soon as French is recognized as the language of social mobility, it tends to be preferred in practice and to progress in its functions (Matthey and Maître, in press). The inhabitants of Évolène do not consider the touristic gain potentially brought by a valorization of this unique linguistic heritage to be sufficiently interesting or important, nor do they feel dispossessed of their language, because they are the ones abandoning it. As a 30-year-old man, born in Évolène but who does not speak the vernacular, told us, '*Patois, it's something proper to Évolène, but it is not what makes an Évolénard*[19]': even if an Évolénard's identity does still hold the emotional value of a linguistic repertoire comprising Patois, in the eyes of the community, it no longer requires an active competence in what has become a symbolic language.

The political authorities did not prove enthusiastic about the idea of spending time or money on a project to provide the local language with a more official status or even to integrate it in school. They behave very differently about spending on the teaching of French, German and English. One must assume that they do not consider Patois likely to provide an interesting return on investments be it in terms of modifications in social practices or anything else.

In these conditions, it would not make sense for the political actors of the canton and the Confederation to finance any action to promote the use of the vernacular. However, there is some relevance in the funds granted by the SNF to linguists eager to collect and analyse precious and ephemeral data: society turns its heritage language into a museum display. This was already the case at the beginning of the twentieth century when the *Glossaire* was funded, and it still is the case 100 years later, if, as we assume, the heritage value attached to our object of research – as well as the theme of language death, a popular theme on the media market – turned out to be in support of our project.

Ultimately, as we mentioned above, seeing that we are Swiss linguists, we are too marked with Swiss consensualism to become 'paladins of endangered languages' (Israel 2001).

We can thus finally answer the question that we raised in our title: who wants to save 'le patois d'Évolène'? It will not be its speakers, nor political authorities, nor the directors of scientific research, nor individual researchers. To sum it up, the answer seems to be: nobody!

References

Althusser, L. (1965), *Pour Marx*. Paris: Maspero.

Berger, P. and Luckmann, T. (1986), *La construction sociale de la réalité*. Paris: Klincksieck.

Berruto, G. (1989), 'On the typology of linguistic repertoires', in U. Ammon (ed.), *Status and Functions of Languages and Language Varieties*. Berlin: De Gruyter, pp. 552–69.

Boyer, H. (1999), 'L'unilinguisme français: une idéologie qui s'essouffle mais ne se rend pas'. *Travaux de didactique du français langue étrangère*, 41, 27–37.

Boyer, H. (2001), 'L'unilinguisme français contre le changement sociolinguistique'. *Travaux Neuchâtelois de Linguistique (TRANEL)*, 34/35, 383–92.

Boyer, H. and de Pietro, J.-F. (2002), 'De contacts en contacts: représentations, usages et dynamiques sociolinguistiques', in A. Boudreau, L. Dubois, J. Maurais, and G. McConnel (eds), *L'écologie des langues – Mélanges William Mackey*. Paris / Budapest / Turin: L'Harmattan, pp. 103–23.

Elmiger, D. and Matthey, M. (2006), 'La diglossie vu du "dedans" et du "dehors": l'exemple de Bienne et d'Évolène. *Travaux Neuchâtelois de Linguistique (TRANEL)* 43, 23–47.

Favret-Saada, J. (1990), 'Etre affecté' *Gradhiva*, 8, 3–9.

Fluckiger, E. (2002), 'Les enquêtes lexicologiques du Glossaire des patois de la Suisse romande', in *Lexicologie et lexicographie francoprovençales. Actes de la conférence annuelle sur l'activité scientifique du Centre d'études francoprovençales, Saint-Nicolas, 16–17 Décembre 2000*. Aoste: Région autonome de la Vallée d'Aoste / Assessorat de l'instruction publique / Bureau régional pour l'ethnologie et la linguistique, pp. 23–40.

Gauchat, L. (1914), 'Notice historique'. *Bulletin du Glossaire des patois de la Suisse romande.* Berne/Zürich 1902–1915: Bureau du Glossaire.

Heller, M. (2002), 'L'écologie et la sociologie du langage', in A. Boudreau, L. Dubois, J. Maurais and G. McConnel (eds), *L'écologie des langues – Mélanges William Mackey.* Paris / Budapest / Turin: L'Harmattan, pp. 175–91.

Israel, P. (2001), 'Acheminement vers la parole unique. Autour du débat sur les langues en danger'. *Cahiers d'études africaines* 163–4. (http://etudesafric aines.revues.org/document123.html)

Knecht, P. (1985), 'La Suisse romande', in R. Schläpfer (ed.), *La Suisse aux quatre langues.* Genève: Zoé, pp. 127–69.

Kristol, A. (1998), La production interactive d'un corpus semi-spontané: l'expérience ALAVAL. *Cahiers de l'ILSL,* 10, 91–104.

Lüdi, G. and Py, B. (eds) (1995), *Changement de langage et langage du changement.* Lausanne: L'Age d'Homme.

Lüdi, G. and Py, B. (2002), *Etre bilingue* (2nd edn). Berne: Lang.

Maître, R. (2003), 'La Suisse romande dilalique'. *Vox romanica,* 62, 170–81.

Maître, R. (in preparation), 'Dynamique variationnelle au sein d'une communauté bilingue – Évolène, îlot francoprovençal en Suisse romande (Ph.D project, Université de Neuchâtel).

Maître, R. and Matthey, M. (2003), 'Le *patois d'Évolène* aujourd'hui ... et demain?', in A. Boudreau, L. Dubois, J. Maurais and G. McConnel (eds), *Colloque international sur l'Écologie des langues.* Paris: L'Harmattan, pp. 45–65.

Maître, R. and Matthey, M. (2004), 'Le patois d'Évolène, dernier dialecte francoprovençal parlé et transmis en Suisse', in J.-M. Eloy (ed.), *Des langues collatérales. Problèmes linguistiques, sociolinguistiques et glottopolitiques de la proximité linguistique.* Paris: L'Harmattan, pp. 375–90.

Matthey, M. (2005), 'Le français à l'école et ailleurs, langue des apprentissages et de la socialisation', in V. Conti and J.-F. de Pietro (eds), *L'intégration des migrants en terre francophone: aspects linguistiques et sociaux.* Neuchâtel: CIIP, pp. 145–59.

Matthey, M. and de Pietro, J.-F. (1997), 'La société plurilingue: utopie souhaitable ou domination acceptée?' in H. Boyer (ed.), *Plurilinguisme: 'Contacts' ou 'conflits' de langues?* Paris: L'Harmattan, pp. 133–90.

Matthey, M. and Duchêne, A. (2000), 'Langues et migration: une approche linguistique', in P. Centlivres and I. Girod (eds), *Les défis migratoires.* Zürich: Seismo, pp. 450–6.

Matthey, M. and Maître, R. (in press), 'Poids relatif du dialecte local et du français dans un répertoire bilingue – Évolène', in D. Trotter (ed.), *Actes du XXIVe Congrès International de Linguistique et de Philologie Romanes (CILPR),* Aberystwyth, 2–5 August 2004. Tübingen: Niemeyer.

Py, B., Kristol, A., Matthey, M. and Maître, R. (2002), *Rapport intermédiaire: Etats de la recherché au 31 octobre 2002.* Unpublished preliminary report, University of Neuchâtel.

Rapp. Gloss. *Glossaire des patois de la Suisse romande: Rapport annuel de la rédaction.* [1899] & [2003–2004].

Schutz, A. (1987), *Le Chercheur et le Quotidien*. Paris: Klincksieck.
Sperber, D. (1997), 'Individualisme méthodologique et cognitivisme', in R. Boudon, F. Chazel and A. Bouvier (eds), *Cognition et Sciences Sociales*. Paris: Presse Universitaires de France, pp. 123–36.

Notes

1   Translated from the French by Sara Cotelli.
2   We chose this adjective rather than the expected 'French-speaking Swiss' for the obvious reason that the territory which it refers to is not solely French-speaking. We coined this word out of the French *suisse (romand)* and will use it in connection with territory, culture and language.
3   In the regions where local dialects are still present, the word *Patois* does not entail the depreciative connotation often linked to this term elsewhere, especially in France.
4   On the proposal of this concept in relation to the Italian situation, see Berruto (1989). On its application to Romand Switzerland, see Maître (2003). For a comparison between two types of diglossic settings, those of Évolène and Biel/Bienne, see Elmiger and Matthey (2006).
5   Swiss National Science Foundation Projects # 1214–064961–01 and 100012–101814.
6   That is to say, three years before the *Société suisse de linguistique appliquée* (VALS-ASLA) held its symposium on the ideological aspect of the discourse on language preservation and diversity, in which we presented a contribution at the basis of this chapter.
7   All the transcriptions quoted in this chapter were produced by Véronique Wild.
8   Let us bet that the procedure started in this chapter will, in turn, be subjected to analyses of ideological motivations that will come to light in three years ...
9   The *Glossaire des patois de la Suisse romande* (abridged thereafter *Glossaire*) is a Swiss research institute working on a large dialectal dictionary of the same name. It is in the process of redaction (6,000 pages for the letters A– to F–/G–). Its original project understood itself as 'both scientific and patriotic', following the example of its Swiss German equivalent, the *Idiotikon* (Rapp. Gloss. [1899]: 1) patriotic by the choice of the research topic, scientific by its method of analysis. Its objective is to describe in a differential perspective language facts that are or have been attested within the borders of Romand Switzerland: the vocabulary of Romand vernaculars, but also any regional form or acceptation of French or Latin.
10 Cf., among others, for an illustration of this conception Lüdi and Py 1995; Matthey and de Pietro 1997; Matthey and Duchêne 2000; Boyer and de Pietro 2002.
11 www.unine.ch/linguistique/Bilbienne/pagebilbienne/projet.html.
12 See Fluckiger (2002) for a description of the corpus of the *Glossaire*; Kristol

(1998) on the corpus of the *ALAVAL* project done by the *Centre de dialectologie*; www.unine.ch/linguistique/Bilbienne/pagebilbienne/methodes.html for the corpus *bil.bienne* of the CLA.

13 The interview is with a women, in her fifties, with passive competence in Patois. In all the extracts that follow, the interventions that we wish to highlight are in **bold**. Transcription conventions: /, \, /\, \/ = intonation patterns; . = pause; <u>underlined</u> = overlapping speech; & = quick linking; : = lengthening; CAPITAL LETTERS = loud.

14 The interviews with a man, in his forties, who is bilingual.

15 The interview is with a woman, in her seventies, who is Patois dominant.

16 This thesis is fully detailed in Lüdi and Py (1995) or in Matthey (2005).

17 In French: *se reprendre* but not *se déprendre*.

18 Some people think, just as the way of dressing, eating, moving, marrying have changed, that the evolution of linguistic practices is a natural process, and do not speak spontaneously of 'death'.

19 *Évolénard* is the name given to Évolène's inhabitants.

6 Français, acadien, acadjonne: Competing discourses on language preservation along the shores of the Baie Sainte-Marie

Annette Boudreau
Lise Dubois

Introduction

Behind every discourse on an endangered language there are not only a definition of what that endangered language is, but also various social and cultural issues attached to that definition. This supports the ideas that language and the criteria defining boundaries between languages are ideological constructions, and that discourses on language endangerment are fertile ground for understanding the issues at stake. Furthermore, discourses on language endangerment and preservation almost invariably recreate the same type of power struggles between speakers that the preservation is supposed to eliminate.

In the following chapter, our main goal is to shed some light on how linguistic debates in general and the question of language survival in particular become ideologized and politicized in conjunction with the symbolic values attributed to languages and linguistic varieties, and to show that the major stakes in these debates carried out on the terrain of language are indeed social. We will attempt to describe the different language ideologies that prevail in the region where we conducted our research, i.e. the municipality of Clare in south-western Nova Scotia (otherwise known as the Baie Sainte-Marie; see below for a brief description). To do so, we will of course have to refer to language ideologies in Canada as a whole and in Francophone minority communities in particular. We will then examine the broad social conditions that have led to the destabilization of a traditional hegemonic discourse on language by a discourse of contestation in the

Baie Sainte-Marie area, and the consequences that this shift has had so far on the construction of Acadian identity in the region. Our data comes from ethnographic observation of community events, analysis of documents regarding community events, institutions and debates and interviews with key producers of discourse on language and identity, notably, in this case, those involved in education, the arts, community organization, community associations, community radio and key sectors of economic activity. We will then focus on how various actors from both sides of the debate appeal to discourses concerning threats to the survival of their language, how they define the variety that they defend as being the legitimate one and how they define themselves as legitimate stakeholders in the power struggle. Special attention will be paid to the strong influence that standard French has on speakers' representations of French, of their variety and of their own linguistic competence.

Since 1996, both authors are part of a research group examining how minority Francophones in Canada,[1] and in particular Franco-Albertans, Franco-Ontarians and Acadians, build discursive spaces in which they can articulate their 'francité', why they do it, what is at stake when they do it, what are the consequences for those included in these processes and for those who are excluded from them, and, finally, how social categories based on language are constructed. A three-pronged approach based on ethnographic field work was developed: we collect documentation on the community under study (books, music, media reports, etc.), do ethnographic observation and interview key social actors.

All the participants interviewed spontaneously broached the subject of the public use of the French local vernacular, a marked variety called *acadjonne* which creates controversy and debate within the community. Some of them defend it, others categorically reject it. The debates concerning this language variety inevitably touch upon language survival and resonate in many sectors of the community. We became interested in language ideologies as a means to understand how language acts as a catalyst for social and political debates. Indeed, language ideologies shed light on power struggles taking place on broader levels, and the ones described in this chapter illustrate that the minority experience and reaction to what appears to be domination by the English-speaking population is ambivalent and certainly not uniform (Blommaert 1999).

Context

1. Canada and its two official languages

Canada has two official languages, French and English. The number of Canadians who in 2001 stated having French as their first language is a little over 6.7 million (23 per cent of the general population), of which almost 5.8 million (85 per cent of all Canadian Francophones) live in the province of Québec (Census of Canada 2001). The other 950,000 are unequally distributed among the nine remaining provinces, in what is generally called in Canada 'official language minority communities'. Francophones therefore constitute an important majority in Québec while maintaining a minority status elsewhere, except in New Brunswick, the only officially bilingual province, where Francophones make up almost 33 per cent of the population. The Canadian Charter of Rights and Freedoms (adopted with the *Constitution Act* of 1982) guarantees various rights for official linguistic communities, such as the right to be educated in the minority language in schools managed by the minority community.

Minority French-speaking communities outside Québec define their 'francité' (Heller 2002; Heller and Labrie 2003) in the context of categories of similarity and difference, that is, through defining relationships with a range of relevant others: the dominant Anglophone society, Québec and its State-territorial model of 'francité', other Canadian Francophone minority communities and the larger world of 'la francophonie'. These relationships also shape their representations of French and its varieties, and of bi- or multilingualism. As we will see, these relationships are key to understanding how people in the Baie Sainte-Marie position themselves.

The minority status of the French language in Canadian communities outside Québec has generated over the last 50 years, both inside and outside these communities, an intense debate on the efforts needed to 'save' them from language attrition and assimilation (language transfer) to English, the dominant language, and, therefore, to guarantee their reproduction and durability. In this debate, the survival of the community is intimately linked to the maintenance of French as the language of use among its members. Questions raised in this debate invariably touch upon issues of legitimacy, exclusion and representations of language: which variety of French spoken in these communities should legitimately be saved; who is legitimately empowered to determine this and who is excluded from the debate; how and by whom are the discourses on legitimacy constructed; what discursive strategies do protagonists develop around the power struggles taking place in these communities as they pertain to the circulation of discourses on endangerment?

The Acadian community of the Baie Sainte-Marie

The Acadian community where we conducted our ethnographic work is made up of a dozen villages strung along the eastern shore of the Baie Sainte-Marie in southwestern Nova Scotia, where Acadia was originally founded by French settlers in 1604. These villages, the first Acadian villages in the Maritimes to be resettled by returning Acadians after the British deported them between 1755 and 1763, have recently been amalgamated into one larger municipality, called Clare, which has a population of approximately 9,000 people, 67 per cent of whom have declared French as their first language (Census of Canada 2001). The French-speaking population of Nova Scotia today makes up about 4 per cent of its total population. The main economic activities of the Baie Sainte-Marie region are the fishing and forestry industries. The narrative of the Deportation (called 'le Grand Dérangement' by Acadians) and of the return of the exiled Acadians to this area is constructed, reproduced and claimed as collective memory through various storytelling, cultural and community events and annual celebrations, e.g. the 'Joseph and Marie Dugas Festival' named after the first couple who resettled from Grand Pré, where they had been deported, to Belliveau Cove in 1768.

In recent years, language issues have generated debate within the community. For instance, in the 1980s, after the Charter of Rights and Freedoms was adopted, the right to manage education was effectively handed over to the minority community, which until then had had to operate in the form of bilingual education within the constraints of English-dominated school boards. This triggered a debate between those who lobbied (eventually successfully) for a change to French-only (so-called 'linguistically homogeneous') schools, and those who had felt comfortable with the status quo, or who at least wished to preserve bilingual schools, fearing that all-French schools would jeopardize their children's competency level in English (Ross 2001). Canada's linguistic duality is characterized by dual education systems, a system for Francophones where subjects are taught mostly in French and another for Anglophones where subjects are taught in English except for second language classes. Because of their minority status outside Québec, Francophones have a very high rate of bilingualism throughout the Anglo-dominant provinces, whereas Anglophones are not generally bilingual (Heller 2003: 70–74, 106–12).

In the 1990s, the Baie Sainte-Marie's francophone community radio station, which had been struggling to survive, started to broadcast programmes and to advertise in the local French vernacular, which increased its popularity and its ratings, making it one of the most successful community radio stations in the country (Boudreau and Dubois 2003; Dubois 2003). Up until then, only standard French and English had been heard on the airwaves, either through public radio stations (which are operated by a federal agency) or through various public radio stations. To this day, the public use of this variety is a bone of contention within the community, as well as outside it, as we shall explain in the following pages.

It is generally accepted among descriptive linguists who have studied the Baie Sainte-Marie variety that the French spoken in the region represents the oldest variety of French spoken in North America (Flikeid 1994). Among its salient features are the widespread use of archaic forms, which have survived since the colonization period, as well as English forms which were introduced into this variety because of the community's close contact with the surrounding dominant English community and its isolation from other Acadian communities over long periods of time. Because contact with other Francophone communities has increased since the middle of the twentieth century, speakers of this variety are acutely aware of the differences in their speech when confronted with speakers of other varieties of French, be they Canadian, Québécois, French or from other parts of the franco-phone world. Paradoxically, these same features which are stigmatized by defenders of the standard and by some speakers themselves become symbolic of the quest to construct a new Acadian language, acadjonne. In reaction to the values attributed to the standard, which is seen by some members of the community as the only variety appropriate for teaching and for broadcasting, defenders of acadjonne have developed a discourse of survival around these features.

Proponents on both sides of the debate want the same thing: the survival of the community as a French-speaking community. At the heart of the debate is the issue of which variety of French is best suited to guarantee the community's survival: the standard variety traditionally used by the educated and moneyed elite, or the local variety which has just recently been introduced during the 1990s into the public linguistic market through the community radio station. Like all public debates in small communities, this one goes beyond the community radio where it originated, and has since been taken into other areas such as education, economic development and associative organizations.

Language ideologies

Before describing the main economic, social and cultural changes which occurred in the Baie Sainte-Marie region and which made a heated language debate possible, we will briefly present the language ideologies which prevail.

Language ideologies are usually defined as a set of beliefs on language or a particular language shared by members of a community (Watts 1999; Milroy 2001). These beliefs come to be so well established that their origin is often forgotten by speakers, and are therefore socially reproduced and end up being 'naturalized', or perceived as natural or as common sense, thereby masking the social construction processes at work. Ideologies become political when they are embedded in the social principles on which a community organizes itself institutionally (Watts 1999).

In this region of Nova Scotia Acadia (as elsewhere for that matter), the ideologies of language that circulate may sometimes compete with each other, while at other times or in certain linguistic markets, one of them may become dominant, but all of them exert pressure on linguistic and non-linguistic issues. In this section, we will present briefly the ideologies that are generally shared by other Canadian francophones; then we will discuss an emerging competing ideology of language which seems to us to be entirely endemic to the Baie Sainte-Marie community.

The ideology of bilingualism posits the social, cultural and economic advantages of being bilingual as an individual and as a country. Canada has developed a positive image of itself as a bilingual, therefore tolerant and progressive country, and its most ardent defenders are various government departments, the media and the Francophone communities themselves. For example, the official site of Nova Scotia's Tourism Department bids tourists to visit the Baie Sainte-Marie region (which is part of the 'Evangeline Trail' tourist area) this way:

> The Municipality of Clare, often referred to as the Acadian Shore, hugs Baie Ste-Marie (...). Route 1 passes through twelve picturesque French-speaking villages (...). The bilingual inhabitants along this shore are descendants of the first European settlers, who came from France in the early 1600's' (http://novascotia.com/en/home/planatrip/travel_guides/downloads.aspx.)

Another website attracts the attention of would-be tourists by pointing out the particularities of the local vernacular: 'The spoken language still rings of 17th century French with a new world twist including Mi'kmaq Indian and English words' (www.evangelinetrail.com/churchpoint.html). But in reality, bilingualism as it is practiced in Nova Scotia is more ideological than it is real; at the very least, it is an asymmetrical bilingualism. Indeed, the only truly bilingual populations are the Acadian ones, who speak English fluently with very little linguistic markers. A visitor to the province of Nova Scotia attracted by the promotional material on Nova Scotia Acadia would be hard-pressed to 'see' and 'hear' bilingualism, as well as to get service in French anywhere other than in the Acadian communities. In fact, in ordinary daily activities, one is led to believe that the ideology of monolingualism is at work here, since the Anglophone majority expects that Acadian French-speakers use English in all public activities, an expectation which does not allow Francophones to exercise their right to use French if they wish to do so.

Another ideology which acts upon language behaviour is the ideology of the standard, which is linked to the perception of language as an essentialized object, that is as a rigid and unchanging system. Despite the fact that it is difficult to define what the standard language is, the idea of its existence is well established in the minds of French speakers and influences how they judge languages, speakers and their own performances.

Lodge (1997) reminds us that French is one of the most standardized languages in the world, and that its speakers have developed strong representations of a unified language with little room for diversity and variation. Furthermore, various studies on French speakers in peripheral regions (peripheral here meaning not in France) have also shown that the idea of a standard is part of the linguistic imagination of Francophones all over the world (see Francard 1993; Francard *et al.* 2001). Because standard French is regarded as prestigious, those who speak vernacular varieties most often accept the symbolic dominance of 'legitimate speakers' since they too aspire to acquire 'an imagined standard language' in order to have access to the economic and social capital associated with standard languages and to a wider range of linguistic markets (Bourdieu 1982).

The ideology of the standard exerts pressure on linguistic practices and on the construction of identity. First, Francophones from minority communities in Canada who have lived in an anglophone dominant environment inevitably show in their linguistic practices the traces of this close linguistic contact through English borrowings and calques. In addition, they have often maintained archaic or older French lexical and syntactic forms.

They are acutely aware of the distance between their variety and the standard. Linguistic insecurity is commonplace in Acadia (Boudreau and Dubois 1991, 2001), and we have found in other studies that some Acadians go as far as to invent various personas to escape negative reactions from other Francophones. For example, in a call centre in Moncton (New Brunswick), where we conducted research on how linguistic skills were used in the new economy, we interviewed a Francophone voice operator who, when dealing with Francophone callers from outside the Maritime Provinces, claimed she was an Anglophone learning French to avoid being criticized by those who preferred dealing with someone speaking a more standard French rather than someone speaking with an obvious southeast New Brunswick accent.

The last ideology presented here, and the one that we posit is unique to the Baie Sainte-Marie within the Canadian context, is the ideology of the dialect. Indeed, we discovered in this community ardent defenders of the dialect who aspire to make it the legitimate language of the community and who have managed to open up the linguistic markets to the local variety by taking control of the community radio. The justifications for their stance regarding this variety are partly historical in nature, claiming that the vernacular was the language spoken by their ancestors when they reclaimed residency in the province at the end of the eighteenth century. According to Watts (1999), when this ideology is acted upon, dialects are then used in the education system (at least in their spoken form) and in certain media, such as radio and television, which is the case in the Baie Sainte-Marie. Language ideologies are therefore linked to the myths that circulate within a community about language (Watts 1999: 72–4). Myths are transmitted and disseminated through shared stories that contribute to the (re)construction of a given cultural group (i.e. the storytelling about the return of the deported mentioned above), and are usually endowed with an explanatory force that can historically frame various group behaviours, including language behaviour and practices. We will see further how the myth of the origins of the Baie Sainte-Marie community is construed today by some of its members as an answer to the various discourses on languages that circulate in the region, and especially how it is being used in the discourses on the survival of French in southwestern Nova Scotia.

Changing social conditions in the Baie Sainte-Marie

There have been many changes over the past 30 years in the Baie Sainte-Marie that can explain the current linguistic debate. The conflict over the increased use of French in the region's schools which emerged in the early 1980s lasted for almost 20 years, divided the community and set the scene for what was to come. The school conflict had indeed polarized the community into two major camps: those in favour of linguistically homogeneous schools where all subjects are taught in standard French and those in favour of maintaining bilingual schools, where only some of the subjects were taught in French in mixed classes (see above). The move towards homogeneous schools was based on the widespread belief that the vitality and the preservation of Francophone minority communities depends largely on the community's access to French-only institutions, schools being the most important. This belief is largely circulated by the communities' traditional educated elites, whereas other groups within the community support bilingual education as a means to upward social mobility. The lines between groups were therefore drawn before the current conflict around the radio station emerged in the late 1990s, in an entirely new context in terms of the community's position within the Canadian 'Francophonie' and within a more globalized economic environment.

In 1994, Acadians organized the first 'Congrès mondial acadien' (CMA – World Acadian Congress), a large popular gathering which unfolded over a period of several weeks, included many types of activities such as large family reunions, concerts, conferences, etc. and has been held every five years since. The 1994 CMA, held in Moncton (New Brunswick, about a six-hour drive from the Baie Sainte-Marie) has come to be regarded as a watershed moment in Acadia's history and in Acadians' awareness of their specificity in the Maritime Provinces and in Canada in general. The CMA's objective was to gather the Acadians from the diaspora (which refers to those of Acadian descent who live outside of the Maritime Provinces) and from all of Acadia in one place: approximately 500,000 people attended and the event generated much enthusiasm. Most importantly, the CMA resulted in the creation of all types of transprovincial and transnational networks – cultural, academic, political and economic – which have not only persisted but have flourished. The second Congress was held in 1999 in Louisiana, and the third, in 2004, in the Baie Sainte-Marie itself. Thus, at the time of our fieldwork, many members of the community were increasingly understanding themselves in the context of discourses, institutions and networks connected to this particular discursive space. The discourses, institutions and networks in question are largely constituted around ideas of language, identity and culture.

If Acadian culture has enabled Acadians to take part in successful cultural exchanges among Canadian Francophones, and between Francophone Canada and connected areas in the United States (notably Louisiana and parts of New England), it has also enabled them to participate in international exchanges, especially within the 'francophonie internationale'. Acadian artists perform regularly in Europe, and a variety of institutions and networks have developed to facilitate this. For example, since 1996, Moncton has been hosting a regional

'Franco-fête', an annual event in various parts of French Canada, spread over several days, whose purpose is to showcase Francophone artists in the fostering of a market for Francophone artistic and cultural products. Several artists and musicians from the Baie Sainte-Marie are now known throughout Acadia, North America and parts of Europe.

Globalization has also enabled traditional businesses from the region to branch out into international markets: one family fish processing business has become in recent years a multinational business exporting its products all over the world, while another small shipyard has specialized in the building of luxury yachts, which again are sold internationally.

Globalization has enabled Francophones from peripheral areas such as the Baie Sainte-Marie to establish links and networks with other communities and interests. These outlying communities have thus been able to redefine their identity and their place in the world without going through traditional channels, such as the State or other agencies dominated by their Anglo-Canadian compatriots. Increased contacts through networking and through increased mobility have deeply modified not only their relationship with the State and with the Anglo-dominant society but also their perception of themselves and of their language.

Discourses on the survival of French in the Baie Sainte-Marie[2]

In the following section, we will attempt to answer the questions raised in the introduction, that is who constructs the discourses on legitimacy, what discursive strategies do protagonists develop around the power struggles taking place, who benefits from the debate and why, and what the repercussions are for Acadians and for other French speakers around them. While our corpus includes a wide variety of forms of data on the debates surrounding linguistic variation and identity in the Baie Sainte-Marie, we will focus here on interviews with key actors in a specific debate surrounding the community radio, which concerns the public use of the local dialect on the airwaves. When we arrived in the region for our fieldwork, we were unaware of the deep divisions within this community caused by the radio station. The use of English words in predominantly French utterances is what offends the majority of participants in the study who oppose the public use of acadjonne, while the use of older archaic forms is more easily accepted. We have heard radio ads using the words 'shirt' for *chemise*, 'pants' for *pantalon*, 'chicken' for *poulet*, etc., which is a source of concern for many participants.

The participants we quote here are those who expressed very strong stances on language as a way of gaining access to important social and economic resources, although they have very different views on how to get there; as such, they represent the extreme positions in the debate. At the outset of our research in the region, we were surprised and intrigued by the strong feelings expressed over the use of a local dialect, which seemed to us to be no more than another variety of language. We were soon to find out that language was at the heart of larger debates connected, on the one hand, to the creation of social categories (who is a real and 'pure' Acadian), and on the other hand, to the redefinition of social structures at the heart of economic developments in the region (what French gets to be legitimized when it comes to attracting tourists in the region, how is acadjonne supposed to be seen as the *real* and authentic language).

The defenders and promoters of acadjonne come from different backgrounds; some are intellectuals like Marcel, who studied abroad and uses his knowledge to reinvent a language aimed at legitimizing what he sees as the 'real Acadian French', while others, who are slightly more educated than the average and who have spent a large part of their lives elsewhere, defend it as they feel that acadjonne is the language through which they construct their sense of belonging in a tight-knit community. The defenders of the standard, such as Paul and Louise, who are members of the intellectual elite, truly believe that the only way for Acadians to have access to social status, good jobs and to be able to be a part of a bigger 'francophonie' is to speak a standard language, even one with some regional features. They feel that not knowing the standard will contribute to further building borders with francophones from elsewhere. Paul was educated by clerics who used standard French as criteria for deciding who belonged to the elite, thus creating social categories based on language, which Paul himself reproduces. Louise is a Quebecker who settled in the area over ten years ago and who believes that people who speak acadjonne are at risk of being trapped in a linguistic ghetto.

As mentioned above, the regional variety of French spoken in the Baie Sainte-Marie was for a long time and is to a large extent today a stigmatized variety. Louise relates that very few people in the Baie Sainte-Marie area were educated enough to teach in the local college. Therefore, a large number of teachers were imported from elsewhere, mostly clerics from Québec, who adopted a superior attitude. Louise, who mostly endorses the pro-standard stance, explains:

Extract 1
Louise   ils sont allés chercher énomément de profs au
                Québec qui disaient 'il faut montrer à ces gens-là à
                parler français' ou encore 'il faut parler un français

standard' (...) les Québécois qui sont venus se
sont posés comme des maîtres de la discipline et
des policiers de la langue (...) ils (les Acadiens)
n'avaient pas le droit d'utiliser les expressions
acadiennes

Louise   *they brought in a lot of teachers from Québec who*
said 'we have to teach these people how to talk' or
'we have to speak Standard French' (...) the people
from Québec who came claimed to be masters of the
discipline and the language police (...) Acadians
did not have the right to use Acadian expressions
when speaking

When the community radio station was launched, the language
used on the air was standard French. After a short period, it almost
went bankrupt. Marcel, a very active voice in the promotion of
acadjonne explains that:

Extract 2
Marcel   toute l'élite du coin était là-dedans et puis ils ont
décidé d'être normatifs et pis à la place de parler
akadjonne / ils avont décidé de parler le bon
français et puis la population l'a boudée

Marcel   *all of the area's elite was involved in the station*
and they decided to use the standard instead of
acadjonne / they decided to speak good French and
the population turned away

What is interesting in this statement is the fact that Marcel, who moves
fluently from one register to the next throughout the entire interview,
makes ostentatious use of certain salient features of acadjonne, such
as 'ils avont décidé' when speaking of the former management of
the station. Marcel explained that acadjonne was always criticized
in schools and Acadians developed a negative attitude towards their
own language. When acadjonne became the dominant language on the
community airwaves, the ratings rose and the station became the most
listened-to station in the region.

As pointed out above, Francophones in the province of Nova
Scotia are a small minority, but in this sub-region (Clare), they are
the majority. Fortified by their unique historic legitimacy as the
direct descendants of the first Europeans to settle in North America,
a certain number of Acadians from this region have reclaimed these
facts and made them the basis of their distinct identity. To legitimize
their way of speaking, they promote the most archaic features of their
variety.[3] Marcel explains: 'notre mission c'est de conserver la langue

de l'ancienne capitale et de continuer le rêve et la mission de nos ancêtres.' ['*our mission is to conserve the language of the old capital and to continue our ancestors' dream and mission*'.]

According to Marcel, not only does the language need to be conserved, but the ancestors' dream also needs to be pursued. Watts has explained that ideologies are born from the right historical circumstances (Watts 1999). The idea of deliberately bringing back to life this 'old language', as Marcel calls it, by increasing the awareness of what makes it distinct, progressively took hold after the CMA in 1994 and the 'Sommet de la francophonie', held in Moncton in 1999, two events which provided Acadians from all three Maritime provinces with a new legitimacy. Furthermore, the idea of constructing acadjonne as a distinct language is meant to lift it from anonymity, to give it a new beginning, but at the same time this idea gives much importance to the historical origins of the community, which are particularly valued by Acadians of the diaspora.

Conserving the archaic forms is one aspect of the intentional construction of acadjonne; another aspect is the acceptance and sometimes deliberate use of English words in French utterances, which, as we mentioned, is what offends the majority of participants in the study who oppose the public use of acadjonne, while the use of older archaic forms is more easily accepted. The arguments used to re-invent a distinct and unique language are based on the idea of a need to distinguish the community from other Francophone communities; to distinguish its speech from other varieties; and, most of all, to distinguish it from standard French. As Marcel puts it, acadjonne is: 'un outil du tonnerre / un outil ultra-moderne qui s'appelerait l'acadjonne et qui se distancierait du français standard' ['*a terrific tool / an ultramodern tool which would be called acadjonne and which would distance itself from standard French*'.]

Very active in this fight, Marcel states that Nova Scotia Acadians will never become French from France, Québécois from Québec nor Acadians from New Brunswick; they might just as well stress their differences by asserting their specificity, therefore their origins. This ideology has given rise to debates, and continues to do so, within the community, especially since ads on the community radio are written in acadjonne (mostly by Marcel). Up until then, because acadjonne was confined to private spaces, there had not been much strife. From the moment that acadjonne was used outside of the family and informal markets, it was condemned by the defenders of the standard. These debates have since been taken into the schools, where once again there are stormy controversies taking place. Parents opposed to 'homogeneous' schools (see above), are now opposing teachers who attempt

111

to eliminate mixed codes from their students' speech, acting out the ideology of the dialect. One of the participants in the study tells the story of his wife, who is a teacher in these schools and whose attempts at correcting her pupils' speech are often met with resistance: students say, 'c'est acadjonne Madame' [*it's acadjonne ma'am*]. Moreover, one of the disc jockeys working at the community radio station who was interviewed claims that more listeners phone in to complain that they do not understand some everyday standard French words than there are listeners who phone in to complain about the use of mixed codes. He alleges that not comprehending standard French is not the problem because in public meetings, these same speakers will speak up to express their opinions to those who have said what they had to say in standard French.

> Extract 3
>
> Leo ils vont dire 'moi je comprends pas le français
> (standard)' / c'est pas vrai / ils vont aller dans une
> réunion pis quelqu'un va s'exprimer dans un français
> standard et si il dit quelque chose qu'ils n'aiment pas
> / ils ont compris (...) ils vont à l'église le dimanche
> et puis si le prêtre dit quelque chose que ils sont pas
> d'accord euh je t'assure qu'ils vont pas dire qu'ils ont
> pas compris le français
>
> Leo *they will say 'me, I don't understand (standard) French'*
> */ it's not true / they'll go to a meeting and if someone*
> *says something in standard French and if it's something*
> *they don't like / they understood (...) they go to church*
> *on Sunday and if the priest says something they do not*
> *agree with euh I can assure you that they will not say*
> *that they have not understood*

The problem is therefore not one of comprehension, but one of resistance. We see here that the comprehension argument is a discursive strategy used to (re)position oneself within the 'francophonie' and to (re)define what is meant by being Acadian. This is comparable to the situation of German Swiss illustrated by Watts, who tells of a mother who says to her child who wishes to buy a book written in German: 'No, don't be silly dear. That's written in Standard German. You won't be able to understand' (Watts 1999: 85). Contrary to the situation in Switzerland, l'acadjonne is rarely written, though it is currently used in songs and has been portrayed in a film (*Les gossipeuses*, 1978), to denounce the parochial mentality of some of the characters in the film. But, in both cases, the comprehension argument is put forward as a discursive strategy to resist the hegemonic influences of those who support the use of the standard.

These discourses on language are linked to strategies to save the language. Some proponents of the dialect think that if the people in the Baie Sainte-Marie were to become confident in their language, they would be better positioned to resist Anglicization and assimilation. However, the public defence of acadjonne has erected yet other language barriers between speakers. Some participants have claimed that speakers who use standard forms are now stigmatized and rejected. Even Marcel, a militant of acadjonne, who attended university outside his community and is capable of using various linguistic registers, says that the typical Acadian:

> Extract 4
> Marcel   adore entendre un Québécois parler québécois,
> un Français de France parler son français, le
> Néo-Brunswickois parler avec son accent, le
> Chéticamptain le Louisianais, il adore ça // mais
> si il y a quelque chose qui fait tenir les cheveux à
> pique sur la tête c'est quand ce qu'il y a un des leurs
> qui s'en va en dehors pis qui s'en revient et puis
> tout d'un coup qu'il peut plus parler dans l'Anse ou
> Meteghan [two villages along the Baie Sainte-Marie]
> ou une affaire de même / la langue acadjonne pour
> un Acadjen de la Baie c'est de quoi de sacré

> *Marcel   loves to hear a Quebecker speak québécois, a*
> *Frenchman speak his French, a New Brunswicker*
> *speak with his accent, a person from Chéticamp*
> *or from Louisiana, he loves that // but if there is*
> *something that makes his hair stand on its ends it's*
> *when one of theirs goes outside then comes back*
> *and all of a sudden can no longer speak in the*
> *Cove or in Meteghan or something like that / the*
> *acadjonne language for an Acadian from the Baie is*
> *sacred*

In this case, maintaining regional structures that were stigmatized in the past instead of using standard forms displays loyalty to the community. Marcel himself reports that he has been excluded, but endorses nonetheless the restrictions of this stance and has even become one of its most ardent defenders:

> Extract 5
> Marcel   beaucoup de fois je me ferais radorsé[4] / t'as dit la
> poubelle / c'est la garbage can // j'ons tout le temps
> dit la garbage can (…) es-tu en train de te comporter
> comme un traître

> *Marcel*   *I have been told to straighten up many times // you*
> *said poubelle / it's a garbage can / we have always*
> *said garbage can (...) are you being a traitor*

The opponents of the ideology of the dialect say they are worried by the social and cultural restrictions put on the members of the community by the widespread use of acadjonne. They feel that using a variety that is too far from standard French may lead to the creation of a linguistic ghetto. Paul, a proponent of the standard, believes that the Baie Sainte-Marie lost its bid to host the *Jeux de l'Acadie*, an annual sporting event in which all Acadian schools of the three Maritimes Provinces have participated since 1978, because of the language issue (which of course we can't confirm).

Extract 6

Paul   l'acadjonne c'est une langue de communication **pour** ici / ça disparaîtra jamais dans les foyers / mais pour les jeunes qui veulent se lancer sur le marché du travail // de faiT nous étions la région française de la Nouvelle-Écosse // pendant des siècles // pis aujourd'hui c'est Halifax qui est la région française de la Nouvelle-Écosse avec le Carrefour du Grand Havre // c'est Halifax qui est la région / on ne l'est plus on ne l'est plus ici (...) parce que: il y a trop d'anglais // il y a /// ben on dit: // les finales des Jeux de l'Acadie ont eu lieu à presque toutes les régions / de l'Acadie // deux ou trois ans passés // Clare ici la municipalité / a fait un gros effort pour avoir la finale ici // ils ont dépensé même dix mille dollars là juste pour préparer un document / pour aller le présenter pour attirer les Jeux de l'Acadie ici / Edmundston les avait déjà eu: // ils sont allés là et la décision c'est que les Jeux iraient à Edmundston /// pis ils se demandaient pourquoi /// à quelques-uns uns j'ai dit : 'regardez les deux personnes qui sont allées là pis écoutez-les s'exprimer' / pis les Jeux de l'Acadie c'est pour promouvoir **la** langue chez les jeunes / et / simplement en les écoutant parler ils ont dit 'on peut pas aller là' /// ils l'ont pas dit (rire) le comité au Nouveau-Brunswick l'a pas dit // mais c'est facile à voir on avait toutes les facilités ici avec l'université pis l'école / tout ce qu'il fallait / et puis la municipalité avait dépensé de l'argent les Jeux étaient jamais venus ici // mais les Jeux sont pas venus ici // alors c'est ce que je vous dis que: // on ne s'attire pas en voulant promouvoir euh / l'acadjonne comme on l'appelle

Paul   *acadjonne is a language of communication for here*
/ it will never disappear from the homes / but for the
young people who want to go into the job market //
in fact we were the first French region of Nova Scotia
// for centuries // but today it is Halifax that is the
first French region of Nova Scotia with the Carrefour
du Grand Havre (name of the French school in
Halifax) // it is Halifax that is the region / we are no
longer it here (...) because there is too much English
// there is /// well it is said // the Jeux de l'Acadie
finals have taken place in almost all the regions of
Acadia // two or three years ago // the municipality
of Clare made a huge effort to have the finals here //
they even spent ten thousand dollars just to prepare
a document / to go present to bid for the Jeux de
l'Acadie here / Edmundston had already gotten them
// they went there and the decision was to give them
to Edmundston /// and then they wanted to know why
/// I told a couple of them 'look at the two people who
went there and listen to them speak' / well les Jeux de
l'Acadie exist to promote the language with the young
people / and / simply to listen to them talk they said
to themselves we can't go there /// they didn't say
(laugh) the New Brunswick committee didn't say // but
it is easy to see that we had all the facilities here with
the university and the school / all that was needed
/ and the municipality had spent all that money
because the Games had never come here // but the
Games did not come here // that's why I tell you this //
we do not attract by by wanting to promote acadjonne,
like we call it here

Extract 6 summarizes the position of those who oppose the use
and promotion of acadjonne. They fear that speakers of this variety
will be barred access to activities taking place in the 'Francophonie'
and to the job market. In opposition to the regional variety, Paul speaks
of his conception of what is Acadian French:

Extract 7

Lise   qu'est-ce qui vous choque dans le dans les la publicité
/ de la radio communautaire

Paul   c'est pas français / c'est que c'est / on prend des
mots anglais ou même on // on invente des mots // tu
sais

Lise   avez-vous des exemples

Paul   je devrais en avoir à conter tu sais là pis je peux pas y
penser

115

Lise	vous avez dit quelque chose d'intéressant vous avez dit qu'ils pensent que c'est de l'acadien mais ça ne l'est pas vraiment / qu'est-ce que c'est pour vous l'acadien
Paul	**l'acadien: / c'est le français classique // du dix-septième siècle** // alors si dire: / si pour du pain je vas dire du 'ponne' (pain) ou à matin je vas dire 'à matonne' (matin) / nous sommes les seuls Acadiens au monde maintenant Nouveau-Brunswick vous êtes pas des Acadiens ni l'Île-du-Prince-Édouard ni Chéticamp // tu sais parce qu'on est on est les seuls qui parlent comme ça alors si on dit si on dit que ça c'est de l'acadien /// ça veut dire qu'on /// on est on est les seuls Acadiens au monde
Lise	*what is it that offends you about the advertisement on the community radio*
Paul	*it's not French / it's that it's / English words are used or even new words are invented you know*
Lise	*do you have any examples*
Paul	*I should have some to tell but now I can't think of any*
Lise	*you said something interesting you said that they thought that it was Acadian but it isn't really / what is Acadian for you*
Paul	*Acadian / it's classic French // from the 17th century // so to say / if for bread I say ponne or for morning I say à matonne / we are the only Acadians in the world today now NewBrunswick you are not Acadian neither is Prince-Edward Island nor Cheticamp // you know because we are the only ones who speak that way therefore if we say that that is Acadian /// then that means that /// we are the only Acadians in the world*

To establish a link between Acadian French and French spoken in France during North America's colonization indicates a fixed and rigid conception of language and a certain nostalgia for the origins of the French language considered to be 'pure, clear and elegant' (Joseph 1987: 158; Walter 1988: 100–14). Language here is seen as detached from real language practices, which explains Paul's difficulty in accepting the particular status given to a regional variety by the community radio station.

This debate on language shows that, in the context under study, the simple choice of using one word over another is filled with significance which cannot be grasped by linguistic analysis alone. The choice to say *ponne* instead of *pain* (bread) is not only an act of identity: it is also taking a stance in relation to a social and political project constructed around the reappropriation of a language, which is seen as the core of the construction of community identity. In this case, the choice to use acadjonne is politically charged and a source of conflict among members of the community.

What is interesting to note here is the fact that positive values attributed to the 'language of the ancestors' are common to both camps and are at the heart of the arguments used for justifying completely different views on language. For the defenders of acadjonne (partici-pants who feel excluded from social structures revolving around the standard), the Acadian language goes back to the beginnings of the colony, and its speakers are the 'purest' of representatives of that state of language which should be conserved even if it means adding English words in order to adapt the language to modern times. For those who oppose acadjonne (the intellectual elite, who exert symbolic power through their use of the legitimate language and who are most aware of the cultural capital gained through the standard, and artists who are now travelling to other parts of the Francophonie and want to diversify their linguistic resources), the Acadian language is also connected to eighteenth-century French as it is imagined, and it cannot be modified without losing its characteristic 'purity'.

Needless to say that the positions presented here are not clear-cut and any single individual's position on the matter is often quite ambiv-alent; in other words, the different discourses concerning the preservation of language sometimes overlap. In fact, on the question of the 'purity' of the language inherited from the ancestors, the two discourses converge, though they diverge considerably on the intended outcome: on the one hand, the aim is to promote the use of a regional language; on the other hand, it is to reassert the value of the standard. This convergence/diver-gence illustrates the power struggle between two groups who wish to gain social advantages on the terrain of language. Therefore, the value attributed to archaisms differs. The proponents of acadjonne seek to assert their identity and their distinctiveness through the concrete use of archaisms derived from a language imagined as being authentic, whereas those who defend the standard pay lip service to the value of maintaining archaisms, distancing themselves from the actual use of these 'old words' and conforming their practices to a fictional standard.

The most obvious aspects of this struggle centre around the language issue, but the real stakes reside in the unequal access to material and symbolic resources in the community. In other words, which group will obtain the funding to operate the community radio and thus to define the community image that is broadcast? Which variety of French will be valued in the various linguistic markets and in individual and collective identity building processes? The most legitimate discourse in the eyes of both groups is the one linked to the historical dimension that is often referred to by politicians and intellectuals alike who value the authenticity of the Baie Sainte-Marie community for various reasons: for example, as a way to promote tourism, as a way to obtain special cultural funding (i.e. the 400th anniversary of the establishment of Acadia), or as a way to participate in the debate surrounding the first French presence on North American soil.

Conclusion

The debate surrounding the 'coming out' of a particular variety of language, a variety which is doomed to be seen by outsiders as impure and contrary to the traditional 'bon usage', is as much about social issues as it is about language. The discourse on the preservation of French via acadjonne can be labelled as a discourse of resistance against the hegemony of standard French whose defenders once monopolized resources in media and educational realms. It challenges long-standing power structures which had been accessed until now only through standard French. However, well-intentioned promoters of the standard language are (aiming as they do at greater access to jobs, social mobility, prestige), many speakers of Acadian French feel left out because of their way of speaking, characterized by hybridity and archaic features. In both cases, language and values attributed to language varieties serve as the bases for social stratification and processes of identity.

In this chapter, we have attempted to show that different groups of social actors from an 'imagined community' have multiple stakes and interests in preserving what they perceive as 'their' variety of French and how they develop different discourses in order to save the language from attrition. In other words, as we stated in the introduction, discourses on language endangerment recreate the power struggles between members of the community that exist already. Discourses aimed at defending a language vary in this case precisely because of the different representations that speakers have of what a language should be ideally, and also because these same speakers develop different language ideologies that shape their political and social actions aimed at preserving the kind of language they want to preserve, imagined as a 'pure' language or as a 'hybrid' one regardless of whether it is rooted in the seventeenth century or not. This case study illustrates that language issues are central to the shaping of a society, especially in minority settings.

Transcription guidelines

1. The apostrophe is used to mark an elision, as it is usually used in French.
2. Capital letters at the end of certain words indicates pronunciation.
3. The slash is used to indicate pauses: one slash indicates a brief pause, two slashes a longer one, three slashes indicate a 4-second pause. The slash also indicates hesitation, such as *la mai/la maison*.
4. Brackets have three functions: (xxx) indicate incomprehensible parts; (laughter) or (ringing), etc. give additional information which cannot be transcribed; (...) truncated parts of the interview.

References

Bloomaert, J. (1999), 'The debate is open', in J. Bloomaert (ed.), *Language Ideological Debates*. Berlin: Mouton de Gruyter, pp. 1–38.

Boudreau, A. and Dubois, L. (1991), 'L'insécurité linguistique comme entrave à l'apprentissage du français'. *Bulletin de l'Association canadienne de linguistique appliquée*, 13, (2), 37–50.

Boudreau, A. and Dubois, L. (2001), 'Langues minoritaires et espaces publics: le cas de l'Acadie'. *Estudios de Sociolingüistica*, 2, (1), 37–60.

Boudreau, A. and Dubois, L. (2003), 'Le cas de trois radios communautaires en Acadie', in M. Heller and N. Labrie (eds), *Discours identités. La francité entre modernité et mondialisation*. Cortil-Wodon: Éditions Modulaires Européennes [coll. Proximités], pp. 269–97.

Bourdieu, P. (1982), *Ce que parler veut dire. L'économie des échanges linguistiques*. Paris: Fayard.

Canada. *2001 Census of Canada*. (www12.statcan.ca/english/census01/home/index.cfm).

Dubois, L. (2003), 'Radios communautaires acadiennes : idéologies linguistiques et pratiques langagières', in A. Magord (ed.), *L'Acadie plurielle. Dynamiques identitaires collectives et développement au sein des réalités acadiennes*. Moncton: Centre d'études acadiennes, Université de Moncton; Poitiers: Institut d'études acadiennes et québécoises, Université de Poitiers, pp. 307–23.

Flikeid, K. (1994), 'Origines et évolution du français acadien à la lumière de la diversité contemporaine', in R. Mougeon and E. Béniak (eds), *Les origines du français québécois*. Sainte-Foy: Les Presses de l'Université Laval, pp. 275–326.

Francard, M. (1993), 'L'insécurité linguistique dans les communautés francophones périphériques'. Actes du Colloque Louvain-la-Neuve, 10–12 November 1993. *Cahiers de l'Institut de linguistique de Louvain-la-Neuve*, 19, (3–4).

Francard, M., Geron, G. and Wilmet R. (2001), 'Le français de référence. Construction et appropriation d'un concept'. Actes du Colloque Louvain-la-Neuve, 3–5 November 1999. *Cahiers de l'Institut de linguistique de Louvain-la-Neuve*, 27, (1–2).

Heller, M. (2002), *Éléments d'une sociolinguistique critique*. Paris: Didier.

Heller, M. (2003), *Crosswords. Language, Education and Ethnicity in French Ontario*. Berlin: Mouton de Gruyter (1st edition: 1994).

Heller, M. and Labrie, N. (2003), 'Langue, pouvoir et identité: une étude de cas, une approche théorique, une méthodologie', in M. Heller and N. Labrie (ed.), *Discours et identités. La francité canadienne entre modernité et mondialisation*. Cortil-Wodon: Éditions Modulaires Européennes [coll. Proximités], pp. 9–39.

Joseph, J. E. (1987), *Eloquence and Power. The Rise of Language Standards and Standard Languages*. New York: Basil Blackwell.

Lodge, A. (1997), *Le français. Histoire d'un dialecte devenu langue*. Paris: Fayard.

Milroy, L. (2001), 'The social categories of race and class', in N. Coupland, S. Sarangi and C. Candlin (eds), *Sociolinguistics and Social Theory*. London: Longman, pp. 235–60.

Ross, S. (2001), *Les écoles acadiennes en Nouvelle-Écosse, 1758–2000*. Moncton: Centre d'études acadiennes, Université de Moncton.

Walter, H. (1988), *Le français dans tous les sens*. Paris: Éditions Robert Laffont.

Watts, R. (1999), 'The Ideology of Dialect in Switzerland', in J. Blommaert (ed.), *Language Ideological Debates*. Berlin: Mouton de Gruyter, pp. 67–103.

Notes

1 The research projects were *Prise de parole 1* (1996–1999) which was funded by the Social Sciences and Humanities Research Council of Canada (SSHRC) (main researcher: Normand Labrie; co-researchers: Jürgen Erfurt and Monica Heller) and *Prise de parole 2: la francophonie canadienne et la nouvelle économie mondialisée* (2000–2003), which also received funding from SSHRC (main researcher: Monica Heller; co-researchers: Annette Boudreau, Lise Dubois, Normand Labrie, Patricia Lamarre and Deirdre Meintel).

2 The translation of each interview extract presented in this section follows each extract.

3 We are not saying that these features were not used before. The fact that they recognize these features as archaic makes their use emblematic.

4 Note: the word 'radorser' is an old French word for 'to straighten up'. The 'j'ons' form in the extract, the first person singular conjugated at the first person plural, is a typical Baie Sainte-Marie structure used as a first person plural 'we'.

7 The future of Catalan: Language endangerment and nationalist discourses in Catalonia[1]

Joan Pujolar

Introduction

In this chapter, I undertake a critical analysis of a recent public debate on the future of the Catalan language on the basis of a corpus of newspaper articles. Catalan is, together with Spanish, the official language of Catalonia and is spoken by over half of the country's population of 7 million. However, Spanish is the language most widely used in large urban centres such as Barcelona, which leads to recurrent debates on whether Catalan will eventually die out as a result of continuous immigration and the internationalization of the economy, politics and the media. My analysis does not address these concerns as such, but the social and political grounds of the debate are analysed, as well as their implications for different sectors of Catalan society. I will show that the debate was not politically neutral, but constituted a site of struggle for power and resources.

As language is widely seen as a component of Catalan national identity, such debates are often sites where competing visions about the Catalan nation are reproduced, reconstructed and transformed. In this context, the *native speakers* of the language emerge as depositaries of an authentic Catalan identity. Philologists and language specialists contribute to the legitimization of these 'authentic' speakers. In the process, bilingual or translinguistic practices and identities become illegitimate or invisible. Insofar as languages and identities are connected with access to material resources and symbolic power, these processes are consequential for the economic and social prospects of different profiles of speakers of Catalan, Spanish or both (or other) languages. The mass media in particular is an important site for the construction of collective, in this case, national consciousness (Billig 1995; Gal and Woolard 2001). In Catalonia, the market of the printed press is dominated by media written in Spanish, which creates a scenario of struggles between Catalan and Spanish political projects in the public sphere. I will begin by laying out the social and historical conditions that render these debates significant as issues of national interest. Then I will move on to analyse a set of newspaper articles in terms of the particular constructions of language and of speech community that they presented. I will finally discuss the significance of the particular debate analysed for the construction of a Catalan nation and the implications for different social groups with different relationships to the language.

Historical background

Discourses over language in Catalonia and Spain have historically played an important role in the articulation of Catalan and Spanish nationalisms. Arguments about language use and policy are intimately connected with struggles over sovereignty, that is, over what social groups wield political power and control over territories and important economic resources within Spain. However, it is useful to appreciate that conflicts over sovereignty long preceded this politicization of language. When the Castilian elites started manoeuvering to obtain political control over Catalonia in the seventeenth century, Catalans met them with bitter resistance through political and military means; however, references to language are absent in contemporary texts. During the times of the Spanish Empire, members of the Catalan nobility often sought to learn Castilian when they had interests or ambitions at court, while a few writers chose to do their work in this language to gain recognition (largely unsuccessfully). After the fall of Barcelona in 1714, the crown imposed Castilian judges and military rulers, and banned Catalan from legal documents and schools (not always successfully) (Ferrer 1985).

In the nineteenth century, a significant section of the Catalan industrial and merchant elite adopted Castilian as a sign of distinction from the Catalan-speaking workers, peasants and the emerging middle classes (McDonogh 1986). However, at the same time, sections of the rural and urban middle classes were taking up the new Romantic ideas on the intimate relationship of language with the 'spirit of nations'. These middle classes were generally literate in both Catalan and Spanish and usually provided the leaders for the various political factions of the time. Conservative, liberal and revolutionary groups, while fighting each other for political hegemony, all contributed to invest language with much of the political significance that it has today. The new romantic focus on language provided a source of legitimacy for a 'Catalan nation', and the mere existence of the language was taken as proof of the existence of the Catalan group as an entity separate from Spanish-speaking Spain. The contemporary political interest in the reproduction of the Catalan speech community originates at this time.

At the turn of the twentieth century, Catalan nationalists concentrated their efforts in the re-establishment of a standard or 'literary' language and the development of a range of prestigious literary genres. It is immigration that explains the recent change of emphasis towards the 'social use of Catalan', which was the focus of the debate analysed in this chapter. During the last century, large numbers of immigrants from other parts of Spain began to settle in industrial towns, thus giving rise to the present demolinguistic structure of Catalonia: urban centres display a predominantly Castilian-speaking profile in working-class areas and a predominantly Catalan-speaking profile in middle-class sectors. The process took place during the economic boom of the 1950s and 1960s, when many Catalans were able to set up businesses for which they needed a workforce that the local population could no longer supply. Large numbers of Catalans became entrepreneurs and managers, as the workforce was filled by the so-called *Castellans*, 'Castilians'. This is how Catalan became the language spoken by those who control the largest part of the administration and the local economy in Spain's top manufacturing and exporting region. In this context, Catalan became an element of prestige and an important resource. Local Spanish-speakers can also profit by using the language to build personal relationships and find good employment, particularly in the public sector. In official surveys, 49 per cent declare Catalan to be 'their own language', but as much as 75 per cent claim to use it in different situations of their everyday life, such as at work with colleagues (GC 2004).

Thus, at the beginning of the millennium the Catalan language embodies not only national identity, but also the type of cultural capital that ensures access to powerful networks and prestigious employment. This sounds like a strong backing for a language. However, Spanish has retained an important position as a public language, particularly in the private sector, as privatized state services (e.g. telecommunications), banks, transnational companies, the cultural industry and the press are not controlled by Catalan capitalists and still treat the Catalan market as just a section of a wider, culturally and linguistically unified, Spanish market. This 'new economy' (which also includes such sectors as tourism, software and the Internet) is thus creating new spaces of penetration for the Spanish language, in addition to the fact that it is the language most widely used to interact with the new immigrants from Africa, Asia and Latin America. Demographic analyses can also be used to provide more pessimistic views of the situation. Subirats (2003), for instance, argues that those who claim Catalan to be 'their own' language ('*la seva llengua*') are diminishing in the younger generations in the province of Barcelona. However, once we arrive at this point, we are treading on shaky ground, as can be shown through the following text:

> A la província de Barcelona predominen les persones que es consideren de parla castellana: és un grup que comprèn més de la meitat de la població, mentre que les que es consideren de parla catalana són només, aproximadament, un terç. La resta està formada per població que considera que català i castellà són per igual les seves llengües; aquest és un grup encara minoritari, però que tendeix a augmentar com a resultat real d'una situació de mestissatge lingüístic en el qual el grup lingüístic numèricament més feble en aquest territori, el català, tendeix encara a reduir-se en les generacions joves. El resultat de les transmissions generacionals, en una situació de tanta desigualtat numèrica, acaba sent desfavorable al català, que com a grup lingüísticament pur tendeix a perdre membres en les generacions joves. (Subirats 2003: 187)

> *In the province of Barcelona, those who consider themselves to be of Spanish language predominate: it is a group that makes up more than half of the population, while those who consider themselves to be of Catalan language only make approximately a third [of the population]. The rest consists of people who consider both Catalan and Spanish to be their languages; this group is still a minority, but is on the increase by means of the real situation of linguistic métissage, in which the numerically feebler language group in this territory, the Catalan one, tends to shrink further in the young generations. The result of intergenerational transmission in a situation of such numeric inequality is disfavorable to Catalan, which, as a linguistically pure group, tends to lose members in the young generations. (my own translation)*

What this text is doing is constructing different profiles of speakers, with self-ascribed bilinguals falling within a category that is implicitly constructed as part of the 'threat' to the Catalan language. This particular perspective is an important component of Catalan discourses on endangerment. Subirats' text actually played an important role in triggering the debate I analyse below. (Interestingly enough, Subirats herself has also provided studies in the past showing that Catalan has so far held ground thanks to the fact that a section of the local Spanish speaking population regularly adopts it as a family language; Subirats 1990; see also GC 2001, 2004.)

Other phenomena that disturb the language-sensitive section of the population are the increasing presence of Spanish in the urban landscape or the fact that it is the main language of communication of children and young people in urban centres. The vigorous colloquial presence of Spanish presents a challenge to Catalan nationalists. If the reproduction of the Catalan speech community cannot be ensured, they may have no case for a Catalan nation as long as language is seen as one of its constitutive features. In fact, the very status of the language as a unifying national symbol is in doubt from the moment that it is not spoken by the whole of the population or is used as an element of social distinction or of differentiation between different types of Catalans.

Thus, debates on the future of the Catalan language are not strictly speaking about the language, but about the reproduction of the national speech community of authentic native speakers and about the means of access to the material and symbolic resources that this community manages. Such a debate gives rise to two constitutive tensions, first over who counts as a Catalan speaker and second over the relationship between *speaking* Catalan and *being* Catalan. As I will show, the former issue is very much dominated by the philological perspective, while the latter is the basis of a division between different strands of Catalan nationalism that can be characterized as either 'ethnic' nationalism or 'civic' nationalism. 'Ethnic' constructions of Catalan identity on the basis of cultural properties – mainly, native language – are confronted by more inclusive, 'civic' conceptions based on citizenship, i.e. participation in political institutions and in civil society.

Most theorists of nationalism suggest that the 'civic' strand may represent a later, more civilized stage (Smith 1986, 1991; Grad Fuchsel and Martín Rojo 2003). However, in the Catalan case, I have my doubts with this view as far as chronology is concerned. The latest historical research on nineteenth-century Catalonia shows that a liberal nationalism, associated with the emergence of labour and revolutionary movements, predated the formation of a conservative culturalist nationalism that may well have been triggered as a response to the former (Hernàndez 2005). Struggles between right-wing and left-wing nationalist sectors continued throughout the twentieth century. However, Woolard's (1989) view that the Catalan language became an emblem not only of national identity, but also of class membership after the massive immigration movements of the 1950s and 1960s, is probably correct too. She also notes, though, that when the autonomous government was established in 1980, all Catalan political parties were committed from an early stage to deconstructing the binary association

125

between language and identity. This is why, as Woolard reports, political leaders adopted the term 'citizens of Catalonia' instead of the traditional 'Catalans' in public arenas. Many sociolinguistic studies have also found that people seek to play down ethnolinguistic boundaries, not only in formal public discourse, but also in everyday social interaction (Tusón 1985; Nussbaum 1990; Boix 1993; Vila 1996; Pujolar 2001; Woolard 2003).

These struggles are further complicated by the pressures of a Spanish nationalism that strives for hegemony too, often through the interests of the media corporations that are instrumental in the constitution of 'public opinion' (Cardús 1995). On the basis of existing data on the Catalan media market, I will also argue that media corporations are important actors in these struggles, probably because of their interests in the markets of the various languages. I will show that, in Catalonia, the media market presents a predominant orientation towards Spanish markets, which contributes to sideline Catalan language issues and benefits Spanish nationalism. By doing this, I hope to show that debates about language endangerment are not only about preserving linguistic diversity in the face of globalized trends towards linguistic and cultural homogenization. These global trends are also deeply implicated in local political struggles over access to political and economic power. Whatever policies and resources are put in place for the development of endangered languages, they must be sensitive to the implications of linguistic policies for the various social groups affected by them.

Data analysis

My corpus consists of 41 articles published between the 1 January and 1 July 2003. I will examine these texts in terms of the differing conceptions of 'Catalan identity' and 'Catalan speaker' that they contained, as well as the connections between these notions and differing views and political interests with regard to the Catalan nation. I collected the articles from the press reports of the Institut de Sociolingüística Catalana and the Institut d'Estudis Catalans in Barcelona, which cover all major newspapers distributed in Barcelona, as well as a number of local publications that are not systematically scanned. As my research approach is heavily invested by ethnographic methods, I tend to resist simple content analyses. Instead, I sought to see these texts as traces of an interaction process, not unlike other forms of human (e.g. face-to-face) conversation. After all, this debate had concrete spatial (the newspapers and magazines) and temporal locations and a set of concrete participants (33 authors plus five interviewees or extensively quoted 'experts'[2]) who often responded to each other before a largely silent audience. This is why I have incorporated some (admittedly few) contextual elements to the analysis, mainly on the basis of publicly available information about the authors of texts, the immediate political context and the print media market in Catalonia.

One interesting way to analyse this type of texts is to examine the 'participant constellation' they tend to construct. I understand by participant constellation the set of individuals who participate in some form in a given social activity and their way of engaging with that activity, i.e. as legitimate speakers, bystanders, overhearers, legitimate audiences and so on. Students of interaction and conversation have long identified and studied these conversational roles (Goffman 1981). Critical discourse analysts have pointed out that they are often not pre-given, but interactionally produced, and hence the object of struggles and tensions (Fairclough 1992). In the media, a common participant is 'the nation' and the reader is often appealed to in subtle ways as a member of that nation (Billig 1995). One useful way to examine processes of construction of national audiences is through the uses of pronouns, particularly the first person plural 'we'. I will show how the shifts and ambivalences of the referents of this pronoun reflected divergent views on the role of language in the construction of Catalan national identities.

The corpus cannot really be seen as a single conversation thematically. There was a clear divide between a 'catalanist' sector (37 items) and a 'non-catalanist' (four items), the latter represented by individuals who could be easily ascribed to various strands of Spanish nationalism. The former discussed issues associated with the *social use of Catalan*, that is, the extent to which the language is used in everyday life. The latter were criticizing Catalan language policies, basically for being 'nationalistic'.

1. Participants

There were four basic types of participant: contributors, journalists, quoted 'experts' and the relatively anonymous audience of readers. The first two categories were projected as both 'authors' and 'animators' of full articles, whereas the others tended to appear either in quotations or in more subtle forms of reporting and reference. Although some contributors may be on the payroll of newspaper companies (columnists), their role is rather that of a person external to the organization whose writings can be argued to have an interest for the public, either because of their content or because of the social position of the writer (or both). Contributors are normally expected to construct a 'personal' position or point of view. They are often identified by name and surname (although pseudonyms are not exceptional) and may address or respond to each other explicitly. Journalists, on the contrary, are supposed to take a stance of professional reporting that formally evacuates issues of personal judgement and perspective. The journalistic voice of news reporting is normally expected to present 'events' in a descriptive way (in terms of the what, who, when and where) rather than arguments. In the corpus, only eight articles (17 per cent) were produced as news reports by professional journalists. The rest were written by regular columnists (also eight) and by other contributors who managed to make their views published by virtue of their social position and their personal contacts.

Beyond the particulars of the journalistic participatory framework, we must also attend to the social characteristics of a large section of the participants. Most belonged to a category I call the 'language professionals'. Language professionals have a special investment in language and play a key role in language debates. The category includes writers, translators, teachers of all educational levels, journalists and linguists (be they academics or not). Language professionals are those who claim expertise on language and on particular uses of language. Philologists (Catalan language professors and teachers, language assistants, writers[3] and publishers) are an important section of these professionals. The discipline of 'philology' has historically played, in many countries, an important role in the production, reproduction and distribution of the traditional discourses that placed language and literature at the centre of the political sphere. Thus philologists have contributed to define communities as monolingual, bounded wholes by constructing sanitized, unified images of all languages. Their sophisticated research on the origins of languages, the canons of literary traditions, dialectal boundaries as well as lexical and grammatical properties has been used to control 'interferences' from other languages and to define the stylistic and formal criteria to write and speak literary or standard forms of languages. In this way, philologists have acted as guardians of an important source of authority, the legitimate language (Bourdieu 1991), which played two fundamental roles in the modern period: (a) it determined the conditions for access to important resources and symbolic power; and (b) it was used to define the national speech community on the basis of the 'authentic' *native speakers* of the language.

Much work in linguistics and literary studies is still amenable to this philological reading of the role of language in society. Writers, in Catalonia and elsewhere, have also seen themselves as actors in the construction of a standard language and a national literary tradition

(Fernàndez 1995). Journalists are a second grouping who play an important role in the contemporary world, not only in the dissemination of legitimate language practices, but also in the regulation of the distribution of discourses in the public arena, although they are also subjected to the interests of the media companies for which they work. In this context, newspapers, radio and television corporations, insofar as they market products that are constitutively linguistic and communicational, can be regarded as 'language companies' that also have important stakes in struggles over language policies, i.e. as to what languages, whose languages, what language ideologies, should be accorded legitimacy in given social contexts or territories. These 'language companies' can thus be seen, as I will show below, as important actors in struggles over languages in Catalonia (see also Cardús 1995).

Language professionals as defined here constitute 75 per cent of the individual characters identified in the texts (all except politicians, activists and teachers not specialized in language). The 'philological' sector makes up 41 per cent of the characters involved. As we can see in Table 7.1, we find women only acting as journalists, which is surprising if one bears in mind the substantial presence of women in the teaching professions and among graduates in philology. Public debates on language remain, for some reason, a masculine concern.

Philologists also played an important role in the debate in that it was largely triggered by a colloquium jointly chaired by the prestigious linguist Solà and the popular writer Quim Monzó (Capdevila 2003; Palomeras 2003; Piñol 2003a, 2003b; Piquer 2003). Solà generally argued that Catalan was receding as a spoken language and that its use had to be promoted without concern for the 'quality' of the language, i.e. people should not be criticized for not using the 'correct' forms. Monzó accused the Catalan government of shirking its responsibilities with relation to the language and proposed, in an ironical key, a linguistic 'euthanasia', i.e. a national agreement to cease speaking Catalan on a certain date. The reactions were varied and will not be extensively glossed here; but most authors recognized the increasing linguistic diversity of Catalonia and lamented that most Catalan speakers would not use the language with most speakers of other languages even if these were able to speak it or at least understand it. This situation, it was argued, gave Spanish its increasingly predominant position in everyday life.

One interesting feature that is common to almost all contributors was that, despite the obvious connection between their own professional roles and their interest in the Catalan language, philologists and language professionals rarely made this connection visible by,

Table 7.1: Professions of active participants in the debate

	Appear in n. articles	n. of persons mentioned	Comments
Language teachers, professors and language assistants	**11** 27%	**7** 19%	They all work specifically on Catalan, not on Spanish.
Other professors	**5** 12%	**4** 11%	Two work in law in the non-catalanist group. Another one is a well-known nationalist ideologist.
Writers	**7** 15%	**7** 19%	They all write fundamentally in Catalan, except one Englishman and except when they write in dailies written in Spanish.
Politicians and cultural activists	**5** 12%	**4** 11%	Three of them belong to clearly pro-Catalan parties or institutions.
Related to publishing	**2** 5%	**1** 3%	In Catalan.
Columnists	**8** 20%	**7** 19%	One of them writes exclusively on (against) Spanish nationalism.
Professional journalists	**8** 20%	**7** 19%	Press reporters. Three of them (in four articles) are signed by women.

Note: the table does not feature authors of texts, but all personal characters active in the debate through different forms of textual presence. The first column presents the number of articles where the characters in question appear in each category. Because each article may contain references to more than one character, the sum of percentages (of articles where the characters appear) exceeds 100. The second column presents the actual number of characters that correspond to each category without repetitions.

for instance, explaining personal experiences. Only the articles by a publisher (Muñoz 2003a, 2003b) clearly focused on the implications of language policies for the publishing industry. One can occasionally find (not in this sample) texts of writers or pop singers who mention the (mostly economic) implications of writing in Catalan for those who seek professionalization (Vallverdú 1975; Bargalló 2005). In some cases (not in this sample either), university professors or secondary school teachers may attest to the language uses of their pupils as supporting evidence for the view that Catalan is receding; but this is very rarely connected with considerations about the specific roles of teachers for language policies. As Billig argues, the social groups implicated in the construction of national consciousness characteristically seek 'to present their particular voice as the voice of the national whole' (1995: 71). Thus, at the moment, the role of speaking for the speech community in Catalonia seems to be largely restricted to those who have a personal investment in the language professions and in the construction of a Catalan national literature.

2. The audience, the speakers and the nation

The general audience, although sometimes explicitly mentioned, was generally not explicitly addressed. However, the texts contain traces of many different and often contradictory forms of audience construction. The most interesting resource for audience construction was the pronoun 'we' and its semantic equivalents (us, our), which were often used to build a sense of the reader accompanying the writer, as in 'However, if we analyze the figures ...' (Sala 2003). As Billig (1995) has pointedly argued, the press is a key site in the construction of the national community and its boundaries, often through implicit means, in which the 'we' plays a key role:

> There is a case for saying that nationalism is, above all, an ideology
> of the first person plural. The crucial question relating to national
> identity is how the national 'we' is constructed and what is meant
> by such construction. (Billig 1995: 70)

In a context where language is being discussed by virtue of its connection with national identity, then we (in this case, author and reader) can expect that first person plurals will point towards the speakers of the languages affected and/or the members of the national group in multiple, ambivalent and contradictory ways.

As is well known, in most languages, the referent of the first person plural may or may not include the audience. Catalan is one of those languages, and there is no linguistic marker that can unambiguously determine who exactly is included in the referent. The key must necessarily be found either in the textual or extratextual contexts, if it can be found at all. Writers may well feel that the disambiguation is not needed or not in their interest. In fact, the shifts between inclusions and exclusions throughout a piece of writing may actually play a key role in the writer's strategy.

For example, in my data, there was one interview article that presented a most interesting itinerary of referents for the first person plural:

> *Text 1: occurrence 1 (L'Hiperbòlic 2003)*
> hem de fer un esforç de revitalització de la societat civil
> *We must make an effort of revitalization of the civil society*

Here we have a restricted 'we' that applied exclusively to the members or the board of a cultural society led by the newly elected president who was interviewed. It is a relatively unproblematic 'we' in the sense that the interview was actually about what the organization wished to present as being of public interest. Later, it emerged that the situation of the Catalan language was at the top of the agenda. In relation to this, the interviewee reportedly said[4]:

> *Text 1: occurrence 2*
> aquí sempre basculem des d'un optimisme més aviat moderat fins a un pessimisme catastrofista
>
> *Here we always stay at a balance between a rather moderate optimism and catastrophist pessimism*

> *Text 1: occurrence 3*
> ... fins a la dictadura del General Franco, tots els avatars que hem tingut ...
>
> *... Up to the dictatorship of General Franco, all the ups and downs we've been through ...*

Up to this moment, the 'we' pointed clearly to the Catalan national community from a historical perspective. It did not necessarily provide clues as to who may or may not be included in this category. There was, however, a significant cohesive connection between the language issue and the destinies of the nation, which built a thematic relationship that did not need explicit elaboration. If we read further, we find sentences such as:

> *Text 1: occurrence 4*
> ... un 50 per cent de la població nascuda a fora, que vénen sense tenir ...
>
> *... a 50 per cent of the population born outside [Catalonia], who [they] come without having ...*

This use of the third person plural to refer to 'outsiders' suggests a contrast between 'us' and 'them', but was still, strictly speaking, ambivalent. Even if the writer considered 'outsiders' to be part of the Catalan group, the use of the third person plural remained grammatically mandatory, except if he would have wished to present himself as a member of the subgroup. However, the contrast between first and third person plural in the following sentence dispelled the ambivalence:

> *Text 1: occurrence 5*
> ... que la mateixa facilitat que tenim els catalanoparlants de passar al castellà, la tinguin els castellanoparlants per passar al català ...
>
> ... *that the same propensity that Catalan speakers [we] have to switch to Castilian, the Castilian speakers [they] have to switch to Catalan ...*

The use of the third person to refer to Catalan speakers would have been correct grammatically, of course if the reported speaker were willing to indicate that Catalan speakers were themselves a subgroup of the nation. This interpretation was not fully excluded by the text, although the stylistic effect of the syntactic juxtaposition was strong. In some way, it contradicted one of the main explicit intentions of the interviewee, namely to construct an inclusive discourse, which was the not fully explicit intention of the following sentence:

> *Text 1: occurrence 6*
> ... tenim unes escoles que no van prou bé (...) hem de pagar peatges ...
>
> ... *We have schools that do not work properly (...) we must pay many motorway tolls ...*[5]

Here the interviewee was precisely trying to identify issues that could be of political interest to all Catalans irrespective of their language. This was a common strategy of the Catalan nationalist left in the period in which the interview was published, in the run up to local and national elections. Many leaders made it explicit by actually adding the coda 'whether one speaks Catalan or Castilian'.

Now if we move on to analyse how first-person plural pronouns are used throughout the corpus to construct different alignments of readers as speakers and as members of the Catalan nation, we can divide them into four categories. The categories involve assumptions as to whether the reader was or was not a speaker of Catalan or Castilian. I shall connect these categories with national belonging below:

> A: 'We' points towards a writer and an audience that was presumed to be Catalan speaking.
> B: The 'we' was more ambivalent. It might be interpreted

like A in the light of the contextual bearing of the discourses on language, but the <u>letter</u> of the text did not unambiguously call forth this interpretation.

C: The 'we' was produced in ways that made clear that the audience included speakers of both Catalan and Castilian.

D: 'We' referred to groups not defined by linguistic or national identities: political parties, professional groups, the writer–reader tandem and so on.

In the corpus, category B is the most present. It appears in 29 articles, though often in combination with all the other categories. Thus, category A appears in 11 articles and category C in five. One article actually includes both A and C first persons, although they are in principle contradictory. Interestingly enough, the three articles with the clearest, least ambiguous occurrences of category C belong to authors who are Spanish nationalists:

Text 2: occurrence 7 (Marhuenda 2003b)
Los catalanes tenemos dos idiomas propios.

[We] Catalans have two languages that are our own.

All in all, we find 26 articles where no explicit claims were made about the linguistic ascription of readers (i.e. they either contain B, B+D or D first person plurals, or none at all).

3. Whose language?

In this subsection, I am going to deal with the connection between language and identity, i.e. the ways in which *speaking* Catalan was associated with *being* Catalan in the texts analysed, which also raises questions as to who counted as a speaker of Catalan. Fifteen articles contained statements presenting or implying rather directly that speakers of both languages were included in the category 'Catalan'. The four items by Spanish nationalists were among these. Five contained these statements in combination with category A first persons, that is, they might recognize that the category 'Catalan' included everyone, but they were assuming that the reader was a speaker of Catalan. However, of these five, three actually contained statements that clearly implied that a Catalan was a Catalan speaker, that is, they were incoherent on this account.

To provide a fuller picture of the discursive resources and processes connecting language and identity, it is necessary to examine the notion of *llengua pròpia* 'own language', as well as the use of the terms *catalanoparlant* 'Catalan speaker' and *castellanoparlant* 'Castilian speaker'.

The expression *llengua pròpia*, present in the Statute of Autonomy of Catalonia and in various Spanish legal texts (Jou 1998), can be treated as equivalent to expressions such as 'our language', or simply 'the language', meaning Catalan. In the corpus, one finds phrases like the following, which in Catalan comes across as remarkably redundant[6]:

> Text 3: occurrence 8 (Solé, 2003)
> Tinc molt respecte pels qui senten el castellà com a llengua pròpia seva …, però és discriminar-los no acollir els immigrants en la llengua pròpia de Catalunya
>
> *I have a lot of respect for those who feel Castilian as their own language (…), but it is to discriminate against immigrants not to welcome them in Catalonia's own language*

The phrase assumed that there was a personal and a collective dimension to language belonging. Castilian-speaking Catalans thus could personally feel that Castilian was 'their own language' and (presumedly) accept that Catalan was Catalonia's own. This undoubtedly reinforced the view that the Catalan language had a privileged relationship with the Catalan community or nation, and thus fostered the assumption that its speakers might also have a privileged access to Catalan identity. My interpretation of occurrence 8 is that the author implicitly proposed a Catalan identity formed mainly by speakers of both Catalan and Spanish *in opposition to* foreign immigrants *in order to* argue that Catalan should be given preference to Castilian when interacting with these immigrants who generally spoke other languages. One additional article by a well-known sociologist contained (besides the sentence 'the natural state of the Catalan is to weep about the language') an explicit discussion on the individual and collective dimensions of the notion of 'own language' (Cardús 2003b). Thus, *llengua pròpia* and related expressions did not necessarily call forth an ethnicizing ideology; but they did not point towards a clear 'civic' framework of equal participation either.

Occurrence 5 above presents another way of constructing who counts as 'Catalan speakers'. The conventional terms *catalanoparlant* 'Catalan speaker' and *castellanoparlant* 'Castilian speaker' arose in public discourse during the eighties as an alternative to the colloquial ethnic labels *Catalan* and *Castilian*, which were unambiguously exclusionary (Pujolar 1995). In the late 1970s, as Woolard (1989) noted, a Catalan was a person who spoke Catalan within the family and to others known to be Catalan. From this viewpoint, the new socio-linguistic labels are not actually descriptive of the specific language abilities of people, but of people's adscription to a language by virtue of the same indicators that served the earlier classification. Thus, while the terms

'Catalan-speaker' and 'Castilian-speaker' have the advantage of not excluding the latter from the group label 'Catalan', they contribute to preserve the notion of what defines a speaker of Catalan. People who speak Catalan (like the *castellanoparlants* in Occurrence 5), but do not use it in the way Catalans do are not considered Catalan-speakers.

The conceptual framework provided by expressions such as '*llengua pròpia*', '*catalanoparlant*' and so on is so widely accepted that official surveys can unproblematically ask residents what *la seva llengua* 'their language' is, to which they may respond 'Catalan', 'Castilian', 'both' or 'others', as is shown by the citation above from Subirats (2003). This also makes possible phrases such as the following:

> Text 4: occurrence 9 (Pla 2003)
> ... els catalans –més ben dit, l'escàs 50% de la gent del país que voldríem poder-hi viure un dia amb normalitat en català-...
>
> ... *The Catalans –to put it more properly, the not quite 50% of people in this country who [we] would like to be able to lead one day a normal life in Catalan-*
>
> Text 4: occurrence 10
> ... un 50% dels catalans senten el castellà com la seva llengua més íntima i personal, a la qual se senten units per un fortíssim vincle d'identificació.
>
> ... *50% of Catalans feel that Castilian is their most intimate and personal language, to which they feel united by a very strong tie of identification.*
>
> Text 5: occurrence 11 (Domínguez, 2003)
> Per què acostumem a ser els catalanoparlants els que ens passem al castellà davant d'un català castellanoparlant?
>
> *Because it is usually [we] Catalan speakers who switch to Castilian before a Castilian-speaking Catalan.*

This implies that, generally speaking, both authors and readers would exclude many 'users' of Catalan from the category 'Catalan-speaker', which in turn implies that articles that assumed a Catalan-speaking readership excluded them too.

4. The print media market

The process through which actors (writers) construct particular relationships with the audience (readers) does not involve just the texts, but the whole social context of communication. From this perspective, the analysis of media texts presents typical limitations when no evidence is available about the processes of text production and reception. However, there are a few interesting points that can be made by simply looking at the print media market in Catalonia. These have to do with the insertion of the language debate in particular sections of the press, mainly the publications written in Catalan, and the discursive differences found in texts published in different media.

An overview of the Catalan market for daily newspapers is useful (see Table 7.2). In 2003, the market was clearly dominated by Catalan-based (mainly Barcelona-based) publications, which made 85 per cent of the net circulation average. However, the market share of the Catalan-written dailies was only 25 per cent.

The four non-catalanist articles appeared in Madrid-based daily newspapers, though two of them in special sections addressed to Catalan audiences only. The rest of the corpus is dominated by the dailies *Avui* (in Catalan, 22 articles) and *La Vanguardia* (in Spanish, 9 articles). The remaining articles (6) were written in magazines,

Table 7.2: Net Circulation average of dailies in Catalonia (2003)[7]

	Based in	In Castilian	In Catalan
ABC	Madrid	10271	
Avui	Catalonia		28368
Diari de Girona	Catalonia		8161
Diari de Tarragona*	Catalonia	15031	
El País	Madrid	61830	
El Periódico	Catalonia	101155	69356
El Punt	Catalonia		23843
La Mañana*	Catalonia	5732	
La Razón	Madrid	Unavailable	
La Vanguardia	Catalonia	205330	
Segre	Catalonia	7209	6365
Diari de Sabadell	Catalonia	5685	
Diari de Terrassa	Catalonia	5611	
El Mundo	Madrid	14486	
Regió 7	Catalonia		8922
TOTAL		**432340**	**145015**
TOTAL PERCENTAGE		**74.9%**	**25.1%**

* Some articles, often on local issues, are written in Catalan.
Source: Oficina de Justificación de la Difusión (www.ojd.es).

regional dailies and the 'cultural' section of the Madrid-based *El Pais*, all written in Catalan. The absence of items in *El Periódico* is interesting, as it is one of the largest newspapers and it is published bilingually, i.e. readers can buy either a Castilian or a Catalan version (largely translated from the Castilian original). The 'opinion' section of this newspaper seems to be more strictly controlled than in the others. There are fewer articles by external contributors and most of them are related to issues addressed in other sections, which suggests that self-appointed contributors may have little chance to get published. In any case, we are sadly left with the question of how would a national 'we' be constructed in a bilingual newspaper (and with the suspicion that this might have been the problem behind the editorial policy of this paper).

Catalan-speaking first-person plurals (category A) and statements that link Catalan identity and language appeared only in Catalan-based, Catalan-written media. To this rule, there were the following exceptions:

1. One article in *La Vanguardia* with the phrase 'We users of Catalan have (...)'.
2. One article in the Catalan-written cultural section of *El Pais*, although the expression was inserted in a quotation of a character separate from the author.
3. Phrases of the 'our language' type also appeared in two articles of *La Vanguardia*, one of them within quoted text.

Otherwise, these features appeared always in 'opinion' articles from external contributors and very rarely in articles by regular columnists (only once) and in the voices of journalistic reporting. Five journalistic reports featured category A pronouns in quotations from the linguist or the writer from the Barcelona colloquium. However, in three interviews, we also find the journalists using these. The need to build some kind of collusive relationship with interviewees may have led journalists to produce these exceptions.

We can draw three main conclusions from these data. First, Catalan professional journalistic discourse tended to avoid expressions that might potentially exclude readers on the basis of language (consistent with general trends towards neutral styles in relation to gender and race). This means that Catalan formal journalistic discourse tactically favoured 'civic' orientations to Catalan nationalism.[8] Second, public debates on the future of Catalan were largely promoted from the (monolingual) Catalan-written press, and particularly by the daily *Avui*, a medium associated with nationalist sectors. Given the market position of the monolingual Catalan-written press, the 2003 debate was marginal in the sense that it reached a small fraction of the potential readership, most of it through the few articles published by *La Vanguardia*. Third, 'ethnic' orientations to Catalan nationalism got expressed almost exclusively in the Catalan-written press, in which they were in a minority position. It was, from this perspective, a clearly marginal discourse.[9]

Discussion

Thus, the 2003 debate on language endangerment in Catalonia was eminently political, not just linguistic, and it involved and affected a variety of social groups in many different ways. It was led by male language professionals, particularly philologists and writers who re-enacted received notions about languages as unified objects that constituted distinct cultural groups. The presence of actors who identified themselves as 'writers' also called forth the symbolic role traditionally ascribed to learned literature in these processes. Pro-Catalan participants were invariably native speakers or people who had adopted native-like patterns of language use (which are also numerous in Catalonia). From this perspective, the participant constellation of the debate claimed the voice of the traditional national community of 'authentic' speakers. It seems to me that it is actually this community – not strictly speaking the language – that was felt to be under threat, as is shown by the deployment of procedures to identify it in the texts themselves and to measure it in official surveys.

The debate had an explicit focus on language use, and a repeated theme was the need to mobilize native speakers of Catalan to use 'their' language when interacting with other Catalans who might have other 'own' languages. Thus, the 'problem' was very much this space of contact with 'other Catalans', and this required an effort to conceptualize their position within the nation, particularly their means of access to Catalan identity. As many actors realized that traditional images of Catalonia as a homogeneous community no longer held, they strived to work out a new framework where language retained its position as a national symbol even for native speakers of other languages. There was the need to produce an image of the nation that could potentially mobilize these 'other' Catalans for the national cause or, at least, avoid their explicit alienation.

However, this agenda was articulated in contradictory ways if we look at it from the perspective of the discourse field that emerged from the texts analysed. First, these 'other' Catalans were often not considered as legitimate participants in the debate itself, which reproduced the notion that authentic speakers must have indeed privileged access to defining and delimiting the Catalan nation. Second, there was virtually no effort to make visible the social, symbolic and economic implications of belonging to the different linguistic groups. The power game remained invisible under a rubric that foregrounded language use as if it was a phenomenon isolated from other aspects of social life.

Thus, the 'other-language' speakers, for whose benefit the nation was supposedly being redefined, were not participating in the very process that was allegedly constituting them as legitimate participants. True enough, the texts point to a shift in Catalan nationalist discourses tilted from the 'ethnic' to the 'civic' poles. The latter were gaining strength, in tune with the principles that legitimize contemporary public discourse within liberal democracies. A number of authors sought to construct a 'civic' discourse that maintained a connection between language and identity by distinguishing between personal linguistic identity and a collective or territorial one, thus reproducing a common distinction used in the definition of language rights and policies. This did not constitute a fundamental challenge to the traditional connection between language and national identity. What it sought to do was precisely to salvage the connection in a way that was in principle inclusive of speakers of other languages. In this way, many Catalan nationalists strove to make room for the large numbers of speakers of Castilian in the representations of Catalonia as a nation, as well as the new foreign immigrants. In some cases, a new picture seemed to emerge of a bilingual Catalan community in the face of the new multilingual population intake.

However, as these ideas were shared by all authors and appeared in contradictory ways, participation in this particular language debates still had an 'ethnicizing effect' for people who might not speak Catalan or might not be seen as native speakers of Catalan. The 'users' of Catalan who did not qualify as actual 'Catalan-speakers' resided in a symbolic limbo. Even in everyday speech there is actually no term to name them (could it be L2 speakers?). Thus, if we sought to follow the discussion from the perspective of a Catalan who might well speak Catalan often, but spoke Spanish at home and with many of her acquaintances, she would encounter 19 articles where no assumptions were made in relation to the languages she spoke or how she spoke them, plus 10 articles that assumed that speakers of both languages were members of the Catalan community. But in the remaining 11 articles, she might feel displaced, as though she were a simple bystander to a conversation between people who saw each other, but not her, as legitimate speakers of Catalan concerned for the future of the language and of the Catalan nation. Thus, the prototypical reader constructed through these debates was the native speaker of Catalan or the speaker with native-like proficiency who spoke predominantly Catalan in everyday life. Opposed to these figures were the 'Castilian' speakers who were assumed to have no substantive interest in learning and using Catalan. The large numbers of people who spoke Catalan as a second language and might have shown more ambivalent forms of language use and identity were left unnamed and ignored.

The absence of references to socioeconomic issues in the debate is also significant, albeit somehow predictable. After all, these questions are not likely to be perceived as problematic by native Catalans, given that their economic position is good if compared with that of first or second-generation immigrants. In the past, a few Spanish nationalist groups have sought to rally Castilian speakers against existing language policies, so far with little success. In these attempts, socio-economic issues have not been stressed either. This is probably because the critique has come either from right wing groups or from sections of a local intelligentsia connected with the upper classes of Barcelona, that is, from sections of the elites, in Catalonia and beyond, who are concerned for their position within the local cultural and political landscape. What these groups generally advocate for is a liberal, non-interventionist language policy, which would not necessarily be to the advantage of the marginalized. Thus, the perspective of the predominantly Castilian-speaking lower middle classes is not present on debates on language, identity and nation. Their voices can only be recovered from a variety of ethnographic and sociolinguistic studies (Woolard 1989; Rodríguez-Gómez 1993; Atkinson 2000; Ros 2000; Unamuno 2000; Pujolar 2001). What these studies show is the explicit awareness of these sectors that Catalan is associated with access to more prestigious employment and more influential social networks. From this standpoint, the relevant questions would be in what ways these social groups are effectively treated as equal citizens, whether Catalan L2 speakers are effectively accepted as legitimate participants in these social networks, how is such legitimization achieved, and so on. This means that the debate analysed in my corpus reproduced both the traditional themes and the traditional silences not only of Catalan nationalistic discourses, but also of the whole range of issues of public interest available for discussion in Catalonia as a whole.

One point that needs to be conceded in this critique: appeals to a restricted Catalan-speaking audience appear basically in Catalan-written media, where it may be legitimate to assume that the reader is an everyday user of the language. Surely native Catalan speakers have every right to construct themselves as a group and discuss their concerns. The university colloquium, whose voices leaked into the

Castilian-written press, was clearly constructed as one such 'insider' space. However, when this kind of debate is potentially important to the construction of Catalonia as a nation, then Castilian speakers as such should also have the means to participate in them. Authors should not act as if the Catalan language concerned only a minority, a fraction or a faction in Catalan society, even if they put forward positive representations of Castilian-speakers. In the corpus, Castilian-speakers were commonly depicted in a favourable light. Their attitudes towards Catalan were positive. Newly created pressure groups of 'new Catalan speakers' were mentioned. Two authors also sought to enact the 'outsider' perspective: one who reflected on the history of his partly Castilian-speaking family (Sáez 2003) and an Englishman, who also used the Catalan-speaking 'we' (Tree 2003). But the large numbers of Catalan L2 speakers were clearly underrepresented in the debate, that is, people generally more fluent in Castilian covering a varied range from the actively bilingual (probably the middle class) to the passively bilingual (probably the lower class). Catalan-medium media should provide a neutral space for Catalans of different backgrounds to negotiate their relationship to the languages they speak and their modes of participation in the construction of the Catalan nation.

It is also necessary to acknowledge that Catalan nationalists who wish to construct more inclusive discourses encounter important limitations in the dissemination of these discourses. The market is dominated by corporations that do not have stakes in the Catalan language. This may be due, in part, to the simple fact that these enterprises benefit from their position in the Spanish linguistic market, which gives them a dominant position in Catalonia too. There is also an argument that could be made as to the role that these companies play in the articulation of new Spanish nationalist projects in which the development of Catalan as a national language is not seen with sympathy. The daily *La Vanguardia*, for instance, has been run throughout the twentieth century by an eminently anti-Catalanist family (see Calvet 1994). In any case, the reserved attitude of the Spanish-speaking press in relation to the Catalan language means not only that the circulation of Catalan nationalist discourses are hampered; it also prevents a substantial section of the population from participating in debates on language and nation and thus to enable other voices to be constructed and heard.[10]

It is also relevant to note that Spanish linguistic nationalism is generally much more 'ethnic' and excluding (Grad Fuchsel and Martín Rojo 2003), though critical analyses of it are rare in academic circles (del Valle & Gabriel-Stheeman 2002; del Valle 2005 are recent exceptions) and non-existent in forms more accessible to the public, even in progressive newspapers like *El Pais*, where 'nationalisms' (meaning Basque or Catalan nationalism) have been subjects of ongoing debate for years. In any case, these issues are pure politics; they belong to the field of struggles for the legitimization of different conceptions of the nation. From this perspective, one should not forget that Catalanist elites have other means of discourse production and distribution which, in some circumstances, can make good the limitations encountered in other sections of public life: a virtually unchallenged hegemony in the public sector, including local and regional institutions, schools and universities. Many actors could also use their strategic position in the local economy to pursue more inclusive policies in the workplace.

Conclusion

Contemporary debates on the future of the language in Catalonia are not simply on language preservation. They concern the social and political organization of linguistic and cultural diversity at all levels, from informal social relations to highly codified institutional practices. Linguistic practices serve to construct and delimit social groups, in this case to distinguish (among other things) between 'native Catalans' and those who do not qualify as such. These distinctions are connected in complex ways with differences of access to symbolic capital and economic resources.

In this chapter, I have shown that language debates in Catalonia are generally led by actors who belong to the group of native speakers of Catalan. These are mainly language professionals and philologists who make claims about the nature of the Catalan nation, basically as centrally constituted by the community of native speakers. This conception of the nation draws from culturalist, romantic ideas on language and the spirit of peoples, which in turn inspired the expert philological discourses that still contribute to the legitimacy of monocultural and monolingual groups. In linguistically and culturally diverse contexts, like Catalonia is, such discourses are potentially alienating for large numbers of people, particularly second-language speakers, bilinguals and speakers of varieties characterized by language contact and hybridization.

In the debate analysed, most actors were seeking to reconstruct a more open, inclusive, 'civic' conception of the nation, which explicitly recognized the legitimacy of speakers of other languages within the Catalan nation. However, although this inclusiveness was often formally honoured, the structure and development of the debate did not confirm it. Apart from the fact that some writers still assumed that 'Catalan' meant a native speaker of the language, quite a few

143

pieces also constructed an exclusively Catalan-speaking audience. The problem of the social use of Catalan was therefore constructed as an 'insider issue' about which other types of speakers had supposedly no say or no interest. This was tantamount to claiming an exclusive right to define the Catalan nation and its corresponding linguistic regime.

This does not necessarily mean that the actors involved in the debate were all intentionally seeking this effect. In fact, many contributors to the debate did not present any textual feature that could be interpreted as ethnicist. There were also important structural conditions that thwarted the development of a more civic framework, such as the fact that the Spanish-written press showed little interest for the debate, probably because of its commitment in the construction of a Spanish nation and probably to avoid a discourse that potentially alienated part of its readership. Had this been otherwise, the debate might have produced a richer range of perspectives and ideas. It would have also forced many authors to acknowledge that language cannot be treated as a simple 'insider' issue among native speakers.

Be that as it may, individual participants may have inclusive intentions but the overall picture of the discursive field is still that of an ethno-national discourse that leaves non-native Catalans in a marginal position. Those who wish to see the Catalan language playing a prominent role in the future must do more than produce inclusive texts. They must organize spaces of communication and participation for a more plural constituency. If all Catalans enjoy the same rights in the construction of the nation, irrespective of the languages they use, then they are entitled to make their views and their experiences heard in all aspects of public life, including the 'national' language.

These considerations point towards the need to deconstruct not only contemporary nationalist discourses (actually, the deconstruction is pretty much under way), but also the expert constructs of language still dominant in linguistics and philology. Linguistics should recognize that language is not politically neutral, but a site of struggles for power and resources. Debates on language survival and language policy cannot be treated as simply 'linguistic' or 'cultural heritage' issues, but as important political questions that may affect the social and economic position of the social groups of a given territory.

References

Atkinson, D. (2000), 'Minoritisation, identity and ethnolinguistic vitality in Catalonia', *Journal of Multilingual and Multicultural Development*, 21, (3), 185–97.

Bargalló, J. (2005), 'Las estirpes condenadas a cien años de soledad'. *La Vanguardia* 6 June 2005. Barcelona.

Billig, M. (1995), *Banal Nationalism*. London: Sage Publications.

Boix, E. (1993), *Triar no és trair. Identitat i llengua en els joves de Barcelona*. Edicions 62: Barcelona.

Bourdieu, P. (1991), *Language and Symbolic Power*. London: Polity Press.

Calvet, A. (Gaziel) (1994), *Història de 'La Vanguardia' 1881-1936 i nou articles sobre periodisme*. Barcelona: Empúries.

Cardús, S. (1995), *Política de paper. Premsa i poder, 1981–1992*. Barcelona: La Campana.

Del Valle, J. (2005), 'Lengua, patria común', in R. Wright and P. Ricketts (eds), *Studies on Ibero-Romance Linguistics Dedicated to Ralph Penny*. Newark: Juan de la Cuesta Monographs (Estudios Lingüísticos no.7).

Del Valle, J. and Gabriel-Stheeman, L. (2002), *The Battle over Spanish between 1800 and 2000: Language Ideologies and Hispanic Intellectuals*. New York: Routledge.

Fairclough, N. (1992), *Discourse and Social Change*. Polity Press: Cambridge.

Fernàndez, J.-A. (1995), 'Becoming normal: Cultural policy and cultural production in Catalonia', in H. Graham and J. Labanyi (eds), *Spanish Cultural Studies: An Introduction: The Struggle for Modernity*. Oxford: Oxford University Press, pp. 342–6.

Ferrer, F. (1985), *La persecució política de la llengua catalana*. Barcelona: Edicions 62.

Gal, S. and Woolard, K. (2001), *Languages and Publics: The Making of Authority*. Manchester: St. Jerome Pub.

GC-Generalitat de Catalunya (2001), *Informe sobre política lingüística. Any 2000*. Barcelona: Direcció General de Política Lingüística.

GC-Generalitat de Catalunya (2004), *Estadística d'usos lingüístics a Catalunya 2003. Estadística Social, Censos i Enquestes*. Barcelona: Generalitat de Catalunya, Institut d'Estadística de Catalunya i Secretaria de Política Lingüística del Departament de la Presidència.

Goffman, E. (1974), *Frame Analysis. An Essay on the Organisation of Experience*. London: Penguin Books.

Goffman, E. (1981), *Forms of Talk*. Oxford: Blackwell.

Grad Fuchsel, H. and Martín Rojo, L. 2003. '"Civic" and "ethnic" nationalist discourses in Spanish parliamentary debates'. *Journal of Language and Politics*, 1, (2), 225–67.

Hernàndez, F. X. (2005), *Història militar de Catalunya. Temps de Revolta. Vol. IV* Barcelona: Rafael Dalmau.

Jou, L. (1998), 'Els principis de llengua pròpia i llengües oficials en l'articulat de la Llei 1/1998, de 7 de gener, de política lingüística'. *Revista de llengua i dret*, 29, 7–22.

McDonogh, G. (1986), *Good Families of Barcelona: A Social History of Power in the Industrial Era*. Princeton, NJ: Princeton University Press.

Nussbaum, L. (1990), 'Contacte de llengües a la classe de francès. Una aproximació pragmàtica' (Ph.D. Thesis. Universitat Autònoma de Barcelona. Bellaterra).

Pujolar, J. (1995), 'Immigration in Catalonia: the politics of sociolinguistic research', in *Catalan Review*, International Journal of Catalan Culture núm. IX.2. Special Issue on Catalan Sociolinguistics. Publicat per la North American Catalan Society (NACS), 141–62.

Pujolar, J. (2001), *Gender, Heteroglossia and Power. A Sociolinguistic Study of Youth Culture*. Berlin: Mouton de Gruyter.

Rodríguez-Gómez, M. G. (1993), *Immigrant Workers Constructing a Nation: Class Formation, the Construction of Social Persons, and the Politics of the Past in Santa Coloma de Gramanet*. Tesi doctoral no publicada. Universitat de Xicago.

Ros, A. (2000), 'Los nuevos significados de la lengua en Cataluña'. *Grenzgänge. Beitrage zu einer modernen Romanistik*, 14, 26–36.

Smith, A. (1986), *The Ethnic Origins of Nations*. Oxford: Basil Blackwell.

Smith, A. (1991), *National Identity*. London: Penguin Books.

Subirats, M. (ed.) (1990), *Enquesta metropolitana de 1986. Condicions de vida i hàbits de la població de l'àrea metropolitana de Barcelona*. Vol. 20: *Transmissió i coneixement de la llengua catalana a l'àrea metropolitana de Barcelona*. Bellaterra: Institut d'Estudis Metropolitans.

Subirats, M. (ed.) (2003), 'Els trets lingüístics. Sobre la situació del català', in *Enquesta de la Regió de Barcelona 2000. Informe general*. Bellaterra: Institut d'Estudis Metropolitans.

Tusón, A. (1985), 'Language, Community and School in Barcelona' (Ph.D Thesis. University of California. Berkeley).

Unamuno, V. (2000), 'Frente a frente: lenguas, diversidad y escuela'. *Grenzgänge. Beitrage zu einer modernen Romanistik*, 14, 37–49.

Vallverdú, F. (1975), *L'escriptor català i el problema de la llengua* (2a edició revisada). Barcelona: Edicions 62.

Vila, X. (1996), 'When Classes are Over. Language Choice and Language Contact in Bilingual Education in Catalonia' (Ph.D Thesis. Vrije Universiteit Brussel).

Woolard, K. (1989), *Doubletalk: Bilingualism and the Politics of Ethnicity in Catalonia*. Stanford: Stanford University Press.

Woolard, K. (2003), '"We Don't Speak Catalan Because We are Marginalized": Ethnic and Class Meanings of Language in Barcelona', in R. Blot (ed.), *Language and Social Identity*. Westport, Connecticut: Greenwood Press, pp. 85–104.

References used as data

Abril, J. (2003), Castigats sense pati? *El Punt* 24/05/2003.

Àlvaro, J. T. (2003), Viure en català amb normalitat. *Diari de Vilanova* 14/03/2003.

Badia, Antoni M. (2003), La llengua catalana, moribunda o envejada? *Avui* 08/05/2003.

Bilbeny, Norbert (2003) La dulce muerte del catalán. *La Vanguardia* 29/05/2003.

Branchadell, Albert (2003a), ¿Tan mal anda el catalán? *La Vanguardia*, culturals 21/05/2003.

Branchadell, Albert (2003b), Clar amb el català. *Avui* 13/06/2003.

Cabré, Jaume (2003), Tu ets Mestre. *Avui* 01/04/2003.

Capdevila, Jordi (2003), Joan Solà creu que el català és a l'UVI però que es pot recuperar. *Avui* 26/03/03

Cardús, Salvador (2003a), Sobrevivir a los sepultureros. *La Vanguardia* 30/04/2003.

Cardús, Salvador (2003b), Remeneu-la abans d'usar-la. *Avui* 13/06/2003.

De Carreras, Francesc (2003), La verdadera normalización del catalán. *El Pais* (Cataluña) 01/05/2003.

Desclot (2003), Retrocessos constatables. *Avui* 07/06/2003.

Domínguez, Lourdes (2003), Hem d'aprendre a estimar tothom en català. *Avui* 27/02/2003.

Huertas, Josep M. (2003), L'aprenent de cadiraire. *Avui* 15/05/2003.

L'Hiperbòlic (2003), Jordi Porta, nou president d'Òmnium Cultural. 'El català se'n pot sortir.' *L'Hiperbòlic* 01/01/2003.

Manent, Albert (2003a), Contra els qui proclamen l'agonia del català. *Avui* 15/04/2003.

Manent, Albert (2003b), De nou els catastrofistes sobre el català. *Avui* 12/05/2003.

Marhuenda, Francisco (2003a), Cataluña y el bilingüismo. *La Razón* 24/01/03.

Marhuenda, Francisco (2003b), Otra polémica con el catalán. *La Razón* 06/02/2003.

Martí, Joan (2003), ¿Es necesaria la lengua catalana? *La Vanguardia* 04/06/2003.

Muñoz, Josep (2003a), El libro no suma. *La Vanguardia* 03/02/2003.

Muñoz, Josep (2003b), ¿Crucifixión? No, gracias. *La Vanguardia* 19/05/2003.

Palomeras, Ramon (2003), L'Eutanàsia per al català? *Avui* 26/04/2003.

Piñol, Rosa Maria (2003a), El catalán, en la UVI. *La Vanguardia* 26/03/2003.

Piñol, Rosa Maria (2003b), El catalán, autopsia en la Central. *La Vanguardia* 26/04/2003.

Piquer, Eva (2003), La llengua del carrer. *Avui* 17/04/03

Pla Nualart, Albert (2003), La normalització lingüística, una ficció que ens volem creure. *Avui* 27/02/2003.

Porta Perales, Miquel (2003), El nuevo impuesto lingüístico. *ABC* 07/02/2003.

Puigcercós, Joan (2003), El pacte de l'eutanàsia del català. *Avui* 08/03/2003.

Puigpelat, Francesc (2003a), El català i el carrer. *Avui* 19/05/2003.

Puigpelat, Francesc (2003b), Llengua i independència. *La Mañana* 22/06/2003.

Sáez, Ferran (2003), Molèsties a la llengua. *Avui* 01/05/2003.

Sala, Josep M. (2003), Hablemos de lenguas. *La Vanguardia* 01/07/2003.

Serra, Màrius (2003), Divergir i divertir. *Avui* 22/05/2003.

Sintes, Marçal (2003), Els catalans i el català. *Avui* 22/04/2003.

Solé, Jordi (2003), Entre el cofoisme i el derrotisme, *Avui* 02/05/2003.

Tree, Mathew (2003), Dit i fet. *El Punt* 02/06/2003.

Vallverdú, Francesc (2003a), Barcelona, bilingüe i mestissa? *Avui* 03/06/2003.

Vallverdú, Francesc (2003b), Barcelona, bilingüe i mestissa? (II). *Avui* 15/06/2003.

Vidal, Pau (2003), Dat i beneït. *El País* 01/05/03.

Vila, Enric (2003), 'Miquel Siguan. Psicolingüista. 'La perduració d'una llengua depèn de la voluntat dels seus parlants'. *Avui* 20/03/2003.

Notes

1 This text is based on the lecture 'Els discursos sobre la desaparició del català: som on érem?' delivered at the lecture series 'Diversitat lingüística: Els fets, els discursos, la gestió (II)' organized by the UNESCO Chair on Languages and Education in Barcelona in February 2004

2 I am using a loose sense of expertise, i.e. any person who is presented as entitled to speak publicly about a given issue on the basis of her or his professional background. Academic sociolinguists have so far kept a low profile in the debates on the future of Catalan. Only three participated in the debate, always with signed articles and were never presented by journalists as 'experts'.

3 The category 'writer' has been applied on the basis of the self-ascription of authors. Most of these are not professional writers, though. What is interesting is the fact that they feel that it is their identity as 'writers' that accords them the legitimacy to participate in this debate.

4 It is important to note that the exact wording of this text may or may not reflect in exact detail what the interviewee actually said in the interview situation. There is an anonymous reporter acting as animator (Goffman 1974) who may have advertently or inadvertently manipulated relevant elements of the text. Thus, the analysis addresses not the interviewee's position, but the version of it that the reporter deemed legitimate or appropriate to circulate.

5 This expression refers to a common complain that motorists must pay to use Catalan motorways, while most Spanish motorways are free.

6 In English, the phrase 'their own language' is a natural semantic redundancy; but in Catalan one should say either '*la seva llengua*' or '*la llengua pròpia*'. This construction is probably rendered possible by the fact that the phrase '*llengua pròpia*' has undergone a process of lexicalization.

7 The missing datum of 'La Razón' does not vary the results significantly. Given that the Catalan editions of other Madrid-based papers constitute only 8.7% of their sales, this one cannot exceed 12,000 copies (and probably not more than 6,000–7,000, given that it is a conservative newspaper).

8 Whether the same could be said in relation to Spanish nationalism remains to be seen. Grad Fuchsel and Martín Rojo (2003) found that ethnic orientations predominated in Spanish nationalist discourse stemming from parliamentary debates, whereas Catalan nationalist leaders articulated an eminently 'civic' nationalism.

9 It is difficult to assess the impact of the predominantly Catalan-written local and regional press, where the publication of responses to national debates is common. In the few instances that appear in this corpus, it appears that this sector is more Catatan-speaker-centred.

10 With respect to this argument, it is interesting to bear in mind that – as far as I can attest by my own experience – the Spanish written press is overwhelmingly managed by native speakers of Catalan too.

8 Language endangerment, war and peace in Ireland and Northern Ireland

Tony Crowley

Introduction: language, war and peace

In 1998 the *Belfast Agreement* was signed by representatives of the British Government, the Irish Government, and the leading political parties in Northern Ireland. The concord was designed to form the basis of the negotiated settlement of the 30-year-old war in Northern Ireland and, more generally, the conflict arising from centuries of English and later British colonialism in Ireland. One significant section of the text dealt with 'rights, safeguards and equality of opportunity' in relation to economic, social and cultural issues; with particular regard to language it declared that:

> All participants recognise the importance of respect, under-
> standing and tolerance in relation to linguistic diversity, including
> in Northern Ireland, the Irish language, Ulster-Scots and the
> languages of the various ethnic minorities, all of which are part of
> the cultural wealth of the island of Ireland (*The Belfast Agreement*
> 1998: 19).

The question may well be posed: why is there any reference at all to linguistic diversity in a text whose primary purpose is to bring an end to a bloody historical dispute? And why is it given such significance in the document? In order to answer these questions and to explain the functions which a variety of discourses of language endangerment have played in Irish history, as well as addressing the more general issue of why such discourses appeared at specific points in that history, it is necessary to analyse the political roles of language on the island of Ireland. Ranging from the earliest examples of colonial legislation in Ireland, to contemporary debates on the treatment of Gaelic and Ulster-Scots in the Northern Irish peace process, this chapter will attempt to show how and for what purposes emphasis is placed either on linguistic and cultural homogeneity or diversity at different

149

points. As will be seen, the discourse of language endangerment is sometimes used as a weapon in these debates, sometimes not, and the analysis will suggest reasons for its variable deployment. One of the central points of the argument will be that far from being the modern invention of linguists, anthropologists or cultural ecologists, the discourse of language endangerment has an established history of involvement in particular types of historical dispute. Long before the current anxieties about language death and the reduction in the number of the world's languages produced by globalization, activists in anti-colonial struggles and nationalist campaigns in Ireland were using the threat to Irish to mobilize social and political forces for a variety of ends.

Colonial language endangerment and the early Irish response

Ireland was Britain's oldest colony and the first in which the colonial practice of language abolition was attempted. Efforts to proscribe Irish and prescribe English date as far back as the *Statutes of Kilkenny* in 1366 (Irish Archaeological Society 1843), though the first language policies proper which sought to achieve this end were formulated by the Tudors. For example, in Henry the Eighth's *Act for the English Order, Habit and Language* (1537) the King's Irish subjects were ordered to conform to English manners, dress and language, since cultural difference, it was argued, created other more telling divisions:

> there is again nothing which doth more contain and keep many of his subjects of this his said land, in a certain savage and wild kind and manner of living, than the diversity that is betwixt them in tongue, language, order and habit, which by the eye deceiveth the multitude, and persuadeth unto them, that they should be as it were of sundry sorts, or rather of sundry countries, where indeed they be wholly together one body, whereof his highness is the only head under God. (*Stat. Ire.* 1786: 28 H 8. c.xv.)

Henry's law is a clear early example of the equation between the use of a language and political identity and allegiance. Linguistic difference was thought to create political division precisely because the use of the native Gaelic language was taken by the colonists as the practical embodiment of Irish national identity. Viewed as an important hindrance to Henry's plan to incorporate all the inhabitants of Ireland as subjects of the crown, the Irish language therefore needed to be eradicated in order to foster a monolingual English cultural and political identity. The law stipulated ominous penalties for those who disobeyed the ordinance: 'his Majesty will repute them in his noble heart ... whatsoever they shall at other times pretend in words and countenance, to be persons of another sort and inclination than becometh the true and faithful subjects' (*Stat. Ire.* 1786: 28 H 8. c.xv.). Thus the adoption of cultural Englishness, with language as its core, was the means of achieving the political and religious loyalty of inter-pellated national subjects, and this became a central policy of colonial rule. Edmund Spenser, poet and colonial servant, proclaimed that 'the speach being *Irish*, the heart must needes bee *Irish*' and used the precept to justify the adoption of Roman imperial practice in Ireland: 'it hath ever beene the use of the Conquerour, to despise the language of the conquered and to force him by all meanes to learne his' (Spenser 1633: 47).

Linguistic colonialism in Ireland brought a slow response from the bardic class, the traditional guardians who maintained the native culture by means of historiography, genealogy, law and poetry, and the evidence suggests that they underestimated the dangers posed by the new colonial regime (Crowley 2005: 33–5). When the attack against the Gaelic political and cultural order was prosecuted vigorously, in the late sixteenth century and then throughout the seventeenth, the fact that the Gaelic social formation crumbled rapidly had a severe impact on the system of patronage which protected the native bards. But despite the fact that some of the native literati were alert to the peril, and lamented the damage as it was occurring, it is interesting to note that the use of a discourse of linguistic endangerment as a means of answering the threat did not appear at the time. The reasons for this are complex and unclear, though a major factor must have been that the principal concern of the learned class, most of whom fled into exile in European seminaries, was with saving the faith of the Catholic Irish in the face of the determined efforts of colonial Protestantism. Thus, although one Irish historian, Seathrún Céitinn, wrote *Foras Feasa ar Éirinn* [*A Basis of Knowledge About Ireland*] in Gaelic in the mid-seventeenth century, most learned writing in the language which was printed in the period was theological. A combination of a simple lack of resources, the scattering of the learned, the dominance of Latin as the language of the Church in Europe, general illiteracy in Irish, and the fact that Irish was still the everyday spoken language of the greatest part of the population, seems to have meant that concern about the vernacular was left to those poets (examples include Ó Bruadair and later Ó Rathaille) who suffered directly and bitterly from the collapse of the native social order (Crowley 2005: 58–61, 75–8).

The first concerted efforts to address the language question date from the middle of the eighteenth century, at which point, although Gaelic was still spoken either monolingually or bilingually by the majority of the inhabitants, English had already made important progress towards its final position as the language of power, commerce and eventually everyday communication in Ireland. But by the mid-eighteenth century the impact of English language and culture on traditional forms of native culture, particularly the use of the Irish language, started to draw hostile responses from commentators. In 1752 a proposal for an Irish Language Society in Dublin noted that 'the mother tongue of this nation, has been long neglected and discouraged by the introduction of strange languages not so full or expressive' (Ó Cuív 1986: 415). And in 1787 Thomas drew attention to the dangers faced by the Gaelic language by comparing its qualities to those of English:

> what, shall a language confessedly derived from one of the first tongues which subsisted among polished nations, be abolished, merely to make room for another compounded of all the barbarous dialects which imperfectly communicated the thoughts of savages to each other? (Thomas 1787: 23)

In the late sixteenth and early seventeenth centuries, members of the bardic class did not appear to see a clear link between the Irish language and Irish identity, not least because the imagined community of the Irish nation simply did not exist in any tangible way (the real threat at the time was perceived to be to the faith). Eighteenth-century commentators, on the other hand, had a keen sense of the connection between language and Irish identity precisely because by that point the unifying tendencies of colonialism had created a nation state which had started to gather to it the types of cultural resource characteristic of the modern definition of nationality (a common language, history or descent). Ironically the linkage which the eighteenth-century observers posited was based on exactly the same principle that lay behind the early colonial legislation (that language and identity were inextricably linked and that a threat to one was a danger to the other). Thus Thomas warned the Bishop of Cloyne about the perils of attempting to abolish Irish:

> Be so good to consider, what is the distinctive mark of natives of different countries? What but language. Any design therefore to destroy the vernacular tongue, is an attempt to annihilate the nation, and let your Lordship well weigh, whether the mouths which you now wish to close, may not soon open with harsh thunder in your ears. (Thomas 1787: 28)

It was, however, only from the mid-nineteenth century that the precarious contemporary situation of the Irish language became a significant focus of resistance to colonial occupation. German Romantic thought, principally in the work of Herder, Fichte and Humboldt, had theorized the insight which had arisen from colonialism and turned it into a philosophical account of the relationship between language and national identity. Such work, which was widely translated in the 1830s and 1840s, influenced the development of Irish cultural nationalism (Crowley 2005: 104–8). Thus Thomas Davis, a leader of the Young Ireland movement, counselled that 'a people without a language of its own is only half a nation. A nation should guard its language more than its territories – 'tis a surer barrier, and more important frontier, than fortress or river' (Davis 1914: 98). Thomas's warning that an attempt to abolish Gaelic would provoke discordant resistance, and Davis's admonition to his countrymen to defend their language and nation, were realized in the social and cultural revolution brought about by the Gaelic Revival.

Language endangerment and anti-colonial cultural hegemony

It was not until the late nineteenth and early twentieth centuries that a discourse of linguistic endangerment in Ireland was fully deployed as a social and political weapon against colonial rule. Its appearance at that particular time was produced by a combination of two factors. The first was that as a result of the success of cultural nationalist movements across Europe, the link between language and national identity had become almost commonplace. The second was the crisis of Irish political nationalism at the end of the nineteenth century. Up to that point Irish parliamentary nationalism had largely scorned the language issue. For example, Daniel O'Connell, the most important leader of the movement in the nineteenth century, had blithely asserted that:

> although the Irish language is connected with many recollections that twine around the hearts of Irishmen, yet the superior utility of the English tongue, as the medium of modern communication, is so great, that I can witness without a sigh the gradual disuse of the Irish. (Daunt 1848: 14–15)

But contradictions within political nationalism in the 1890s, centred upon the downfall and death of its leader Parnell, were disabling and opened up a discursive space for cultural nationalism, a movement which had been relegated to a secondary position for most of the century. And the main tactic of cultural nationalism, particularly of the central organization, the Gaelic League, was the use of a discourse which centred upon the dangers faced by the national language. Patrick Pearse, one of the leaders of the 1916 Rebellion against British rule, correctly forecast in 1913 that 'the coming revolution' would be undertaken by 'the men and movements that have sprung from the Gaelic League' (Pearse 1952: 91). And in many ways the campaign launched and sustained by the League is a paradigmatic example of the way in which a discourse of language endangerment can be used to forge a form of cultural hegemony for political purposes. The League used the danger of the extinction of Gaelic (by this point the vast majority of Irish people used English as their everyday medium) as a motivating issue by tying it closely to questions of Irish national identity, personal morality, social well-being and, ultimately, political independence. If Irish was lost, the League argued, then Ireland, as a country with a history, literature, identity of its own would also be lost: 'gan teanga, gan tír' (no language, no nation).

Douglas Hyde, one of the founders of the Gaelic League, appealed to 'every Irish feeling Irishman':

> to encourage the efforts which are being made to keep alive our once national tongue. The losing of it is our greatest blow, and the sorest stroke that the rapid Anglicisation of Ireland has inflicted upon us. In order to de-Anglicise ourselves we must at once arrest the decay of the language. (Ó Conaire 1986: 160)

Hyde's comments were not simply a rallying call to defend Gaelic, but also an appeal for the creation of a particular type of identity for Irish people through the use of their endangered language. And one of the effects of the Gaelic League's activities was the formation of a specific model of Irishness which was to endure for most of the twentieth century. There were various identity features which were inculcated through the League's highly influential pamphlets, language classes and social programme by means of a rigid opposition between the oppressive English and the endangered Irish languages. On the one hand there was English and all it stood for: 'English is the language of infidelity. It is infidels who for the most part speak English' (Ó Braonáin, quoted in O'Leary 1994: 24). And on the other hand there was Irish and all it represented: 'Irish is pre-eminently the language of prayer and devotion. Its dignity and impressive majesty admirably suit the themes of religion' (Morris 1898: 8). English and Irish, according to this model, were engaged in what one Irish language activist (the most important modern lexicographer of Gaelic) called 'the struggle between the languages', which was 'a deeper, a more far-reaching struggle than appears on the surface, it is a struggle between the civilisations which these languages represent' (Dinneen 1904: 28).

At stake in this conflict, couched in Darwinian terms, was the future identity of Ireland, including its racial character. Another Gaelic

League pamphleteer asked rhetorically if the Irish were 'a totally distinct and wholly superior race, ever zealous for the better gifts that God made the soul of man to desire and enjoy, clinging ever to the spirit-world? ... Are we mere planters and marchmen of the Pale, or are we Celts, Gaels, Irish?' Thanking God that they knew what they were, Gaelic Leaguers proclaimed their recognition of the true racial identity of Ireland and the pressing duty which followed from it. Irish was the imperilled but only means of sustaining Irishness:

> if this nation is to live on, or the Church of this nation, the Irish mind will have to be preserved; and to try to preserve it without the Irish tongue, is to endeavour to hold it while choosing the best means for letting it go. (O'Reilly 1901: 5)

From this perspective, the unique means by which Ireland could be kept faithful to its true nature (moral and pure, poetic and spiritual, authentic and organic, Gaelic and Catholic) was through the use of the native Gaelic language, but because the colonists had sought to banish this medium for centuries through legislative and economic action, it was now in serious danger of disappearance. Accordingly, the task which at least one form of cultural nationalism took to itself was to alert the Irish people to the significance of this calamitous historical moment in order to foster the preservation and restoration of Irish as the national language. Paradoxically, the deeply conservative cultural revolution which such activists desired (though it would be inaccurate to say that all activists thought the same way), would also be a contribution to the radical overthrow of colonial rule and the achievement of an independent, politically sovereign Ireland.

There can be no doubt that the Gaelic League and the Irish language movement in general made a significant contribution to the revolutionary campaign to overthrow British rule in Ireland, a struggle which resulted in independence for 26 of the 32 counties of the country in 1921. There is also no disputing the fact that Irish cultural nationalism used the discourse of language endangerment as a weapon in its fight to produce a new cultural hegemony in Ireland. It is likewise incontestable that this new cultural order was achieved and that it was extraordinarily influential in the formation and development of the new Irish State. The 1937 *Bunreacht na hÉireann* (Constitution of Ireland), which created the Republic of Ireland and which was passed by plebiscite, re-emphasized the place of Irish as the national language which had been enacted in the 1922 Constitution of the Irish Free State:

Airteagal 8.
1. Ós í an Ghaeilge an teanga náisiúnta is í an phríomhtheanga oifigiúil í.

155

2. Glactar leis an Sacs-Bhéarla mar theanga oifigiúil eile.
3. Ach féadfar socrú a dhéanamh le dlí d'fhonn ceachtar den dá theanga sin a bheith ina haonteanga le haghaidh aon ghnó nó gnóthaí oifigiúla ar fud an Stáit ar fad nó in aon chuid de. (*Bunreacht na hÉireann* 1999: 8–11)

Article 8.
1. *The Irish language as the national language is the first official language.*
2. *The English language is recognized as a second official language.*
3. *Provision may, however, be made by law for the exclusive use of either of the said languages for any one or more official purposes, either throughout the State or in any part thereof.*

In addition to the constitutional position, other measures were taken to preserve the language. From the mid 1920s to the 1970s a 'compulsory Irish' policy in schools was coupled with a stipulation that Irish was a pre-requisite for specific types of state employment. These policies combined to make the language a central locus of national life and national identity.

Nonetheless, after the consolidation of independence, the Irish State continued to use a discourse of language endangerment in order to create a constant sense of cultural crisis and to encourage zealous efforts to preserve the national tongue. This had negative effects both politically and in regard to the language itself. Irish, constructed as being always in peril of extinction, became the crucial focus around which reactionary ideological forces were able to forge an Irish identity which was based largely on a homogenizing view of the language and its ties to tradition and Catholicism. Unlike its use in the anti-colonial struggle, the representation of Irish as an endangered language in independent Ireland was one of the factors which have contributed to its decline. One of the great peculiarities of twentieth-century Irish history is that it was precisely the link between the language and a specific conservative ideology which proved so damaging to the health of Gaelic. Rather than saving the language, the actions of the state, the Catholic Church and the language movement placed it further in jeopardy.

Political status and language rights: Irish in Northern Ireland

In 1921 Britain ceded the greater portion of the land mass of Ireland but retained as part of the United Kingdom six counties wherein the majority of the population were Protestant and wished to preserve the

Union with Britain. If the fate of Irish in the Republic of Ireland was to form part of an unholy trinity of language, nationality and religion, then what happened to it in Northern Ireland, the state created by the partition of Ireland on sectarian grounds? Given the centrality of the Irish language to the revolution which brought about the independence of most of Ireland, it is no surprise to find that in the newly created Northern Irish State the language attracted considerable antipathy from the ruling Unionist powers. In 1933 even minimal state funding for the teaching of Irish was abolished; the Prime Minister defended the decision precisely on the grounds of the need to foster good British citizens:

> What use is it to us here in this progressive, busy part of the Empire to teach our children the Irish language? What use would it be to them? Is it not leading them along a road which has no practical value? We have not stopped such teaching ... We have stopped the grants simply because we do not see that these boys being taught Irish would make them any better citizens. (Maguire 1991: 11)

On both sides of the border children were given a linguistic education intended to fulfil nationalist purposes: compulsory Irish for the Irish, compulsory English for the British.

The problem for a significant minority of the population of Northern Ireland was that they didn't consider themselves British but laid claim and allegiance to both Irish identity and citizenship. For the Irish nationalist community in the North, therefore, the treatment of the Irish language was but one among many forms of discrimination and disenfranchisement. In fact, in the scheme of things, the state's treatment of the symbolically significant but practically irrelevant national language of Ireland was a minor matter (the use of Irish among the nationalist community was very limited indeed) since jobs, housing and political suffrage were of more immediate concern. But when the conflict which was integral to the Northern Irish State finally reached a critical point, that is to say when the campaign began to achieve full civil and political rights for nationalists, the role of the Irish language gradually began to change.

Though there had been a history of enthusiastic and determined Irish language organizations from the inception of the state, these were small-scale acts of resistance in the face of the opposition of the official authorities to the Irish language. One such group was Cumann Chluain Ard in West Belfast (founded in 1936), where a small number of language activists met in the 1960s. Their decisions and actions were, indirectly, to have a durable and important impact on the cultural and political landscape of Northern Ireland. Given the attitudes of the state

157

in both the Republic of Ireland (where despite the official policy the practice was one of at best indifference to the national language) and Northern Ireland (studied hostility which reached as far as banning the language from the local BBC), what this group proposed was extraordinary: the creation in Belfast of an all-Irish speaking community (Gaeltacht) and school. In 1969 the first Irish-speaking families moved into a small number of self-built houses on the Shaw's Road in Belfast and in 1971 the community opened Bunscoil Phobal Feirste, a primary school.

The motivation behind the Shaw's Road Gaeltacht is significant. The small number of families who began this project did not do so because the Irish language was endangered in Northern Ireland (though by the late 1960s it existed only as a school subject in Catholic schools and in a small number of adult classes), nor even because the language was endangered in Ireland as a whole (in the Republic by this time the government was moving towards abandoning the policy of compulsory Irish and each census return revealed fewer and fewer active speakers). In fact a discourse of language endangerment hardly figured at all in the reasons given for beginning what was an extremely implausible venture. Instead those involved specified a simple love of the language itself, a cultural nationalist regard for the language as part of a specific historical heritage, and a sense that the language was tied to a form of identity which they wished to practice despite the general contempt in which it was held.

The unpropitious circumstances in which the undertaking commenced and continued meant that the community had to engage in politics, in the sense of the struggle for rights and resources (Bunscoil Phobal Feirste was not funded by the state for the first 13 years of its existence and relied on the support of parents and sympathizers). But despite the fact that it was notable for its detachment from larger political disputes and its concentration on local activism, the Shaw's Road Gaeltacht became the focus and inspiration of the Irish language movement in Northern Ireland. It is remarkable to note that starting with this community in West Belfast, and then spreading to nationalist areas throughout the country, an Irish language revival has taken place which was simply unimaginable at the beginning of the 1970s. In the 2001 census 10.35 per cent of the Northern Irish population (167,490) claimed at least some knowledge of Irish. All-Irish education has become increasingly popular with the establishment of infant or primary schools in each of the six counties, and a secondary school, Méanscoil Feirste, in Belfast. Various other initiatives include the Council for Irish medium education, Gaeloiliúint; a development agency, Forbairt Feirste, an e-tech organization, An Telelann; a weekly newpaper, *Lá*; and an arts centre, Cultúrlann McAdam Ó Fiaich. The net effect has been that Irish, viewed as a serious issue only among a tiny minority of mainly middle-class people in the early 1970s, has risen to the centre of political and cultural debate in Northern Ireland.

It needs to be stressed again that this significant development has taken place with only minimal recourse to a discourse of language endangerment. Why did this happen? If Irish has not been revived in Northern Ireland because it was in danger of dying out, then what is the explanation? The fact is that, despite the stimulus provided by the Shaw's Road example, the real interest in the Irish language in the late 1970s and 1980s was directly linked to the struggle of the Irish Republican movement against British rule, especially in the prisons. Republican prisoners engaged in a sustained campaign of resistance which culminated in the Hunger Strikes in 1981; as part of that process the prisoners started to learn and use Irish both as a symbol of their defiance and as an expression of their identity. The language became an important element in their battle with the British, and the prisons became known as the Jailtacht:

> When the men in the H-Blocks of Long Kesh jail and the women in Armagh prison were stripped of everything, they realised that the most Irish thing they had was their Irish language. Learning it, speaking it all day, was a way of resisting, of asserting your identity, of crying out your defiance against a system that sought to rob you of all identity, and break in you all spirit of defiance (Sinn Féin 1986: 9).

This political rhetoric belonged to what one commentator has called 'decolonising discourse' (O'Reilly 1999); one of its common reflexes was the claim not so much that the language was endangered but that it was being repressed by the British authorities. But assertions such as that made by a Sinn Féin policy pamphlet that children learning Irish in Belfast would thereby 'not feel the alienation of Irish people with only the language imposed upon them by imperialism in their mouths' (Sinn Féin 1986: 8) seemed implausible in light of the fact that Irish people north and south of the border didn't actually seem particularly alienated by the English language at all. A more convincing comment on the language revival and the importance of the prison campaign to it was made by an activist in retrospect:

> At the time of the Hunger Strikes it was a political reaction with me, because Irish was the language I should be speaking and it's the least I could do for those men who were dying. I wanted to make it clear that I supported them standing up for their civil rights and

human rights. If this hadn't happened I don't think that the Irish language would be as strong as it is today (O'Reilly 1999: 58).

The crucial point here is that the discourse of decolonization, based on the postulated links between contemporary Republican activity and earlier national-liberation struggles in Ireland and the Third World, was used as part of the justification for armed struggle against the British State. As the Republican movement turned to a dual strategy of violence and politics, however, the rhetoric of decolonization was gradually displaced by a discourse which was concerned, as O'Reilly has demonstrated, with achieving civil and political rights for nationalists. And it is this rights discourse which eventually came to dominate, because it enabled Republican activists to tie the language question to a much broader and therefore more attractive political strategy. Many who were antagonistic to British rule but did not support violent resistance saw in the language rights issue a way of both expressing their identity and making their political point in a non-violent form.

In the discussions which led to the *Belfast Agreement* (1998) the basic principles were set out by the British and Irish governments in the *Downing Street Declaration* (1993) and the *Framework Document* (1995). They consisted of the non-negotiable tenet of consent with regard to the border question, new constitutional arrangements between Britain, the Republic of Ireland and Northern Ireland and an internal negotiated settlement within Northern Ireland itself. It was emphasized that 'full respect for the rights and identities of both traditions in Ireland' (*Joint Declaration* 1993: para. 4), and an emphasis on 'parity of esteem, and on just and equal treatment for the identity, ethos and aspirations of both communities' (*New Framework* 1995: para. 20) would have to form the basis of the internal settlement. In the *Belfast Agreement* (1998) itself this resulted in the British government agreeing to a set of undertakings with regard to the Irish language:

- take resolute action to promote the language;
- facilitate and encourage the use of the language in speech and writing in public and private life where there is appropriate demand;
- seek to remove, where possible, restrictions which would discourage or work against the maintenance or development of the language;
- make provision for liaising with the Irish language community; representing their views to public authorities and investigating complaints;
- place a statutory Department of Education to encourage

and facilitate Irish medium education in line with current provision for integrated education;

- explore urgently with the relevant British authorities, and in co-operation with the Irish broadcasting authorities, the scope for achieving more widespread availability of Teilifís na Gaeilige [sic] in Northern Ireland;
- seek more effective ways to encourage and provide financial support for Irish language film and television production in Northern Ireland; and
- encourage the parties to secure agreement that this commitment will be sustained by a new Assembly in a way which takes account of the desires and sensitivities of the community.

(pp. 19–20).

This set of measures constitutes an extraordinary reversal of the British State's hostility to the Irish language which, as noted earlier, stretches back to the beginnings of colonial rule. It also signifies a new British attitude to Irish nationalism. Over a decade or so in the 1980s and early 1990s the Irish language became both a cipher for the question of nationalist identity and the focus of demands for equal treatment and status recognition of nationalists by the state. Thus what the state's cultural, legal and financial commitments to the language in the *Belfast Agreement* amounts to is an acknowledgment of the nationalist/Republican linguistic rights agenda and, by extension, recognition of the legitimacy and status of Irish nationalism itself. But it is worth noting again that a discourse of language endangerment played no significant role in the achievement of this goal. Unlike their predecessors at the beginning of the twentieth century, who used the peril of the extinction of Irish by English as a way of fostering revolutionary cultural hegemony, the Irish nationalist/Republican movement in Northern Ireland has had little use for the terms of language endangerment. This is perhaps unsurprising, given the embarrassing fact that the Irish Republic, the state to which they pledged allegiance and from which they claimed nationality, had allowed the Irish language, which they took as central to the national identity, to wither away. It would be difficult for Northern Irish nationalists to attack the British State for endangering the Irish language without implicitly criticizing the equally disastrous policies of the Irish Republic, whose citizens they wished to become. Instead nationalists and Republicans turned to a discourse of choice, opportunity and right with regard to a language which was taken to express an identity and perhaps a political allegiance rather than embodying a political goal in itself. Yet

161

although they did not deploy the discourse of language endangerment in their tactical strategy, this does not mean that it has been absent from Northern Ireland in the past 30 years. Indeed one of the more peculiar developments of the cultural-political scene in Northern Ireland has been the adoption of this discourse by the opponents of Irish nationalism/Republicanism.

Identity and rights: Ulster-Scots in Northern Ireland

Though the *Belfast Agreement* made specific provision for measures to encourage to facilitate, promote and encourage Irish, it also stressed the importance of linguistic diversity, and recognized Ulster-Scots as a form worthy of 'respect, understanding and tolerance'. At the start of the troubles some 40 years ago such a claim would have been puzzling if not bizarre to any but a handful of scholars and antiquarians. In order to understand the significance of this development it is necessary to trace the story of how Ulster-Scots was transformed in status from a spoken dialect to a fully fledged language, and the role which the discourse of language endangerment played in the process.

Though there are a few scattered references to a distinct language variety to be found in Ulster, with the exception of Joseph Wright's treatment of the Antrim dialect in his *English Dialect Grammar* (1905), there is little evidence of any sustained interest in the form until the mid-twentieth century when the Folklore and Dialect section of the Belfast Naturalists Field Club started to garner materials for the purposes of regional and antiquarian interest. This led to the establishment of the Ulster Dialect Archive at the Ulster Folk Museum in 1960, a long-term dictionary project and a symposium on Ulster's language varieties, which resulted in the publication of *Ulster Dialects: An Introductory Symposium* in 1964. This collection of essays contained a seminal statement by Adams in which he declared that 'Ulster English consists essentially of two primary dialects: the north-eastern or Ulster-Scots dialect, and the central or mid-Ulster dialect, together with a number of marginal contact dialects' (Adams 1964: 1). A decade later, the established poet and critic John Hewitt published an important piece of scholarly recovery, *Rhyming Weavers and other Country Poets of Antrim and Down* (1974), in which he gave an account of a long-standing Ulster-Scots literary tradition. But in the bloodiest phase of the civil war in Northern Ireland, literary-historical attempts to draw attention to what seemed to be but a lost local cultural form seemed doomed until the intellectual and Unionist politician Ian Adamson (sometime Lord Mayor of Belfast and Member of the Northern Ireland Assembly) published a text which was to change the debate in the long term. Adamson's *The Identity of Ulster: The Land, the Language and the People* (1982) marked the beginning of an ideological challenge to received notions of cultural identity, partly based on Ulster-Scots, which was to have significant political repercussions.

Adamson's argument was that the Ulster-Scots dialect (he refers to both Ulster Lallans, his coinage for Ulster-Scots, and Ulster English as 'two varieties of the English language') has played a constitutive role in the formation of Ulster identity. He proposed that Britain and Ireland were both inhabited by the ancient British and that one branch of this people, the:

> British Cruthin or 'Cruithne' formed the bulk of the population of
> both Ulster and North Britain in early Christian times and that they
> are therefore the earliest recorded ancestors not only of the people
> of Ulster but those of Scotland as well. (Adamson 1982: 1)

These early inhabitants of Ulster spoke a language, Brittonic, or Old British, which was subjugated by the language of a set of invaders: 'Old British was displaced in Ireland by Gaelic just as English later displaced Gaelic'. (Adamson 1982: 73).

Such revisionism undermined one of the perpetual grievances of Irish nationalism, that Gaelic had been destroyed by colonial invaders, by claiming that Irish was not simply the language spoken by the victims of linguistic colonization but was itself in fact a language of conquest. Ulster-Scots, the form which developed in Ulster from Old British origins and the language of the Scottish Planters, was therefore a linguistic variety which was tied to a unique ancient history and which marked off the distinctive identity of Ulster from the rest of Ireland.

Adamson's version of history provided a counter to Irish nationalism's discursive use of the concepts of primary possession, origins, indigeneity and colonial dispossession by producing what is in effect a version of Ulster nationalism (which even stretched to include Ulster Gaelic as one of the historical language varieties of the area). For the Ulster Unionist community, who wished to retain the constitutional link with Britain, Adamson's account offered a useful support in terms of language and identity: Ulster could be shown to be British in more than the legal and political senses. For if Adamson was right, then Ulster was not just politically but also culturally British, and the proof lay in the Ulster-Scots dialect.

There were, however, two problems with Adamson's description of Ulster-Scots as a dialect of English rather than a language in its own right. The first arose from the powerful history of the association between language and nationality in the European cultural nationalism which was noted earlier. It was exemplified in Fichte's dictum that 'wherever a separate language is found, there a separate nation exists' (Fichte 1968: 184). The second derives from Adamson's identification of Ulster-Scots as a dialect of English (rather than Scots as was later claimed). If Ulster-Scots was merely a dialect of English, then it was difficult to see how it could be the basis of an independent Ulster nationality (unless the other forms of dialect in Britain were also putative foundations of distinct nationalities). Thus rather than being the focal point of a unifying national identity, Ulster-Scots as a dialect form served merely as a marker of local difference. Only if Ulster-Scots were a language tied to a national identity could it be used in debates which had previously been dominated by Irish cultural nationalism (specifically in recent history those involving cultural identity and civil rights). The difficulty therefore for its supporters was to shift the status of Ulster-Scots from dialect to language. And the major means by which this has been achieved has been through the Ulster-Scots Language Society, formed in 1992, whose principal objective was set out in the first issue of its journal *Ullans* (1993): 'our aim is to promote the status of Ulster-Scots as a language, and to re-establish its dignity as a language with an important part to play in our cultural heritage' (*Ullans* 1983: 2).

The success of the Ulster-Scots language movement has been remarkable. Adamson had used the standard description of Ulster-Scots as a dialect in his pioneering text in 1982, but barely 20 years later a panoply of initiatives, institutions and events had combined to establish it as a language tied to a particular cultural and political identity. In 1994 Belfast city council pronounced its recognition of the linguistic and cultural diversity of the city and awarded equal recognition to the Irish language and Ulster-Scots. The same year saw the formation of the Ulstèr-Scotch Heirskip Cooncil (Ulster-Scots Heritage Council), an umbrella group for Ulster Scots interests, and in 1995 the Cultural Traditions Group, a body sourced by the British government, funded a development officer for the Heritage Council. In 1996 the Minister of State in Northern Ireland gave notice of the British government's intention to treat Ulster-Scots in Northern Ireland in the same manner as Scots in Scotland. But the most important developments came with the reference to Ulster-Scots in *The Belfast Agreement* (1998) and the formal recognition of Ulster-Scots as a language with the British government's ratification of the European Charter for Minority and Regional Languages in 2001.

The transformation in the status and standing of Ulster-Scots can best be explained by reference to a number of discursive strategies deployed by its supporters. One example was the appropriation of a discourse of grievance and oppression, wrongs and remedies, identity and rights which had formerly belonged to Irish nationalism. Thus the submission of the Ulster-Scots Language Society and the Ulster-Scots Academy to the Northern Irish Forum in 1996 stressed the importance of the principles of 'mutual respect and cultural pluralism': 'that within Northern Ireland Ulster-Scots and Irish (Gaelic) be afforded parity of esteem, equal status and equality of treatment' (Ulster-Scots Language Society and the Ulster-Scots Academy 1996: n.p). But another significant discursive strategy used both to consolidate the status of Ulster-Scots as a language rather than a dialect and to place it at the heart of contemporary political debates was the deployment of a discourse of language endangerment by its supporters. For example, Philip Robinson, one of the leading players in the Ulster-Scots movement, has claimed that the number of Ulster-Scots speakers has decreased from 170,000 to 100,000 in 30 years (though as a matter of fact both figures are untested estimates since there are no reliable independent surveys) (Robinson 2003: 113). Other assertions which are typical of language endangerment protest include claims that Ulster-Scots is scorned 'as a socially stigmatized language with low social status', that it is marginalized as 'an ignorant rural dialect or as some form of bad English', and that this 'leads to an undermining of the self-esteem of individuals and communities by whom the language is still used' (Ulster Scots Language Society and the Ulster-Scots Academy 1996: n.p.). Demands were made that the state should prevent the extinction of the native language of Ulster by making use of it on official documents and in advertisements for public employment, sponsoring the reprinting of the available literature and encouraging new writing, funding the publication of a full grammar and dictionary and promoting its 'cross-community understanding and appreciation' by its use in schools and other educational institutions. In a telling accusation the Ulster-Scots language movement declared that refusal to provide such supportive measures to a language under threat, while at the same time offering sustenance to the Irish language, would be tantamount to 'endorsing the culture of one minority language community while denying the validity of the other' which would be 'communally divisive' (Ulster-Scots Language Society and the Ulster-Scots Academy 1996: n.p.).

The political aspect to the Ulster-Scots language campaign is revealed in an editorial in *Ullans* in 1998 which reported on an abortive meeting with a British minister in the Northern Ireland Office to discuss state recognition and funding for the language (the disregard with which the society's representatives were met is reflected in the fact that the minister did not even have the civil service papers for the meeting). The editorial, however, records the fiasco as fortuitous given that the society was 'unaware that the Ulster-Scots issue was being simultaneously negotiated by politicians and the two [British and Irish] governments in the Stormont talks themselves' (*Ullans* 1998: 4). In one sense it is clear that the Ulster-Scots Language Society representatives were not involved in the talks precisely because the discussions were not about the language per se but concerned larger political issues. But the point is that the fact that the politicians were discussing Ulster-Scots as one of these issues demonstrates that the work of the society had been achieved. Ulster-Scots, a fully fledged but endangered language, gave the Unionist community precisely what the Irish language gave the nationalist community: a medium through which identity-claims and demands for civil rights could be articulated.

Conclusion: the political uses of discourses of language endangerment

The point that debates about language are very rarely simply debates about language is now so familiar that it has become almost commonplace. Given its role in such debates, it is no surprise to find that it is also the case that the discourse of language endangerment is very rarely simply about the endangerment of a language. As the examples from the island of Ireland demonstrate, under particular historical circumstances discourses of language endangerment have been used by social groups which are opposed to each other in order to achieve similar political purposes (though to different ends). One form of this discourse was used as a weapon in an anti-colonialist struggle by the forces of Irish nationalism in order to produce a form of 'Irish' subjectivity, centred upon the Irish language, which was in a binary opposition to the language, culture and politics of the colonizers. Later in the historical process another form was used by anti-nationalist forces whose aim was to guarantee the link between Northern Ireland and the United Kingdom which is a legacy of colonialism.

In one sense this may tell us nothing more than the plastic nature of the language endangerment discourse: it has been used in this case to help wage a war and to attempt to forge a specific peace. But the historical examples analysed here also offer an insight into the fearful, aggressive and non-reflexive stance which the discourse can generate. The non-reflexivity lies in the fact that what is presupposed by language endangerment discourse is precisely the language in question – in the two cases examined here, Irish and Ulster-Scots. What may in fact happen is that this discourse does not so much defend a language

166

which already exists in practice (through the call for grammar books, dictionaries, educational measures, language rights and so on) as create a recognizable institutionalized language through such means. The fearfulness often appears as a recourse to a simplistic version of tradition, specifically a reliance on a vision of an organic past in which a language and culture were wholly unified. And the aggressiveness manifests itself in both an absolute insistence on the link between language and identity and a refusal to view history in other than binary terms. For example, with regard to the Irish and Ulster-Scots debates, little notice has been given to those hybrid forms which have arisen out of a history of linguistic contact and intermingling – Hiberno-English and Ulster-English. As with language debates in general then it is necessary to consider deployment of the discourse of language endangerment in the specific historical and political conditions in which it is produced. This is of course not to dismiss it but rather to see its significance as lying outside the area of 'pure' language studies, whatever that means. But given that language lies at the core of our social being, the real surprise would be if the discourses used to defend languages were not in essence a matter of politics and history.

References

Adams, G. B. (1964), 'Ulster Dialects', in G. B. Adams (ed.), *Ulster Dialects: An Introductory Symposium*. Holywood, Co. Down: Ulster Folk Museum, pp. 1–4.

Adamson, I. (1982), *The Identity of Ulster: The Land, the Language and the People*. Belfast: Pretani Press.

Bunreacht na hÉireann. Constitution of Ireland 1999. Dublin: The Stationery Office.

Céitinn, S. (Geoffrey Keating) 1902–14. *Foras Feasa ar Éirinn* (A Basis of Knowledge About Ireland) (1634) 4 vols. (ed. and trans. D. Comyn and P. S. Dinneen). London: Irish Texts Society.

Crowley, T. (2005), *Wars of Words: the Politics of language in Ireland 1537–2004*. Oxford: Oxford University Press.

Daunt, W. J. O'Neill. (1848), *Personal Recollections of the Late Daniel O'Connell, M.P.* Dubin.

Davis, T. (1914), *Essays Literary and Historical*. Dundalk: Dundalga Press.

Dinneen, Rev. P. S. (1904), *Lectures on the Irish Language Movement*. Dublin: Gill.

Downing Street Declaration. Joint Declaration by An Taoiseach, Mr. Albert Reynolds, T.D., and The British Prime Minister, The Rt.Hon. John Major, M.P. (1993).
www.irlgov.ie/iveagh/angloirish/jointdeclaration/default.htm.

Fichte, J. G. (1968), *Addresses to the German Nation (1808)*, George Kelly (ed.). New York: Harper.

Hewitt, J. (1974), *Rhyming Weavers and other Country Poets of Antrim and Down*. Belfast: Blackstaff Press.

Irish Archaeological Society (1843), *Statutes of Kilkenny* (1366) in *Tracts Relating to Ireland*. Dublin: Irish Archaeological Society, pp. 1–23.

Maguire, G. (1991), *Our Own Language: An Irish Language Initiative*. Clevedon: Multilingual Matters.

Morris, H. (1898), The loss of the Irish language and its influence on the Catholic religion in Ireland, *Fáinne An Lae*, I, 13, 1.

New Framework for Agreement (1995)
www.irlgov.ie/iveagh/angloirish/frameworkdocument/default.htm.

Ó Conaire, B. (ed.) (1986), *Language, Lore and Lyrics: Essays and Lectures of Douglas Hyde*. Dublin: Irish Academic Press.

Ó Cuív, B. (1986), Irish language and literature, 1691–1845, in T. W. Moody and W. E. Vaughan (eds), *A New History of Ireland*, vol. IV, 'Eighteenth Century Ireland, 1691–1800'. Oxford: Clarendon, pp. 374–423.

O'Leary, P. (1994), *The Prose Literature of the Gaelic Revival, 1881–1921, Ideology and Innovation*. Pennsylvania: Pennsylvania University Press.

O'Reilly, C. (1999), *The Irish Language in Northern Ireland. The Politics of Culture and Identity*. Houndmills: Macmillan.

O'Reilly, Rev. J. M. [n.d.1901], *The Threatening Metempsychosis of a Nation*. Dublin: Gaelic League.

Pearse, P. (1952), *Political Writings and Speeches*. Dublin: Talbot.

Robinson, P. (2003), 'The historical presence of Ulster-Scots in Ireland', in M. Cronin and C. Ó Cuileanáin (eds), *The Languages of Ireland*. Dublin: Four Courts Press, pp. 112–26.

Sinn Féin (1986), *The Role of the Language in Ireland's Cultural Revival*. Belfast: Sinn Féin.

Spenser, E. (1633), 'A View of the State of Ireland' (1596), in Sir James Ware (ed.), *The Historie of Ireland Collected by Three Learned Authors*. Dublin.

The Belfast Agreement: An Agreement Reached at the Multi-Party Talks on Northern Ireland (1998), London: The Stationery Office.

The Statutes at Large Passed in the Parliaments Held in Ireland (1786–1801) 1310–1800, 20 vols., Dublin.

Thomas, D. (1787), *Observations on the Pamphlets Published by the Bishop of Cloyne, Mr. Trant, and Theophilus, On One Side, and Those by Mr. O'Leary, Mr. Barber, and Dr. Campbell On the Other*. Dublin 'Printed from the Author'.

Ullans. The Magazine for Ulster-Scots (1993–), Nos. 1–8. Belfast: Ulster-Scots Language Society.

Ulster Scots Language Society and Ulster-Scots Academy (1996), 'Submission to the Northern Ireland Forum', unpublished manuscript.

Wright, J. (1905), *English Dialect Grammar*. Oxford: Henry Frowde.

9 Voices of endangerment: A language ideological debate on the Swedish language

Tommaso M. Milani

Introduction: from language indifference to language endangerment

There is no doubt that Sweden is not famous for heated language debates in a cold climate, to paraphrase Monica Heller's (1999) suggestive characterization of the Canadian context. Rather, the image which emerges from a review of literature on what one could broadly call the 'linguistic culture'[1] (Schiffman 2006) in Sweden is that of a country with a low level of 'linguistic consciousness' (Lund 1986), that is, a country whose 'population takes the prevailing language situation for granted' (Vikør 2001: 184). As an example, one often hears references to the absence in Swedish legislation of a law which sanctions the status of Swedish as the official language. Moreover, some scholars have underscored the role played by English as a communicative and symbolic resource in Sweden. Phillipson (1992: 25) argues that English has become a second rather than a foreign language in Sweden, and Oakes (2001) claims that English, rather than Swedish, played an important role as an overt marker of national identity in the post-war period until the 1990s. In the light of this, it may sound surprising that, throughout the 1990s, the status and future of Swedish in the national and international arena became the major topic of a debate involving some linguists and politicians, in which Swedish is represented as an entity under some forms of *endangerment*.

In this chapter, I propose that the Swedish debate is not about language per se, but is a prime example of a complex *ideological* contention about conceptualizations of language practices, and their ties to other culturally-bound categories (e.g. nation, state, community, etc.), which Blommaert (1999) calls a *language ideological debate*. In accordance with Blommaert, a debate can be described as a discursive nexus of voices – not just politicians, but also academics, journalists, and individual citizens – engaging in the process of policy-making. Blommaert goes on to argue

169

that language ideological debates are specific types of debates which deal with the production, reproduction or contestation of *language ideologies*, understood as 'cultural (or subcultural) system[s] of ideas about social and linguistic relationships, together with their loading of moral and political interests' (Irvine 1989: 255). To put it simply, language ideological debates are textual/discursive battlegrounds on which social actors struggle with each other in producing, reproducing and/or challenging culturally situated conceptions of the social world enmeshed in representations of language(s) or language practices. Furthermore, given that in such debates language plays a crucial role both as the *medium* and the *object* of discourses whereby the collective order is enacted, language ideological debates are crucial sites where power imbalances and relations of domination tied to the *representations* and the *perceived value* of certain language practices may be upheld, negotiated or even overturned (see the essays in Blommaert 1999 for an illuminating sample of studies on language ideologies in different socio-political contexts).

By taking Blommaert's definition as a point of departure, the focus of the chapter will be twofold: on social actors and on texts. First, I will give a historical overview of the *origins* of the Swedish language debate. The question I want to address is why the debate on the Swedish language emerged when it did and how it developed over nearly ten years. The texts analysed cover the period 1990–2002[2] and include: (1) motions submitted by members of the Swedish parliament,[3] government directives, and legislative proposals, which have been retrieved from the electronic database of the Swedish parliament (www.riksdagen.se/debatt)[4] through a search for the expression 'Swedish language' (*svenska språket*); and (2) academic writings published in *Språkvård* and *Språk i Norden,* which are respectively the official publications of the Swedish Language Council (*Svenska språknämnden*) and the Nordic Language Council (*Nordiskt språkråd/Nordens språkråd*).[5]

Second, I will concentrate on one specific policy document – the draft action programme for the Swedish language, entitled *Mål i mun*[6] (SOU 2002) – which can be regarded as the most comprehensive textual result of ten years' debates on the Swedish language. On the basis of two manual annotations of the whole policy document, I will show the patterns of lexical choice used to conceptualize the Swedish language, and its interplay with other languages in Sweden (English, national minority languages and immigrant languages). Against the backdrop of textual analysis, I will highlight the language ideologies underpinning *Mål i mun* and see whether there is a tension between them in representing the Swedish sociolinguistic situation. At this juncture, it is important to emphasize that an analysis of the ideologies underlying a specific text does not aim at tracing the intentions of those who contributed to and/or eventually wrote the text, but to shed light on the covert and implicit meaning of that text, which is the site where '[the] unformulated premises of an ideology' (Verschueren 1999: 245) are most tangible.

The analysis will be based on a multidisciplinary theoretical framework, which encompasses performativity theory (Butler 1997), Critical Discourse Analysis (hereafter CDA) (Wodak *et al.* 1999; Fairclough 2003) and the notion of voice (Bakhtin 1981, 1986). The aim of bringing together notions belonging to different scholarly traditions (see Blommaert 2005 for a critical overview of CDA) is to initiate a poststructuralist approach to CDA (cf. Pennycook 2001), which can be particularly adequate to study the historically-situated and dynamic relationship between texts, discourses, ideologies and social actors.

Before proceeding further, and at the risk of falling into undue oversimplifications, it can be useful to give a definition and delimitation of these contentious notions for the purpose of the present study. I understand texts in a broad sense as any 'kind[.] of semiotic phenomena [...] connected by virtue of their sign-based character' (Cobley 2001: 276). However, the focus of the chapter will be exclusively on written language. By discourses, I mean sets of historically and socio-culturally situated social practices which provide social actors with semiotic resources for acting together and making sense of – that is, representing and signifying – social reality. Given that making meaning of the social world always entails assumptions about truth, knowledge, values, order, social relations, etc. (Foucault 1980; Butler 1999), discourses are tied to the notion of ideology, in the sense of 'any constellation of fundamental or commonsensical, and often normative, ideas and attitudes related to some aspect(s) of social "reality"' (Blommaert and Verschueren 1998: 25). In other words, discourse and ideology are deeply interrelated insofar as discourses are the site where ideology is materialized (Blommaert and Verschueren 1998; Blommaert 2005). Finally, I do not view social actors as inert shapes moulded by discourses, but as dynamic Bakhtinian voices which repeat, cite and recontextualize creatively available semiotic resources in always new fashions, and thus produce, reproduce, but also rearticulate, discard or contest existing discourses and ideologies.

The debate opens

At the end of the 1980s, more or less at the same time as Sweden was negotiating accession to the European Community (later the European Union), some Swedish linguists and politicians publicly expressed their concern about the future of the Swedish language. A review of

Språkvård and *Språk i Norden* shows that a group of Swedish and Nordic linguists began to discuss the effects that a closer European integration might have on the status and the future of Swedish and the other Nordic languages. The first to draw attention to a potential change in the Swedish sociolinguistic situation as a consequence of Sweden's membership of the EU was probably Ulf Teleman, Professor of Swedish at Lund University and Chairman of the Swedish Language Council, who pointed out that increased Europeanization might result in a higher use of English at the expense of Swedish in the industrial, political and cultural sectors (Teleman 1989).

In the following years, other linguists expressed similar fears. As Svanlund and Westman (1991) recount in an article entitled 'The position of Swedish in the European integration' (*Svenskans ställning vid europeisk integration*), Swedish linguists had two main concerns. On the one hand, they were afraid that Swedish would not be recognized as an official language in the EU. Svanlund and Westman (1991) explain that this fear seems to have been generated by an interview published in the newspaper *Arbetet* (28 July 1991), in which the Swedish EU delegation explicitly expressed their doubts that Swedish would be granted the status of an official EU language. On the other hand, linguists were concerned about the effects that an increased political and economic integration might have on the use of Swedish in public domains.

In October 1992, Teleman took up the relationship between Swedish and European integration and made it the main topic of an influential lecture he held at the annual meeting of the Swedish Language Council, in which he examined whether 'Swedish would be weakened in an integrated Europe' (Teleman 1992: 7). The lecture was later published in an issue of *Språkvård* (1992), and had major resonance in the press (Hyltenstam 1996). After presenting three factors that can weaken a language, namely lexical loans/borrowings, loss of functional domains and loss of language users, Teleman argued that the most interesting and significant aspect in order to understand what was going to happen to the Swedish language was the eventual loss of functional domains. According to Teleman, the use of Swedish in different domains would be affected as a result of the interplay of four processes, which are partially or totally related to European integration: the internationalization of higher education, the weakening of national autonomy, the Europeanization of the private sector and the internationalization of popular culture. Of these, Teleman underscored the primacy of national autonomy as decisive for the future of Swedish.

In those years, the future and the status of the Swedish language was also raised by some members of parliament (MPs) in a number of parliamentary motions. MPs wanted the government to guarantee two conditions: (1) that Swedish should be one of the official languages in the EU (1992/93:U514); and (2) that Sweden should defend the status of Swedish as an official and working language on a par with the other EU languages (1994/95: U502).

After Sweden's official membership in January 1995, Swedish indeed became an official and working language in all EU institutions in accordance with Council Regulation 1. This entailed *inter alia* the establishment and management of a translation and interpretation body to accomplish the needs of the Swedish delegates, an enterprise which did not prove to be without problems. As a matter of fact, the Swedish government commissioned in May 1995 an official inquiry with the aim to explore 'the measures that need to be taken in the Swedish public administration and in the EU, in order to secure the quality of Swedish EU texts', and to propose 'what claims (*krav*) Sweden should make for the use of Swedish as a working language in the institutions of the EU' (Dir. 1995). 'Claims' refers in this context to requirements aiming to guarantee the right to use spoken and written Swedish in meetings in EU institutions.

Also in May 1995, Professor Kenneth Hyltenstam, Director of the Centre for Research on Bilingualism at Stockholm University, gave a plenary lecture, entitled 'Swedish, a minority language in Europe, and in the world?' (*Svenskan, ett minoritetsspråk i Europa – och i världen?*), at the annual conference 'Describing Swedish' (*Svenskans beskrivning*), which that year was dedicated to the topic of languages in contact (see Ivars *et al.* 1996). As was the case for Teleman in 1992, Hyltenstam's main concern was the possible linguistic scenarios following Sweden's entry into the EU. Unlike Teleman, though, Hyltenstam presented the status of Swedish in the light of a broad theoretical framework on power relations between majority and minority languages, language shift, language maintenance and language endangerment (Hyltenstam and Stroud 1991; Krauss 1992; Phillipson 1992). Drawing on Krauss' taxonomy of safe, moribund and endangered languages, Hyltenstam claimed that Swedish definitely belongs to the group of safe languages, as it fulfils both criteria established by Krauss. That is, Swedish is a *de facto* official language, and it has a large number of speakers. Nevertheless, Hyltenstam went on to argue that the position of Swedish as a safe language might be affected by EU membership, because the EU, with unequal status among its official languages, higher status accorded to English, and diminished political autonomy of the Member States, represents a 'typical frame for language shift' (Hyltenstam 1996: 29).

The language issue became even more salient when both MPs and the government expressed the necessity to develop practical

173

strategies and measures in order to strengthen the status of Swedish (1994/95: Kr239; Bet. 1995/96: Kru07; Prop. 1996/97; 1996/97: Kr221). In April 1997, the Swedish government directed the Swedish Language Council to draft an action programme for the promotion of Swedish (Regeringsbeslut, 30 April 1997). The text of this government directive explicitly formulated the same concerns expressed earlier by academics about what 'can happen to the language [i.e. Swedish] in the future' and what 'an increased European and global integration may imply for the Swedish language' (Regeringsbeslut, 30 April 1997).

The work around the draft action programme began with an article under the title 'Do we need a national language policy?' (*Behöver vi en nationell språkpolitik?*), written by Ulf Teleman, Chairman of the Swedish Language Council, and Margareta Westman, Secretary of the Council (Teleman and Westman 1997). The authors proposed guiding principles for language policy, and used a terminology which would be referred to and re-elaborated in later policy documents (see below). According to Teleman and Westman, Swedish is a fully-fledged language which needs to be preserved and strengthened for two reasons. First, Swedish needs to be maintained in order to avoid social inequalities, tied to lack of skills in one language, which might arise on the way to societal bilingualism (Swedish/English). Second, Swedish is the *bearer* of Swedish culture. Therefore, Swedish needs to be preserved in order to maintain Swedish culture as an independent entity in interaction with other cultures, and consequently in order to avoid cultural uniformity. On the basis of these two arguments, Teleman and Westman suggested two goals for Swedish language policy, which would be incorporated in the draft action programme elaborated by the Swedish Language Council (Svenska språknämnden 1998): (1) Swedish should be a 'complete'[7] language; and 2) Swedish should remain a *samhällsbärande*[8] (lit. society bearing) language, and an official language in the EU. In order to fulfil these two goals, the Swedish Language Council proposed (among other things) that the status of Swedish as the 'principal language' (*huvudspråk*) should be ratified by law. It is relevant to point out that, despite the exclusive concern with the Swedish language in the government directive, the Language Council did not focus on Swedish only, but it also took into consideration national and immigrant minorities, their languages and their rights to maintain their mother tongues, and to learn the Swedish language.

On the basis of the Language Council's proposal, the Swedish government recognized the necessity to continue the work of promoting the Swedish language (Prop. 1998/99). In October 2000, a parliamentary committee was appointed with the aim of formulating a concrete action programme for the promotion of Swedish and of giving everyone in Sweden, irrespective of their social and linguistic

174

background, equal opportunities to learn Swedish (Dir. 2000). After two years' work, the committee, named the Committee on the Swedish Language (*Kommittén för svenska språket*), published an ambitious language policy proposal entitled *Mål i mun* (SOU 2002). In the proposal, the committee formulated a large number of recommendations to achieve three aims: 'Swedish shall be a complete language, serving and uniting our society, Swedish in official and public use shall be correct and shall function well, everyone shall have a right to language: Swedish, their mother tongue and foreign languages' (SOU 2002, official translation contained in the English summary: 2). At the time of writing (December 2005), the Swedish government presented a bill entitled 'Best language – a comprehensive Swedish language policy' (*Bästa språket – en samlad svensk språkpolitik*) (Prop. 2005/06), in which the three main aims previously formulated in *Mål i mun* were reiterated. Moreover, the government proposed that Swedish should be the 'principal language' (*huvudspråk*) in Sweden. Yet, the government pointed out that this would not need to be ratified by a law. This stance was ultimately confirmed by the vote of the parliament against a law on the Swedish language.

Discussion: the actors

On the basis of the historical data presented in the previous section, the first question the present chapter addresses is why the debate on the Swedish language emerged when it did, and how it developed over nearly ten years. Blommaert (1999: 11) reminds us that 'there is no public opinion, no social consensus which can be detached from real processes of hegemonization. For this reason, analyses of debates have to make references to the forms of *stasis* preceding or following them' (emphasis in original). Therefore, an analysis of the reasons and conditions underlying the debate on the Swedish language cannot leave out an understanding of the political, economic, cultural and linguistic situation antecedent to the emergence of the debate itself.

The current Swedish constitution can be taken as a useful example to illustrate the linguistic situation before the 1990s. The constitution does not contain any regulation which sanctions the status of Swedish as official or national language. Nevertheless, that Swedish is the *de facto* official language emerges implicitly in the sections in which the legislation deals with the 'ethnic Other', i.e. immigrant and national minorities.

The absence in the Swedish legislation and the reference to the 'ethnic Other' can be interpreted as a result of the interplay of several factors: (1) the long historical territorial unity of Sweden as a political entity; (2) the unchallenged tradition since the eighteenth century of a codified and standardized Swedish variety (*rikssvenska*) (Hyltenstam 1999; Teleman 2003); (3) the lower role attributed by social democracy to the notions of nation and language as collective symbols in the period following the Second World War (Oakes 2001; Teleman 2003); and (4) the importance attributed to Swedish language instruction and interpretation services for non-Swedish speakers. Whereas the first two factors contributed to naturalizing the hegemonic position of standard-Swedish as the *de facto* official language variety to be used in all public domains to a degree that it did not even need to be ratified by law, the third and fourth factors can be understood respectively in the light of the social democratic nation-building project after the Second World War and increased immigration in the 1970s.

In the post-war period, the Social Democratic party aimed at shaping the image of Sweden as a neutral, international and socially equal welfare state model, the so-called *folkhemmet*. According to Löfgren (1993) and Stråth (2000), neutrality and the welfare state, based on the principle of social equality (*jämlikhet*), played a major role as symbolic resources for mobilizing and organizing Sweden in the national arena while demarcating and distinguishing Sweden from the 'continent' (Europe) in the international arena. However, neutrality and the welfare state as elements of identity demarcation did not entail isolationism. On the contrary, they gave rise to an active third-way internationalism, in which Sweden presented itself as a political and economic model, a sort of world conscience 'standing outside big-power ties' (Stråth 2000: 371). As far as language is concerned, the historically 'natural' position of Swedish as *the* official language in the national arena, together with the Social Democratic priority accorded to internationalism, played down the symbolic function of Swedish nationally while at the same time enhancing the symbolic function of English as the language representing Sweden internationally (Oakes 2001). In sum, neutrality, social equality and the welfare state, rather than the Swedish language and nation, constituted the explicit symbols whereby Swedish national identity was constructed.

This claim can be substantiated by a comparison of the importance given to the notion of nation in school subjects at the beginning and at the end of the 1900s. According to Teleman (2003), the nation was a keyword in the instruction of Swedish, geography and history at the beginning of the 1900s. Likewise, in a study of the discourse of the nation in literature anthologies and textbooks used in Swedish secondary schools in the 1920s and 1980s, Englund (1997) demonstrates that the nation and cultural heritage were fundamental categories for what counted as literature in the 1920s. Most interestingly, Englund's study also shows that the nation was no longer central for the definition of literature in the 1980s. It had been replaced by human relations, pluralism and social education. These results are consistent with the claim that 'a nation that seeks international hegemony must deny that it is nationalist. It must claim to speak with the voice of universality, whilst protecting its own particular interests' (Billig 1995: 92).

The Swedish language, however, became a major topic of debate among politicians and academics in connection with an increased immigration during the 1970s. Although immigration was not a new phenomenon to Sweden, in the 1970s and 1980s, it was different from previous periods in nature and volume. In the 1950s immigration was still numerically contained and was broadly welcomed as a means to sustain Swedish economic expansion. By contrast, the people who moved to Sweden from the 1970s onwards were fleeing their countries for political, personal and economic reasons. Whereas in the 1950s and 1960s immigrants had been largely expected to leave their cultural traditions and be assimilated into Swedish society, the nature and volume of immigration in the 1970s brought about the abandonment of assimilationism in favour of multicultural policies (Hyltenstam 1999). As for language, the debate focused, on the one hand, on the importance for immigrants to learn Swedish as a prerogative for a successful integration, and, on the other, on rights of immigrants to maintain and develop their 'home-languages' (Hyltenstam and Tuomela 1996; Hyltenstam 2004).

This multilayered sociolinguistic order, in which Swedish, English, immigrants and national minorities and their languages were intertwined to accomplish different communicative and symbolic functions, underwent a significant turn at the beginning of the 1990s, when the heretofore uncontested and naturalized position of Swedish as official language suddenly became an explicit and pivotal topic for some linguists and politicians. One has to note that linguists and politicians became concerned with the future of Swedish during a period of economic, political and identity crisis. In those years, the Swedish welfare state model was challenged by negative economic growth, rising unemployment and inflation rates. Moreover, prompted by the crisis, Social Democrats were shifting from a skeptical to a positive attitude towards the European Union. The new interest in the status of the Swedish language, the emergence and development of a language debate, and its link to Sweden's membership in the EU can be explained by the help of two notions, which are the core of performativity theory, namely iterability and interpellation (Butler 1997), to which I will now turn.

Iterability can be defined as the never-ending process whereby texts repeat, cite and recontextualize previous texts and discourses.

177

According to Butler (1997), iterability is not a static textual repetition, but a dynamic one. Iteration implies change through the break with an original context and the inauguration of new contexts, and hence of new meanings.

If one reads the academic texts mentioned in the previous section in the light of the concept of iterability, one can see that Swedish linguists attempt to explain the possible consequences an EU membership might have on the status of the Swedish language by citing and recontextualizing two interrelated academic discourses, the discourse of language endangerment and the discourse of English as a global language. Despite their different focus (i.e. minority languages and English respectively), these discourses share the assumption that some 'dominated' languages are exposed to the threat of other more powerful and 'dominating' languages (Calvet 1974, 1987). Moreover, these discourses are based on the analogy between languages and organisms and between language diversity and biological diversity. It is also relevant to point out that two groundbreaking works within these discourses came out at the beginning of the 1990s: the book *Linguistic Imperialism* by Robert Phillipson (1992) and the article 'The world's languages in crisis' by Michael Krauss (1992), published in *Language*. Phillipson focuses on English, and, in particular, on the relationships between the dominance of English and the deliberate maintenance of 'structural and cultural inequalities between English and other languages' (1992: 47) by certain groups, states and institutions. Krauss, on the other hand, is more generally concerned with the future of linguistic diversity in the world, and pessimistically predicts that 'the coming century will see either the death or the doom of 90% of mankind's languages' (1992: 7).

Teleman (1992) refers to several key notions and features from these discourses, and applies them to the Swedish context, e.g. Calvet's *glottophagie* (or linguistic cannibalism), that is, the notion of dominant languages 'eating up' dominated languages; language death; and the increasing anglo-americanization of Swedish education, the private sector and popular culture. This leads him to conclude that European integration might make Swedes, and by implication the Swedish language, 'more vulnerable' (Teleman 1992: 16). Teleman's analysis, however, is concentrated on the threats to the communicative, rather than the symbolic, function of Swedish in various societal domains. By contrast, despite citing and iterating Teleman's argumentation, Hyltenstam (1996) recontextualizes Teleman's scenario in a broader framework. Hyltenstam argues that the status of Swedish is multi-layered. On the one hand, Swedish is a majority and dominant language in the national arena. However, English plays an important symbolic function in relevant segments of society, including the educational system. On the other hand, in the international arena, Swedish can be viewed as a 'minority' language within the new context of power relations represented by the EU, in which Swedish is not directly under the threat of, but 'in competition with' English (Hyltenstam 1996: 16).

In this way, Hyltenstam contributed to uphold and, at the same time, to reshape the debate on the future of Swedish, shifting the focus from communicative functions to power inequalities between languages and the symbolic functions attached to them by their speakers. It is not irrelevant to point out that the stance Hyltenstam took in the debate could be partly explained as the effect of his long professional experience with immigrant and minority languages. In the 1970s, Hyltenstam had played a major role in the debates on the rights of immigrants to maintain and develop their 'home-languages', and at the beginning of the 1990s he had worked on language shift and language maintenance among the Sámis.

The importance of the communicative function of Swedish was also reiterated by Teleman and Westman (1997). In fact, they suggested that Swedish should remain a *complete* language, that is, a language to be used in all public domains. Yet, Teleman and Westman (1997: 14) went a step further and claimed that Swedish needs to be maintained as *samhällsbärande* (lit. society bearing). What the authors meant is explained in the following extract:

> Kulturer hålls ihop av språk. Inte minst i dagens genomkommer-sialiserade värld hotas kulturerna av likriktning om inte språkliga gränshinder bromsar och ger en viss tid för eftertanke. Argumentet utgår också ifrån att olika kulturer är kreativa på olika sätt och att denna pluralism är en viktig motor för utvecklingen i vår värld. [...] Det som ger kulturerna självkänsla och rikedom är att de språk som bär upp dem är samhälleliga språk, att de bär upp offent-ligheter. [...] Om de olika språken inte längre är bärare av olika offentligheter är fältet fritt för kommersialisering och likriktning av politik, ekonomi och (språkbunden) kultur.
> (Teleman and Westman 1997: 9–10)

> *Cultures are kept together by languages. Especially, in today's totally commercialized world, cultures are threatened by homoge-neity if it were not for linguistic boundaries to hold up and give some time for reflection. The argument also presupposes that cultures are creative in different ways, and that this pluralism is an important engine for the development of our world. [...] What gives cultures self-esteem and richness is that the languages that bear them are societal languages – they bear publics. [...] If*

*different languages are no longer bearers of different publics, there
will be free room for commercialization and uniformity of politics,
economy, and (language-borne) culture.*

Similarly to the remarks May (2001: 132–35) makes on an excerpt
from Fishman (1991), I want to draw the attention to the assumptions underlying Teleman and Westman's argumentation. Language
and culture are linked here in three ways: instrumentally, indexically
and symbolically. First, language is the cohesive instrument which
binds a culture together. Second, language indexes – that is points
to – a culture. Teleman and Westman echo a 'weak version' of the
Sapir–Whorf hypothesis, according to which 'one's social and cultural
experiences are organized by language and thus each language represents a particular worldview' (May 2001: 133). This entails that every
language expresses a specific conceptualization of the world, and that
diversity in the world is produced by the multiplicity of different
realities which each language conveys. Therefore, every language
is worth being preserved if one wants to maintain diversity, and
counteract homogenization. Third, by way of a metaphor, language is
conceptualized as an entity, which 'bears' culture and publics. This
means that language symbolically stands for both a culture, and the
collectivity which speaks that language. In sum, language (in this
case, Swedish) is viewed as a resource at a civic and symbolic level.
It produces societal integration, that is, it makes communication
possible among individuals and, accordingly, constitutes publics (for
discussion on the relationship between language and publics see the
essays in Gal and Woolard 2001), and it enables social identification,
that is, the definition of who 'we' are.

That European integration, global integration and the spreading
of English were also viewed as major threats to the communicative
and symbolic functions of Swedish by some politicians is manifest
in the policy documents referred to in the previous section. In the
international arena, MPs were engaged in the recognition of Swedish
as an official language in the EU and the organization of a translation
and interpretation service for Swedish delegates (1994/95: U502;
Dir. 1995). MPs and the government explicitly cited the concerns
expressed by linguists and pleaded for concrete measures aiming at
strengthening the Swedish language both as a means of communication, and – this time it is stated *explicitly* – as a symbol of national
and cultural identity (1994/95: Kr239; Prop. 1996/97; Regeringsbeslut
30 April 1997). Moreover, the notion of Swedish as 'society bearing'
(*samhällsbärande*) was incorporated into and became pivotal in policy
documents on language (SOU 2002; Prop. 2005/06). In this way,
through citation and recontextualization of concepts developed by

linguists and their concerns, MPs and the government contributed to extending the language debate from the academic to the political field. What remains to be demonstrated now is the role played by Sweden's accession to the EU in relation to the emergence of the debate on the Swedish language.

The relationship between the EU and the Swedish language debate can be understood only if we view EU membership not as an economic and political event per se, but as one dimension of the large-scale process of globalization, which entails the ' "re-structuring" of relations between the economic, political and social domains [...], and "the re-scaling" of relations between the different levels of social life' (Fairclough 2003: 4). Accession to the EU entails for a new member country the re-shaping of an existing political, economic and, most interesting for us, sociolinguistic situation. As a matter of fact, the official language(s) of each new Member State receive(s) the status of both official and working languages in EU institutions (Council Regulation 1). However, what is not and cannot be said explicitly – because it would go against the EU's policy of multilingualism – is that some languages are 'more equal' than others (Phillipson 2003). In the case of Sweden, Swedish was for the first time *de jure* recognized as an official language in a political/economic entity, but also occupied a *de facto* lower position of power, if compared to other official EU languages (e.g. English, French and German).

These discourses on language linked to EU accession can be viewed *pace* Butler (1997) as *interpellations*. Interpellation is a concept which was originally used by the French philosopher Louis Althusser (1971) to explain the way in which ideology 'hails' individuals, thereby transforming them into subjects with specific ideological and social positions. By appropriating Althusser's notion of interpellation, Butler argues that interpellations are 'powerful and insidious ways in which subjects are called into social being from diffuse social quarters' (Butler 1997: 159ff), and that interpellation 'is not descriptive, but [...] introduce[s] a reality rather than report[s] on an existing one' (Butler 1997: 33).

As for Sweden's entry into the EU, this brought into being (among other things) a new language regime (Kroskrity 2000), that is, a new sociolinguistic order embedded in power relations, in which Swedish is at the same time an official language, but less powerful than other official EU languages. Moreover, the discourses on language tied to the EU interpellated some social actors, who, because of their expertise, could claim authority in the field of language (linguists), or whose possibility of using Swedish in the new political and economic entity (the EU) was called into question by the new regulations (politicians).

On the one hand, some linguists, familiar with the discourses of language endangerment and English as a global language, feared that accession to the EU would further weaken the already problematic position of Swedish, challenged by English in the national and international arena. On the other hand, the proclamation of Swedish as official language in the EU introduced in political discourse a category – that of official language – which was previously taken for granted and covertly defined, and, at the same time, entitled Swedish politicians to speak Swedish in the EU institutions. This entailed that politicians had to make decisions about the status of the Swedish language in the EU (for example, about the establishment of translation and interpretation services for Swedish). Moreover, prompted by the *de facto* status of Swedish as a less powerful language in the EU, and influenced by the fears shown by academics, politicians became worried about the relationship between Swedish and English. In responding to the call of interpellation, linguists and politicians took specific stances about the Swedish language in the public sphere (e.g. in newspapers, journals and in the parliament), and thereby became public *voices*, which initiated and upheld the language debate.

To sum up, language discourses tied to EU accession stressed the element of threat exerted by English, already present in the discourses on language endangerment and on English as a global language. In this way, EU membership played a major role in amplifying existing academic discourses on language. This, together with the introduction of official language as an overt category in political discourse, contributed to extending an academic debate to the political field.

A key text: the policy document *Mål i mun*

Whereas the previous section dealt with the emergence and development of the debate among linguists and politicians, the present and the following sections aim to address the second question of the present chapter, namely which lexical items are used and how they co-occur to represent the Swedish language in one specific policy document, the Draft action programme for the Swedish language, *Mål i mun* (SOU 2002).

The introductory sections of *Mål i mun*, which cannot be reproduced here for reasons of space, are representative of the way in which the Swedish language is conceptualized in the whole policy document. The titles of some sections in the first chapter are instructive: 'A complete and society bearing language' (*Ett komplett och samhällsbärande språk*), 'Swedish is strong' (*Svenskan står stark*) (p. 45), 'A language in good conditions' (*Ett språk i gott skick*) (p. 53),

'No general language decay' (*Inget allmänt språkförfall*) (p. 54). If one looks at the content of these sections, one can notice that the positive characteristics of Swedish are presented first, followed by a ranking, in which Swedish is compared to the other languages of the world. Swedish is said to be strong because it is well-documented, codified, and with a long literary tradition. Moreover, a trait of uniqueness is added: Swedish is claimed to be particularly susceptible to precise grammatical description ('[it] has been [...] [grammatically] described in a way which for precision has few equivalents' [*har [...] fått en beskrivning som i noggrannhet har få motstycken*]) (p. 54). These examples show that a non-physical thing such as the Swedish language is viewed as a bounded material entity – metonymically represented here by a descriptive grammar – with a specific physical condition.

Although Swedish is said to be one of 'the big and favoured languages' (*de stora och gynnade språken*) (p. 45) against the backdrop of a taxonomy building on the relationship between the number of languages in the world and their speakers, internationalization, multilingualism and multiculturalism are singled out as the factors that have changed the conditions of existence for the Swedish language.

Extract 1
I en värld som förändras snabbt förändras också språkens villkor – språk och samhälle hänger nära samman. Svenskan är inget undantag. Framför allt är det i två avseenden som situationen har blivit annorlunda. För det första har engelskan fått allt starkare internationell ställning, och därigenom även ökande användning inom vårt land. För det andra är Sverige inte ett lika språkligt homogent land som tidigare. [...] Dessa utvecklingar gör att svenskans förutsättningar förändrats: den måste på ett annat vis än tidigare samspela med andra språk inom ett samhälle som präglas av internationalisering, mångspråkighet och multikultur (p. 47–8).

In a world which changes quickly, language conditions also change – language and society are closely interrelated. Swedish is not an exception. The situation has become different especially in two respects. First, English has received an increasingly stronger international position, and thus also a growing use in our country. Second, Sweden is not as linguistically homogeneous as before. [...] As a result of these developments, the conditions of the Swedish language have changed. In a different way from before, it must interplay with other languages in a society which is characterized by internationalization, multilingualism and multi-culture

Extract 2
Svenskans ställning som komplett och samhällsbärande språk är inte ohotad, bl.a. är användningen av svenskan inte längre

183

självklar inom vissa funktionsområden. Andra språk, speciellt engelskan, har fått en allt starkare ställning, såväl internationellt som nationellt. Vidare har Sverige blivit ett mångspråkigt samhälle. Fem minoritetsspråk har erkänts som nationella minoritetsspråk. Genom invandringen har ett stort antal språk kommit till Sverige. Det är av vikt att man i ett sådant samhälle har ett språk som befolkningen kan ha gemensamt, ett språk som är huvudspråk. Detta är i Sverige svenskan (p. 465).

The position of Swedish as a complete language serving and uniting Swedish society is not unthreatened – among other things, the use of Swedish is no longer obvious in certain functional domains. Other languages, especially English, have received an increasingly stronger position, internationally as well as nationally. Furthermore, Sweden has become a multilingual society. Five minority languages have been recognized as national minority languages. Through immigration, a great number of languages have come to Sweden. It is important to have in such a society a language which the population has in common, a principal language. In Sweden, this is Swedish.

Extract 3
Samtidigt har svenska språket fått hård konkurrens från engelskan och inom några av språkets bruksdomäner finns risk för att svenskan tappar mark (p. 415).

At the same time, the Swedish language is in tough competition with English and in some domains there is the risk that Swedish may lose ground.

In the extracts above, one can see that Swedish is not only an entity with a physical state, it also occupies a specific position together with other languages in co-existing spaces (Sweden, the world), the control of which is at stake. In the case of Swedish and English, their relationship assumes the form of economic competition and war of domination. As an effect of societal changes, Swedish is portrayed in a 'tough competition' with English. Therefore, Swedish might be 'losing ground', and in need of 'promotion'.

Besides being represented in economic terms, English and Swedish are portrayed as engaged in a struggle for domination of the spaces of language use, the so-called language domains. Keywords here are 'dominate' (*dominera*) – together with its derivates – and 'domain loss' (*domänförlust*). Swedish is said to be 'losing' domains in favour of English, and English, in turn, is 'taking over', 'pushing aside' Swedish, and consequently 'dominates' the spaces previously controlled by Swedish. This view of language relations in economic and war terms is consistent with findings in cognitive studies on metaphors (Lakoff and Johnson 1980; Koller 2004). As a matter of fact, Lakoff and Johnson (1980) point out that war is a common metaphor to structure argument in Western culture, and Koller (2004) shows that war metaphors are particularly productive in the representation of marketing processes.

Extract 4

Att språket har en oerhörd betydelse för oss kan ingen ifrågasätta. Vår identitet och självbild är knuten till språket. Genom språket upplever och förstår vi människor vår tillvaro, uttrycker våra tankar och känslor och samspelar med andra. Språk och tanke hänger nära samman; när ett språk dör försvinner också det sätt att uppleva och förstå världen som är kopplat till detta språk. Språket ger oss tillgång till litteratur och andra kulturalster, språket är bärare av vårt kulturarv och nyckeln som öppnar dörren till detta. Ett rikt och levande språk – både om vi ser till språket som övergripande samhälleligt fenomen och till de olika individernas enskilda språkförmåga – är en förutsättning för att vi skall kunna växa och utvecklas som människor. Vill vi verka för ett samhälle präglat av humanism måste därför alla ha rätt till språket.

Men språket är också ett redskap. Skall man kunna hävda sin rätt måste man ha språket i sin makt: språket är förutsättningen för att man skall kunna delta i det offentliga samtalet och den allmänna debatten, för att man skall kunna verka i politiskt och fackligt arbete, för att man skall kunna ta strid med makthavare inom företag och myndigheter m.m. Språket är nyckeln till framgång i skolan, och kraven blir allt större för allt fler; exempelvis går ju numera nästan alla elever vidare till gymnasieskolan och skall där skaffa sig grundläggande behörighet till högskolestudier. Inom arbetslivet blir språkanvändningen allt centralare. I dagens Sverige finns mycket få arbeten som skulle kunna utföras av den som inte alls kan läsa och skriva; [...] (p. 58–9)

No one can call into question the fact that language has an enormous importance for us. Our identity and self-image is tied to language. Through language, we human beings experience and understand our life, express our thoughts and feelings, and interact with others. Language and thought are closely interrelated. When a language dies, the way of experiencing and understanding the world tied to that language also dies with it. Language gives us access to literature and other cultural products. Language is the bearer of our cultural heritage and the key which opens the door to it. A rich and living language – both if we see language as a comprehensive social phenomenon and as the ability of different individuals – is a prerequisite for us to be able to grow and develop as human beings. If we want to work for a society characterized by humanism, everybody has to have the right to language.

185

> *But language is also a tool. If one has to be able to assert one's own right, one has to have language in one's power: language is a prerequisite for being able to participate in public debates, for working in politics and the trade-unions, for being able to struggle with those in power in private companies and public authorities, etc. Language is the key for success in school, and [language] demands are becoming higher and higher for everyone. For example, nearly all pupils go on to study in upper secondary school and there acquire necessary qualifications for access to university studies. Language use is becoming more and more important in working life. In today's Sweden there are only a few jobs which could be pursued by somebody who cannot read or write; [...].*

Extract 4 is taken from a section entitled 'Everybody's right to language' (*Allas rätt till språk*). Here the language as an entity metaphor is elaborated into three other metaphors: language is portrayed as a 'bearer', a 'tool' and a 'key'. There are no explicit references to Swedish in this very extract, and the argumentation is carried out at a high level of abstraction. The deictics 'we' and 'our' in the first four sentences have an all-inclusive meaning, which encompasses all human beings, and their relationships to each other. Nevertheless, the meaning of 'language' and of 'our' seems to shift when language is described as the 'bearer of our cultural heritage'. There are indeed no references to any specific languages. But if one looks at the patterns of co-occurrence of the noun 'bearer' throughout the whole text, one can notice that it co-occurs with the Swedish language, Swedish dialects, Swedish national identity and Swedish cultural heritage, and with language in general. Similarly, the related present participle 'bearing' (*bärande*) occurs only in its compound form *samhällsbärande*, with the function of attributive adjective, in contexts where the Swedish language is clearly stated. The presence of these instances throughout the policy document increases the vagueness of 'language', 'we' and 'our' in this very extract, and contributes to make their meaning slide from the universal (i.e. language, human beings) to the particular (i.e. Swedish language, Swedes). Further evidence of this gradual shift of meaning is given by the analysis of the second section of the extract.

In this part, language is described in its function of a *lingua franca*, whose possession enables communication between individuals, whatever linguistic and ethnic background they may have, and allows their participation in society as active citizens in the public debate. The power and the importance that language has for all citizens is amplified by the image of social struggle produced by the use of 'struggle' (*strid*) and 'those in power' (*makthavare*). In the following sentence, 'key' (*nyckel*), a hyponym of 'tool', in combination with success (*framgång*), reinforces the instrumental image of language, at the same time as it shifts the focus from the public sphere of political debate and social struggle to the more private domain of personal success at school. Furthermore, through several references to a specific school system (*gymnasieskola, grundläggande behörighet, högskolan*), the Swedish one, and through the locative 'in today's Sweden' (*i dagens Sverige*), it becomes evident, though again not explicitly expressed, that the language in question is Swedish.

Discussion: conflicting voices in *Mål i mun*

As the extracts above show, the new sociolinguistic situation resulting from the interplay of economic, political and cultural factors appears to be a reality with both positive and negative aspects. Multilingualism is repeatedly heralded as a 'resource for society', but 'English has received stronger international position', and the 'position of Swedish as a complete and society bearing language is not unthreatened'. Moreover, it is clearly stated that 'we need a common language – Swedish – in order to be able to recognize and benefit from the richness a multilingual and multicultural society offers' (SOU 2002: 26). It is evident that these statements are not about language(s) alone. They are rather about language(s) and their relationship to what is alleged or assumed as good and/or desirable for a polity. In other words, these statements are textual manifestations of what Irvine (1989) calls language ideologies (see definition in the introductory section), and their relationship to the nation state. Two language ideologies tied to the nation state seem to be at work here: (1) the ideology of multilingualism, according to which language diversity is a positive societal phenomenon, which needs to be supported; and (2) the ideology of social cohesion, according to which social cohesion is the foundation of civil society and is achieved by means of one common language (Swedish), which therefore needs to be preserved. Drawing on Bakhtin's (1981) distinction between 'centrifugal' and 'centripetal' voices, and applying it to these two ideologies, one could say that multilingualism and multiculturalism represent centrifugal voices because they work for the recognition and legitimation of a multiplicity of languages and cultures within a polity, while social cohesion represents centripetal voices because it operates for the accomplishment of a unity – be it at a civic/political or symbolic/cultural level.

There is no doubt that *Mål i mun* is an attempt to propose a viable solution for the recognition and management of language diversity and multiculturalism in Sweden (Swedish, national and immigrant minority languages, and foreign languages, especially

English), and, at the same time to pin down the communicative and symbolic functions of Swedish as a resource whereby social cohesion is achieved. However, focusing on the notion of language as 'society bearing' (*samhällsbärande*), I want to show in the remaining part of this section that there is a tension between centrifugal voices of multilingualism and multiculturalism and centripetal voices of social cohesion in representing a symbolic/cultural dimension of the nation state.

I illustrated in the previous section that Swedish is conceptualized as an entity which assumes different facets: a tool, a key and a bearer. Whereas the tool and key metaphor are used to represent the communicative function of Swedish in relation to other languages, one has to bear in mind that the communicative function of Swedish is just one aspect, though a predominant one, in *Mål i mun*. Swedish is also presented as a right of every individual living in Sweden, whatever linguistic background s/he may have, and as a symbolic resource, which marks national belonging. All these three aspects are co-present in the metaphor of Swedish as a bearer. As noted before, a search for the occurrences of the present participle *bärande* ('bearing') and the noun *bärare* ('bearer') shows that *bärande* occurs only in its compound form *samhällsbärande*, to define the Swedish language, and that *bärare* is used as a predicative of the Swedish language and its dialects, and of language in general. What is interesting is that language (be it Swedish or language in general) is portrayed as a 'bearer' of different entities: 'culture, history and traditions' (1), 'cultural heritage' (3), 'culture' (3), 'information' (1), 'literature' (1) and 'national identity' (1).

The expression *samhällsbärande* seems to have been employed for the first time to characterize the Swedish language in Teleman and Westman (1997), in which *samhällsbärande* is undoubtedly conflated with *kulturbärande* (lit. 'culture bearing') (see above). That is, Swedish is not only viewed as an instrument of communication, but also as a symbolic resource for imagining the nation and its culture (Anderson 1991). In other words, Swedish is regarded as a strong cohesive resource for two co-existing dimensions of the nation state: a civic dimension and a symbolic/cultural one. Nevertheless, the meaning of *samhällsbärande* given in a definition in *Mål i mun* explicitly emphasizes the civic dimension rather than the symbolic/cultural one.

Extract 5
Att språket är samhällsbärande betyder för det första att svenskan har rollen som det gemensamma språket i Sverige och alltså är det språk som i ett mångspråkigt samhälle gör det möjligt för personer med olika språklig bakgrund att mötas och samverka. För det andra innebär det att svenskan skall vara det språk vi använder i

offentliga sammanhang i Sverige: i politik, i administration, inom
rättsväsendet, som skolspråk m.m. (p. 419).

That language [Swedish] is samhällsbärande *means first that
Swedish has the role of the common language in Sweden, that
is, the language which in a multilingual society makes it possible
for people with different language backgrounds to meet and act
together. Second, it entails that Swedish is the language we use
in official situations in Sweden: in politics, administration, the
judicial and educational system, etc.*

This definition underscores the function of Swedish as a *lingua franca*
and a right of every citizen, which makes a sort of ideal Habermasian
public sphere possible and opens its access to everyone, irrespective of
their linguistic background. That is, Swedish is viewed as a resource
that makes societal integration and political participation possible. At
the same time, one has to bear in mind that minority and immigrant
language 'rights' are also recognized, and thereby those languages
are given a legitimate position in society. Taking these two considerations together, one could claim that there is an attempt to mediate
between what I called the centrifugal voices of multilingualism and
the centripetal voices of social cohesion. This means that an eventual
tension between these voices is neutralized at a civic level. At the
symbolic/cultural level, the picture is quite different.

As Bakhtin (1986: 89) points out, '[the] words of others carry
with them their own expression, their own evaluative tone, which
we assimilate, rework and re-accentuate'. Likewise, *Mål i mun* incorporates and recontextualizes Teleman and Westman's metaphor and
accentuates the civic dimension of language. Nevertheless, the original
focus on cultural identity is not completely lost. There are in fact few,
though relevant, instances in which language and culture are tied
together and Swedish is represented as a bearer of *culture* and *cultural
heritage*.

Culture is a significant concept, because '[it] is a way of summarizing the ways in which groups distinguish themselves from other
groups. It represents what is shared within the group, and presumably
simultaneously not shared (or not entirely shared) outside it'
(Wallerstein 1990: 32). Therefore, together with deixis (e.g. 'we', 'our',
'Sweden', etc.) it can be a powerful instrument for the construction in
discourse of a symbolic sense of 'an imagined community' (Anderson
1991; Billig 1995). In other words, culture can be useful to trace how a
group defines itself and what and/or who is included or excluded.

The frequency of 'culture' and 'cultural heritage' amounts
respectively to 107 and 20 instances in the whole text. Despite the

outweighing prevalence of 'culture', a qualitative analysis shows that 'culture' is most often employed as a highly abstract category in chapter, section or book titles, or in lists of domains. '(The) Swedish culture' (*svensk kultur/den svenska kulturen*) occurs four times, and it is also used as a general and all-encompassing term. An overview of the section entitled 'Culture and media' reveals that this domain includes print media, popular music, theatre, radio, television and film. There are no occurrences of expressions such as 'our culture' (*vår kultur*), 'our Swedish culture' (*vår svenska kultur*), or 'our common culture' (*vår gemensamma kultur*), but there are two instances of 'our cultural identity' (*vår kulturella identitet*) in the same sentences in which it is claimed that 'Swedish is our utmost bearer of culture' (*svenska är vår främsta kulturbärare*), and one instance of 'our cultural environment' (*vår kulturmiljö*) with reference to the Act concerning ancient monuments and finds (*Kulturminneslag*). Thus, the highly abstract meaning of 'culture' and the nearly total absence of deixis in connection to it seem to reveal that 'culture' is not particularly productive in the text for constructing a sense of 'we-ness'.

A different picture emerges from the patterns of co-occurrence of 'cultural heritage' (*kulturarv*). This expression co-occurs with 'common' (3), 'important' (4), 'language' (3), 'linguistic' (3), 'national minorities' (4), 'our' (6), 'Sweden's' (3), 'Swedish language' (2) and '(Swedish) dialects' (4) in different mutual combinations (therefore the sum of the single instances is higher than the total frequency of 'cultural heritage').

Four observations can be made. First, the word 'cultural heritage' (*kulturarv*) is itself indicative because it underscores a relation – be it factual or imagined – with a historical tradition, which legitimizes what counts as cultural heritage and thereby gives it authenticity. In addition, cultural heritage bears intrinsically the facet of a static and uniform entity which has been handed over from the past and has been transmitted over generations. Second, by claiming that Swedish, (Swedish) dialects and national minority languages 'are an important part of our cultural heritage', specific language varieties are alternately included into the cultural heritage. This entails that the meaning of 'our' shifts accordingly from including all those who historically have lived on the Swedish territory (Swedes together with national minorities), to encompassing only one ethnic group (Swedes). Third, the fact that cultural heritage is determined along an historical axis leads to the implicit and apparently 'natural' exclusion of other language varieties (e.g. immigrant languages) from this domain. Fourth, although national minority languages are heralded as 'an important part of the cultural heritage', only Swedish and Swedish dialects are said to be 'bearers' of this very heritage. Thus, there is a discrepancy in the text between what is *incorporated* into cultural heritage and what *stands* for this very heritage. This can be taken as an example of what Billig (1995: 87) calls a 'syntax of hegemony', that is, the attempt of a part of a polity or of a culture to stand for, or, in *Mål i mun*, 'to bear' the whole.

Postmodernist approaches to text and discourse analysis have taught us that textual discrepancies are the manifestation of an under-lying tension between different discourses and ideologies in their attempt to secure closure for one meaning among an infinite number of possible ones. In the case of the expressions related to the metaphor of the bearer, one can note that, on the one hand, this metaphor is built on the assumption that each language indexes a specific culture and consequently each language and culture is worth being preserved. This can be interpreted as an attempt to account for and accentuate multiculturalism. On the other hand, the same assumption, by linking one language to one culture, contributes to the erasure of both linguistic and cultural diversity, and thereby to the homogenization of language and culture, and to an intrinsic negation of linguistic and cultural hybridity. Moreover, the recourse to an intrinsically static notion – that of cultural heritage – to imagine a symbolic sense of social cohesion, further operates towards the essentialization of a historically bound cultural tradition and the exclusion of certain groups and language varieties from it. Finally, despite the recognition of other language varieties within the cultural heritage, the metonymic representation of Swedish as the 'bearer' of it, instead of highlighting linguistic diversity as a prerogative for cultural diversity, reproduces a static relation between one language indexing and symbolically standing for one, in reality diverse, blended and always changing culture.

To conclude, there is no doubt that *Mål i mun* focuses on Swedish, but it is also a step in a process of recognition of linguistic diversity in Sweden. It is an attempt to mediate between unity and diversity at the civic and symbolic levels of a nation state. At a civic level, the possible tension between a unifying *lingua franca* (Swedish) and the multiplicity of languages spoken in Sweden is neutralized by the recognition and legitimation of the 'right' of every individual to learn and use other language varieties (than Swedish) in certain societal domains, and also by the recognition and tolerance of a large spectrum of variation within Swedish (sociolects, dialects, ethnolects, etc.). By contrast, the symbolic dimension of imagining a culture and a nation displays a more complex picture. Expressions related to the metaphor of the bearer reveal a tension between multiculturalism and social cohesion working to represent and construct the symbolic dimension of the nation state by way of a notion of culture, and what is included and excluded from it.

Conclusion

In the present chapter, I set out to illustrate two aspects of a language ideological debate on the Swedish language, which can be brought together under the common denominator of *voice*. First, the notions of interpellation and iterability have helped show how language discourses tied to Sweden's accession to the EU interpellated linguists and politicians, who became public voices by taking specific stances about the Swedish language, and thereby initiated a language debate. Moreover, it was possible to illustrate how the debate was upheld by the mutual interaction between linguists and politicians through repetition, citation and recontextualization of existing texts and discourses (the discourse on language endangerment and the discourse on English as a global language). Second, textual analysis of one relevant policy document, *Mål i mun*, showed the existence of different, co-existing and competing voices drawing on previous voices and discourses to represent the impact that different phenomena related to globalization (e.g. EU-integration, immigration and the spread of English as a global language) had on the position of Swedish in a multilingual Sweden. The common element these voices share is that Swedish is undergoing some form of endangerment. On the one hand, Swedish is represented as an entity (tool/key) threatened (by English) with regard to the communicative function of *de facto* official language to be used in all public domains. On the other hand, it is portrayed as an entity (bearer) put at risk with regard to both its communicative and symbolic functions, which respectively enable public participation and the imagining of a nation by way of a notion of culture. Regarding the symbolic function, textual analysis revealed a tension between centrifugal voices of multilingualism and multiculturalism which push towards the recognition of a multiplicity of languages and cultures in Sweden and centripetal voices of social cohesion which aim at the achievement not only of a civic/political, but also of a symbolic/cultural national unity.

Acknowledgements

I would like to thank Monica Heller (OISE/University of Toronto), Alexandre Duchêne (University of Basel), Kenneth Hyltenstam (Stockholm University), Sally Johnson (University of Leeds), Aneta Pavlenko (CALPER/Penn State University) and my colleagues at the

Centre for Research on Bilingualism at Stockholm University for their invaluable insights and precious comments on previous draughts of the present chapter. All translations from original texts are mine unless otherwise specified.

References

Althusser, L. (1971), 'Ideology and ideological state apparatuses', in L. Althusser (ed.), *Lenin and Philosophy*. New York/London: Monthly Review Press, pp. 85–126.

Anderson, B. (1991), *Imagined Communities. On the Origin and Spread of Nationalism* (revised edn). London: Verso.

Bakhtin, M. (1981), *The Dialogic Imagination: Four Essays*. Austin, TX: University of Texas Press.

Bakhtin, M. (1986), *Speech Genres and Other Late Essays*. Austin, TX: University of Texas Press.

Billig, M. (1995), *Banal Nationalism*. London: Sage.

Blommaert, J. (1999), 'The debate is open', in J. Blommaert (ed.), *Language Ideological Debates*. Berlin/New York: Mouton de Gruyter, pp. 1–38.

Blommaert, J. (2005), *Discourse: A Critical Introduction*. Cambridge, UK: Cambridge University Press.

Blommaert, J. and Verschueren, J. (1998), *Debating Diversity: Analysing the Discourse of Tolerance*. London: Routledge.

Butler, J. (1997), *Excitable Speech: A Politics of the Performative*. New York/London: Routledge.

Butler, J. (1999), *Gender Trouble: Feminism and the Subversion of Identity* (revised edn). New York/London: Routledge.

Calvet, L.-J. (1974), *Linguistique et colonialisme: petit traité de glottophagie*. Paris: Payot.

Calvet, L.-J. (1987), *La guerre des languages et les politiques linguistiques*. Paris: Payot.

Cobley, P. (ed.) (2001), *The Routledge Companion to Semiotics and Linguistics*. London: Routledge.

Englund, B. (1997), *Skolans tal om litteratur: Om gymnasieskolans litteraturstudium och dess plats i ett kulturellt åter-skapande*. Stockholm: HSL Förlag.

Fairclough, N. (2003), *Analysing Discourse: Textual Analysis for Social Research*. London/New York: Routledge.

Fishman, J. (1991), *Reversing Language Shift: Theoretical and Empirical Foundations of Assistance to Threatened Languages*. Clevedon, U.K.: Multilingual Matters.

Foucault, M. (1980), *Power/Knowledge*. New York: Pantheon Books.

Gal, S. and Woolard, K. (2001), *Languages and Publics: The Making of Authority*. Manchester, UK: St. Jerome.

Heller, M. (1999), 'Heated language in a cold climate', in J. Blommaert (ed.), *Language Ideological Debates*. Berlin/New York: Mouton de Gruyter, pp. 144–70.

193

Hyltenstam, K. (1996), 'Svenskan, ett minoritetsspråk i Europa – och i världen?', in A.-M. Ivars, A.-M. Londen, L. Nyholm, M. Saari and M. Tandefelt (eds), *Svenskans beskrivning 21. Förhandlingar vid tjugoförsta sammankomsten för svenskans beskrivning, Helsingfors den 11–12 maj 1995*. Lund: Stundentlitteratur, pp. 9–33.

Hyltenstam, K. (1999), 'Inledning: Ideologi, politik och minoritetsspråk', in K. Hyltenstam (ed.), *Sveriges sju inhemska språk*. Lund: Studentlitteratur, pp. 11–40.

Hyltenstam, K. (2004), 'Engelskan, skolans språkundervisning och svensk språkpolitik', in Svenska språknämnden (ed.), *Engelskan i Sverige*. Småskrift utgiven av Svenska språknämnden. Stockholm: Norstedts, pp. 36–107.

Hyltenstam, K. and Stroud, C. (1991), *Språkbyte och språkbevarande: Om samiska och andra minoritetsspråk*. Lund: Studentlitteratur.

Hyltenstam, K. and Tuomela, V. (1996), 'Hemspråksundervisningen', in K. Hyltenstam (ed.), *Tvåspråkighet med förhinder*. Lund: Studentlitteratur, pp. 9–109.

Irvine, J. (1989), 'When talk isn't cheap: Language and political economy'. *American Ethnologist*, 16, 248–67.

Ivars, A.-M, Londen, A.-M. Nyholm, L., Saari, M. and Tandefelt M. (eds) (1996), *Svenskans beskrivning 21. Förhandlingar vid tjugoförsta sammankomsten för svenskans beskrivning, Helsingfors den 11-12 maj 1995*. Lund: Stundentlitteratur.

Koller, V. (2004), *Metaphor and Gender in Business Media Discourse: A Critical Cognitive Study*. Basingstoke: Palgrave Macmillan.

Krauss, M. (1992), 'The world's languages in crisis'. *Language*, 68, 4–10.

Kroskrity, P. V. (2000), 'Regimenting languages: Language ideological perspectives', in P. V. Kroskrity (ed.), *Regimes of Languages: Ideologies, Polities and Identities*. Santa Fe: School of American Research Press, pp. 1–34.

Lakoff, G. and Johnson, M. (1980), *Metaphors We Live By*. Chicago: The University of Chicago Press.

Löfgren, O. (1993), 'Nationella arenor', in B. Ehn, J. Fyrkman and O. Löfgren (eds), *Försvenskningen av Sverige. Det nationellas förvandlingar*. Stockholm: Natur och Kultur, pp. 22–118.

Lund, J. (1986), 'Det sprogsociologiske klima i de nordiske lande. Kommentarer og påstande'. *Språk i Norden*, 1986, 34–45.

May, S. (2001), *Language and Minority Rights: Ethnicity, Nationalism and the Politics of Language*. London: Longman.

Milani, T. M. (2006), 'Language planning and national identity in Sweden: A performativity approach', in C. Mar-Molinero and P. Stevenson (eds), *Language Ideologies, Policies and Practices: Language and the Future of Europe*. Basingstoke, UK: Palgrave Macmillan, pp. 104–17.

Oakes, L. (2001), *Language and National Identity: Comparing France and Sweden*. Amsterdam/Philadelphia: John Benjamins.

Pennycook, A. (2001), *Critical Applied Linguistics: A Critical Introduction*. Mahwah, NJ: Lawrence Erlbaum.

Phillipson, R. (1992), *Linguistic Imperialism*. Oxford: Oxford University Press.

Phillipson, R. (2003), *English-Only Europe? Challenging Language Policy.* London: Routledge.

Schiffman, H. (2006), 'Language policy and linguistic culture', in T. Ricento (ed.), *An Introduction to Language Policy: Theory and Method.* Malden, MA: Blackwell Publishing, pp. 111–25.

Stråth, B. (2000), 'The Swedish image of Europe as the other', in B. Stråth (ed.), *Europe and the Other and Europe as the Other.* Brussels: P.I.E. Peter Lang, pp. 359–83.

Svanlund, J. and Westman, M. (1991), 'Svenskans ställning vid europeisk integration', *Språkvård,* 4, 9–11.

Teleman, U. (1989), 'Det nordiska språksamarbetet. Idéer och framtidsuppgifter'. *Språk i Norden,* 1989, 14–32.

Teleman, U. (1992), 'Det svenska riksspråkets utsikter i ett integrerat Europa'. *Språkvård,* 4, 7–16.

Teleman, U. (2003), *Tradis och funkis. Svensk språkvård och språkpolitik efter 1800.* Stockholm: Nordstedts Ordbok.

Teleman, U. and Westman, M. (1997), 'Behöver vi en nationell språkpolitik?'. *Språkvård,* 2, 5–22.

Verschueren, J. (1999), *Understanding Pragmatics.* London: Arnold.

Vikør, L. (2001), *The Nordic Languages: Their Status and Interrelations.* Oslo: Novus Forlag.

Wallerstein, I. (1990), 'Culture as the ideological battleground of the modern world-system'. *Theory, Culture & Society,* 7, 31–55.

Wodak, R., de Cilla, R., Reisigl, M. and Liebhart, K. (1999), *The Discursive Construction of National Identity.* Edinburgh: Edinburgh University Press.

Policy documents

Bet. 1995/96: Kru07. *Språkfrågor.* Kulturutskottets betänkande.

Dir. 1995. *Svenskan i EU.* Kommittédirektiv 1995:81.

Dir. 2000. *Handlingsprogram för det svenska språket.* Kommittédirektiv 2000: 66.

1992/93: U514. *Sverige i EG.* Motion till riksdagen av Ylva Annerstedt m.fl. (fp).

1994/95: U502. *Sveriges agerande i EU.* Motion till riksdagen av Marianne Samuelsson m.fl. (mp).

1994/95: Kr239. *Svenska språket.* Motion till riksdagen av Inger Lundberg och Britta Sundin (s).

1996/97: Kr221. *Svenska språket.* Motion till riksdagen av Lena Larsson (s).

Prop. 1996/97. *Kulturpolitik.* Regeringens proposition 1996/97: 3.

Prop. 1998/99. *Budgetpropositionen för 1999,* Regeringens proposition 1998/99: 1.

Prop. 2005/06. *Bästa språket – en samlad svensk språkpolitik.* Regeringens proposition 2005/06: 2.

Regeringsbeslut 30 April 1997. *Uppdrag till Svenska språknämnden att utarbeta förslag till handlingsprogram för att främja svenska språket* (Stockholm: Riksdagen).

195

SOU 2002. *Mål i Mun. Förslag till handlingsprogram för svenska språket.* Statens Offentliga Utredningar (SOU), 2002: 27. Stockholm: Fritze.

Svenska språknämnden 1998. *Förslag till handlingsprogram för att främja svenska språket.* Stockholm: Svenska språknämnden.

Notes

1 Schiffman (2006: 112) defines linguistic culture as 'the cultural "baggage" that speakers bring to their dealings with language from their culture'.

2 The texts analysed for the purpose of this study are only a part of a larger corpus of academic essays and policy documents covering the period 1970–2003 (see Milani 2006). The cut-off dates of the present study (1990 and 2002) coincide respectively with Sweden's negotiations with the EU and the publication of the Draft action programme for the Swedish language *Mål i mun* (SOU 2002).

3 When the government presents a bill before parliament, MPs are allowed to submit a counter-proposal in the form of a motion on the same topic of the bill. In connection with the Budget Bill, MPs can submit motions on any subject under the jurisdiction of the parliament.

4 At the time of writing, the link has been moved to: www.riksdagen.se/templates/R_SubStartPage___5029.aspx.

5 *Nordiskt språkråd* has been replaced by *Nordens språkråd* since January 2004. Nevertheless, the English denomination Nordic Language Council has been maintained.

6 In the English summary, *Mål i mun* has been translated with *Speech. Draft action programme for the Swedish language.*

7 *Komplett språk* (complete language) refers to the possibility of a language to be used in all domains.

8 The adjective *samhällsbärande* poses translation problems. Literally it means 'society bearing'. In the English summary of *Mål i mun* it has been rendered with 'serving and uniting our society'.

10 Defending English in an English-dominant world: The ideology of the 'Official English' movement in the United States

Ronald Schmidt, Sr.

English has become the dominant language in the world today in the domains of commerce, industry, politics and telecommunications, to name just a few. Within the United States, moreover, the English language holds such sway that virtually all migrant newcomers to the country are clear that their economic and political futures are bound up with their ability to speak and read the country's dominant language as quickly as possible. Further, no immigrant can become a US citizen without first passing an English language exam.

Within this hegemonic, English-dominant environment, nevertheless, the past several decades have witnessed the emergence of a powerful and popular political movement dedicated to defending English as the sole public language of the United States. How can we explain this political movement and the power that it wields in American politics? What motivates those who devote their considerable sums of money, time and energy in this seemingly unnecessary political campaign? What has been their impact on language policy in the United States? Employing critical discourse analysis, this chapter seeks to understand the origins and impacts of the political movement to defend English in an English-dominant world.

The 'Official English' movement in the 'United' States: Description

Political movements to secure English as the sole public language of the United States have existed before in US history. The most prominent of these erupted in the early twentieth century as the country absorbed the several million immigrants who arrived between the 1880s and the 1920s. This movement was especially powerful during and just after the first World War when anti-German sentiment reached a fever pitch in many states, resulting in restrictive legislation and strongly prescriptive policies designed to ensure language shift to English (see e.g. Kloss 1977; Baron 1990; Wiley 1998). With the dramatic decline in immigration that followed the US Congress' adoption of an immigration restriction law in 1924, however, the movement died down.

The contemporary 'Official English' movement – known to its detractors and to some supporters as the 'English Only' movement – formally began on a national level on 27 April 1981, when then-US Senator S. I. Hayakawa (R-California) introduced into the Senate a proposed amendment to the US Constitution which would have designated English as the sole 'official' language of the United States. The movement had been building for some time before that, however, bringing together a variety of individuals and groups united primarily by their opposition to the noticeable expansion of languages other than English in US public and civil society domains (e.g. in schools, hospitals, courtrooms, public parks, recreation facilities, sidewalks, stores, shopping malls, television and radio shows, etc.).

In addition to its goal of amending the Constitution, the movement's primary political efforts have been directed at eliminating most forms of governmental support for the use and reproduction of languages other than English in the US public domain (e.g. bilingual education in the public schools, ballots and elections materials in languages other than English as required by amendments to the *Voting Rights Act* of 1965, provision of public services in languages other than English, etc.). Put differently, the contemporary Official English movement is not opposed to the public schools teaching 'foreign' languages to English speakers, but it is adamantly opposed to the recognition and public support of languages other than English that might be recognized as not 'foreign' but as other 'American' languages. Adherents of the movement believe that the public provision of bilingual education, non-English election materials, and so on, fall into the latter category and therefore must be eliminated from public policy.

An English Language Amendment to the Constitution has been proposed to each US Congress since Hayakawa's initial effort in 1981, but none has ever been brought to a vote in either house. At the state and local levels, however, 'official English' legislation has been much more successful.[1] Proponents have persuaded legislators and voters to adopt policies designating English as the official language in a number of states and localities. By 2005, 27 states had adopted English as their *sole* official language, including many of the states with the highest numbers of speakers of languages other than English (e.g. California, Arizona, Colorado, Florida) (Crawford 2005). Most of these policies are purely symbolic (i.e. they have no enforcement mechanism, simply declaring that English is the state's official language), but others have attempted to limit the public use of languages other than English by public officials and/or service workers. The most far-reaching of these, in Arizona and Alaska, were overturned by the courts.

The movement also has been somewhat successful in its goal of reducing governmental support for the reproduction of non-English languages in the United States. Bilingual education, for example, which was once supported by US Department of Education guide-lines, and by the *Bilingual Education Act* at the national level, has been reduced to a much diminished role under President G. W. Bush's '*No Child Left Behind*' Act.[2] At the state level, moreover, bilingual education has clearly been on the defensive for over a decade, with anti-bilingual education initiatives being approved by voters in several states with large numbers of limited English speaking students (e.g. California, Arizona and Massachusetts). At a time when the number of non-English speaking students has continued to mount dramatically, then, the availability of bilingual education classes has been sharply reduced, in favour of various forms of English immersion classes. Similarly, the *Voting Rights Act*, which serves as the legal foundation for the provision of election materials and ballots in languages other than English, is due to expire in 2007, and there appears to be strong sentiment among majority party Republican legislators to eliminate these aspects of the law.

At the organizational level in the realm of language politics, the two most prominent Official English groups are 'US English' and 'English First' US English is a mass-based organization co-founded in 1983 by former Senator Hayakawa and John Tanton, a retired ophthal-mologist who was previously president of Zero Population Growth and had also founded the Federation for American Immigration Reform (FAIR). The latter organization is one of the nation's leading lobbying groups supporting efforts to limit immigration to the United States. 'US English' is the largest official English group in the country with well over a million members, and has recruited a number of 'star power' names to be on its board of directors over the years, including Walter

Annenberg, Jacques Barzun, Saul Bellow, Bruno Bettelheim, Alistair Cook, Walter Cronkite, Norman Cousins, Angier Biddle Duke, George Gilder, Barry Goldwater, Sidney Hook, Norman Podhoretz, Arnold Schwarzenneger and Karl Shapiro. Some of these luminaries resigned in protest after an embarrassing memo written by John Tanton was inadvertently made public. In the memo, Tanton expressed fears about the nature and character of Latin American immigrants to the US, asking:

> Will Latin American migrants bring with them the tradition of the *mordida* [bribe], the lack of involvement in public affairs? Will the present majority peaceably hand over its political power to a group that is simply more fertile? ... Perhaps this is the first instance in which those with their pants up are going to get caught by those with their pants down! (quoted by Henry 1990: 28).

Also resigning at the time was the organization's first executive director, Linda Chavez, a prominent conservative Republican activist, who went on to found the Center for Equal Opportunity in New York City, a think-tank that has provided a platform for Chavez and other movement activists to mount campaigns against bilingual education, affirmative action and other multiculturalist and race-based policy initiatives.

Meanwhile, the second mass-based official English organization, 'English First', was formed in 1986, founded by Larry Pratt, president of Gun Owners of America, and affiliated with the anti-abortion group Committee to Protect the Family (Henry 1990: 32; Tatalovich 1995: 10). More strident in tone and smaller in size than US English, English First has not achieved the prominence of US English, but both of these groups are mass membership organizations that use mass mailings and the Internet to recruit and mobilize opponents of 'bilingualism' across the country. Both are also quite active in lobbying members of the US Congress and state legislatures across the country in support of their English-only cause.

The rationale for Official English

How does the Official English movement make its arguments? What is the rhetorical strategy deployed by the movement in its defence of the English language in the United States? My previous research[3] has concluded that the movement focuses its rhetoric on two primary arguments. One argument aims to convince the public and public officials that the *common good* requires the US to have only one public language, English. The movement's rationale for this position is that multiple languages would destroy the country's unity by promoting inter-ethnic discord. Thus, for example, a 1984 articulation by US English claimed:

> The United States has been spared the bitter conflicts that plague so many countries whose citizens do not share a common tongue. Historic forces made English the language of all Americans, though nothing in our laws designated it the official language of the nation.
>
> But now English is under attack, and we must take affirmative steps to guarantee that it continues to be our common heritage. Failure to do so may well lead to institutionalized language segregation and a gradual loss of national unity. (US English 1984: 144)

Former Senator Hayakawa was even more pointed in his call for adoption of the Official English amendment to the US Constitution, singling out Latinos in particular as a new source of social division and conflict in US society:

> The ethnic chauvinism of the present Hispanic leadership is an unhealthy trend in present-day America. It threatens a division perhaps more ominous in the long run than the division between blacks and whites. Blacks and whites have problems enough with each other, to be sure, but they quarrel with each other in the same language. Even Malcolm X, in his fiery denunciations of the racial situation in America, wrote excellent and eloquent English.
>
> But the present politically ambitious 'Hispanic Caucus' looks forward to a destiny for Spanish-speaking Americans separate from that of Anglo-, Italian-, Polish-, Greek-, Lebanese-, Chinese-, Afro-Americans and all the rest of us who rejoice in our ethnic diversity, which gives us our richness as a culture, and the English language, which keeps us in communication with each other to create a unique and vibrant culture. (Hayakawa 1985: 11–12)

A more recent articulation of this argument, made by Harvard political scientist Samuel P. Huntington, received widespread notice in newspapers and magazines in the United States in 2004. In several journal articles (2004a, 2004c) and a new book (2004b), Huntington charged that Latino immigrants (and especially Mexican immigrants) are undermining the cultural foundations on which the United States has stood since its inception as an independent country. The abstract of Huntington's widely circulated article in *Foreign Policy* summarizes the point:

> The persistent inflow of Hispanic immigrants threatens to divide the United States into two peoples, two cultures, and two languages. Unlike past immigrant groups, Mexicans and other Latinos have

not assimilated into mainstream U.S. culture, forming instead their own political and linguistic enclaves—from Los Angeles to Miami—and rejecting the Anglo-Protestant values that built the American dream. The United States ignores this challenge at its peril. (Huntington 2004a)

In short, those pushing for an Official English policy in the United States argue that acknowledging and supporting the country's non-English languages, and particularly the Spanish language, would provide a structural foundation for those languages that would lead to intensified inter-ethnic conflict, undermining the national unity of the country. It is for this reason, they argue, that the common good necessitates English as the single common language.

The second rationale for providing public policy support for English as the country's sole official language is couched in the political rhetoric of *justice*. Most English-only political activists begin from the premise that languages other than English exist in the United States only because of recent immigration. They assume, that is, that English has been historically the sole 'American' language, and that it is only because of 'foreign' immigrants that other languages are found in the country. In this context, justice requires that immigrants adopt English as their sole public language for two reasons. First, voluntary immigrants are obligated to adapt to the country (a manifestly English-speaking country) they have chosen freely to migrate to; it is not the obligation of that country to adapt to the languages of its multiple immigrant communities (see, e.g. Imhoff 1990; Huntington 2004a).

And second, becoming fluent in English is the only means for immigrant newcomers to successfully adapt and take advantage of the manifold opportunities for social and economic mobility that exist in the country. Any policy that encourages immigrants to cling to their non-American languages and cultures is an obstacle to immigrants' success in their new country, and thereby does them an injustice. This is the primary argument made by two well-known Hispanic opponents of bilingual education in the United States, Linda Chavez (1991) and Richard Rodriguez (1982). Both argue that Spanish-speaking Latino children are made worse off by bilingual education because it prevents them from acquiring English language fluency, thereby depriving them of full and equal membership in US society. In making this argument, of course, both Chavez and Rodriguez assume that individual bilingualism is not really possible, so that refusing to make English one's *primary* language in effect makes one incapable of English language fluency.

Critique of the rationale for Official English

I have criticized both of these lines of argument for Official English in previous writings (see e.g. Schmidt 2000: Chapter 7), and it is not my purpose here to reiterate that criticism. In very brief summary, my argument is that the historical evidence clearly defeats the claim that English is the sole 'native' language of the United States. Other languages, and especially Spanish, have been native to several large regions of the country (and especially the southwest) since before the United States became an independent state. Moreover, both Spanish speakers, and the speakers of numerous other languages (especially the indigenous populations), initially became 'Americans' not through voluntary immigration but through conquest and annexation. And other ethno-racial communities, too, were initially incorporated through means not accurately described as 'voluntary' immigration. Among these are African Americans (whose communities were established initially via the international slave trade) and, more recently, refugees of a diverse number of foreign policy ventures undertaken by the United States (e.g. Cubans, Filipinos, several Southeast Asian ethnic groups, etc.). I argue that these historical facts undermine the claim that the United States is best understood simply as an 'English-speaking society' in which other languages are derived solely from voluntary immigration. The United States has never been a country in which only English was spoken by virtually all of its population, and many of its other language communities were established through violent acquisition.

In the face of these historical realities, the language policy claims made by Official English advocates are also undermined. For example, if Spanish has been an 'American' language since the US conquered and annexed nearly half of Mexico's territory in 1848, it is not clear that Spanish speaking immigrants have an 'obligation' to adopt English as their primary language as quickly as possible after moving to this country. 'Justice' for non-English speakers is a much more complex problem than that.

It *is* true that English is the *dominant* – indeed, *hegemonic* – language in the country, and has been so since its inception. And given this reality, nearly all immigrants – including Spanish speaking immigrants – are clear that mastering English quickly is in their interests in a variety of ways (e.g. economically, politically, socially). Not surprisingly, then, most students of the subject point to evidence that contemporary non-English speaking immigrants (including those speaking Spanish) are learning English more rapidly than was true during earlier periods of high international migration to the US, such as in the nineteenth and early twentieth centuries.

203

Within this multilingual but hegemonic English-dominant context, moreover, it is not clear that seeking to acknowledge and support the continued existence of non-English speaking cultural communities is a primary source of social and political conflict. Equally compelling, I argue, is that seeking to *impose* English as the *sole* public language in the United States is an injustice that is bound to generate social and political conflict for years to come. Put differently, the evidence is powerful that social and economic incentives for English language shift are so strong in the laissez-faire hegemonic English-dominant environment of the US that mounting a social movement in opposition is highly unlikely *in the absence of direct English-only pressure mounted by the Official English movement.* In short, 'national unity' is undermined far more powerfully by the Official English movement than by the feeble efforts of the relatively weak political groups supporting bilingual education and other policies seeking to acknowledge and support language communities other than those speaking English in the United States. My claim, then, is that both 'justice' *and* the 'common good' require a pluralistic, not an assimilative English-only, language policy.

How to explain the Official English movement?

If English is so clearly the dominant language of the United States, and is not under any realistic 'threat' by other language communities, how then are we to understand the powerful emotional force that is so evident among those assimilationists who make extraordinary efforts to 'defend' English in contemporary American politics? While there are many possible avenues to explore that might bear analytic fruit in trying to answer this important political question, the line of inquiry I want to follow here is one that tries to unpack the social psychology of individual cultural 'threat' from within a culturally hegemonic context. This analysis may help to deconstruct the ideological foundations of the English-only movement.

The best point of departure for this analysis, I think, is to keep firmly in mind the *hegemonic cultural context* of the United States. That is, English *is* the dominant language in the United States and has been so since the country's founding, and this 'English fact' is so powerful that English becomes the de facto, 'common sense' national language. This is what is meant when I claim that English is the *hegemonic* language of the United States.[4] Within this context, English is 'normalized,' and any public actions (by individuals or by social and political groups) that implicitly or explicitly challenge that apparent social reality are experienced as 'abnormal' and 'illegitimate' by those for whom the English fact has been normalized. In this manner, cultural power operates ideologically to legitimate itself.

Within this ideological context, moreover, English-speaking monolinguals may easily experience the presence of non-English language speakers within 'their' public spaces as demeaning or subversive of a legitimate cultural 'reality'. Thus, they experience efforts to gain recognition of the manifest social reality of non-English languages in the United States as attempts to dislodge English from its 'rightful' place in the public life of US society. They feel excluded, 'put down' and often outraged by such counter-hegemonic efforts. In sum, then, a hegemonic language functions to blind most monolingual English-speaking Americans to the social reality of their own privileged position in an ethno-linguistically diverse society. And reminders of this complex social reality operate ideologically to engender feelings of loss, anger or both in the minds and hearts of many monolingual Anglophone Americans. This sense of being displaced by non-English language communities has been captured well by one of political science researcher Joanne Bretzer's respondents in Miami, Florida:

> Before we had our revolution, it was laid back. You could start out in the morning and go down to Matheson Hammock [a local park], take the kids down and stop at Shorty's on the way home. Of course, people, their language--it was very easy to conduct your business, and I miss it, I miss it. I have *lost my city* ... [my emphasis] (Bretzer 1992: 210)

Thus, despite the social and historical 'facts' that English has *never* been the sole language of the people of the United States, and that non-English ethno-linguistic communities have been present in the country since its founding, English language exclusivity is so taken for granted that being confronted with the social and historical facts is experienced as 'abnormal' and 'un-American'. The irony (and injustice) of these ideologically-driven perceptions may be grasped quickly by seeing and hearing (as I have done) recently arrived 'Anglo'[5] residents of *Los Angeles* or *Santa Ana* or *Santa Barbara* express their disgust and revulsion at having to hear the 'foreign' language of Spanish spoken in 'their' (Spanish-named) city.

Underlying this experience of being 'displaced' from one's rightful position in an English-only society by the presence of other ethno-linguistic communities, of course, is a profound ignorance of one's own social and historical context. The ideological power of the hegemonic 'English fact' of the United States functions to keep most contemporary Americans unaware that they and their culture are in such a dominant position in the world today, and that other cultural communities have been part of the fabric of their national life throughout the history of the United States. Thus, if the dominant culture in the world has been one's own since birth, it comes 'for free' just as does (seemingly) the air one breathes. It is (again) 'normal'. And since this culture *is* so dominant, one's own interests provide little incentive to familiarize oneself with, or to master, other languages and cultures. One can simply expect that everyone, everywhere, will know how to speak one's own language – because so often it happens in a US dominant world that these expectations are met by others throughout the world. In this context, being confronted with a 'foreign' cultural community in one's own backyard, so to speak, can seem not only outrageous but downright dangerous.

But what drives the emotional intensity of the English-only movement within such a context? My answer to this question will take its bearings from another aspect of the cultural context of the United States, its *dominant political ideology of liberal individualism*. The argument I want to make relies on the insights of two prominent political theorists, one a nineteenth-century aristocrat, Alexis de Tocqueville, and the other a contemporary radical democrat, Sheldon Wolin. Both argue that the dominant liberal individualist ideology of the United States generates a high degree of individual anxiety that results in a powerful impulse towards conformity. It is this anxiety-driven need for conformity, I think, that best explains the emotional intensity of the English-only movement.

Believing that the European-centred world was being swept by an irresistible movement toward 'equality of condition', Tocqueville came to the United States in 1830 to study what the American experience might teach Europeans about the nature of social and political life under the newly dominant culture of egalitarian democracy. His two volume treatise, *Democracy in America* (Vol. 1, 1835; Vol. 2, 1840), quickly became recognized as among the most astute observations on the culture, and the social and political institutions, of the new country. While Tocqueville had much to praise about democracy in America, he also had many critical judgements to offer about the dangers that accompany the kind of social egalitarianism he encountered in the United States. Among the most insightful of these was his belief that social conformity is a powerful reality in the highly individualistic culture of the United States. The theme of social conformity runs throughout the two volumes, but is succinctly summarized by Tocqueville near the end of the second volume:

> If the influence of individuals is weak and hardly perceptible among such a people, the power exercised by the mass upon the mind of each individual is extremely great; I have already shown

for what reasons. I would now observe that it is wrong to suppose that this depends solely upon the form of government and that the majority would lose its intellectual supremacy if it were to lose its political power. ... [In democratic countries], public favor seems as necessary as the air we breathe, and to live at variance with the multitude is, as it were, not to live. The multitude require no laws to coerce those who do not think like themselves: public disapprobation is enough; a sense of their loneliness and impotence overtakes them and drives them to despair. (Tocqueville, Vol. 2, 1840: 275)

Tocqueville's central explanation for the power of mass opinion on individuals in a democratic country points to the combination of both a highly individualistic culture and the widespread condition of social equality in the United States, so that '*everyone is at once independent and powerless*' (Tocqueville, Vol. 2, 1840: 311, my emphasis). This lack of individual power is traced directly to the equality of social condition:

As men grow more alike, each man feels himself weaker in regard to all the rest; as he discerns nothing by which he is considerably raised above them, he mistrusts himself as soon as they assail him. Not only does he mistrust his strength, but he even doubts of his right; and he is very near acknowledging that he is in the wrong, when the greater number of his countrymen assert that he is so. (Tocqueville, Vol. 2, 1840: 275).

The political effects of this conformism are powerful, in Tocqueville's view, and among them is a strong push for 'uniformity' in public policy:

The very next notion to that of a single and central power which presents itself to the minds of men in the ages of equality is the notion of uniformity of legislation. As every man sees that he differs but little from those about him, he cannot understand why a rule that is applicable to one man should not be equally applicable to all others (Tocqueville, Vol. 2, 1840: 306).

As noted above, Tocqueville wrote from the perspective of a nineteenth-century European aristocrat bent on assessing what was to be gained and lost from the new spectacle of democracy sweeping over his world. Sheldon Wolin, in contrast, writes from the perspective of a contemporary radical democrat bent on exposing the sources of anti-democratic thought that stand as obstacles to democratization. Among the most important of these, he believes, is the belief system of liberal individualism which leads to an anxiety supportive of social conformism.

207

Wolin's chapter on 'Liberalism', first published in the 1960 edition of his highly influential text, *Politics and Vision* (2004 [1960]), asserts that contrary to the claims of many mid-twentieth century scholars of liberalism, the origins of liberal individualistic politics do not lie in an optimistic faith in the perfectibility of humans and society through scientific progress and a free market, but rather lie in an obsessive and gloomy anxiety rooted in '... a fundamental hostility between man and nature' (Wolin 2004: 283). That is, liberal philosophers (e.g. John Locke, Adam Smith) based their understandings of the processes leading to increased human wealth and material progress on a view of nature as a hostile force needing to be subdued, transformed, subjected to human will and conquest. Subsequently, Wolin writes, the nineteenth-century liberal philosopher John Stuart Mill, anticipating Freud, articulated the view that '[t]he irony of progress lay in the fact that it could be achieved only at the expense of man's natural desires and hence of his happiness' (Wolin 2004: 285). This alienation of humans from nature, including their own natures, leads to 'a guilt complex about nature' (Wolin 2004: 283), thus inducing widespread anxiety among adherents of liberalism.

Adding to this anxiety derived from being perpetually at odds with nature, Wolin asserts that liberal philosophers also substituted human 'interests' (rooted in 'passion' and 'desire,' honed by instrumental reason) for the traditional understanding of conscience, and that this substitution was made in the belief that each individual is the best judge of her own welfare (Wolin 2004: 297). This individuation of human well-being was 'disastrous', in part because it easily pits the interests of each individual against those of all others but leaves the individual bereft of traditional (e.g. Christian) sources of moral guidance, all of which leads once again to a heightened and perpetual anxiety.

Partly as a consequence of this heightened anxiety, Wolin argues, liberalism – an avowedly individualistic political ideology – in fact is 'addicted' to social conformity:

> Liberalism has always been accused of seeking to dissolve the solidarities of social ties and relationships and to replace them by the unfettered, independent individual, the masterless man. In reality, the charge is almost without foundation and completely misses the liberal addiction towards social conformity. (Wolin 2004: 307)

The path from liberal individualism to social conformity is traced by Wolin through the understandings of Locke, Smith and the later Utilitarians, and is derived initially from Locke's separation of 'society' from the political community. Existing prior to, and apart from, political authority, society and social norms are viewed by Locke, for example, as the real foundations for individual conscience. In reasoning remarkably similar to that of Tocqueville, Wolin articulates liberalism's move towards social conformity as based on 'the law of opinion or reputation' deriving from Locke's

> ... observation that men exercised 'the power of thinking well or ill, approving or disapproving of the actions of those whom they live amongst.' These judgments tend to become 'the common measure of virtue and vice' and, in many ways, to punish violators more effectively than positive law. No man, Locke noted, can endure being at odds with his 'club' and no man can live conscious that he is disliked by all. 'This is a burden too heavy for human sufferance.' (Wolin 2004: 307–8).

Thus, Wolin concludes, 'the heavy sanctions which society could bring to bear – economic, social, and psychological – rendered an act of defiance far more consequential to the individual than any action of a private variety' (Wolin 2004: 308). Ultimately, in Wolin's analysis, what drove liberalism to its addiction to social conformity was that the philosophy's foundation was not, as later liberals claimed, its commitment to individualism, but rather its commitment to avoid any form of authority that is 'personal or personified'.

In Wolin's view, in short, it is precisely the anonymity and deper-sonalized nature of social conformity that makes its power acceptable to liberalism, along with the power of the market and other mecha-nized forms of decision-making (Wolin 2004: 311–13). But this very anonymity undermines liberals' ability to see that their 'individuals' are performing very public and tightly scripted social roles, thereby enabling them to see themselves as autonomous individuals. The contemporary political philosophy claiming to be the foundation for individual 'freedom', in short, is rather a philosophy that paradoxically undermines the bases for genuine individuality, driving its hapless adherents toward social conformity. Under these circumstances, what happens when the Other is inescapably part of, or introduced into, this social and political setting? More specifically, how does a political culture founded on beliefs in 'invisible hands' guiding social and political development towards greater progress deal with the realities of social and cultural difference?

A recent analysis of the relationship between 'democracy and the foreigner' by political theorist Bonnie Honig (2001), is very helpful, I think, in answering these questions in a way that illuminates the emotional power that drives the English-only movement in the United

States. More specifically, Honig's analysis of the special role played by American myths about immigrants helps to explain Americans' ability to shore up (but also undermine) their ideological understandings of their national identity and their understandings of how the United States 'works' as a political economy and society. Articulating her analysis here will, I hope, help to further unpack the social psychological forces driving the emotional intensity of the English-only movement.

Honig begins from the premise that all national identities are socially constructed (and endlessly re-constructed) through discourses among competing political elites. Unlike many theorists, however, she argues as well that these discourses take place *within* our individual selves (elites and non-elites alike), as tensions or ambivalences in our perceptions, values and beliefs, embedded in the complexities of the human psyche.

Within this context of national identity formation in the United States, moreover, Honig argues that *immigrants* play a vital role in maintaining and resurrecting central myths that sustain Americans' understanding of themselves as a nation. In particular, Honig posits four key mythic themes of national revival in which immigrants play the central redemptive role. These themes are the 'capitalist, communal, familial, [and] liberal' (Honig 2001: 74). In the capitalist version of the American myth, first, 'the immigrant functions to reassure workers of the possibility of upward mobility in an economy that rarely delivers on that promise, while also disciplining native-born poor, domestic minorities, and unsuccessful foreign laborers into believing that the economy fairly rewards dedication and hard work' (Honig 2001: 74).

The second, 'communitarian immigrant', myth 'responds to the dissolution of family and community ties' generated by 'a capitalist economy's unresisted need for a mobile labor force' (Honig 2001: 74). Third, the 'familial' myth portrays immigrants as 'saviors of traditional patriarchal family arrangements that have been variously attenuated by capitalist mobility and materialism, liberal individualism, and feminism' (Honig 2001: 74).

And finally (fourth), 'liberal consent theorists' look to immigrants to solve the problem of political legitimacy in a country in which government claims to be based on the 'consent of the governed', but native-born citizens are rarely given opportunities to explicitly consent to be governed. As Rousseau understood, Honig states, 'merely periodic practices such as voting do not position citizens to experience the law as their own' rather than as imposed by undemocratic authoritarian rulers (Honig 2001: 74). Genuinely experienced consent of the governed requires more than occasional voting by a shrinking electorate and the 'tacit consent' said by some liberal theorists to have been given by those of us who continue to live unexamined political lives in our country of birth. Under these conditions, Honig suggests, immigrants come to the rescue 'through the agency of foreignness': 'The regime's legitimacy is shored up by way of the explicit consent of those celebrated foreigners – immigrants – who, almost daily are sworn into citizenship in the nation's naturalization ceremonies' (Honig 2001: 75).

These four themes of the positive, even redemptive, contributions made to American well-being by immigrants, Honig asserts, combine into an iconic 'supercitizen' who

> somehow manages to have it all – work, family, community, and a consensual relation to a largely nonconsensual democracy – even though these very goods are experienced by the rest of us as contradictory or elusive: work in late modern capitalist economies often demands hours and mobilities that are in tension with family and community commitments; meaningful consent eludes the native born ... (Honig 2001: 78)

While these images of iconic supercitizens help to revitalize Americans' faith in their nation's virtues and opportunities, the elusiveness of their achievement by the native-born at the same time reinforces a mirror-image *negative* symbol for each of the contributions made to American national identity by immigrants. Thus, xenophilia is intimately intertwined with xenophobia in Honig's gothic analysis. The negative side of the economically upwardly mobile immigrant's supercitizen image, for example, is that of the foreigner who takes from the country's economy to enrich himself and his family without accepting and sharing the burdens of contributing to the well-being of the local or national community.

More directly related to the 'Official English' policy debate, the negative side of the communitarian supercitizen is the 'clannish' immigrant who insists on living in ethnic 'enclaves' where he/she continues to speak a 'foreign' tongue and resists integration into the larger (individualistic, anomic, conformist) society. Similarly, the negative side of the politically 'consenting' supercitizen is the foreigner, probably an 'illegal' immigrant, who takes the government's services and tax-dollars without ever naturalizing as a citizen.[6]

Honig's point is that each of these intertwined images of immigrants, those generating both xenophilia and xenophobia, is a powerful symbol performing important work in shoring up the ambivalent and fragile hold on our psyches of our assumptions about American nationalism. It is through these powerful ideological images

– negative *and* positive – that we see the emotionally powerful stakes that Americans might have in the behaviour of the immigrant. To restore and revive the health and vitality of their American national identities (particularly, the communal and the liberal), they *need* to see the immigrant choose to transform her/himself into an 'American', which is to actively replay the national mythic drama of Americanization, moving out of the ethnic enclave and adopting English as her/his only public language. In the absence of such recurring reinforcement, the grasping materialism, alienating and divisive de-communalization and coercive manipulation experienced in the contemporary American political economy become all too evident. Failure of the immigrant to perform her/his 'work' in the service of our (conformist) national identity, accordingly, is experienced as ingratitude, rejection and an opportunistic exploitation of 'real' Americans.

The problem with this scenario, as noted above and as Honig points out as well, is that it fails to capture important parts of the American national experience. Puerto Ricans living on the mainland, for example, are not immigrants at all, but US citizens whose origins lie in a Spanish-language dominant Caribbean island that the US forcibly took from Spain in 1898. Unlike immigrants, Puerto Ricans do not have to pass an English language test to become US citizens – like other native-born Americans, they acquire their membership through birth and not through a voluntary (and self-transformative) act of 'consent'.

Similarly, Mexicans who migrate north to the southwestern US are 'returning' to a land that was taken from their country by force (after the US military invaded Mexico City) in 1848, and from which their culture and language (as well as the people practising them) have never been erased. In the historical context in which Mexican immigrants find themselves after arriving in the US, 'assimilation' as Americans need not imply substituting English for Spanish in their public lives, but might instead mean learning to live a bilingual, bicultural life both privately and publicly, as do many native-born Mexican-origin U.S. citizens. Attending to *these* realities of the American experience would enable Americans to see other stakes in the Official English debate that might have equally powerful emotional impacts leading in directions different from that of an English-only approach. The question, of course, is how such a counter-hegemonic political move might be made more effective. That question, however, must wait for another analysis at another time.

Conclusion

This paper has raised the question of how we might explain the extraordinary (and seemingly inexplicable) political efforts made in the United States to 'defend' the English language in a global and national context in which English is clearly the dominant language in the world today. After describing and critiquing the claims made by the Official English political movement in the contemporary United States, the paper has aimed at understanding the motivations underlying that movement. My analysis has focused on the ideological power of the English 'fact' of the United States which derives from the hegemonic position of the English language in US society. That power, I claim, blinds most Americans to their own privileged position in US society and to the social reality of non-English languages and ethnolinguistic minority communities. Further, it functions to legitimate the feelings of loss and displacement experienced by monolingual Anglophone Americans at the sound and sight of non-English languages in 'their' public spaces. The analysis is extended by drawing upon the arguments of both a nineteenth-century conservative European aristocrat (Tocqueville) and a contemporary radical democrat (Wolin), both of whom claim that America's uniquely liberal individualistic public philosophy pushes individuals under its sway towards a powerful social conformity that is emotionally driven by heightened anxiety towards an unusually intense hostility to social and cultural difference. The analysis is illuminated, finally, by Honig's insightful deconstruction of the ideological 'work' performed by immigrants in shoring up certain central myths that sustain Americans' understanding of their society. In sum, it is hoped that this analysis has shed some light on the seemingly inexplicable political efforts to defend English in the contemporary United States.

References

Baron, D. (1990), *The English-Only Question: An Official Language for Americans?* New Haven: Yale University Press.

Bretzer, J. (1992), Language, power and identity in multiethnic Miami, in J. Crawford (ed.), *Language Loyalties: A Source Book on the Official English Controversy.* Chicago: University of Chicago Press, pp. 209–16.

Chavez, L. (1991), *Out of the Barrio: Toward a New Politics of Hispanic Assimilation.* New York: Basic Books.

Crawford, J. (2002), 'Obituary: The Bilingual Education Act, 1968–2002'. Article posted on Crawford's Language Policy Website: http://ourworld.compuserve.com/homepages/JWCRAWFORD/T7obit.htm.

Crawford, J. (2005), Language Policy Website: http://ourworld.compuserve.com/homepages/JWCRAWFORD/langleg.htm.

213

Hayakawa, S. I. (1985), *One Nation ... Indivisible? The English Language Amendment*. Washington: The Washington Institute for Values in Public Policy.

Henry, S. (1990), 'English only: the language of discrimination'. *Hispanic: The Magazine For And About Hispanics* (March), 28–32.

Honig, B. (2001), *Democracy and the Foreigner*. Princeton: Princeton University Press.

Huntington, S. P. (2004a), 'The Hispanic challenge'. *Foreign Policy*, (March/April). Available at www.foreignpolicy.com/story/cms.php?story_id=2495&PHPSESSID=5e2867aff94461a7a95dd8fe49c70dc1.

Huntington, S P. (2004b), *Who Are We: The Challenges to America's National Identity*. New York: Simon and Schuster.

Huntington, S. P. (2004c), 'One nation, out of many'. *The American Enterprise* (September). Available at www.taemag.com/issues/articleid.18144/article_detail.asp.

Imhoff, G. (1990), 'The position of U.S. English on bilingual education'. *The Annals of the American Academy of Political and Social Science*, 508, 48–61.

Kloss, H. (1977), *The American Bilingual Tradition*. Rowley, MA: Newbury House Publishers, Inc.

Laitin, D. D. (1986), *Hegemony and Culture: Politics and Religious Change among the Yorubas*. Chicago: University of Chicago Press.

Rodriguez, R. (1982), *Hunger of Memory: The Education of Richard Rodriguez*. Boston: David R. Godine, Publisher.

Schmidt, R. Sr. (2000), *Language Policy and Identity Politics in the United States*. Philadelphia: Temple University Press.

Schmidt, R. Sr. (2002), 'Racialization and language policy: the case of the U.S.A'. *Multilingua*, 21, 141–61.

Tatalovich, R. (1995), *Nativism Reborn? The Official English Language Movement and the American States*. Lexington: The University Press of Kentucky.

de Tocqueville, A. (1945 [1835, 1840]), *Democracy in America*. New York: Vintage Books.

US English, (1984), in defense of our common language ..., reprinted in J. Crawford (ed.), *Language Loyalties: A Source Book on the Official English Controversy*. Chicago: University of Chicago Press, 1992, pp. 143–7.

Wiley, T. G. (1998), 'The imposition of World War I era English-only policies and the fate of German in North America', in T. Ricento and B. Burnaby (eds), *Language and Politics in the United States and Canada: Myths and Realities*. Mahwah, NJ: Lawrence Erlbaum Associates, pp. 211–42.

Wolin, S. S. (2004 [1960]), *Politics and Vision: Continuity and Innovation in Western Political Thought* (Expanded Edition). Princeton: Princeton University Press.

Notes

1 See Tatalovich 1995, for a detailed study of this movement at the state and local levels.
2 See Crawford 2002, for an analysis of the language policy provisions of the *No Child Left Behind Act.*
3 The fullest exposition of this research is in Schmidt 2000; see also Schmidt 2002.
4 That is, hegemonic cultural power exists when one set of cultural relations is so powerful that operating within it is experienced as 'common sense'. My use of the term 'hegemony' has been shaped importantly by David Laitin's interpretation of Gramsci's pathbreaking work on the subject (see Laitin 1986).
5 'Anglo' is a term often used in California and the US Southwest to describe an Anglophone person of European ancestry.
6 US naturalization, of course, involves taking an exam to demonstrate one's proficiency in one language, English, as well as renouncing one's former citizenship.

11 Protecting French: The view from France[1]

Claudine Moïse

France's ideological position is clear, affirmed since the Age of the Enlightenment and strongly advanced by the Revolution of 1789. From a social contract perspective, the *nation* rests on the political willingness of individuals to live in a society from which flows a common cultural vision. The Revolution of 1789 imposed a unique citizenship, indifferent to distinctiveness and, consequently, to minority groups. The fight for the French language and French cultural values then allowed for the reproduction of the dominant ideology and asserted the legitimacy of the Republic as nation state. But today, the two oft-brandished sections of the Constitution, section 1 'La France est une République indivisible, laïque, démocratique et sociale' ['*France is an indivisible, secular, democratic and social Republic*'], and section 2, 'La langue de la République est le français' ['*The language of the Republic is French*'], are largely challenged by values that are considered as threatening, i.e. multiculturalism and multilingualism.

We will see in this chapter how French is construed as an endangered language. The French language was constructed throughout the centuries around the unification of the state and territory. The discourse on language has contributed to the construction of the nation state, and political authorities have always tried to maintain, until the 1990s, the values attributed to French in order to achieve national cohesion and international influence. Fears of seeing the language undermined and corrupted are not new. It is a matter of fighting against the heterogeneous forces perceived as threatening for the public space and for the construction of national order, forces that could run counter to power and the reproduction of the dominant elite. Today, however, the protection strategies used both inside and outside the territory are wearing out and numerous political crises and ideological tensions (e.g. the legislation which prohibits Muslim girls from wearing a veil in public schools and the elimination of dialectal Arabic from the school curriculum), indicative of the social changes caused in part by globalization, seem to be moving from the field of language to that of cultural identity.

216

The French language, foundation of the Republic

1. The historic making of a social body

The link that has been established between language and power, since the Carolingians and the division of Charlemagne's empire between Charles the Bald and Louis the Germanic into a Francophone part and a German one, is particularly ancient. Very early on, French was used to ensure centralization and state control of the territory. With the reign of Louis XIV, which was followed by that of the Age of Enlightenment, of reason and of universalism, the French language – like the arts or dance for other areas – served the political in a way which was both understood and expected. Social control and public order were dictated by words and the body. The codification of the language (what is correct and what is not), begun in the sixteenth century, intensified throughout the seventeenth century. A distinctive sign of social belonging, the right way of speaking, devoid of dialect or social variation, drew marked boundaries. Standardized language still defined correct behaviour as a means of recognizing various groups, more specifically the elite, the king's court, which was exposed to the public sphere. If, from 1500 to 1660, it was the language spoken by the people of the 'better world' (Lodge 1997), and if it hunted down dialectal features under the pretext of precision and rigour, French became, in the Age of Enlightenment, from Louis XIV to the Revolution, the language of clarity and reason, an ideology set as unshakeable dogma, a language legitimized by the dominant classes for the dominant classes. Rational order as expressed through language was also called upon in the defence of the natural order of words while the inversion of the subject was brandished as belonging to the domain of passions and emotional disorder, an old quarrel between the Ancients and the Moderns from Descartes to Condillac. Thus, right from that time, reason's primacy over the sensual saturated? Maybe permeated – the consciousness of the French, and, from control of the body to the restraint of the word, the model of propriety and excellence began with the disciplined mind. Civility, as advocated in the seventeenth century, most likely helped to move away from the religious civil wars and to rebuild the social body (Merlin-Kajman 2003); but it was also a form of socio-political domination by the political body and it defined contours of the public space, keeping out any variations or other languages.

We know how, afterwards, the French Revolution and the third Republic used the French language to build citizenship, how an egalitarian, unifying and homogeneous public space was defined, how language, through the school system as reproducer of republican values, espoused secular values. The nation language became sacred and its authority rested on the 'French genius', worthy of divine power (Balibar 1995: 288). Secularism became a religion and was relayed by the sacred book, the French language dictionary as Bernard Cerquiglini[2] (2003) expresses it:

> Ainsi, le monolinguisme institutionnel semble bien avoir pris rang et fonction de religion d'Etat, par déplacement du sacré, dans le temps que l'Etat se laïcisait. Religion monothéiste, qui reconnaît un seul dieu : la langue française ; religion du Livre (LE diction-naire, tenu, contre toute évidence, pour infaillible et immuable); religion prosélyte, comme toutes les religions du Livre : on sait l'ambition internationale du français, le messianisme quasi constitutif de cette langue et l'ardeur diplomatique en la matière (Cerquiglini 2003).

> *Thus, institutional monolingualism seems to have taken up rank and function as state religion, through the displacement of the sacred, while the state was secularizing itself. A monotheistic religion, which recognizes only one god: the French language; a religion of the Book (THE dictionary, held, against all evidence, as infallible and unchanging); a proselytizing religion, as are all religions of the Book: the international ambition of French, the near-constituent messianism of this language and the diplomatic ardour in the matter are all well known.*

To these secular virtues, one must add the moral and civic values attributed to the French language (Gadet 2003: 21): the public space was to be built in French, the long hard road to learning how 'not to make mistakes' became a distinctive sign and a force for empow-erment. Access to 'correct French', through the idea of democracy, via equality and meritocracy, contributed to the reproduction of the elite.

2. The invention of universalism

National homogeneity – beyond the citizen's social and political contract – manifests itself through a universalist ideology, as advocated by Rivarol (1783) in his essay on the universality of the French language which, in 1783, won the Berlin Academy of Science and Literature Prize, and as carried by a language worthy of thought and reason, a pure, structured and civilizing language. When Alexandre Dumas' ashes were transferred to the Panthéon, many newspapers dedicated articles to this national writer. Above comments by Jean Dutourd, of the Académie française, and by Denise Bombardier, high priestess of beautiful French, one of these articles, published in the 25 July 2002 edition of *Paris Match*, declared 'Dumas est la preuve que l'on peut être d'origine africaine, devenir français, et maîtriser mieux que personne notre langue'. ['*Dumas is proof that one can be of African origin, become French and master our language better than anyone.*'] (p.7). As if one has to be French to master the French language, as if the French language could not belong to Africans. In short, as if French were a possession of France and capable of civilizing,[3] an old hymn of the colonial empire brought back to life from time to time through media discourse. French and the values it holds are a possession of France and a civilizing issue; it is only recently, as we shall see, that the question of regional varieties – such as the metropolitan French variety, diverse varieties from other Francophone regions, post-colonial varieties or languages of immigration – is raised. In fact, the sought-after purity echoes the fear of the multiple and the fear of complexity so dear to Edgar Morin (2004), a fear linked to strangeness in a need to reproduce a homogeneous social body favourable to the national elite which takes strength in its self-legitimacy. If there is any democracy in the French language, inside and outside of national boundaries, there are always some citizens who are more equal than others. Within the colonial empire, where universalist and civilizing ideas were meant to be spread through the French language, the languages of the concerned countries were foreign languages. The code of nativeness, established in Algeria in the 1830s and abolished only in 1945, introduced a specific legal system for natives. Areas of daily life, like dress codes or the banning of traditional holidays, could be subject to particular offences and special violations.

Feelings of threat and political resistance

Even if the reality of languages lies in the multiple, the centralizing building of the national order has crossed the centuries against all heterogeneous forces, constantly reaffirming its unifying republican strength in the French language.

1. The theme of threat

Threat metaphors have been perpetuated from one century to another since complaints were made against Italian borrowings in the sixteenth century, and they are still numerous today in books on the correct use of the language or in readers' columns. The purity image of a disappearing homogeneous language is an old fear; this fear concerns the integrity of the language, the system itself, and often leads to political decisions regarding corpus and status,[4] as means to recover the affirmation of an identified, identifiable and unified social body. The

seventeenth century was characterized by the search for a common
language, a classical language, through dictionaries and the Académie,
and the hunting down of provincialisms and borrowings (Wionet
2005). The late nineteenth and early twentieth centuries, with the
implementation of compulsory, free and secular schooling, witnessed
the blacklisting of regional demands and liberation movements, such
as Félibrige in Provence.[5] These opposition forces were later rejuve-
nated in the regional minority movements of the 1970s. Let us now
take a look at some recent actions and protective reactions of the
1990s with respect to language. There was, in 1989, an attempt made
to reform spelling. Although the proposed changes were very limited,
reactions were numerous, highly critical and impassioned. These were
not so much about how the language itself works, but more about larger
themes of national protection, 'de défense de la patrie ou de l'âme du
peuple' ['*the defense of the homeland or the soul of the people*'] (Eloy
2000: 101). There was the 1994 Toubon law, which related to the 'usage
of the French language', especially in advertising, work contracts and
instruction manuals, and was in fact a measure against anglicisms,
symbols of linguistic impurity. Although the law was criticized by the
Constitutional Council in the name of freedom of expression, it was
highly symbolic of the state's affirmation, with the establishment of the
European Union and the advent of globalization, of the need to defend
the French fact and national unity. There was also a certain media
coverage of the decisions made by the terminology commissions which
were put in place in government departments in the 1970s and which
reaffirmed the use of French and unborrowed neologisms as a way to
legitimize once again the merits and values of the French language.

The main focus of the fears of losing and undermining the language
was nevertheless on the school system as reproducer of the national
ideology. The theme of the language crisis in education appeared at the
beginning of the twentieth century, and is still alive today. We still hear
people speak about the poor quality of French and its degeneration,
exemplified by the lack of vocabulary among young people and their
deficient spelling skills. After cutting budgets for artistic activities in
2003, the department of education reinforced the teaching of grammar
at the primary level. In October 2004, following a major national
debate on the future of the school system, the commission chaired by
Claude Thélot (2004) submitted a report in which it insisted on the
need for a 'common core':

> Pour éclairer des orientations possibles, le socle commun des
> indispensables pourrait comprendre les fonctions primordiales
> suivantes : lire, écrire, maîtriser la langue et les discours, compter,
> connaître les principales opérations mathématiques, s'exprimer (y

compris en anglais de communication internationale), se servir de l'ordinateur, vivre ensemble dans notre République. (p. ii)

To shed light on potential directions, the common core of essential tools could include the following key functions: reading, writing, mastering the language and discourses, adding, knowing mathematical operations, speaking (including in international English), using computers, living together in our Republic.

This once again reasserted the primary role of the school in learning to master French and the Republic's values. In her time, Nicole Gueunier (1985) researched what the term 'crisis' covered and had suggested the following: deprofessionalization, linguistic insecurity of the middle classes, population explosion in the schools and media influence. In short, French, more visible and present in the social space which had been invested by a certain idealized standard associated with the elites whose legitimacy was now threatened, was displaying greater variations which could give rise to fears of seeing the language of reference undermined.

2. A loss of benchmarks and power

The age-old discourse on language and the threats it faces is very much present at times of crises and social transformations. The language crisis 'n'est qu'un aspect particulier d'un phénomène plus vaste: celui d'un effondrement des valeurs' ['*is but a specific aspect of a wider phenomenon: that of the collapse of values*'] (Klinkenberg 2001: 110). As Gadet has shown (2003: 21), the discourse on language protection gets more strident during political moments of social debate: in the 1900s (clash of two models of society, the rural and the urban), in the 1930s (economic crisis, threat of war), in the 1960s (persistence of school failure, decline of the international status of French, loss of the colonial empire). I would add the 1990s (Maastricht Treaty, globalization). The republican model is confronted with the collapse of the past grandeur of a conquering nation and of its world influence; it also feels threatened from the inside by various groups, especially immigration groups, which challenge the established social stratification and their own invisibility in the public space. It is then a crisis of *conscience or confidence* (Klinkenberg 2001: 109) which affects all majority languages; French, for its part, tries to counter the malaise by becoming a unifying and aesthetic element in a world which has lost its benchmarks.

At this stage of our reflection, it is interesting to look more closely, among other things, at a recent form of protection strategy, which has

221

shown once again how, through lively debate and legal argumentation, the French state has tried to protect the French language against the varieties that exist on its own territory.

3. The European Charter for Regional or Minority Languages: an example of a protectionist strategy

The objective of the *European Charter for Regional or Minority Languages* is to recognize, essentially as heritage property, regional languages within Member States. It was signed by France on 7 May 1999; this led to a general outcry and exacerbated the passions in a cult of the nation. The Minister of the Interior, J.-P. Chevènement, talked of the balkanization of France. The Constitutional Council, to which the case was referred on 20 May 1999 by the Head of State, declared publicly on 16 June that the commitments made by France under the Charter were contrary to several fundamental principles, namely the indivisibility of the Republic. To move towards the ratification of the Charter, French authorities had to accept a constitutional review. Although the concrete commitments (i.e. those sections which were signed) did not infringe on the constitutional standards, the preamble to the Charter, along with section 7, which was of a constraining and general nature, were judged (Décision 99–412, 1999) to be contrary to the Constitution 'en ce qu[ils confèrent] des droits spécifiques à des groupes de locuteurs de langues régionales ou minoritaires, à l'intérieur de territoires dans lesquels ces langues sont pratiquées' ['*in that they conferred specific rights to groups of regional or minority language speakers inside territories in which these languages are practiced*'] (Décision 99–412, 1999). These provisions were contrary to the 'principes constitutionnels d'indivisibilité de la République, d'égalité devant la loi et d'unicité du peuple français' ['*constitutional principles of indivisibility of the Republic, of equality before the law and of the unicity of the French people*'] (Décision 99–412, 1999). The Council argued that these three principles 's'opposent à ce que soient reconnus des droits collectifs à quelque groupe que ce soit, défini par une communauté d'origine, de culture, de langue ou de croyance' ['*were opposed to the recognition of collective rights to any group, as defined by a community of origin, culture, language or belief*'] (Décision 99–412, 1999). Who would have dared to engage in a discussion on the indivisibility of the Republic? The provisions of the Charter were also contrary to the rule established by section 2 under which 'la langue de la République est le français' ['*the language of the Republic is French*'] (Décision 99–412, 1999). Now, according to the members of the council, 'la Charte tend à reconnaître un droit à pratiquer une langue autre que le français non seulement dans la vie privée mais également dans la vie publique' ['*the Charter tended to recognize the right to practice a language other than French not only in private life but also in public life'*] (Décision 99–412, 1999). The media themselves understood to what extent these decisions were motivated by ideological considerations:

> Peine perdue : la timidité du texte volontairement consensuel, qui visait à donner satisfaction aux régionalistes tout en calmant les ardeurs jacobinistes, n'a pas convaincu les gardiens de la loi fondamentale. Lesquels se sont livrés à une gymnastique juridique pour le moins contestable : les arguments du Conseil pour censurer la ratification de la carte ressemblent plus à un manifeste idéologique qu'à un exercice de droit. (Vallaeys 1999: 6)
>
> *It was of no use: the timidity of the voluntarily consensual text, which was intended to satisfy regionalists as well as to calm jacobinist ardours, did not convince the guardians of the constitution. The latter engaged in somewhat questionable legal gymnastics: the arguments of the Council to suppress the ratification of the Charter looked more like an ideological manifesto than a legal exercise.*

On 23 June, 1999, the President of the Republic, Jacques Chirac, made public his refusal to engage in a constitutional review process in the matter. Thus, in the name of the high principles of indivisibility of the nation, of private/public separation, of the non-recognition of groups, the Charter could not be ratified. It must be noted that the authors of the Charter had always taken care not to undermine the prerogatives of member countries.

Thus, in spite of phrasing whose ideological scope was felt to be weak, the objections raised showed to what extent France could be disturbed about its language. Fortunately, and in spite of the perceived threat against the state's unilingualism, the Charter was signed by the President of the Republic[6] and 75 languages were recognized as languages of France (metropolitan France, departments and overseas territories). In addition to the languages 'without territories' that he preferred to call 'historical languages', Bernard Cerquiglini (1999) revisited the concept of *territorial* languages, but in the end from a political rather than a linguistic perspective:

> Ce désir d'une assise géographique des langues régionales [...] s'oppose en outre aux principes républicains français, qui tiennent que la langue, élément culturel, appartient au patrimoine national; le corse n'est pas la propriété de la région de Corse, mais de la nation [...]. Le vrai territoire d'une langue est le cerveau de ceux qui la parlent.

> *The desire for a geographic basis for regional languages runs against the French republican principles which state that language, a cultural element, belongs to the national heritage; Corsican does not belong to the region of Corsica, but to the nation [...]. The real territory of a language is the brain of those who speak it.*

Even though he lent himself to an ideological discourse, even though he used arguments that were more political than socio-linguistic (Moïse 2000), we can be thankful to the author for having drawn a complete and precise socio-linguistic landscape of the languages found on the French territory,[7] and for having admitted into the languages of France[8] the 'non-territorialized' languages related to France's national history, which are not official languages of other countries, languages not of migrants but of French citizens, i.e. Maghrebian Arabic, Western Armenian, Berber, Yiddish, Romani, Judaeo-Spanish.

This lengthy ideological debate about the Charter is especially interesting as it revealed the different threats evoked against national unity: the obliteration of the French language by regional languages, the loss of purity, the break-up of the republican cohesion, the inter-penetration of the public and private spheres. One of the foundations of the French model is the '"neutralisation" de l'espace public' ['*"neutralization" of public space*'] (Semprini 1997: 109), a neutralization which has been given a particularly rough ride these last few years. According to this principle, cultural, religious and ethnic differences are only expressed in private space. The public space is for the expression of citizenship by citizens detached from their distinctiveness, from their cultural identity; secular, free, brotherly citizens, strongly bonded together in their republican commitments. The public space is therefore considered the space for the political, the space assigned to common affairs and the separation of private and public guarantees 'le dépassement des intérêts individuels ou de groupes, elle est le lieu de débat démocratique, du déploiement de la raison, de la mise en forme et de l'application du droit' ['*the surpassing of individual or group interests; it is the place for democratic debate, for reasoning, for the development and application of the law*'] (Wieviorka 1997: 21). Equality is therefore inherent to this model, rational and necessary; it is shaped and becomes tangible thanks to the social contract between citizens, a symbolic act which marks everyone's agreement with the Republic's values. A rally beyond differences. The law, 'expression of the general will', under section 6 of the Declaration of the Rights of Man and of the Citizen (1789), is the gatekeeper and guarantor, a way of maintaining in public reality the ideological and social order. But everything falters when equality, as decreed by the holders of the dominant power, is questioned by those who feel wronged by it, when access to their own recognition, through their language among other things, is denied.

If the contentious forces, particularly around regional languages, were very much present before the events surrounding the Charter, especially in the 1970s, all dominant certainties wavered in the late 1990s, and it seems that the vested national power was no longer so clear-cut. There are many reasons for these changes and they are strongly linked to the ideological upheaval brought about by globalization as well as by North–South relations.

The years 2000: crystallization of the crisis of the French Republic

With the end of the previous century, the opening up of Europe, globalization and new tensions with the South, symbolized by September 11, power struggles changed and greatly undermined the French conception of nation. Among other things, in France, these world changes shifted the open debate on language to more cultural issues. Though not completely absent, the French language is indeed no longer in the forefront, it is no longer at the heart of the debates, and has become part of cultural tensions, as we shall see. Fears are no longer driven by the omnipresence of English, by regional languages nor by spelling, in short by the preservation of a homogeneous language, but by the cultural links with Mediterranean countries, often identified and stigmatized through their religion, indeed through dialectal Arabic. Nonetheless, debates on language or culture, or on culture through language, always refer to challenging of the dominant and unifying ideology.

France's domestic crisis has crystallized over these last few years around its colonial past through its immigrant populations that have established themselves on its territory since the 1950s. The French identity and language are now challenged and the 'republican model' no longer seems to build a unified citizenry in the public space. The airtight separation between the two spaces, private and public, is an ideological construct which no longer has any great hold on reality. The France that is experiencing an identity crisis from a world perspective – loss of its political and cultural pre-eminence, decline of the French language, weak influence of the Francophonie – seeks to reassert, both inside and outside, its national specificity and uniqueness. The hardening of its universalist vision, and thus of the separation of the private and the public and the withdrawal into a national ideological identity, reflect the fear of an opening onto certain world values, those which, for example, make it a political necessity to recognize

225

differences in order to counteract the standardization and negation of individuals by the economic.

We will now see which events have led to societal changes and consequently to changes in the prevailing discourses.

1. The social crisis

At the time I finished writing this chapter, the Parisian suburbs were in flames. Burnt cars and ransacked schools, violent outbreaks and provocations against the public order were reminiscent of the 1981 car 'rodeos' in the Lyon area, events which launched important political measures aimed at the country's cities, the 'suburb measures',[9] which did nothing to prevent the 1990 crisis nor, once again, the explosion of the neighbourhoods. Events and authors bear witness to the social crisis that France has been going through for over 20 years and the failure of the social measures taken these last few years with regards to housing, integration or education for example (Maurin 2004). Multiple social and economic factors, often interrelated, have contributed over time to the worsening of life situations in the suburbs and to exclusion phenomena. The establishment of these peripheral urban areas – between major highways as is sometimes the case in the Parisian region or in territorialized dead ends, like the 'Northern neighbourhoods' of certain provincial cities – and the confining architecture of the buildings often contribute to the isolation of their inhabitants (Vieillard-Baron 2001: 145). The desertion of peripheral neighbourhoods by the middle classes, through individualized access to property, has left the most underprivileged populations among themselves. Everything seems to show that a great social proximity to the neighbourhood (this being true a contrario for the bourgeois classes and neighbourhoods of city centres) promotes the reproduction of failure (or success) (Maurin 2004). The economic changes of the last few years, such as the entry into globalization and the shift from a commodity-based economy to a service-based one, requiring higher qualifications, have left by the wayside, on the one hand, the 'immigrated workers' who came to France to find work and, on the other, the younger ones who are failing school and are the first to be hit by unemployment and insecurity.[10] The generalized pauperization of these neigbourhoods,[11] which affects the old immigrated population as well as more recently arrived ones, is relayed by violence, especially among younger people, by the disintegration of social links between inhabitants, by the parents' feelings of guilt and by the media's mises-en-scène (Boyer and Lochard 1998). Negative representations of these neighbourhoods and their inhabitants can only generate racism,

226

on the one hand, and feelings of injustice, on the other (Mucchielli 2002).

Although they reflect increasing forms of exclusion and banishment, the 'suburb malaise'[12] and the 'social rift'[13] are also telling of the political and national ideological crisis, and the social changes underway show how the French nation remains frozen in the rigidity of its 'abstract universalism' (Khosrokhavar 1997).

2. The breach of the social contract

Social and economic changes are also causing a breach in the contract between nation and citizens. The return on equality traditionally guaranteed by the social contract is no longer honoured – as political integration can only be achieved through economic and social integration – and resentment, frustration and bitterness keep on growing. Of course, part of the population whose parents were immigrants from North Africa has succeeded in its social development and partakes of the new configuration of France,[14] particularly through the arts (Moïse 1999, 2004; Caubet 2004a). Of course, social links in the suburbs are maintained through many citizen associations and actions. Of course, women 'prennent place parmi les actrices d'une société réconciliée avec sa diversité' ['*are taking their place among the actors of a society reconciled with its diversity*'] (Guenif-Soulimas 2000: 370). Of course, our Minister responsible for the promotion of equal opportunities, Azouz Begag, was raised in the slums of Lyon and remains an example of the school-based integration and a model of success. However, one can also point to dereliction in the suburbs, the parallel economy, an unemployment rate which is well above the national average, marginalization, discrimination for access to jobs or housing (Mucchielli 2002) and the submission of women, all of which are emphasized in numerous life stories (Amara 2003; Méliane 2003; Guerfi 2004). For many, neither equality nor the promise of social progress that could justify integration, renunciation and sacrifice are any longer persuasive. Equality often remains a right of the majority. In countries claiming to draw from a universalist ideology, equality is a formal, administrative equality belonging to the public space and, consequently, only partly illusory. Inequality exists from the moment that it is felt socially and individually, that it is central to the building of the self or the group, and that it stems from subjective feelings of marginalization or exclusion. Granting public equality does not take into account the daily discriminations, the setting of distances, the marginalization processes. In the absence of recognition, particularly of that which should have been granted to previous generations, namely to the fathers who through their work took part in the building of France, rebellions and the assertion of differences speak to idleness, the loss of benchmarks, the feelings of injustice and the inequalities experienced. Rebellions and demands are again rising in the public space, and the assertion of a collective identity makes it possible to break the isolation and marginalization in order to impose one's existence. From the demands for more visibility of minorities in the audio-visual field through quotas to the 'Indigènes de la République'[15] movement or the 'veil affair', the French Republic has been challenged because it can no longer fulfill its contract of insuring equal opportunities and economic and social integration. How then can people be asked to let go of a part of themselves in the public space, of their singularity when this same public space, marked by too many biases, seems to be closed to the social progress of minority groups? When the children of North African immigrants have so little access to political representation,[16] when they are too often branded according to their origin or religion, when they are an electoral non-entity and therefore not part of the French public space? And when positive discrimination, which exists in France without being named, does not yet seem to be sufficiently motivated to be efficient. In education, the *Zones d'Education Prioritaire*[17] (Priority Education Zones) allows more resources from the state for lesser performing colleges and recruitment incentives in certain large schools like *Sciences politiques*, but the results are not equal to expectations.

A shifting of the feeling of threat, from the linguistic to the cultural

With this new landscape and with the social and identity malaise which is rocking France, the feeling of threat faced by the French language now involves immigration languages, particularly Maghrebian Arabic. At the same time, it seems that linguistic issues (regional languages and secularity at the beginning of the century) have always underlain cultural and religious questionings, as if linguistic issues have always been the seismographs of crises and tensions in the established order. Today, however, the most visible components of these tensions are related to cultural issues ... even if, once again, the linguistic refers back to the cultural.

1. New linguistic practices and vitality of Maghrebian Arabic

'Urban' or 'youth' speech refers to particular practices influenced, in particular, by Maghrebian Arabic. This speech or those speeches that are contrary to the standard norm, the one conveyed by the school system, have been largely described from a lexical perspective (Merle 1986; Goudailler 1997; Binisti 1998, among others). This urban speech would seem to be a language constructed from the high variety, French, and would be functionally differentiated to replace the ethnical languages which have disappeared, have become useless or are confined to the family environment (Calvet 1994). That is not to say that these ways of speaking – and such is the fate of any linguistic variety – comprise lexical characteristics that are far from the standard models. These creations stem from semantic processes such as borrowing from Arabic [*être fellèh* = *être nul* from *fellah* = *peasant*], Occitan or African languages (Binisti 1998) or metonymy [*airbags* = *breasts*] (Goudailler 1997). Other lexical processes found are formal effects, like the use of verlan [*Il a kécla* (claqué, or blew, in verlan) *tout son gencaille, sa race!* (*Gencaille*, a hybrid word mixing *argent* and *caillasse/caille* = money) (quoted by Caubet 2001a: 740)] or apocopes and aphaereses [*plème* for *problème*, *lèz* for *balèze*, tasse for *pétasse*, *zic* for *musique* (quoted in Goudailler 1997)].

From another standpoint, the urban speeches, those at the margin or at the periphery and different from the more standard varieties, refer to various language functions which are already well identified, such as cryptic and playful functions. The identity function of these speeches remains no doubt stronger today. Through linguistic assertion of their differences, young people are trying to 'overcome the stigma' (Billiez 1992), which often catches up with them.

If suburban speakers remain for the most part stigmatized, some of their linguistic practices are making their way in society. It is easy to see that lexical borrowings, from *zarma* to *khalouf*, which come from Maghrebian Arabic, called *darja*, are numerous and commonly used among the young (Caubet 2004b; 2005). We therefore find 'des lexèmes sans cesse renouvelés mais également une intonation générale du français, des emphatisations très influencées par l'arabe maghrébin, adoptées par des jeunes quelle que soit l'origine de leurs parents' ['*lexemes that are constantly renewed, but also a general intonation of French, words that are emphasized under the influence of Maghrebian Arabic and adopted by the young whatever their parents' origin*']. (Caubet 2004b: 42). This influence of Maghrebian Arabic over French accounts for the vitality of practices in France:

> Lors du recensement de 1999, une enquête 'famille' a été menée par l'INSEE et l'INED. 380000 adultes de plus de 18 ans ont été interrogés sur la transmission familiale des langues. A la question: 'quelle(s) langue(s), dialecte(s) ou patois vous parliez, quand vous aviez 5 ans, votre père et votre mère', un adulte sur

quatre a répondu que ses parents lui parlaient une autre langue que le français. Pour 23.000 d'entre eux, il s'agissait de l'arabe, maghrébin pour l'essentiel, puisque la question portait sur la transmission familiale. A partir de ces réponses, on est arrivé au chiffre de 1.170.000 adultes à qui l'un des parents parlait arabe, auxquels il convient d'ajouter les moins de 18 ans. Le Secrétaire d'État aux affaires étrangères, Renaud Muselier, lors d'un colloque à l'Université d'Austin au Texas,[18] a donné des chiffres très intéressants, en disant que, sur 4 à 5 millions de musulmans en France, 70% étaient originaires du Nord de l'Afrique, soit entre 2,9 et 3,5 millions de personnes, auxquels il faudrait ajouter environ 400.000 juifs et les pieds-noirs. (Caubet 2004a: 142)

In the 1999 census, a 'family' survey was conducted by INSEE and INED. 380,000 adults over 18 years old were questioned on the transmission of languages in the family. To the question: 'in which language(s), dialect(s) or patois did your mother and father speak to you when you were 5 years old', one out of four adults said that their parents spoke to them in a language other than French. For 23,000 of them, it was Arabic, mostly Maghrebian, since the question dealt with family transmission. From these responses, it was calculated that there are 1,170,000 adults to whom one of the parents spoke Arabic, to which the under 18 year-olds should be added. At a symposium held at Austin University, Texas, the State Secretary to Foreign Affairs, Renaud Muselier, provided very interesting numbers, saying that, out of 4 to 5 million Muslims in France, 70% were from North Africa, i.e. between 2.9 and 3.5 million people, to which approximately 400,000 Jews and pieds-noirs should be added.

Similarly, it cannot be denied how much artists who have ties with the Maghreb (Moïse 1999, 2004; Caubet 2004a, 2004b) are contributing to the richness and the transformation of the French cultural and linguistic landscape (as is claimed by the protagonists themselves, and despite all 'metis', 'traditional' or 'authentic' labelling), thereby asserting a contemporary plurality of expression. They are imposing, without hammering it in, a new conception of French society. While remaining faithful to all the general principles of national community, they are imposing, by the acknowledgement of who they are and not by any deliberate political action, subtle changes in the representation of the French identity and in linguistic practices; they are perhaps opening a new avenue by shaking up the homogeneous French nation, which sees its old defence models profoundly weakened.

2. New fears, new resistances

But the fight of the central state persists, in spite of it all.

2.1 Dialectal Arabic in the baccalauréat[19]

In February 2001, the optional Maghrebian Arabic exam was abolished by Jack Lang, Minister of National Education, while there were 10,000 students registered with a 72 per cent pass rate. Aside from international pressures to promote classical Arabic, now the sole Arabic language at the baccalauréat level, Maghrebian Arabic was perceived as confined to an ancestral identity. But this was both a linguistic and ideological distortion. *Darja* is in fact the language of neutrality, the language of family and personal stories, the language which told of the meeting of communities (Jews, Arabs, pieds-noirs), free of religious, pan-Islamic or pan-Arab representations which are carried by the sacred language, that of the Koran, Classical Arabic. This exam recognized not only a culture of the family and a precise identity, but also the richness represented by this type of linguistic transmission, as well as cultural element of a diverse France. It promoted pride and institutional recognition. Classical Arabic, a distinct language from Maghrebian Arabic, is mostly unknown by students and to offer them only this language to learn is, once again, to assign them to an identity, a religious one among others, and to references far removed from their practices. This school situation can only give rise, because of a certain contempt which permeated the process, to reactions of shame, if not of withdrawal and rejection. As if the behaviours condemned by politicians were induced by their own decisions.

2.2 The Bénisti report

In October 2004, a preliminary report by the parliamentary commission on domestic security, chaired by Jacques Alain Bénisti, member for Val-de-Marne, was submitted to the Prime Minister. This report would require professionals to report to the Mayor 'all persons with social, educational and material problems'. But, far from any educational prevention purpose, this project focused on repression and punishment as ways of penalizing social exclusion. Many educational measures were mentioned, aimed at both parents and children. Sanctions could be imposed for what is stigmatized as abdication of parental responsibility, school absenteeism by children or using family languages. What is of greater interest to us here were the language recommendations? In particular, the report stated that:

seuls les parents, et en particulier la mère, ont un contact avec leurs enfants. Si ces derniers sont d'origine étrangère, elles devront s'obliger à parler le français dans leur foyer pour habituer leurs enfants à n'avoir que cette langue pour s'exprimer. (Bénisti 2004: 9)

only the parents, and particularly the mother, have any contact with their children. If the latter are of foreign origin, the mothers should force themselves to speak French at home in order to get their children used to having only this language to express themselves.

And further, that 'si cette mère persiste à parler son patois l'institutrice devra alors passer le relais à un orthophoniste' ['*if the mother persists in speaking her patois, the school teacher will then have to refer the case to a speech therapist*'] (Bénisti 2004: 9).

Of course, this report gave rise to much criticism, which in particular highlighted the shortcut between language learning, delinquency and the disqualification of Arabic or immigration languages. We are in a discourse of deviance, the like of which was also aimed at colonized peoples or women in their time and, although the basis of the arguments has changed little, the social and ideological consequences are new. Groups that had until then remained unobtrusive in the public space are now stigmatized, and we are also witnessing upheavals and world tensions in relation to the rise of the religious. In response to such intentions, a letter, a form of argumentative resistance, was written by the Réseau Français de Sociolinguistique (2005) to question once again the shift from the public to the private:

Les rédacteurs du projet préconisent que les parents s'obligent 'à parler le français dans leur foyer pour habituer les enfants à n'avoir que cette langue pour s'exprimer' (p. 9). L'État n'a pas vocation à réglementer les usages linguistiques au sein des espaces privés que sont les familles, même si les témoignages abondent de personnes à qui il a été déconseillé de parler leur langue à leurs enfants, au motif de risques d'échec scolaire.

The project's authors recommend that parents force themselves to speak French at home in order to get their children used to having only this language to express themselves (p. 9). It is not the state's responsibility to regulate linguistic practices within the private space of the family, even if there are abundant testimonies from people who were advised not to speak their own language to their children, for fear of potential school failure.

I would like to point out once again the public oversight over the private (education and language surveillance of parents), the shift of the symbolic and ideological boundary when it serves national interests, and the defence of the dominant prerogatives and the social order.

3. The school system in crisis, the nation in crisis

Linguistic tensions are now accompanied by strong cultural and religious tensions, brought to light especially in the school system as reproducer of the social order. Following a series of crises on the wearing of the Islamic veil in schools, between 1989 and today, an act was passed on 15 March 2004 and implemented in September, stating that, in public schools and colleges, signs and clothes that conspicuously indicate a student's religious affiliation are forbidden. Throughout this crisis over the legislation on the wearing of the veil, the debate centred above all on secularism and religion, i.e. the separation of the public and private spaces. The politicians and the media played a significant role in the politicizing process, no doubt more so than the Muslims themselves or the teachers, the first ones concerned by the issue. Although they did not always accept the veil in schools, those who were opposed to the legislation, in particular those represented by the *Islam et laïcité* commission,[20] were not able to get themselves heard by the government. In reality, therefore, the veil issue revealed less on Islam and the place of religion in our political system and more on how the old community which emigrated from North Africa is treated, on the discrimination it suffers and on the fears it generates. And finally on the 'deviant' citizens themselves, as were the colonized peoples and women in their time, who threaten the reproduction of the dominant elite.

Without going as far as the extreme right's discourse, it can be said that this crisis has replayed stereotypes by its generalizing effect and has demonized Islam through the issues of the submission of women, religious fanaticism and the non-integration to the republican model. Yet, the reasons or motivations for wearing the veil were multiple (Amara 2003: 48) – an identity and origin banner, a teen statement, a guarantee of the freedom of movement in the city and outside – and were not really questioned. But in the face of these reactions, given that it seemed to be difficult to identify those that stemmed from more extreme convictions such as anti-democratic practices or a true belief in the submission of women to the male model, the legislation's goal was to bring back social and national order. Therefore, the veil affair served to trigger a politicizing process (Lorcerie 2005) whereas it probably had more to do with both an identity search, whatever it was, and the school system malaise. Politicians and intellectuals

233

brandished the fear of the religious as well as of the destabilization of the Republic instead of looking more closely at the manifestation of individualities and at education. It was probably more radical, visible and political to reassert the republican principles than to revisit the school system's functioning or the identity question within the French nation state.

If schools are at the centre of linguistic reproduction, they are also at the centre of cultural reproduction, something that the education system is currently trying to reactivate under the cover of secularity, just like at the onset of public education. The secularity principle, established primarily in schools by the law of 1905, was not put forward as an anti-religious model, but was put forward in an enlightened spirit of tolerance and rationalism. It was not only aimed, in an anticlerical perspective, at the separation of Church and State but was part of an educational project that was more global and universal. The school institution was where a common national culture was reproduced, separate from particular popular cultures, and constituted the building block of citizenship. Beyond knowledge, schools were engineered as holders of a federative ideology and providers of the learned culture. Contrary to the myth of an ideal era, schools, as implemented under the reign of Jules Ferry, were also inegalitarian, but this inequality emanated from social classes with well-defined boundaries and was admitted by the school; a certain form of social determinism was largely admitted in society, and finally within the school's walls. Although they reproduced inequalities, schools at least seemed not to be causing them or making them worse. The 'republican elite' even made an effort to recruit certain students who met standards of excellence, thereby contributing to social mobility (Dubet 1997). More than an anti-religious statement, secularity represented an education model, partaking of the universalist ideology. Today, through the veil debate, secularity has become stuck in a religious debate and, instead of questioning identity claims, which are sometimes driven by feelings of inequality and non-recognition within the school system, the danger of 'communitarianism' and 'fundamentalism' is brandished.

However, schools can no longer insure the reproduction of the citizenship model, as holders of a universal culture. They are part of a world where they play upon meritocracy and profit. They provide access to the spheres of power to the most deserving students or those who have understood various success strategies, which are recognized and facilitated by the social class to which they belong, the most well-off, holder of the expected codes. More than the acquisition of humanistic and republican values, school competition is an affirmed and integrated mode for accessing social mobility for which the

234

dominant classes are the best trained. Furthermore, schools are being mobilized – away from their primary purpose – for school-to-work transition, family mediation, psychological difficulties of children, civility, which weakens them and catches them off guard because they have always been focused on the transmission of a universal common knowledge while leaving at their doors the private, the intimate, popular knowledge, home languages other than French, if any, and parents themselves. Thus, schools now seem to produce inequalities because they can no longer leave them behind with impunity in the social sphere.

Secularity, which provided this distance between the private and the public, between schools and society, is now subject to social change. The religious issue is one element which is more visible and more ideologically marked than other issues, more than languages themselves (unless, again, it is associated with them, as was the case at the beginning of the twentieth century, in a regional language versus Catholicism relationship), but it is a reflection of the changes that the school institution is undergoing in the same way.

Conclusion: impossible change or ideological impasse

It now therefore appears that the national crises surrounding linguistic issues are giving way to cultural or religious ones. But we are still talking about the same thing. Tensions are rising just as power struggles are intensifying and the ideologies in place becoming less flexible: whether it is on the side of the dominant and conservative monocultural assertions, underlaid by the fear and rejection of strangeness, or on the side of identity demands which, from a sign of resistance can become an identity quest in a cult of the lost origin and authenticity, a quest relayed by a social malaise and feelings of non-belonging. These assertions are vigorously redrawing boundaries (who is inside and who is outside) without, for all that, considering other ways of being together. Today, some community members are rejecting a homogeneous package which would still serve the majority and accentuate their own cultural marginalization; they are upsetting the established order, the notion of homogeneity and national unity. To a certain extent, they are pushing each one of those who are on one side of the boundary to try a possible meeting. Minority groups are asserting the French fact (for the most part, their children are now born in France) while insisting on a wider recognition of cultural and linguistic specificities by challenging the airtight boundary between the private and the public. Always reminding the groups who are feeling excluded from the French specificity of the nation, of its values of freedom and equality, of its language – without admitting to its rigidity and dysfunction – stigmatizing them because they are undermining the model, and even rejecting it, can only create tensions and blockages.

The old world France, moulded by its language with its sovereign surges and by its universal culture, leaves little room for the recognition of cultural plurality. For this reason, thinking the nation differently would lead to the break-up of established patterns and would force the doors of imagination, which would be a real modernity challenge. It is probably a matter of accepting and bringing to light, as the basis for the construction of a new society, the conflicts and the words said in the public space, as we do with everything cultural and artistic. Accepting these demands as reflections of the real historical path of France, the violence of the decolonization and immigration processes of the 1960s, the children and grandchildren of wounded migrants, the daily discriminations and humiliations, the multilingualism. When the old protection reflexes remain fruitless, listening to and considering the social demands of the minority would help to avoid any hardening and would help assert a plural nation.

France will not be able to solve its domestic tensions without questioning the political order and universalism; a political and ideological order which only serves to reproduce the social assets of the dominant group and legitimize the power holders. In the end, it is the whole social functioning that needs to be rethought before the break occurs too violently from the margins. And before France withdraws into an ideological impasse. It cannot rid itself of this national and linguistic conception that hinders it, while making it also an 'exception'. The French nation is in an ideological crisis and the more it closes its doors to diversity and change because on its abstract universalism, the more it nourishes the demands and dissatisfactions from the margins. It is as if the national neurosis has become a figure of identity and the French language contributes to this neurosis, especially when it is called upon to delineate the public and the private space.

References

Amara, F. (2003), *Ni putes ni soumises*. Paris: La Découverte, Poche.

Bachmann, C. and Le Guennec, N. (1996), *Violences urbaines. Ascension et chute des classes moyennes à travers cinquante ans de politique de la ville.* Paris: Albin Michel.

Balibar, R. (1995), Qualité et personnalité de la langue française', in J.-M. Eloy (ed.), *La qualité de la langue française ? Le cas du français*. Paris: Champion, pp. 285–89.

Bénisti, J.-A. (2004), 'Sur la prévention de la délinquance'. Rapport préliminaire de la Commission prévention du groupe d'études parlementaire sur la sécurité intérieure. Assemblée nationale, XIIe législature, October 2004.

Binisti, N. (1998), 'La construction de l'identité à travers les pratiques discursives de jeunes des quartiers Nord de Marseille'. *Les langages de Marseille!* Actes de la journée d'études, IUFM Académie d'Aix Marseille, 7 November 1998, Aix en Provence: Editions Skolê.

Billiez, J. (1992), 'Le "parler vernaculaire interethnique" de groupes d'adolescents en milieu urbain', in *Des langues et des villes*. Actes du colloque de Dakar, 15–17 December 1990, Paris: Didier Erudition, pp. 117–26.

Bombardier, D. (2002), 'Les cendres d'Alexandre Dumas au Panthéon'. *Paris Match*, 25 July 2005, 7–8.

Boyer, H. and Lochard G. (1998), *Scènes de télévision en banlieues*. Paris: l'Harmattan.

Calvet, L.-J. (1994), *Les voix de la ville*. Paris: Payot.

Caubet, D. (2001a), 'Du baba (papa) à la mère, des emplois parallèles en arabe marocain et dans les parlures jeunes en France'. *Cahiers d'Etudes Africaines*, 163–64, 735–48.

Caubet, D. (2001b), 'L'arabe dialectal en France', in M. Pontault (ed.), *Arabophonie. Les cahiers de la francophonie* 10. Haut Conseil de la Francophonie: Paris, pp. 199–212.

Caubet, D. (2004a), *Les mots du bled*. Paris: L'Harmattan.

Caubet, D. (2004b), 'La *darja*, langue de culture en France'. *Hommes et Migrations*, 1252, 34–44.

Caubet, D. (2004c), 'L'arabe maghrébin-darja, langue de France'. *La Célibataire*, 8, 139–45.

Caubet, D. (2005), 'Ce français qui nous (re) vient du Maghreb, mélanges linguistiques en milieux urbains'. *Notre Librairie*, 159, 18–24.

Cerquiglini, B. (1999), *Les langues de la France*. Rapport au Ministre de l'Education Nationale, de la Recherche et de la Technologie et à la Ministre de la Culture et de la Communication, April 1999. Available at www.culture. gouv.fr/culture/dglf/lang-reg/rapport_cerquiglini/langues-france.html

Cerquiglini, B. (2003), 'Le français, religion d'Etat'. *Le Monde*, 25 November 2003.

Constitution de la République Française (1958). Available at www.legifrance. gouv.fr

Décision n° 99-412. (1999), Charte des langues régionales ou minoritaires. Conseil constitutionnel de la République française. Available at www. conseil-constitutionnel.fr/decision/1999/99412/99412dc.htm

Loi Deixonne sur l'enseignement des langues et des dialectes locaux (1951), Loi 51–46 published at *Journal Officiel* (13 January 1951).

Dubet, F. (1997), 'La laïcité dans les mutations de l'école' in M. Wieviorka (ed.), *Une société fragmentée? Le multiculturalisme en débat*. Paris: La découverte/Poche, pp. 85–112.

European Charter for Regional or Minority Languages (1992), Council of Europe, adopted 5 November 1992.

Eloy, J.-M. (2000), 'G, comme gérer la langue', in B. Cerquiglini, J.-C., Corbeil, J.-M.

Klinkenberg, and Peeters, B. (eds), *Tu parles!? Le français dans tous ses états*. Paris: Flammarion, pp. 95–107.

Gadet, F. (2003), *La variation sociale en français*. Paris: Orphys.

Goudailler, J.-P. (1997), *Comment tu tchatches! Dictionnaire du français contemporain des cités*. Paris: Maisonneuve et Larose.

Guénif-Soulimas, N. (2000), *Des 'beurettes' aux descendantes d'immigrants nord-africains*. Paris: Grasset.

Gueunier, N. (1985), 'La crise du français en France', in J. Maurais, *La crise des langues*. Québec et Paris: Conseil de la langue française et le Robert, pp. 4–38.

Guerfi, N. (2004), *Le sauvageon*. Paris: Le manuscrit Editions.

Histoire. La colonisation en procès. No 302, October 2005.

Khosrokhavar, F. (1997), 'L'universel abstrait, le politique et la construction de l'islamisme comme forme d'altérité', in M. Wieviorka (ed.), *Une société fragmentée ? Le multiculturalisme en débat*. Paris: La découverte/Poche, pp. 113–50.

Klinkenberg, J.-M. (2001), *La langue et le citoyen*. Paris : PUF.

Kloss, H. (1969), *Research Possibilities on Group Bilingualism: A Report*. Quebec: Centre international de recherche sur le bilinguisme.

Lodge, A. (1997), *Le français, histoire d'un dialecte devenu langue*. Paris: Fayard.

Lorcerie, F. (2005), *La politisation du voile: l'affaire en France, en Europe et dans le monde arabe*. Paris: l'Harmattan.

Marianne (no 445), 29 October – 4 November 2005.

Maurin, E. (2004), *Le ghetto français, enquête sur le séparatisme social*. Paris: Seuil.

Méliane, L. (2003), *Vivre libre*. Paris: Oh éditions.

Merle, P. (1986), *Dictionnaire du français branché*. Paris: Seuil.

Merlin-Kajman, H. (2003), *La langue est-elle fasciste?* Paris: Seuil.

Moïse, C. (1999), *Les danseurs du défi, rencontre avec le hip hop*. Montpellier: Indigène Editions.

Moïse, C. (2000), 'De la politique à la politique linguistique, quelle place du chercheur dans la cité?' *Grenzgänge*, 13, 38–48.

Moïse, C. (2004), *Danse hip hop, respect*. Montpellier: Indigène Editions.

Mucchielli, L. (2002), *Violences et insécurité. Fantasmes et réalités dans le débat français*. Paris: La Découverte.

Réseau Français de Sociolinguistique (2005), *Lettre en réaction au rapport Bénisti*. Available at www.univ-tours.fr/rfs/lettre.htm#lettre

Rivarol, A. (1783), *Discours sur l'universalité de la langue française*. Available at www.bribes.org/trismegistre/rivarol.htm

Semprini, A. (1997), *Le multiculturalisme*. Paris: Que sais-je? PUF.

Thélot, C. (2004), *Pour la réussite de tous les élèves: Rapport de la Commission du débat national sur l'avenir de l'école*. Paris: la Documentation française.

Vallaeys, B. (1999), 'Le Conseil Constitutionnel tire sur les langues', *Libération*, 6, 18 June 1999.

Vieillard-Baron, H. (2001), *Les banlieues. Des singularités françaises aux réalités mondiales*. Paris: Hachette.

Wieviorka, M. (1997), 'Culture, société et démocratie', in M. Wieviorka (ed.), *Une société fragmentée? Le multiculturalisme en débat*. Paris: La découverte/ Poche, pp. 11–56.

Wionet, C. (2005), 'Les langues régionales au XVIIIe siècle'. *Marges Linguistiques*, www.marges-linguistiques.com.

Notes

1 Many thanks to Pierre Bériault and Lise Dubois for the translation from the French and stylistic revision.

2 Cerquiglini is the head of the Institut National de la Langue Française (National Institute for the French Language), and was responsible for a report published in 1999 for the French Ministry of Education, Research and Technology on the languages of France.

3 And along the same lines, the National Assembly rejected in December 2005 a socialist document that wanted to repeal in the Act of 23 February 2005 references in school history books to the 'positive role of the French presence' during the colonization period, particularly 'in Northern Africa'. Following this controversy, the President of the Republic, Jacques Chirac, removed this section by decree.

4 In language planning, interventions on the corpus of a language, i.e. the system, are opposed to those on the status of a language, i.e. its recognition and prestige, since Kloss (1969).

5 A literary school founded in Provence in 1854 with, as figurehead, the Nobel prize winner Frédéric Mistral, who unrelentlessly worked for the recognition of Provençal through a strong willingness to standardize this language.

6 Caught between the objections expressed and the image that had to be given to Europe of France's democratic values, the President signed the Charter knowing that it would not be ratified by Parliament.

7 The 1951 *Deixonne Act* on teaching only dealt with Basque, Occitan, Catalan and Breton.

8 Thus, the *Délégation Générale* à la Langue Française became the DGLFLF, or *Délégation Générale à la Langue Française et aux Langues de France*.

9 For a precise history of the urban policies, see the particularly well documented book by Bachmann and Le Guennec (1996).

10 De 1974 à 1995, le secteur industriel a enregistré une perte de 430 000 emplois pour la seule région Ile de France, alors même que la croissance du secteur des services ne permet pas de compenser les licenciements d'un personnel peu qualifié et mal préparé à d'autres tâches'. ['*From 1974 to 1995, the industrial sector recorded a loss of 430,000 jobs for the sole region of Île de France, while the growth of the service sector has not compensated for the lay-off of workers who are little qualified and ill-prepared to take on other tasks*'] (Vieillard-Baron 2001:153).

11 Although one must remain cautious and always conduct alternate studies on urban changes to also draw attention to the wellbeing of certain territories where social and civic work is paying off…

12 This expression has been repeatedly used by the media.

13 This formula was extensively used by the 1995 presidential candidate, Jacques Chirac, during his campaign.

14 The 29 October – 4 November 2005 edition of *Marianne* (no 445), a weekly magazine, ran this headline: 'Enquête : immigration, intégration. Quand Fadila et Ahmed incarnent la France qui réussit'. [Special report: immigration, integration. When Fadila and Ahmed personify the France which succeeds].

15 In the face of numerous difficulties, children of immigrants, the 'Indigènes de la République' [natives of the Republic], supported by French intellectual figures, are denouncing discrimination as measured against the colonial ideology which is still alive in France. They are also telling of the humiliations sustained by their fathers, and of the non-recognition of the French government's responsibilities at the time of the colonization and the war of Algeria. This would also be a way of avenging their wounded honour. 'Derrière la normalisation apparente des relations, il reste le souvenir très vivant des guerres coloniales, en particulier de la guerre d'Algérie, et d'un renversement de domination qui n'a pas encore été accepté par tous' ['*Behind the apparent normalization of relations, there remains the vivid memory of the colonial wars, in particular the war of Algeria, and of a domination reversal which has not yet been accepted by everyone*'] (Vieillard-Baron 2001: 165). Today, the debate is lively and historians (see in this regard *Histoire*, 'La colonisation en procès' No 302, October 2005) are warning us about the danger of decontextualizing the situation while forgetting to consider the current socio-economic factors and the international situation (Israeli–Palestinian conflict, Iraq war) to reactivate a past history.

16 Certain events, such as the 'Marche pour l'égalité des droits dite Marche des Beurs' in 1984, the 'Ni putes ni soumises' movement of 2003, the publishing of a list of 'motivés' during the municipal elections of Toulouse, led by a group of Toulouse artists among whom were Zebda, represent a political conscience on the move but without any patent electoral representation.

17 'Le classement en Zep offre un surcroît de moyens aux établissements sous forme de postes et d'heures supplémentaires d'enseignement, l'un des objectifs étant de réduire la taille des classes. Au total en 1998 et 1999, le supplément de ressources allouées aux Zep représentait environ 1,2% du total des dépenses pour les activités d'enseignement. L'effort est toutefois saupoudré sur une telle quantité de zones et une telle masse d'enfants qu'au total les ressources allouées pour un élève de Zep sont à peine 8% à 10% supérieures à celles allouées à un élève hors Zep' ['*The ZEP classification provides institutions with additional means in the form of extra teaching positions and extra hours, one of the goals being the reduction of class sizes. In 1998 and 1999, the total additional resources allocated to ZEPs represented approximately 1.2% of the total teaching expenditures. The effort is however spread over so many ZEPs and so many children*

that the total resources allocated for one ZEP student are barely 8 to 10% higher than those allocated to a non-ZEP student'] (Maurin 2004: 64).

18 *Language and (Im)migration in France, Latin America and the United States: Sociolinguistic Perspectives*, 25–26 September 2003.

19 For this whole question, see Caubet (2001b; 2004c).

20 The goal of this commission initiated in 1997 by Michel Morineau and Pierre Tournemire within the Ligue de l'enseignement was to conduct, through discussion and knowledge sharing, a detailed analysis of the issue of the presence of Muslims in French society to search for avenues that would lead to their harmonious integration in the intangible framework of secularism and its political philosophy.

12 Embracing diversity for the sake of unity: Linguistic hegemony and the pursuit of total Spanish

José del Valle

'Hay que preservar la unidad del español porque corre peligro'
['*We must protect the unity of Spanish because it is in danger*']
(Santiago de Mora-Figueroa, Marquis of Tamarón and Director of
the Cervantes Institute between 1996 and 1999, quoted in EL PAÍS,
24 May 1996).

Introduction

A brief survey of academic discussions and public debates on language
in the Spanish-speaking world reveals that endangerment and diversity
have been and continue to be prominent linguistic themes (Rama 1982;
Caballero Wanguemert 1989; del Valle and Gabriel-Stheeman 2002a,
2002b). On the one hand, especially in recent decades, we find voices
that present Spanish as a powerful homogenizing force that threatens
to erase linguistic and cultural diversity[1]; on the other, we also come
across discourses of endangerment in which, conversely, it is the
quality, status and, as the epigraph to this essay indicates, unity of
Spanish that is felt to be under threat (e.g. Grijelmo 1998; Lodares
2000).

Deborah Cameron has argued that verbal hygiene – the impulse
to 'meddle in matters of language' (1995: vii), by defining its nature,
by suggesting ways of cleaning or improving it, and by attempting to
regulate and control it – is a natural component of the linguistic life of
any human society, and it is often deployed as a response to not only
linguistic but also, and most importantly, non-linguistic concerns.
Consequently, we are not surprised to find that a territory as vast as

242

the Spanish-speaking world – that such a varied assembly of cultural, social and economic concerns – has yielded an equally complex set of discourses on language in which the notions of endangerment and diversity are variously defined and forms of verbal hygiene differently instrumentalized (Kroskrity 2000: 12).

In this chapter, I will focus on a particular kind of discourse that, emerging from within Spain's language policy agencies and in response to concerns about the possible fragmentation of Spanish, espouses not the elimination but the enthusiastic embrace of intralingual diversity. On the basis of previous research on the topic (del Valle and Gabriel-Stheeman 2002a, 2002b, 2004; del Valle 2005; del Valle and Villa forthcoming), I will approach these fears of fragmentation, affirmations of unity and celebrations of internal diversity as discursive sites where anxieties over Spain's desire to build a privileged economic and political relationship with Latin America are worked out. While these desires and anxieties are not new (they can in fact be traced back to the period following the independence of most of Spain's American colonies after 1810 and Cuba and Puerto Rico's in 1898), here I will concentrate on their most recent manifestation after the 1990s, in the context of Spain's economic take-off and the subsequent landing of Spain-based corporations in Latin America (Bonet and de Gregorio 1999; Casilda Béjar 2001). Under these new conditions, Spanish governments in collaboration with the business sector (e.g. Telefónica, PRISA, Iberdrola, Banco de Santander, Repsol) and with the complicity of certain sectors of Latin America's societies have mobilized cultural and linguistic institutions (the Spanish Royal Academy and the Cervantes Institute)[2] in order to promote a conceptualization of the Spanish-speaking community that will secure it as a market where the presence of Spanish capital is felt to be both natural and legitimate.

Against this cultural and economic *land-guage-scape*, in this chapter I will analyse the ideological bases of the Spanish Royal Academy's main policy lines in the contemporary construction of the *hispanofonía*: first, the pursuit of a pan-hispanic policy through the creation of a seemingly consensual discursive space in which all Spanish-speaking nations supposedly converge on equal terms, and second, the embrace of intralingual diversity as the political and theoretical foundation of linguistic and cultural unity. In my analysis, I will rely mainly on three theoretical concepts whose relevance will be justified in due course: Jürgen Habermas' notion of public sphere (Habermas 1991), Richard Watts' analysis of discourse communities (Watts 1999), and Antonio Gramsci's elaboration of hegemony (Williams 1977; Gramsci 1991).

Hispanofonía and its discontents

As mentioned above, Spain's efforts to engage in post-colonial community-building with Latin America can actually be traced back to the nineteenth century and to the development of *hispanismo*. While this cultural trend was mostly discursive, it also materialized in the form of a number of cultural initiatives that included congresses and symposia (such as the Ibero-American congresses of 1892 and 1900 organized by the *Unión Íbero-Americana*) as well as journals (such as *La Ilustración Ibérica, La Revista Española de Ambos Mundos,* and *La Ilustración Española y Americana*) (Fogelquist 1968; Pike 1971). *Hispanismo* was grounded in the belief that a common Spanish culture embodied in the Spanish language existed on both sides of the Atlantic and was the basis for an economically and politically operative entity, for a true *hispanofonía*. In my use of the term, *hispanofonía* is not an objective fact, a group of nations, a network of interaction threaded by a shared communicative code; it is rather, following Anderson's (1983) notion, an imagined community grounded in a common language, itself imagined, that ties together in an emotional bond those who feel they possess it and those who have a sense of loyalty to it (del Valle 2005). It is, therefore, according to Gal and Woolard's definition of the term (2001), a language ideology, a historically situated conception of Spanish as an enactment of a collective order in which Spain performs a central role.

The explicit defence of unity that constitutes the core of *hispanismo* emerged in part as a response to a number of centrifugal forces that challenged Spain's own nation-building demands: on the one hand, the threat posed to Spain's integrity by nationalist movements emerging in the Basque Country, Catalonia and Galicia; and on the other, its loss of prestige and influence in Latin America (especially after Spain's defeat in the Spanish–American war of 1898), where the former colonies were now engaged in their own nation-building projects, managing the linguistic, cultural and social specificity of their territory and facing the North American colossus' moves towards regional hegemony. Thus, against these fragmentationist challenges, *hispanismo* offered, first, a proud affirmation and embrace of the national signs of identity which towards the end of the 1900s some Basque, Catalan and Galicians began to deny, and second, a strategy to build a unified cultural field that would allow Spain to retain some of the privileges of empire without actually having one.

The scope and purpose of this section does not allow us to trace the complex history of Spain and Latin America's post-colonial relations (but see for example Fogelquist 1968; Pike 1971; Rama 1982;

Sepúlveda 2005). However, as background to my analysis of Spain's contemporary language policies, it seems appropriate to underline, first, the fact that *hispanismo* has provided us with one of the most powerful narratives (though certainly not the only one) for imagining Spain and the pan-hispanic community; and second, the fact that *hispanismo* has tended to express itself through profoundly colonialist discourses.

One of the first journals to embrace this ideology was *La Revista Española de Ambos Mundos* ['The Spanish Journal from Both Worlds'] which in its first issue (1853) stated:

> Destinada a España y América, pondremos particular esmero en estrechar sus relaciones. La Providencia no une a los pueblos con los lazos de un mismo origen, religión, costumbres e idioma para que se miren con desvío y se vuelvan las espaldas así en la próspera como en la adversa fortuna. Felizmente han desaparecido las causas que nos llevaron a la arena del combate, y hoy el pueblo americano y el ibero no son, ni deben ser, más que miembros de una misma familia; la gran familia española, que Dios arrojó del otro lado del océano para que, con la sangre de sus venas, con su valor e inteligencia, conquistase a la civilización un nuevo mundo. (quoted in Fogelquist 1968: 13–14; all translations throughout the chapter are mine, JdV)

> *The journal is meant for both Spain and [Latin] America, and we will make a particularly careful effort to help tighten the relationship between the two. Providence does not bind two different peoples with the bond of a common origin, religion, customs, and language so that, whether in prosperous or adverse times, they look at each other in suspicion or turn their backs on each other. Fortunately the reasons that brought us to the field of battle have now disappeared, and today the [Latin] American and Iberian people are nothing but—should be nothing but—members of one and the same family, the great Spanish family, which God sent across the ocean so that, with their blood, courage and intelligence, they would conquer a new world for civilization.*

This type of colonialist rhetoric has in fact continued to be one of the central impediments to building pan-hispanic solidarity and earning loyalty to the *hispanofonía*. A perfect example of the problem posed by the persistence of imperial impulses was the polemic between Colombian philologist Rufino José Cuervo (1844–1911) and Spanish writer and essayist Juan Valera (1824–1905). In 1899, Cuervo, drawing an analogy between Latin and Spanish, expressed his concern over the still distant and unfortunate but likely development of new languages from the dialectal remains of Spanish. Fragmentation would be, according to Cuervo, a consequence of dialectal diversity, low communication among Latin Americans, and the absence of a common cultural beacon for all Hispanic nations as a result of Spain's decadence. In response to these claims, Valera published an article on 24 September 1900 in a Madrid daily in which he rejected Cuervo's prediction and, undoubtedly injured by the Colombian's pessimistic view of Spain's intellectual life, called on men of letters to protect unity by serving as models not only through their linguistic practices but also through their exemplarily optimistic attitudes towards Spanish (see del Valle 2002 for a fuller analysis of the polemic). This exchange had a telling ending. In a 1903 article, Cuervo put aside all linguistic argumentation for a moment and wrote:

> [Valera] pretende que las naciones hispanoamericanas sean colonias literarias de España, aunque para abastecerlas sea menester tomar productos de países extranjeros, y, figurándose tener aún el imprescindible derecho a la represión violenta de las insurgentes, no puede sufrir que un americano ponga en duda el que las circunstancias actuales consientan tales ilusiones: esto le hace perder los estribos y la serenidad clásica. Hasta aquí llega el fraternal afecto. (Cuervo 1950: 332)

> *[Valera] wants Latin American nations to be literary colonies of Spain, even if, in order to supply them, he has to resort to foreign products; and, thinking that he still has the inalienable right to violent repression of the insurgent colonies, he is unable to tolerate that an American question such a possibility given the present circumstances: this makes him lose his temper and his customary serenity. Here ends the fraternal love.*

Thus, for much of the nineteenth and twentieth centuries, Spain's ability to satisfy its hegemonic desires was limited: on one hand, as we just saw, the egalitarian proclamations of *hispanismo*, enveloped as they were in colonialist rhetoric, were naturally received with profound skepticism; on the other, the material circumstances of Spain's political life and economic development limited the intensity of its efforts and constrained its ability to commit the necessary resources to such a mission. However, in the late 1980s and the 1990s Spain's profile drastically changed under new cultural and economic conditions that included the consolidation of democracy, membership in NATO and the European Union, economic growth and the spread of Spain-based corporations throughout Latin America.

Interestingly, even in the late twentieth and early twenty-first century the spectre of empire continues to haunt the *hispanofonía*. In 1991, Manuel Alvar (1923–2001), distinguished Spanish philologist and dialectologist and Director of the Spanish Royal Academy between 1988 and 1991, still echoed the view of colonialism as a *mission civilisatrice*:

> México sabía mejor que nadie el valor de tener una lengua que unifique y que libere de la miseria y del atraso a las comunidades indígenas ... Salvar al indio, redimir al indio, incorporación del indio, como entonces gritaban, no es otra cosa que desindianizar al indio. Incorporarlo a la idea de un estado moderno, para su utilización en unas empresas de solidaridad nacional y para que reciba los beneficios de esa misma sociedad ... El camino hacia la libertad transita por la hispanización. (Alvar 1991: 17–18)

> *Mexico knew better than anybody else the value of having a language that unifies, that liberates the indigenous communities from their backwardness and misery ... Saving the Indian, the redemption of the Indian, the incorporation of the Indian, as they used to say, is nothing but de-indianizing the Indian, incorporating him into the idea of the modern State, in order to use him in projects of national solidarity, and in order to extend to him the benefits of belonging to that same society ... The path to freedom runs through hispanization.*

More recently, emotive narratives of Spain's 'new' role and commercial enterprises in Latin America have been equally coloured by colonialist imagery:

> Un siglo después del repliegue definitivo de España al perder Cuba, se vuelve a un continente que de ninguna manera a nadie nos es ajeno: Iberoamérica. Ahora con otras ideas, perspectivas e ilusiones que nos confieren las nuevas armas: las empresas españolas, que se han expandido con los nuevos vientos de la globalización. (Casilda Béjar 2001)

> *One century after Spain's definitive withdrawal after losing Cuba, we return to a continent that in no way is alien to us: Iberoamerica. Now with other ideas, perspectives, and hopes provided to us by the new weapons: Spanish corporations, which have spread with the new winds of globalization.*

Yet, things have changed. Now even the very same economic actors who engage in colonialist discourse are well aware of its dangers. Casilda Béjar – an economist and guest speaker at the II International Conference on the Spanish Language (see below) – stated in his speech:

> [l]a transferencia de la propiedad de empresas importantes de manos nacionales [i.e. Latin American] a manos extrajeras [i.e.

Spanish] puede verse como un hecho que socava la soberanía nacional y que es equiparable a una 'recolonización'. (2001)

transferring the property of important companies from national [i.e. Latin American] to foreign [i.e. Spanish] hands may be perceived as a process that undermines national sovereignty and that can be equated with a 're-colonization'.[3]

But this concern, in his view, could be alleviated:

adviértase que la extraordinaria posición alcanzada [por España] en este continente, ha sido posible gracias a nuestro extraordinario aliado: el idioma, causa y efecto de nuestra afinidad cultural, psicológica y afectiva. (Casilda Béjar 2001)

notice that the extraordinary position reached [by Spain] in this continent has been made possible by our extraordinary ally: the language, cause and effect of our emotional, psychological, and cultural affinity

This emotional, psychological, and cultural affinity grounded in a common language is nothing but the *hispanofonía*, a community that sits on an ideological fault line and therefore needs constant reinforcement. It is in this context that Spanish governments and business leaders, under new and more favourable conditions, have strategically mobilized linguistic and cultural institutions in order to assure that the presence of Spain's economic actors in Latin America be perceived not as a high-modern version of the old colonial relationship but as 'natural' and 'legitimate':

Iberoamérica es un área de expansión *natural* para las entidades y empresas españolas, porque las raíces culturales y el idioma común facilitan el acceso a los mercados y la clientela. (Casilda Béjar 2001, emphasis added)

*Iberoamerica is a **natural** area for the expansion of Spain's institutions and companies, because the common cultural roots and language facilitate access to markets and clients.*

Iberoamérica es un objetivo político, económico y empresarial *legítimo* para los españoles ... Estamos mucho menos lejos de América Latina de lo que nadie puede pensar. (Jesús de Polanco, President of the Spanish media conglomerate PRISA, quoted in EL PAÍS, 24 July 1995, emphasis added)

*Iberoamerica is a **legitimate** political, economic, and business objective for Spaniards ... We are a lot less far from Latin America than anyone might think.*

The Spanish Royal Academy's verbal hygiene: moderate prescriptivism

The Spanish Royal Academy (henceforth RAE, the acronym for *Real Academia Española*) has existed since 1713, when it was created under the inspiration offered by the *Accademia della Crusca* (Italy) and the *Académie Française*. Throughout its history, the Academy's mission has been defined by three codification projects – a dictionary, a grammar and an orthography – and, not surprisingly, by an essentially puristic and Eurocentric ideology that seriously damaged its prestige in Latin America and its ability to contribute to the *hispanismo* movement. In the late twentieth and early twenty-first century, corpus planning remains the responsibility of the RAE which, as mentioned, through intense activity and support from a number of political and economic actors, has modernized its image and strengthened the Association of Academies of the Spanish Language (henceforth AALE, acronym for *Asociación de Academias de la Lengua Española*).[4] Among the many objectives of the new RAE, two are of special interest for the present chapter since they clearly illustrate Spain's efforts to erase the memories of empire and overcome the colonialist rhetoric of the old *hispanismo*: the definition of Spanish as a pluricentric language and of their policy as pan-hispanic.

It is appropriate to begin our analysis of the RAE's new discourse on language with a quotation from a brief but representative text: *The New Pan-hispanic Language Policy* (henceforth *NPLP*), a mission statement of sorts signed by the AALE and published by the RAE in 2004:

> Las funciones atribuidas tradicionalmente a las Academias de la Lengua consistían en la elaboración, difusión y actualización de los tres grandes códigos normativos en los que se concentra la esencia y el funcionamiento de cualquier lengua y que aseguran su unidad: la *Ortografía*, el *Diccionario* y la *Gramática*. Hasta hace algunos años, el modo de alcanzar esos objetivos se planteaba desde el deseo de mantener una lengua 'pura', basada en los hábitos lingüísticos de una parte reducida de sus hablantes, una lengua no contaminada por los extranjerismos ni alterada por el resultado de la propia evolución interna. En nuestros días, las Academias, en una orientación más adecuada y también más realista, se han fijado como tarea común la de garantizar el mantenimiento de la unidad básica del idioma, que es, en definitiva, lo que permite hablar de la comunidad hispanohablante, haciendo compatible la unidad del idioma con el reconocimiento de sus variedades internas. (AALE 2004: 3)

> *Traditionally, the tasks associated with Language Academies were the creation, promotion, and elaboration of the three main*

249

> *normative codes that represent the essence and inner workings of*
> *the language and that safeguard its unity: the **Orthography**, the*
> ***Dictionary**, and the **Grammar**. Until a few years ago, the strategies*
> *advanced to reach these objectives were grounded in a desire to*
> *keep the language 'pure' – based on the model of the linguistic*
> *practices of a small group of its speakers – and to protect it against*
> *contamination from foreign words and changes that might result*
> *from the language's internal evolution. In our days, the Academies,*
> *with a more adequate and realistic orientation, have established*
> *as their common task the protection of the language's basic unity,*
> *which is, ultimately, what allows us to speak of a Spanish-speaking*
> *community, making the unity of the language compatible with the*
> *recognition of its internal varieties and evolution.*

While the RAE unquestionably engages, by its very nature, in verbal hygiene, the *NPLP* document displays a moderate, almost inconspicuous, form of prescriptivism. In elaborating the concept of verbal hygiene, Cameron was careful to separate it from prescriptivism, insisting that it may actually represent a wide range of positions with respect to language: it may, for example, promote change in the name of progress (as in the case of efforts to eradicate practices felt to be sexist or racist) or it may oppose it as a sign of decaying intellectual standards (as in the multiple manifestations of what Milroy and Milroy (1999) have called the complaint tradition); it may embrace diversity (as in the Universal Declaration of Linguistic Rights) or it may reject it as a threat to social order (as in the English Only movement in the United States).

While authoritarian, elitist and purist forms of verbal hygiene are alive and well, the RAE, as the *NPLP* document shows, has distanced itself from the rhetoric of linguistic conservatism and embraced instead a more 'adequate and realistic' view of language: protecting the purity of Spanish is no longer its goal, and variation and change are now accepted as facts of language that do not interfere with its value.

This new permissiveness, however, is not to be mistaken for an 'anything goes' approach to verbal hygiene. While in general the RAE has steered clear of extreme forms of prescriptivism, it still retains and publicly declares a moderately prescriptive responsibility:

> El conocimiento de las características que presenta actualmente
> nuestra lengua en todos los países que integran el mundo hispánico
> permite llevar a cabo una auténtica política panhispánica, que
> recoge lo consolidado por el uso y, en los casos necesarios, se
> adelanta a *proponer las opciones que parecen más aconsejables en*
> *aquellos puntos en los que el sistema muestra vacilación.* (AALE
> 2004: 4, emphasis added)

*Knowledge of the features characteristic of our language in all the countries that make up the Hispanic world allows us to implement a truly panhispanic policy that collects what has already been consolidated by actual usage and that, whenever necessary, takes the initiative **to propose more appropriate choices in those points in which the system hesitates.***

Teams of 'experts' carefully study the language, focusing mostly on new forms and singling out those that have not yet been consolidated by usage in order to intervene and provide speakers with 'appropriate' guidance. It was precisely this moderately prescriptive attitude that triggered the publication in 2005 of the *Pan-hispanic Dictionary of Doubts* (henceforth *DPD*, for *Diccionario Panhispánico de Dudas*), a volume in which the academies have collected frequently asked questions about the correctness of specific aspects of Spanish grammar, lexicon and orthography. During its highly publicized presentation, the Madrid daily EL PAÍS reported:

> De la Concha no ha ocultado su 'enorme satisfacción' ante la publi-cación de esta obra, de 880 páginas y 7.250 entradas que recogen, en un lenguaje de fácil comprensión y accesible a los no especia-lizados, las dudas más habituales que asaltan cotidianamente a quienes desean *hablar y escribir correctamente español*. (EL PAÍS, 10 November 2005, emphasis added)

> De la Concha [the RAE's Director] did not hide his 'great satis-faction' over the publication of this 880-page, 7250-item work that collects, in a style easily accessible to non-specialists, the most frequent questions faced by those who want **to speak and write Spanish correctly**.

The new RAE: modern, popular and pan-hispanic

Like all institutions with normative responsibilities, the RAE is deeply concerned with legitimacy and profoundly aware of the impact that its public image may have on its authority. Consequently, since the early 1990s, it has taken careful steps towards cleansing the old image of a conservative, elitist and Eurocentric institution. First, as we just saw, against the old accusations of conservative purism, the RAE now acknowledges the inevitability of change and emphasizes its modernity and commitment to technological progress.

Second, against the accusation of elitism, the RAE now claims to speak for the people. We already saw that the *NPLP* document, in contrast with the previous approach, which selected the classics of the Spanish Golden Age as the principal linguistic model, declares actual usage as the main criterion in deciding on correctness. The public presentation of the *DPD* offered a perfect opportunity to project this down-to-earth image: 'Lo único que hemos hecho es estar atentos a lo que oímos en la calle, hacerlo nuestro y devolvérselo a los hablantes en forma de norma' ['*The only thing we did was pay attention to what we hear in the street, make it ours, and send it back to speakers in the shape of a linguistic norm*'] (García de la Concha quoted in EL PAÍS, 10 November 2005). Of course, no reference was made (literal or metaphorical) to the specific neighbourhoods whose streets the academicians walked in their search for the language of the people. What is clearly stated, though, and from the very title of the dictionary, is that, in the streets selected for the elaboration of the new linguistic norm, all Spanish-speaking countries are represented.

Therefore, third, against the old accusation of Eurocentrism, the RAE now commits to a pan-hispanic approach both to language and to language policy. In fact, the *NPLP* document is itself a declaration of principles that, first, defines Spanish as an internally variable language and, second, places agency and responsibility for language policy not in the hands of Spain but in those of the pan-hispanic community.

> Esta orientación panhispánica, promovida por la Real Academia Española y que las Academias han aplicado sistemáticamente y se plasma en la coautoría de todas las obras publicadas desde la edición de la *Ortografía* en 1999, procede de la voluntad política de actuar en una determinada dirección. (AALE 2004: 3)

> *This panhispanic orientation – promoted by the Spanish Royal Academy, systematically applied by the Academies, and manifest in the co-authorship of all works published since the* **Orthography** *in 1999 – comes from the political will to act in a specific direction.*

At a meeting of the AALE held in Salamanca, Spain, in September 2005, its President, García de la Concha (who – as the reader may have noticed – is also the Director of the RAE), stated that

> La esencia de todo lo que estamos haciendo es la unidad de lo que llamamos política lingüística panhispánica ... [lo cual] consiste en que los tres grandes códigos en que se sustenta y expresa la lengua española ... sean obra no sólo de la Academia Española, sino del conjunto de las academias. (EL PAÍS, 15 September 2005)

> *The essence of everything we are doing is the unity of what we call panhispanic language policy ... [which] means that the three main codes that support and express the Spanish language ... are the work not only of the Spanish Academy, but of the academies as a whole.*

A few weeks after the Salamanca meeting, the presentation of the *DPD* (again, in another Spanish city, Madrid) offered yet another opportunity to showcase the spirit of pan-hispanic cooperation that the RAE so enthusiastically upholds. EL PAÍS's coverage of the event highlighted the authorship by the 22 academies and the completion of the work as the result of an agreement, as a political alliance of sorts: 'Las 22 academias de la Lengua presentan el *Diccionario panhispánico de dudas*' ['*The 22 academies of the language launch the **Panhispanic Dictionary of Doubts**'] (EL PAÍS, 10 November 2005); 'El gran acuerdo para la unidad del idioma' ['*The great agreement for the unity of the language*'] (EL PAÍS, 10 November 2005). One aspect of the newspaper's coverage is notable in that it cues us in to the political nature and specific ideological roots not only of the event but also of the pan-hispanic policy as a whole: the almost frantic repetition of the word *consensus*:

> No ha sido difícil de hacer, gracias al gran consenso ['*it hasn't been difficult, thanks to the great **consensus**'] (EL PAÍS, 10 November 2005); no estaba claro si sería posible *consensuar* ['*it was not clear if it would be possible to reach **consensus**'] (EL PAÍS, 10 November 2005); primer trabajo de consenso América-España. Un hito ['*First America–Spain work that reaches **consensus**. Quite a landmark*'] (EL PAÍS, 10 November 2005); resultado de un consenso que consolida ... ['*the result of **consensus** that consolidates ...*'] (EL PAÍS, 11 November 2005); Y se ha llegado a esto, dicen, por consenso ['*and they have reached this goal, they say, through **consensus**'] EL PAÍS, 11 November 2005); La ministra de Educación destacó la voluntad de consenso ['*the Education Minister highlighted the willingness to reach **consensus**'] (EL PAÍS, 11 November 2005) (all emphases added).

Consensus and the constitution of a linguistic public sphere

By promoting the strategic alliance and permanent collaboration among the 22 academies, the RAE can claim to foster what I will refer to – using, somewhat liberally, Habermas' (1991) notion – as a linguistic public sphere: a series of real or virtual places of encounter and channels of communication through which members of the academies allegedly openly, rationally and democratically discuss linguistic issues of common concern and design and implement policy through consensus. Habermas' notion captures the idea of 'private people com[ing] together as a public' and claiming an active role in the 'debate over the general rules governing' social and economic

253

relations (1991: 27). These debates, which take place through the medium of 'people's public use of their reason' (*ibid.*), may become the 'authoritative bases for political action' (Calhoun 1992: 1) and for the legitimate exercise of formal democracy. The democratic adequacy of the public sphere depends, according to Calhoun, 'upon both quality of discourse and quantity of participation' (1992: 2).

The notion of a public sphere is illuminating in the analysis of Spain's language policy inasmuch as the RAE carefully projects an image of itself and its operations that formally complies with the protocols of a legitimate democracy grounded in open and rational debate: quality of discourse is protected by the careful watch of language 'experts' – the RAE is careful to recruit institutionally sanctioned linguists and philologists – and quantity of participation is pursued through a permanent 'dialogue' with the people and representative social institutions.

The 'debates' fostered by the RAE actually materialize in a variety of forms: in the conferences that regularly bring together all the academies of the Spanish language, in the interacademic committees created for specific projects, or in the fellowship programme, developed by Spain's Agency for International Cooperation, to sponsor Latin Americans while they collaborate with the Academy in their respective countries. But, in order to project an image of openness and democracy and consolidate its widespread legitimacy, the RAE must go beyond interacademic exchanges by creating a credible connection with the people whose linguistic loyalty is their target. In this quest for popularity, the RAE builds a down-to-earth image in a number of ways: first, as we saw above, by claiming to produce a norm that directly emerges from the people; second, by using the Internet as a channel of communication with speakers:

> Desde que, en 1998, la Real Academia Española abrió en su página electrónica el servicio de consultas lingüísticas ... no ha dejado de crecer el número de personas que se dirigen a esta institución en busca de una respuesta autorizada a las dudas que a diario plantea el uso del idioma. Actualmente se recibe una media de 300 consultas diarias, procedentes de todas las partes del mundo. (AALE 2004: 8)

> *Since, in November 1998, the Spanish Royal Academy initiated on its web page a service to answer linguistic questions ... the number of people coming to this institution in search of an authorized response to the questions raised by daily language use has not stopped growing. Currently we receive an average of 300 questions a day from all over the world.*

And, finally, by justifying its very existence as a response to popular demand: 'Es verdad que hay buenos libros de estilo en los medios de comunicación, pero *los hispanohablantes quieren oír la voz de las academias*' ['*It is true that the media have good style manuals, but Spanish-speakers want to hear the voice of the academies*'] (García de la Concha quoted in EL PAÍS, 10 November 2005, emphasis added).

The reference to the media is neither sporadic nor coincidental: the RAE, in its effort to broaden the social base of the linguistic public sphere, has carefully cultivated its relationship with them. In the 1990s, two distinguished journalists and media entrepreneurs became members of the RAE: in 1997, Juan Luis Cebrián, founder and editor of the centre-left Madrid daily *EL PAÍS*; and one year later, Luis María Anson Oliart, former editor of the rightwing newspaper *ABC* and founder of the even more conservative *La Razón*. The relationship between the RAE and the media seems to be more than just symbolic: not only was the *DPD* conceived as a response to questions of linguistic correctness posed by speakers; it was developed, we were told, in close consultation with the press: 'El diccionario se ha elaborado con su ayuda, sus críticas y sus aportaciones' ['*The dictionary has been elaborated with their help, their critiques, and their contributions*'] (García de la Concha quoted in EL PAÍS, 10 November 2005).

Perhaps the most inclusive and spectacular materializations of the linguistic public sphere have been the international conferences on the Spanish language, jointly organized by the RAE, the Cervantes Institute and other private and public institutions.[5] These conferences bring together prominent political figures, business people and experts from a wide range of fields, and the proceedings are made public through the Institute's website:

El Centro Virtual Cervantes se complace en publicar ... cientos de estudios que analizan, desde las más diversas perspectivas y con rigor científico, el pasado, el presente y el futuro del español ... Los congresos constituyen significativos foros de reflexión acerca de la situación, los problemas y los retos del idioma español ... Participan de los Congresos de la Lengua Española personas de todos los países de habla hispana: escritores, artistas, especialistas y profesionales de los más diversos campos del quehacer cultural. (http://cvc.cervantes.es/obref/congresos/)

The Cervantes Virtual Center is pleased to publish ... hundreds of studies that analyze, from different perspectives and with scientific rigor, the past, present, and future of Spanish. ... The conferences are important forums for reflection on the situation, problems, and challenges of the Spanish language. ... People from all

> *Spanish-speaking countries participate in the conferences: writers,*
> *artists, experts, and professionals from the most diverse fields of*
> *cultural production.*

In sum, the RAE, in collaboration with the AALE and the Cervantes Institute, strives to constitute a network of interaction that it can present as a truly representative linguistic public sphere: it welcomes the people and the experts, journalists and politicians, writers and businessmen, and, in all cases, careful attention is paid to the necessary presence of the Spanish-speaking world as a whole. It is this alleged convergence of all in an open and reasoned dialogue that, the RAE hopes, will certify it as a democratic institution and consequently invest it with the legitimacy and authority that it so covets (Gal and Woolard 2001).[6]

The discourse community and the linguistic public sphere

The linguistic public sphere promoted by the RAE has produced a significant corpus of texts dealing with language: the conference proceedings I just discussed, the annual reports (*Anuarios*) on the status of the language sponsored by the Cervantes Institute, press coverage of linguistic events, etc. In previous work (del Valle and Gabriel-Stheeman 2004; del Valle 2005; del Valle and Villa forthcoming), I have analysed different components of this corpus, concluding that one of Spain's main language policy strategies has been the projection of a meticulously crafted image of the language: first, Spanish is promoted as a language of encounter, that is, as an instrument for the expression of multiple cultures and a symbol of the spirit of democratic harmony; second, Spanish is a global language, one that is successfully spreading beyond the Spanish-speaking world; third, as a result of being the common language of many nations, Spanish is a symbol of universalism that overpowers the dangers of ethnic and national loyalties; and finally, Spanish is a useful and profitable language and knowledge of it may constitute a valuable economic asset, a source of cultural capital – to use Bourdieu's (1991) term – for those who possess it. From a language policy perspective, it is hoped that this image will further the acceptance of Spanish, first, as Spain's common language – against the constant questioning of its status by Basque, Catalan and Galician nationalists – second, as a prestigious and valuable international language, and third (the most relevant here), as the fundamental building block of the *hispanofonía*.

Thus, what the analysis shows so far is a group of individuals and institutions converging into a common set of metalinguistic practices, and producing a coordinated and, at times, highly choreographed discourse of verbal hygiene that defines and hopes to control the nature of Spanish. The internal consistency of this discourse and the frequency with which it is reproduced in a series of well-defined institutional settings suggests that we are dealing with what Watts has called a discourse community:

> a set of individuals who can be interpreted as constituting a community on the basis of the ways in which their oral or written discourse practices reveal common interests, goals and beliefs, i.e. on the degree of institutionalization that their discourse displays. (Watts 1999: 43)

One aspect of Watts' proposal is of particular interest to the present analysis: discourse communities are defined not only by producing common discursive practices but also by representing socially situated interests. Because of this social specificity, the view of language produced by the community is necessarily partial and, therefore, always contestable. Consequently, discourse communities that hope to become or remain dominant must constantly renovate their sources of legitimacy.

Antonio Gramsci's notion of hegemony (Ives 2004) offers a view of domination that may help elucidate the mechanisms through which the discourse community that has formed around the RAE secures its power. Hegemony is a form of domination based not on coercion but on control and naturalization of a specific system of values:

> It is a whole body of practices and expectations, over the whole of living ... It thus constitutes a sense of reality for most people in the society, a sense of absolute because experienced reality beyond which it is very difficult for most members of the society to move. (Williams 1977: 110)

What better way of naturalizing the discourse community than presenting it not as a socially situated and interested group that projects a specific point of view but as a linguistic public sphere where all converge to produce a common vision of language through consensus? The total dominance of a community, its hegemonic power, will rest on its ability to absorb dissent and ideologically merge with the linguistic public sphere:

> Any hegemonic process must be especially alert and responsive to the alternatives and opposition which question or threaten its dominance ... to the extent that they are significant the decisive hegemonic function is to control or transform or even incorporate them. (Williams 1977: 113)

257

By absorbing dissent, the discourse community erases (Irvine and Gal 2000) its social roots and grounds its views not in specific interests but in consensus, in an open and democratic debate, in an anonymous public. If it successfully merges with the linguistic public sphere – if it manages to be perceived by all as *being* the public sphere – the hegemonic vision of language that it produces will be a vision from nowhere, a perspective paradoxically assumed to contain all points of view (Gal and Woolard 2001).

Within this theoretical framework, for the power of a discourse community to be truly hegemonic, dissent must be negotiated internally and in compliance with the community's institutionalized practices. In other words, alternatives and opposition must not threaten the ultimate (extralinguistic) social order represented by the discourse community. While Spain's linguistic agencies have striven (with great success, we must say) to create an appearance of openness and democracy, our survey of the recent history of Spain's language policy finds a number of incidents that expose the imperfect fit between the dominant discourse community and the linguistic public sphere.

Perhaps the most strident happened on 23 May 2001. At a literary award ceremony, King Juan Carlos I of Spain stated:

> Nunca fue la nuestra lengua de imposición, sino de encuentro; a nadie se le obligó nunca a hablar en castellano: fueron los pueblos más diversos quienes hicieron suyo por voluntad libérrima, el idioma de Cervantes.
>
> *Ours has never been a language of imposition; instead, it has been a language of encounter. No one has ever been forced to speak Castilian; different peoples, through their free will, have chosen to make the language of Cervantes their own.*[7]

These words, of course, triggered the immediate and angry protest, within Spain, of Basque, Catalan and Galician nationalists; to which the Royal House quickly (and clumsily) responded: the King was referring to America![8] The episode offers a perfect example of an excessively conspicuous erasure: an ideological deletion so extreme that it ends up revealing precisely the object whose erasure was intended (Irvine and Gal 2000). In an effort to affirm the pan-hispanic community by rooting it in an unproblematic shared language, the King and his speech writers take the 'encounter' metaphor – widely used within the discourse community to which they all belong – too far. The fumbled sleight of hand exposes the traumatic historical experiences and profound inequalities that brought about the *hispanofonía* and, thus, reveals the constructed (interested) nature of the image.

A second incident took place in Zacatecas, Mexico, in 1997, during the First Conference on the Spanish Language. One of the keynote speakers was the renowned Colombian novelist and Nobel Prize winner Gabriel García Márquez. In a lecture mischievously entitled '*Message in a bottle for the god of all words*' ['Botella al mar para el dios de las palabras'] he called for orthographic reform:

> Jubilemos la ortografía, terror del ser humano desde la cuna: enterremos las haches rupestres, firmemos un tratado de límites entre la ge y jota ... Y qué de nuestra be de burro y nuestra ve de vaca, que los abuelos españoles nos trajeron como si fueran dos y siempre sobra una?

> *Let's retire the orthography, that monster that haunts humans from the cradle: let's bury the old h, let's sign a border agreement between **g** and **j**, ... and what about **b** as in **burro** and **v** as in **vaca**, brought by our Spanish grandparents as if they were two when actually there is always one too many?*[9]

García Márquez's speech made a splash whose ripples were felt all over the Spanish-speaking world. He had been invited to celebrate the language and lend legitimacy to the event with his enormous symbolic capital; and instead he unexpectedly opened the can of worms of orthographic reform. After the initial upheaval, and once the conference was over, the discussion slowly faded ... until 1999, when the RAE and the rest of the language academies published the *Orthography*, 'el fruto de un consenso alcanzado tras largas negociaciones entre las 22 academias [que] despejan definitivamente cualquier temor sobre una fragmentación del español' ['*the result of a consensus reached after long negotiations by all 22 academies [that] finally removed any concerns about the possible fragmentation of Spanish*'] (EL PAÍS, 9 October 1999). The *anonymous* prologue contains a few paragraphs devoted to 'dealing with' orthographic mavericks:

> [S]on muchos los arbitristas de la Ortografía que acuden a esta Institución o salen a la palestra, con mejor intención que acierto, pidiendo u ofreciendo radicales soluciones a los problemas ortográficos o cebándose con fáciles diatribas en el sistema establecido ...
> A todos estos entusiastas debería recordárseles que ya Nebrija ... advirtió que 'en aquello que es como ley consentida por todos es cosa dura hacer novedad'. (Real Academia Española 1999: xv)

> *There are many eccentric utopians that come to this Institution or appear in public (with good intentions but poor judgment) asking for or offering radical solutions to orthographic problems or attacking the established system with simplistic diatribes. ... Those enthusiasts should be reminded of Nebrixa's warning ...:*

259

*'in matters of law that have been agreed upon by all it is hard to
introduce things that are new'.*

Thus, without naming names, García Márquez and other orthographic
idealists were guided as to 'correct' procedure within the discourse
community. Interestingly, this direct admonition was not the most
severe warning against eccentric initiatives. The most threatening
caution actually came in the form of a history lesson:

> En 1843, una autotitulada *Academia Literaria y Científica de
> Profesores de Instrucción Primaria* de Madrid se había propuesto
> una reforma radical, con supresión de *h*, *v* y *q*, entre otras estri-
> dencias, y había empezado a aplicarla en las escuelas. El asunto
> era demasiado serio y de ahí la inmediata oficialización de la
> ortografía académica, que nunca antes se había estimado necesaria.
> Sin esa irrupción de espontáneos reformadores con responsabi-
> lidad pedagógica, es muy posible que la Corporación española
> hubiera dado un par de pasos más, que tenía anunciados y que la
> hubieran emparejado con la corriente americana, es decir, con las
> directrices de Bello. (Real Academia Española 1999: xv)[10]

> *In 1843, a self-proclaimed **Scientific and Literary Academy of
> Teachers of Primary Education** in Madrid proposed a radical
> reform that included the elimination of **h**, **v**, and **q** among
> other eccentricities, and began to use it in schools. The matter
> was too important and triggered the immediate officialization
> of the Academy's orthography, which had never until then been
> considered necessary. Without this irruption by spontaneous
> reformers with pedagogical responsibilities, it is quite likely that
> the Spanish Academy would have taken a couple of the already
> announced extra steps that would have brought it closer to the
> American trend, that is, to Bello's norms.*

In this passage, the anonymous author/s of the Prologue remind
the readers, through an old linguistic episode, of the fragmentation
debates, of a time when several orthographic models circulated, both
in Spain and Latin America, threatening the unity of the language.
It is remarkable how gently the Prologue treats Andrés Bello (1781–
1865) – proponent of the most successful alternative orthography in
the Spanish-speaking world, but a highly respected (especially in
Latin America) grammarian and man of letters – and how harshly,
in contrast, it portrays the Madrid teachers as dangerous mavericks
('self-proclaimed', 'spontaneous reformers with pedagogical responsibilities'). It is the teachers – their independence and autonomous
actions – who are actually blamed for the Spanish government's
'emergency' decision to exercise its linguistic authority and make
the RAE's orthography official before reaching an agreement – the

coveted consensus – with Bello's Latin America. Regardless of how things actually played out in 1843 (an interesting topic in its own right), the present context highlights the strategic use of the episode as a deterrent to anyone tempted to engage in verbal hygiene outside the jurisdiction of the RAE's discourse community. The indirect threat of coercion contained in the Prologue reveals the imperfect match between the interests of the discourse community and the true openness that would define the ideal public sphere. Open and democratic debate is possible as long as the linguistic/social order represented by the dominant discourse community is not placed under threat.

Diversity: theoretical imperative and political necessity

The episode recalled by the RAE brings us back to the times when fears of linguistic fragmentation and the consequent breakdown of communication were a significant concern in public discussions of language. While the fetish of communication (Cameron 1995: 24) is still present in the RAE's contemporary discourse of verbal hygiene (i.e. Spanish must be cared for in order to preserve its communicative transparency), the fragmentation prophesies have been notoriously absent from linguistic debates for decades now. Academicians no longer feel that dialectal variation threatens the unity of Spanish and can therefore celebrate unity while simultaneously embracing internal diversity. They also seem aware that selection is a delicate process in language planning and that strict prescriptivism and the pursuit of homogeneity would in all likelihood severely damage the image of openness and modernity that they so carefully cultivate.

The *NPLP* document is clear in this regard: the academies must make the defence of unity compatible with the recognition of the language's internal varieties. Interestingly, this favourable attitude towards variation has gone well beyond tolerance and the old fragmentation argument has now been turned on its head: in the image of Spanish being projected by the dominant language agencies, diversity is embraced as an asset, as the best protection against atomization. Spain's King Juan Carlos I unequivocally subscribes to this view: 'el arraigo de la lengua española ... tiene en su diversidad su más firme garantía de unidad' ['*The roots of the Spanish language ... have in their diversity the strongest guarantee of unity*'] (quoted in EL PAÍS, 11 May 2005).

Most importantly, this ideology – that pronounces the unifying power of diversity – has actually informed the RAE's normative activity. When the publication of the new grammar of Spanish was

261

announced, García de la Concha stated: '[Será] la primera no peninsular, descriptiva del español en todas sus variantes, una norma policéntrica' ['*It will be the first non-peninsular descriptive grammar of all varieties of Spanish; a pluricentric norm*'] (EL PAÍS, 15 October 2005). Not only is Spanish embraced as a diverse language from which the norm is extracted; the norm itself – the synecdoche, to use Joseph's (1987: 58) concept – is pluricentric. Thus, the pan-hispanic policy is two-sided: on one hand, design and implementation are overseen by all Spanish-speaking nations; on the other, the norm itself represents them all. Like the makers of that old map of China in Jorge Luis Borges' story (1972), so concerned with accuracy that they created a map that literally covered the whole territory, the writers of the normative Spanish grammar exhibit a similar desire for totality and hope to cover the language in all its diversity: 'se busca que "se reflejen y expresen no sólo el español peninsular, sino el español total"' ['*we want to "reflect and express not just Peninsular Spanish, but total Spanish"*'] (García de la Concha quoted in EL PAÍS, 15 September 2005).

In view of such confidence, it is intriguing that the RAE would adopt precisely the defence of unity as its main objective and that language policy agents would feel compelled to affirm unity over and over again as they do. Repetition is, of course, a strategy through which culturally constructed categories become naturalized: public celebrations of the language (such as conferences) and the normative monuments that represent it (such as grammars and dictionaries) are the very acts that constitute it; and similarly, apparently descriptive statements of its unity are in fact performative acts that create it. However, the perseverance in the assertion of unity and the centrality given to the topic by the RAE's discourse community reveal the presence of a (mostly latent but at times loudly voiced) fragmentation anxiety. Santiago de Mora-Figueroa, Marquis of Tamarón and Director of the Cervantes Institute in the 1990s, said shortly after taking office: 'Hay que preservar la unidad del español porque corre peligro' ['*We must protect the unity of Spanish because it is in danger*'] (quoted in EL PAÍS, 24 May 1996). Voicing similar concerns, a few years later, an editorial in which EL PAÍS celebrated the publication of the *DPD* also warned against excessive optimism: 'la formidable expansión de nuestra lengua en el mundo ... no por ello menos sometida al peligro de atomización ['*the international spread of Spanish ... does not mean that it is less vulnerable to the danger of atomization*'] (EL PAÍS, 11 November 2005).

Obviously, some fears of disintegration still linger. But, if dialectal diversity has been ruled out as the possible cause of a linguistic breakup, then what exactly is the source of this fragmentation anxiety?

Not dialectal but ideological diversity: a conflicting view of Spanish that might gain support, a possible fracture in the discourse community that would disrupt the prevailing linguistic order and expose the socio-political roots of the dominant linguistic ideology. New forms of verbal hygiene claiming their right to participate in the linguistic public sphere on their own terms, that is, outside the carefully guarded boundaries of the discourse community, would threaten the latter's hegemonic power and jeopardize the social order that it supports.

I have argued in previous work that Spain's contemporary language policies and the image of Spanish that they project play a major part in controlling the political instrumentalization of the *hispanofonía*. As we have seen, Spanish 'is, ultimately, what allows us to speak of a Spanish-speaking community' (AALE 2004: 3), a *hispanofonía* that, since the 1990s, has acquired great economic significance for Spain-based corporations and their partners (wherever in the globe they may come from). But, like Ernest Renan's nation (1996), this multinational community is a daily plebiscite, a permanent campaign against those who might choose to imagine it differently. This constant threat posed by possible ideological dissidence, by alternative views of Spanish – of what it is, what it represents and who has the authority to settle linguistic disputes – is confronted by the RAE through the production of a powerful image that now more than ever must include the enthusiastic embrace of diversity. In order for the RAE's discourse community to become truly hegemonic it must present its vision of Spanish as emerging, not from an interested socio-economic position, but from the open, rational and democratic debates of a public sphere, from the consensus reached by an anonymous and aperspectival public that represents all because it represents no one in particular (Gal and Woolard 2001). There is no legitimacy without democracy, no democracy without consensus, and no consensus without diversity. In sum, in the contemporary construction of a hegemonic *hispanofonía*, diversity has become a theoretical imperative as well as a political necessity:

> La variedad ... es una garantía para la democracia [*Diversity ... is the guarantee of democracy*]. (Pedro Luis Barcia, Director of the Argentinean language academy, quoted in EL PAÍS, 11 November 2005)

Conclusion

In the present chapter, I have argued that, in the wake of Spain's recent economic take-off, Spanish governments have mobilized cultural and linguistic institutions in order to strengthen and legitimize their influence

in Latin America and facilitate the operation of Spain-based corporations in that continent. Faced with the possibility that this scenario be
perceived as neocolonial, these institutions have striven to conceptualize and publicly portray Spain's presence in its former colonies as both
'natural' and 'legitimate' and have unequivocally promoted the notion of a
fraternal community of Spanish-speaking nations – a construct that I have
chosen to call *hispanofonía*. In this process, the Spanish Royal Academy
has been a central actor, designing and promoting images of itself and of
Spanish that would function as iconic representations of the idealized
egalitarian and democratic pan-hispanic community.

In my studies of Spain's contemporary language policies and
ideologies, current discourses of endangerment surrounding Spanish
have emerged as sites where anxieties over Spain's struggles to achieve
relative prominence within the international arena are worked out.
Thus, present worries about linguistic fragmentation do not only or
necessarily reflect concerns about the purely 'linguistic' integrity of
the language. Instead, I contend, they mirror fears of an 'ideological'
fracture that would expose inequality and dissent and thus hamper
the consolidation of the *hispanofonía*. In response to the potentially
dangerous identification of Spain as a privileged and interested player
within the fraternal language community, I suggest that the Spanish
Royal Academy has structured its activity around a linguistic public
sphere, an open space where, allegedly, representatives from all
Spanish-speaking nations converge in order to 'democratically' decide
on the future of the language. In this ideological context, the language
itself must necessarily reflect the egalitarianism that allegedly charac-
terizes the *hispanofonía*: consequently, intralingual diversity is now
embraced and, thus, its meaning, its subversive potential, controlled.

References

AALE [Asociación de Academias de la Lengua Española] (2004), *La nueva
    política lingüística panhispánica*. Madrid: Real Academia Española.
Alvar, M. (1991), *El Español de las Dos Orillas*. Madrid: Mapfre.
Anderson, B. (1983), *Imagined Communities: Reflections on the Origin and
    Spread of Nationalism*. London/New York: Verso.
Bonet, L. and de Gregorio, A. (1999), 'La industria cultural española en América
    latina', in N. García Canclini and C. Moneta (eds), *Las industrias culturales
    en la integración latinoamericana*. Buenos Aires: Editorial Universitaria de
    Buenos Aires, pp. 77–114.
Borges, J. L. (1972), 'Del rigor de la ciencia', in *El Hacedor*. Madrid: Alianza
    Editorial.
Bourdieu, P. (1991), *Language and Symbolic Power*. Cambridge, MA: Harvard
    University Press.

Caballero Wanguemert, M. M. (1989), 'Las polémicas lingüísticas durante el siglo xix'. *Cuadernos Hispanoamericanos*, 500, 177–87.

Calhoun, C. (ed.) (1992), *Habermas and the Public Sphere*. Cambridge, MA: The MIT Press.

Cameron, D. (1995), *Verbal Hygiene*. London/New York: Routledge.

Casilda Béjar, R. (2001), 'Una década de inversiones españolas en América Latina (1990–2000) El idioma como ventaja competitiva'. Available at http://cvc.cervantes.es/obref/congresos/valladolid/ponencias/activo_del_espanol/1_la_industria_del_espanol/casilda_r.htm.

Cecchini, D. and Zicolillo, J. (2002), *Los nuevos conquistadores*. Madrid: Ediciones Foca.

Cuervo, R. J. (1899), 'Prólogo', in F. Soto y Calvo, *Nastasio*. Chartres: Durand, pp. vii–x.

Cuervo, R. J. (1950), *Disquisiciones sobre filología castellana*. Bogotá: Instituto Caro y Cuervo.

Del Valle, J. (2002), 'Historical linguistics and cultural history: the controversy between Juan Valera and Rufino José Cuervo', in J. del Valle and L. Gabriel-Stheeman (eds), *The Battle over Spanish between 1800 and 2000: Language Ideologies and Hispanic Intellectuals*. London/New York: Routledge, pp. 64–77.

Del Valle, J. (2005), 'La lengua, patria común: política lingüística, política exterior y el post-nacionalismo hispánico', in R. Wright and P. Ricketts (eds), *Studies on Ibero-Romance Linguistics Dedicated to Ralph Penny*. Newark: Juan de la Cuesta, pp. 391–416.

Del Valle, J. and Gabriel-Stheeman, L. (eds) (2002a), *The Battle over Spanish between 1800 and 2000: Language Ideologies and Hispanic Intellectuals*. London/New York: Routledge.

Del Valle, J. and Gabriel-Stheeman, L. (2002b), ' "Codo con codo": the Hispanic community and the language spectacle', in J. del Valle and L. Gabriel-Stheeman (eds), *The Battle over Spanish between 1800 and 2000: Language Ideologies and Hispanic Intellectuals*. London/New York: Routledge, pp. 193–219.

Del Valle, J. and Gabriel-Stheeman, L. (2004), 'Lengua y mercado', in J. Del Valle and L. Gabriel-Stheeman (eds), *La batalla del idioma: la intelectualidad hispánica ante la lengua*. Frankfurt/Madrid: Vervuert/Iberoamericana, pp. 253–63.

Del Valle, J. and Villa, L. (forthcoming), 'Spanish in Brazil: language policy, business and cultural propaganda', *Language Policy*, 5, (4).

DPD [Real Academia Española and Asociación de Academias de la Lengua Española] (2005), *Diccionario Panhispánico de Dudas*. Madrid: Santillana.

Fogelquist, D. F. (1968), *Españoles de América y Americanos de España*. Madrid: Gredos.

Gal, S. and Woolard, K. (eds) (2001), *Languages and Publics: The Making of Authority*. Manchester, UK: St. Jerome.

Gramsci, A. (1991), *Selections from Cultural Writings*. Cambridge, MA: Harvard University Press.

Grijelmo, Á. (1998), *Defensa apasionada del idioma español*. Madrid: Taurus.

Habermas, J. (1991), *The Structural Transformation of the Public Sphere.* Cambridge, MA: The MIT Press.

Irvine, J. T. and Gal, S. (2000), 'Language ideology and linguistic differentiation', in P. V. Kroskrity (ed.), *Regimes of Language: Ideologies, Polities, and Identities.* Santa Fe, NM: School of American Research Press, pp. 35–83.

Ives, P. (2004), *Language and Hegemony in Gramsci.* London/Ann Arbor, MI: Pluto Press.

Joseph, J. E. (1987), *Eloquence and Power: The Rise of Language Standards and Standard Languages.* New York: Basil Blackwell.

Kroskrity, P. V. (2000), 'Regimenting languages: language ideological perspectives', in P. V. Kroskrity (ed.), *Regimes of Language: Ideologies, Polities, and Identities.* Santa Fe, NM: School of American Research Press, pp. 1–34.

Lodares, J. R. (2000), *El paraíso políglota.* Madrid: Taurus.

Milroy, J. and Milroy, L. (1999), *Authority in Language: Investigating Standard English* (3rd edn). London: Routledge.

Pike, F. B. (1971), *Hispanismo, 1898–1936.* Notre Dame/London: University of Notre Dame Press.

Rama, C. M. (1982), *Historia de las relaciones culturales entre España y la América Latina. Siglo XIX.* México: Fondo de Cultura Económica.

Real Academia Española. (1999), *Ortografía de la Lengua Española.* Madrid: Espasa.

Renan, E. (1996), 'What is a nation?', in G. Eley and R. G. Suny (eds), *Becoming National.* New York: Oxford University Press, pp. 42–55.

Sepúlveda, I. (2005), *El sueño de la Madre Patria. Hispanoamericanismo y nacionalismo.* Madrid: Marcial Pons.

Valera, J. (1900), 'Sobre la duración del habla castellana', *Obras Completas,* 1961, 2, 1036–40.

Velleman, B. (2004), 'Linguistic anti-academicism and Hispanic community: Sarmiento and Unamuno', in J. Del Valle and L. Gabriel-Stheeman (eds), *La batalla del idioma: La intelectualidad hispánica ante la lengua.* Frankfurt/Madrid: Vervuert/Iberoamericana, pp. 14–41.

Watts, R. J. (1999), 'The social construction of Standard English: Grammar writers as a "discourse community"' in T. Bex and R. Watts (eds), *Standard English: The Widening Debate.* London/New York: Routledge, pp. 40–68.

Williams, R. (1977), *Marxism and Literature.* Oxford: Oxford University Press.

Notes

1 Many are related to the emergence of nationalist movements in parts of northern Spain after the late nineteenth century; others appear in Latin America, especially after the 1960s, in connection with efforts to empower indigenous cultures and revitalize their languages.

2 The Spanish Royal Academy, founded in 1713, is the main Spanish institution in charge of the codification of the language (see below and www.rae.es). 'The Cervantes Institute is a public institution created by Spain in 1991 in order to promote and teach Spanish and to spread Spanish and

Spanish American culture'. It was originally created under the umbrella of the Ministry of Foreign Affairs and is currently also overseen by the Ministry of Culture. (www.cervantes.es/seg_nivel/institucion/Marcos_institucionprincipal.jsp).

3 A number of labour disputes involving Spain-based corporations in Latin America have in fact been codified as neocolonial conflicts (see del Valle 2005). An excellent example of this perception is *The New Conquistadors* [*Los_nuevos conquistadores*] by two Argentinean journalists: Cecchini and Zicolillo (2002).

4 All Spanish-speaking countries (including the USA) have a Spanish language academy. They all come together, under the leadership of the *Española*, in the Association. More information at www.rae.es.

5 The first was held in 1997 in Zacatecas, Mexico, and organized by the Cervantes Institute in collaboration with this country's Office of Public Education; the second took place in 2001 in Valladolid, Spain, and was organized then by both the Cervantes and the RAE; the third, held in Rosario, Argentina, in 2004, was planned by the Spanish institutions in collaboration with the Argentinean Academy of Letters and an executive committee representing the host country.

6 My purpose in this chapter is to analyse the mechanisms through which the RAE responds to endangerment through the embrace of diversity and how in the process it creates an image of itself and of Spanish. While my immediate goal in this particular chapter is not to expose specific distortions, it is worth noting a couple of flagrant glitches in the image of representativeness, democracy and egalitarianism. Out of 40 current members of the RAE, only three are women. The veteran among the women is Ana María Matute, who joined the institution in 1998. Since then, there have been thirteen additional appointments out of which two went to women and eleven to men. In the corpus of texts that I have analysed, I have encountered references (some quoted above) to Latin America as a space where Spain's presence is 'natural' and 'legitimate'. However, in the same texts, I have not found any references to Spain as a 'natural' and 'legitimate' space for, say, Ecuadorian or Dominican workers.

7 The speech can be read at www.casareal.es/casareal/home – Discursos y Mensajes: 23/4/01.

8 More details on the incident and its aftermath in Chapter 10 of del Valle and Gabriel-Stheeman 2004.

9 The speech can be read at http://cvc.cervantes.es/obref/congresos/zacatecas/voces/. It is also available at numerous websites.

10 In that period, the University of Chile was engaged in a well-known controversy which resulted in the relative generalization of Andrés Bello's orthographic proposal. In Spain, around the same time, and as the Prologue relates, an organization of teachers also put forth a new spelling project. See Velleman 2004 for more information on these nineteenth-century orthographic debates.

13 Language endangerment and verbal hygiene: History, morality and politics

Deborah Cameron

During the past ten years, the plight of endangered languages has attracted increasing interest from the mainstream media. A study carried out by the communication researcher Nancy Rivenburgh (2004) found, for example, that 'between 1996 and 2004, the issue of endangered languages appeared on some international news wire, on average, 1.5 times a month'. Though as Rivenburgh observes, this is hardly saturation coverage, it does show that the subject is featuring in news stories with some regularity. This steady trickle of reporting suggests that language endangerment has ceased to be seen as a 'fringe' issue, of little interest to anyone outside a small group of activists and academics, and has found a niche – albeit a modest one – on the mainstream news agenda.

Since the representation of any issue for a mass audience has implications for the way it is understood, it is of interest to inquire how – that is, through what kind of representation – language endangerment has been able to move into the mainstream. A useful parallel here is with climate change, an issue which made the same move somewhat earlier. One thing the two issues have in common is that they do not fit the prototype for news stories. According to the classic work of Galtung and Ruge (1965) on 'news values', issues and events are most likely to be treated as newsworthy when they involve dramatic events, occurring in spatiotemporal proximity to the target audience, and involving either 'important' people or people with whom the audience can readily identify. Climate change and language endangerment, by contrast, are both gradual processes, whose most immediate negative effects are felt by poor people in remote places; presenting the bigger picture depends heavily on using statistical models which deal in probabilities rather than certainties. To make such issues newsworthy, it is necessary to inject drama and urgency by framing them as grave crises which we ignore at our peril. But while 'crisis' framing may give an issue greater mainstream visibility, it can also lead to unbalanced and misleading coverage, as Allan Bell points out in a discussion of the climate change case (Bell 1991). In an effort to fit the facts to the frame, statements about the extent of the problem may be reproduced shorn of the caveats their expert sources were careful to include; disagreement among experts may be glossed over in formulations like 'many scientists believe...'; prominence may be given to the most extreme and alarmist expert predictions, or even to predictions no expert has made, but which journalists have extrapolated from their inexpert reading of the evidence.

Reporting on endangered languages shows many of these tendencies. In the sample of mainstream media sources I examined, most repeated at least one of the following assertions: that the number of languages spoken in the world will have halved by 2050; that 90 per cent of the approximately 6,800 languages in use today are destined to disappear completely (some reports specified 'by the end of this century', others left the time-frame vague); and that ultimately 'fewer than a dozen languages' will be spoken by the overwhelming majority of humans. None of these predictions was clearly attributed to a source in any of the texts in which I found them (though '[many] linguists believe' was a common formula). It was never explained how such predictions might be arrived at, and no reference was made to dissenting opinions.

It is also evident that the 'crisis' of language endangerment is generally presented in emotive and moralistic terms. While I would not go so far as to describe the result as a 'moral panic' in the classic sense (Cohen 2002) – for most people language endangerment is not enough of a threat to engender the requisite fear and loathing – it does arguably share some features with moral panic, such as the presupposition of a dire and rapidly deteriorating situation (cf. the statistical claims cited above), the repeated expression of alarm about the scale of the problem, and the use of emotionally loaded terms to describe it (e.g. *death, endangerment, extinction, threat*[1]). As with most phenomena which become the focus of moral panic, there is no attempt to present a 'balanced' argument about whether or not endangered languages should be preserved. Rivenburgh reports that all the press stories in her sample took a 'neutral to sympathetic' stance: 'No article', she notes, 'stated that language extinction was a good thing'. This is unsurprising, for the 'crisis' frame presupposes that it is not a good thing: even what Rivenburgh classes as 'neutral' (i.e. descriptive) reports are implicitly 'sympathetic' to the extent that they make use of that frame.

269

In sum, then, language endangerment is presented by the mainstream media as one of those causes which axiomatically call for a moral response – if not panic, then certainly indignation – from the imagined community of right-thinking people. By implication, no right-thinking person would entertain the proposition that 'language extinction is a good thing', nor even that it is simply a thing, on which right-thinking people might have differing opinions, or no very definite opinions at all. *Not* deploring the rapidity with which human languages are apparently being lost once the matter has been brought to your attention would be as odd as not deploring world hunger, the HIV–AIDS epidemic, the destruction of tropical rainforests or the dying out of many animal and plant species.

This last is of course a particularly salient parallel, since the English phrase 'endangered language' clearly trades on the analogy with 'endangered species'. In addition to being moralized, then, the issue of language endangerment has been *biologized* or *ecologized* (see Muehlmann, this volume). What I mean by that is that moral indignation about the plight of endangered languages is generated by linking the issue to ecological concerns about biodiversity and the conservation of the earth's resources (which are seen in this context as including its array of human cultures), rather than – as would also be possible – to political concerns about human rights, social justice and the distribution of resources among more and less powerful groups. Of course it should be acknowledged that these two sets of concerns are not in principle mutually exclusive: they can be connected, and have been by various commentators (e.g. Phillipson *et al.* 1994; Nettles & Romaine 2000). But below I will suggest that in most mainstream discourse, it is the 'ecologizing' idea of diversity as a good in itself – and conversely, the loss of that diversity as an injury to humanity as a whole – that is presented as the central moral issue. Far less attention is given to the overtly political, redistribution and recognition struggles in which many language preservation and revitalization movements are actually embedded.

Rivenburgh's criticisms of the media provide a good illustration of the way it has come to be taken for granted that language endangerment is primarily an environmental issue. Rivenburgh complains that most media coverage:

> ... gives no sense that the loss of indigenous languages is *an indicator of trends, environmental or otherwise*, that will affect the general public in any way ... The rapid pace of vanishing languages is definitely not portrayed ... as the *'miner's canary'*, *indicating the diminishing health of our planet* (Rivenburgh 2004, emphasis added).

The italicized sections of this passage show how Rivenburgh evidently feels the issue *should* be portrayed. Her complaint is puzzling, however, for as I will try to demonstrate below, the issue is very commonly represented in precisely the ecologizing terms she castigates the media for failing to use. After looking at some illustrative examples taken from mainstream media sources (encyclopaedia entries, news stories, science journalism aimed at non-specialists and contributions to online discussion groups), I will go on to consider in more theoretical terms the ideological underpinnings and effects of what I take to be the currently dominant, ecologizing discourse on language endangerment. I will suggest that the understanding of language that is mobilized (and reproduced) in this discourse has its roots in language ideologies which were historically connected to the rise of nationalist movements in nineteenth-century Europe, and which also entered into the racialized linguistics of the National Socialist era in Germany. I will further argue that this history is not irrelevant for our understanding of contemporary discourse on language endangerment. Without suggesting that today's language preservation movements are in any sense nationalist, still less fascist, I do want to suggest that their rhetoric often relies implicitly on assumptions which, in the light of history, can hardly be considered unproblematic.

Representing language endangerment: languages and (other) living things

Let us begin with an example of 'ecologizing' discourse. It comes from a report on a recently-published study that appeared in the science section of CNN's website on 22 May 2003:

Extinction fear for languages

LONDON, England. New research on human communication suggests that languages may be more threatened by extinction than previously thought.

Using the same standards applied to bird and mammal populations, Professor Bill Sutherland of the University of East Anglia in England examined the threat to the world's 6,800 languages. His findings – that nearly 1,700 languages are either endangered, critically endangered or vulnerable – are reported in the May 15 edition of the science journal, Nature.

'The threats to birds and mammals are well known, but it turns out that languages are far more threatened', Sutherland says. About 27 percent of the world's languages are threatened, compared to about 9 percent of the bird population, his study shows.

271

Sutherland also notes similarities in areas where languages and birds were endangered or extinct. 'Countries with the most endangered and extinct languages also have more endangered and extinct birds', he writes in Nature. Likewise, 'areas with high language diversity also have high bird and mammal diversity, and all three show similar relationships to area, latitude (and) area of forest'. (www.cnn.com/2003/TECH/science/05/22/extinct.language/ [accessed 22 May 2003])

This extract is not the whole of the report, which contains a further paragraph actually naming several endangered languages, followed by a quote from a different expert source (the Foundation for Endangered Languages) positing essentially socio-political causes for their decline, such as 'urbanization, westernization and the growth of global communications, which diminish the self-sufficiency of small and traditional communities'. But the key part of the report, consisting of the headline, lead and summarizing quotes from the main source, is premised entirely on the equation of languages with animal species. The piece is even illustrated by a large photograph of an endangered bird, the Kirtland's Warbler.

The aspect of this report which is most striking from a language ideological point of view is its matter-of-fact acceptance of what we might call, following Lakoff and Johnson (1980), the conceptual metaphor LANGUAGES ARE BIOLOGICAL SPECIES. Something like 'Saami' (an endangered language spoken by the reindeer-herding Saami people of northern Scandinavia) can be compared directly with something like 'the Kirtland's Warbler' (an endangered bird species), on the grounds that each is 'threatened' with 'extinction'. What the comparison obscures, however, is that the mechanism of that 'extinction' is completely different in the two cases. In the case of the Kirtland's Warbler, environmental changes affecting their habitat have impaired the birds' ability to reproduce. This has led to a decline in their numbers, which if it continues will lead inexorably to the loss of the species as a genetically-defined entity. In the case of the Saami language, by contrast, the threat of 'extinction' arises from the cultural process of language shift, i.e. the adoption by the people in question of other languages such as Swedish and Norwegian. This assimilation to other groups' languages is possible (whereas it would not be possible for Kirtland's Warblers to turn themselves into blackbirds or sparrows) because Saami is *not* a genetically-defined entity. Indeed, it is not a life-form of any sort; as Milroy once observed (1992: 23): 'it is not true that language is a living thing (any more than swimming, or birdsong, is a living thing): it is a vehicle for communication between living things, namely human beings'. But texts like the CNN report bear eloquent witness to the persistence and continued potency of the 'organicist' view, according to which languages are indeed living organisms.

The organicist view of language had its intellectual heyday in the philological scholarship of the nineteenth century (when it influenced Darwin as he formulated his views on evolution and the origin of species). In that period it came with other kinds of ideological baggage – in particular, the notion that the language of a people was a repository of their history and cultural heritage, an expression of their characteristic nature or spirit (*Volksgeist*), and the vehicle through which all these were transmitted to each new generation. These ideas were taken up in some European nationalist movements, and also in those later forms of inquiry which concerned themselves with elucidating the distinctive characteristics of different racial and ethnic groups. Modern linguistic science has dismissed the ideas in question as intellectually misguided and, in their racialized forms, politically repellent; yet something of their flavour would appear to linger on in contemporary discourse about endangered languages. That the continuities go beyond the cliché of 'language as a living thing' is illustrated by the following extract from the entry for 'endangered languages' in a popular online encyclopaedia, www.yourdictionary.com. The passage quoted comes from a section of the entry headed 'Why does it matter?':

> Language is the most efficient means of transmitting a culture …. Every culture has adapted to unique circumstances, and the language expresses those circumstances. …All peoples identify their culture as closely with their languages as with their religion. What we talk about, think, and believe is closely bound up with the words we have, so the history of a culture can be mapped in its language.
> (www.yourdictionary.com/elr/whatis.html)

The sentence 'what we talk about, think and believe is closely bound up with the words we have' may look like a folk-rendering of the Sapir–Whorf hypothesis (in its popular 'Eskimos have a lot of words for snow' version), but the way the sentence continues – 'so that the history of a culture can be mapped in its language' – points, as does the observation that every language expresses the unique circumstances to which its speakers have adapted – to a source in the earlier ideas of thinkers like Herder and Humboldt.[2]

Another variant of organicism is seen in the following quotation, from a 2005 press announcement that the US National Endowment for the Humanities (NEH) and National Science Foundation (NSF) would jointly fund a major project to document endangered languages before they became extinct:

> 'This is a rescue mission to save endangered languages', says NEH
> Chairman Bruce Cole ... 'Language is the DNA of a culture, and
> it is the vehicle for the traditions, customs, stories, history, and
> beliefs of a people. A lost language is a lost culture'.
> (www.scienceblog.com/cms/node/7780 [accessed 6 May 2005])

The statement 'language is the DNA of a culture' exemplifies a
discursive move that is becoming increasingly common, and not only
in relation to endangered languages. This move involves recasting
cultural phenomena in biological, typically Darwinian, terms, so that
without anyone actually denying that the issue under discussion is
cultural rather than biological, biology becomes the 'master discourse'.
The implication is that cultural processes work, and can best be
modelled, on the analogy of biological processes. The *Nature* study
reported by CNN, which used 'the same standards applied to bird
and mammal populations' to model 'the threat to the world's 6,800
languages' is one application of this belief.[3] Similarly, the metaphor
'language is the DNA of a culture' seeks to explain the phenomenon of
cultural transmission by analogizing it to the genetic transmission of
traits like eye colour or blood group.

Apart from claiming the authority of modern genetics for an
argument which in essence belongs to the nineteenth century, the
rhetorical effect of Cole's metaphor is to block certain objections to the
organicist view of language and culture. As Lakoff and Johnson have
pointed out, conceptual metaphors work by describing something that
is more difficult to grasp in terms of something that is experientially
and cognitively more 'basic': for instance, temporal phenomena are
often represented using spatial metaphors. The implication of Cole's
metaphor, then, is that genetic transmission via DNA is the prototype
for the cultural transmission of 'traditions, customs, stories, history
and beliefs'. This helps to strengthen the argument that the survival of
a culture's worldview is dependent on the preservation of the language
in which it has traditionally been expressed. No one doubts that DNA
is the only vehicle through which a heritable trait can pass from one
generation to the next. If language stands to cultural inheritance as
DNA stands to the genetic kind, that lends rhetorical force to the
(otherwise disputable) idea that a community's language is the only
vehicle through which new generations can inherit their ancestors'
cultural wisdom.

So far, then, I have suggested that two figures are common
in mainstream discourse on endangered languages. The first is the
metaphor LANGUAGES ARE SPECIES/ENDANGERED LANGUAGES ARE ENDANGERED
SPECIES. The second is more difficult to gloss in this way, for the core
of it could be considered a metonym or synecdoche (substitution of

274

part for whole) rather than a metaphor: in this figure the language of a people stands in for the entire edifice of their culture, their history and their accumulated knowledge, and if the language is lost, the whole edifice is lost. While it might seem that there is some tension between these two ways of figuring endangered languages, one clearly organicist while the other treats languages as cultural phenomena, for various reasons they are not generally apprehended as incompatible. One reason is that both have historical roots in the language ideologies of the nineteenth century: they grew up together, as it were, and have fused into a single package of folk linguistic common sense. Another reason is the discursive tendency to biologize culture itself (which is arguably not new either, but has undoubtedly received a boost from recent advances in genetic and evolutionary science). In any case, it is common to find the two figures juxtaposed without comment in the same piece of discourse, which suggests they are seen as reinforcing rather than contradicting one another.

A good illustration of this comes from the record of an online discussion group hosted by the BBC's website. Below I reproduce two contributions[4]:

> I don't believe in one universal language. We need to preserve cultures that are now dying! Human languages are more threatened than birds and mammals. Many linguists predict that at least half of the world's languages will be dead or dying by the year 2050! Languages are becoming extinct at twice the rate of endangered mammals and four times the rate of endangered birds. If this rate continues, the world of the future could be dominated by a dozen or fewer languages. When you lose a culture your [sic] not only losing humanity. You are losing a unique set of answers to the question of what it means to be human. Language is a main concept in culture.

> Preserving endangered languages is a vital part of securing the culture and heritage of our rich human landscape. Language keeps traditions alive, it inspires knowledge and respect about our past and the planet on which we live, and it links communities across borders and beyond time.
> (www.bbc.co.uk/languages/yoursay/200506/587.shtml   [accessed 28 June 2005])

These writers make no clear separation between biodiversity arguments and cultural preservation arguments. The first writer shifts between the two from sentence to sentence, apparently seeing no need to spell out any logical connection between a statement like 'we need to preserve cultures that are now dying' and the following assertion that 'human languages are more threatened than birds and mammals'. The second writer too weaves bits and pieces of environmentalist discourse into what is basically a plea for 'keeping [cultural] traditions alive', via otherwise unmotivated references to 'landscape' and 'respect about... the planet on which we live'.

These texts also provide some evidence for a claim I made earlier, that in mainstream discourse on language endangerment it is the 'ecologizing' idea of linguistic and cultural diversity as a good in itself that has come to carry most ideological weight: the cry is not 'justice for the X, Y and Z people', but 'protection for our diverse human heritage'. The moral fervour in both cases is directed not to any particular group's unjust situation but to a completely abstract ideal of cultural and linguistic diversity. This abstraction is evident in the terms the two writers use. They refer to 'culture(s)', 'language(s)', 'heritage', 'traditions' and 'communities', but 'people' and 'speakers' are conspicuously absent: the multifarious inhabitants of 'the planet on which we live' have become, ironically, an undifferentiated mass, 'our rich human landscape'. Could these writers give names and geographical locations to any of the groups whose cultures are said to be dying, or to the languages that are threatened with extinction? Could they say anything specific about the cultural traditions they are so eager to preserve, beyond the trite observation that each offers 'a unique set of answers to the question of what it means to be human?' Would their passion for diversity be diminished if, for the sake of argument, they discovered that the traditions in question included slaughtering your tribal enemies and then ritually consuming their flesh, or torturing community members suspected of witchcraft?

Perhaps I had better say that these are hypothetical examples, constructed not in order to argue that some cultures and languages are unworthy to survive, but to call attention to the prevalence of the opposite assumption, that any and every expression of 'what it means to be human' should axiomatically be preserved in the name of 'diversity'. The reified notion of 'culture' in play here is contentless and static: it admits neither the possibility of internal dissent and conflict, nor that of change, except for the kind that is introduced from outside and leads inevitably to the culture's destruction. I was going to write that this conception of culture is 'apolitical', meaning inattentive to the struggles between opposing interests which are part of the history and the current state of any culture; but of course it is far from apolitical. By representing (other people's) cultures and languages in particular ways, commentators like the ones I have quoted in this section are following, whether they know it or not, in the footsteps of earlier language ideologists and verbal hygienists; they are reworking ideas about language and culture whose origins and earlier political applications will bear closer and more critical examination.

Organicism, history and politics

In 1934, a European linguist 'contemplated the possibility that one day all the inhabitants of the earth would speak the same language, perhaps some kind of "Basic English"'. That, he argued, 'would be a great loss to humanity, even if economic and diplomatic communication would be facilitated, for the rich diversity of human cultures would be lost' (Hutton 1999: 4). Seventy years on, these remarks may seem both prophetic and enlightened; but few right-thinking people today would want to be associated with the linguist who made them. His name was Georg Schmidt-Rohr, and he is unfondly remembered now for his scholarly contributions to the 'race science' that flourished in Germany during the Nazi era.[5]

Before I continue, I should make clear that I am not preparing to indict today's language preservationists as fascists. Plainly they are not fascists. But one of the key arguments of Hutton's study *Linguistics and the Third Reich* – my source for the views of Schmidt-Rohr – is that fascists did not invent the connection between language and race, nor distort a previously untainted body of linguistic scholarship with their bizarre racial obsessions. In Hutton's view, the influence ran in the other direction: 'race science took its lead from the study of language' (Hutton 1999: 3). Nazism built on already-established traditions of linguistic thought, and to portray the linguistics of the Third Reich as a wholly aberrant chapter in the discipline's history is to deny the continuing influence of certain ideas on our own ways of thinking. Of linguistics then and now, Hutton observes that:

> Many of its descriptive or methodological principles reflect the politics of European nationalism in the last two centuries. Notions such as 'native speaker' and 'native speaker intuition', 'natural language', 'linguistic system' [and] 'speech community' have their roots in nationalist organicism, and the fundamental vernacularism of linguistics needs to be seen as an ideology with a complex history and real political consequences. That ideology is alive and well today... (1999: 1).

This is the point I want to explore in relation to contemporary concerns about language endangerment.

When Hutton says that 'race science took its lead from the study of language', he is alluding in the first instance to the philological scholarship that followed Sir William Jones's famous observation, made in

1786, that the systematic resemblances among Sanskrit, Greek and Latin suggested all three must share a common ancestor. The comparative-historical method that was subsequently developed, leading to the reconstruction of Proto-Indo-European and the compiling of a detailed genealogy for the Indo-European 'family' (or '[Indo-]Aryan', as it was commonly also called by scholars until 'Aryan' became tainted by its association with the Nazis), was seen from the start as a method for reconstructing the otherwise inaccessible narratives of racial groups. Indeed, for this purpose it was considered both more reliable and more illuminating than archaeology or physical anthropology. Whereas bones or pottery fragments were mute, requiring interpretive leaps on the part of the investigator to tell their stories, linguistic evidence 'spoke' more directly, shedding light not only on the material landscapes inhabited by ancestral peoples, but also on their conceptual universe.

But in using linguistic evidence to write the history of races – their origins, migrations, contacts and conquests – scholars were making assumptions that derived from the language ideologies of nineteenth-century European nationalism. In particular, they were assuming as both a norm and an ideal the organic connection between a people (*Volk*) and its 'mother tongue', a single, natively-acquired vernacular which defined the people as a group and distinguished them from other groups. For Humboldtians, this connection between language and group was not just a matter of 'the A people speak A while the B people speak B', with the difference of language functioning simply to mark the group boundary – a function that could equally well have been fulfilled by the A people speaking C and the B people D. Rather, as noted earlier, a people's native language was considered to be imbued with its history, culture and (national or racial) character. The link between 'being A' and 'speaking the A language' was thus not arbitrary and contingent, but organic and necessary.

It was this aspect of nationalist organicism that was taken up most enthusiastically in Nazi linguistic thought. For Hutton, the most distinctive feature of Nazi language ideology was not racism in and of itself, but the fetish of the mother tongue. Nazis were not linguistic imperialists who sought to impose the German language on other nations – but their rejection of linguistic imperialism was based on racism. The superiority of the German language arose from its expressing the character of a superior race: it followed that far from wanting others to adopt it, the Nazis wanted to restrict its use to those who were truly, that is, racially, German. More generally, their linguistic philosophy was, in Hutton's phrase, 'mother tongue fascism', the view that every people should speak a vernacular to which it was organically linked by ancestry, land and spirit.

278

This view had clear reflexes in Nazi anti-semitism. One of the Jews' offences was that they lacked the organic connection and natural sense of loyalty that in Nazi thought bound every true *Volk* to its ancestral mother tongue. The Jews' deepest linguistic allegiance was to a learned 'father tongue', Hebrew, and they had no vernacular which was uniquely, ancestrally theirs. Yiddish, spoken widely by Jews in some parts of Europe, did not conform to the Nazi ideal of a mother-tongue because of its 'hybrid' character – mixing elements of Germanic, Slavic and Semitic, it broke what for the Nazis was the all-important link between vernacular language and race. So too, in a different way, did the practice of those more assimilated Jews who did not speak Yiddish, but rather adopted the native language of the surrounding speech community. In other words, they claimed as a 'mother tongue' a language which was not 'theirs' by virtue of ancestry and racial character. Hitler himself, in *Mein Kampf*, condemned the use of German as a vernacular among Jews. Since for them German could only be a means of communication, and not an expression of the German racial character which Jews by definition could not possess, their speaking it threatened the integrity of the mother tongue by severing the mechanics of language from the vital – and race-specific – quality of *Geist*.

Yet the same language ideology which licensed this anti-semitism also prompted the Nazis to take positions that would now be considered progressive: they advocated, for instance, the preservation of traditional German dialects under pressure from standardization, and championed the cause of the Celtic languages spoken by oppressed minorities in France and Britain. Schmidt-Rohr was not alone among the linguists and ideologues of the Third Reich in his desire to preserve the 'rich diversity of human cultures', expressed most iconically in their diverse mother tongues.

As I have already said, I do not want to suggest that contemporary movements for endangered language preservation are fascist in character, nor that the cause itself is tainted because it was also espoused by Nazis. However, I do want to argue that contemporary mainstream discourse on language endangerment supports Hutton's contention that 'the ideology [of vernacularism rooted in nationalist organicism] is alive and well today'. I also agree with Hutton that this is properly a matter for critical reflection, since as he says, it has real political consequences, albeit not the same ones it had in 1930s Europe.

It might seem that contemporary discourse on endangered languages has little in common with vernacularist nationalist organicism beyond the organicist notion of languages as living things.

279

To my mind, however, there is a deeper, if less obvious, affinity in the idea of an organic connection between 'being A' and 'speaking A'. Many exhortations to preserve endangered languages depend overtly or covertly on the understanding that a group's mother tongue is not an instrument of communication only, but in Bruce Cole's words, 'the vehicle for the traditions, customs, stories, history, and beliefs of a people'. Of course, it is uncontroversial to suggest that language is the main vehicle through which ideas of all kinds are circulated among members of a group; but this cannot be all that is implied in arguments like Cole's, for if it were, any language adopted by a group to communicate would *ipso facto* take over the function of being a vehicle for the group's ideas. What Cole and others appear to be suggesting is that particular languages are the only authentic vehicles for particular traditions. Similarly, when www.yourdictionary.com asserts (not altogether accurately, but let it pass) that 'all peoples identify their culture... with their languages', it is not simply echoing the modern socio-linguistic axiom that the use of a particular language or variety can index group identity. In the socio-linguistic version, that indexical relationship is neither organic nor fixed for all time: it is not impossible for a group to retain its identity while varying the linguistic resources used to mark it. Thus, for instance, Welsh identity today does not depend on speaking Welsh; it can just as well be marked by speaking English with a Welsh accent. It is also possible for group identity to be maintained in the absence of distinctive linguistic markers, using non-linguistic cultural resources like genealogies, rituals, music or visual art styles. But most rhetoric about endangered languages holds that any shift away from the language of your ancestors must entail a catastrophic loss of identity and culture.

The whole moral force of this kind of preservationist argument lies in the perception of a natural bond between a community and the mother tongue that uniquely expresses its culture and worldview; this natural bond makes the mother tongue's preservation (or in other circumstances, its recognition as a legitimate language and/or its use as a medium of education or official transactions) a natural right. Could any such moral force, even now, become attached to the converse argument that people like the Jews in Nazi Germany or Black South Africans living under apartheid have a natural right to speak, or to be educated in, a language that is not their ancestral mother tongue (and by implication, a right *not* to be defined linguistically and culturally in terms of the ethnic, racial or religious affiliation somebody else considers the most important thing about them)? The question surely does have to be asked, whether behind the organicism and vernacularism of mainstream rhetoric on language endangerment, there lurks something which looks suspiciously like the old concept of the *Volk*, with its at least potentially racial (and racist) overtones.

Volk is a concept we associate strongly with European nationalism (and Nazism), whereas the discourse I have been discussing on endangered languages and cultures seems very markedly a discourse about non-European peoples. One way to get a critical handle on arguments like those examined above is to ask whether it would be plausible, or acceptable, to say the same things about 'us' as are frequently said about 'them'. In many cases, I submit that it would not. For instance, I would be extremely surprised to come across the argument that English culture had essentially been destroyed by the Norman Conquest of 1066, though the effects of Anglo-French contact were great enough to make it possible to argue that English was not the same language afterwards. I would be only a little less surprised to encounter the argument that the people of Britain's Celtic regions, where today very few people acquire Celtic languages as their mother-tongues and many do not speak a Celtic language at all, have on that account lost any connection to the 'traditions, customs, stories, history, and beliefs' of the Irish, Gaels, Welsh, Cornish or Manx. Of course that is not to say that they are still living the lives of their ancestors, but in these cases we do not have any difficulty grasping that 'cultures' are dynamic and syncretic.

I am suggesting, then, that as well as a vernacularist nationalist organicist strain, there is an exoticizing or 'orientalist' strain in some preservationist rhetoric. Arguably, too, this both reinforces and is reinforced by the paralleling of endangered languages and endangered species. Though I have already said I think the roots of the LANGUAGES ARE SPECIES metaphor lie elsewhere – it is not about dehumanizing speakers by comparing them to exotic animals, but rather about attributing animacy to languages – I do think this metaphor contributes to, or at least does nothing to deter, the implicit exoticism of images like 'our rich human landscape', and more generally, the discursive depoliticization of preservation and revitalization movements.

This depoliticization is accomplished not only by making 'languages' (and other abstractions such as 'cultures' and 'traditions') more salient in discourse than human beings, but also by portraying (certain) human beings as lacking all agency and choice. One variant of that portrayal is seen in Bruce Cole's description of the NEH/NSF documentation project as 'a rescue mission', to be carried out, as he goes on to say, 'with the aid of modern technology and these federal funds'. This is a picture of concerned and enlightened westerners doing their bit to help the less fortunate, who are not apparently doing much to help themselves. Certainly you would not know from most mainstream

281

media coverage that many struggles around language are intimately linked to other political struggles for, say, land rights, compensation for past injustices, the withdrawal of military or corporate forces from indigenous lands, or political independence.

Another variant makes Westerners the villains rather than the heroes, but this move depends on the presupposition that if a community is shifting away from its ancestral mother tongue, this can only be a course of action forced upon it by outsiders against its will. Nettles and Romaine (2000), for instance, refer to the case of Taiap, a language spoken only in the remote village of Gapun in Papua New Guinea, where it is now yielding increasingly to the national language Tok Pisin. The implication of their remarks is that Gapuners would preserve Taiap if they had any real choice in the matter. But Kulick's detailed ethnographic study of language shift in Gapun (Kulick 1992) makes clear that the situation is more complex. While the villagers made no deliberate decision to abandon Taiap, and sometimes expressed regret that children did not seem to be learning it any more, they clearly had made other choices that significantly contributed to this outcome, embracing for instance the Christian religion, money and the goods it could be exchanged for, schooling and schooled literacy, and the goal of economic and social 'development' – all of which favoured the increased use of Tok Pisin. Even though they did not foresee the linguistic effects, it is clear from Kulick's account that the villagers would not now be willing to repudiate these innovations in exchange for Taiap's survival. Of course it would be wrong to suggest that Gapuners had a 'free' choice about these things, or that they made their choices on the proverbial 'level playing field'. Nevertheless, it is inaccurate to represent them as lacking *any* choice or agency. They were and are (just as we Westerners were and are) in the situation described by Marx's axiom that '[humans] make their own history, but not in circumstances of their own choosing'.

The defence of diversity and the horror of homogenization

In my book *Verbal Hygiene* I suggested that evaluative discourse on language has 'a moral dimension that goes far beyond its overt subject to touch on deep desires and fears' (Cameron 1995: xiii). Hutton argues that Nazi mother-tongue fascism was animated by a 'horror of assimilation': what animates today's concerns about language endangerment and 'death' might be thought of as a 'horror of homogenization', rooted, as were the Nazis' fears, in contemporary geopolitical realities.

282

One of those realities may be, in fact, the political shadow that the Third Reich still casts over Western democracies. The cultivation of more positive attitudes towards diversity (or what we now call 'multiculturalism') is part of a liberal consensus which was constructed at least partly in opposition to fascism: the rainbow flag represents, among other things, a symbolic rejection of the swastika. But probably a more important contemporary reality is the anxiety prompted by globalization. 'Globalization' is a shorthand term for a complex set of processes, any and all of which may be apprehended as threatening for a variety of reasons; but it is often figured discursively as a single, unified force whose aim and effect is to *homogenize* – to destroy long-established traditions and flatten out what is locally distinctive, imposing on everyone the same values, economic disciplines and political systems (in most versions of this story, these are essentially the values/disciplines/systems of western and especially US neo-liberalism). 'Diversity', signifying the opposite of homogenization, becomes a code-word or condensation symbol for everything globalization is felt to threaten.

The unease globalization generates could be compared with the kind of fear which in Cohen's classic account of moral panic gets projected on to the figure of the 'folk-devil'. In the globalization case, however, where the threat cannot be seen to emanate from some demonized representative of an 'underclass' (cf. such classic 'folk devils' as the juvenile delinquent and the mugger), anxiety is projected in a different way – not by scapegoating the 'enemy within', but by idealizing a more remote Other whose way of life, unlike ours, remains untouched and pristine, and then projecting on to that Other our own feelings of threat, loss, and guilt. The result is a discourse exhorting others to resist the forces to which we have already capitulated, and promising our support for that resistance. But it surely needs to be asked just whose anxieties are being assuaged by this gesture. Like the villagers of Gapun, we Westerners have embraced at least some aspects of globalization with enthusiasm rather than reluctance; we have integrated them into our culture, and would resist any proposal to return to the *status quo ante*.[6] So, when we represent other people's cultures and languages as being 'destroyed' by contact with the modern, globalized world, are we defending their real, self-defined interests, or are we objectifying their 'traditions' and their 'diversity' to serve our own?

I do not intend that question to be purely rhetorical: on the contrary, I think it is a real question which needs to be posed, and then answered, in relation to each particular case. Language preservation and revitalization movements, like all verbal hygiene movements, have

283

their own specific histories and political contexts; as other contributors to this volume show clearly, the interests at stake are not always and everywhere the same. Preservationist struggles may, indeed, be part of a broad popular movement serving the causes of equality and justice; they may also be motivated by exclusionary ethnic nationalism, or strategically appropriated by local vested interests in a bid to consolidate their own position. But the 'ecologizing' discourse I have examined in this chapter does not make such distinctions: culture becomes a branch of nature, and local political interests are subsumed into a global celebration of 'diversity'. What this obscures, paradoxically, is the diversity and complexity of the concrete situations in which endangered language speakers find themselves.

References

Bell, A. (1991), *The Language of News Media*. Oxford: Blackwell
Cameron, D. (1995). *Verbal Hygiene*. London: Routledge
Cohen, S. (2002), *Folk Devils and Moral Panics* (3rd edn). London: Routledge.
Galtung, J. and Ruge, M. H. (1965), 'The structure of foreign news'. *Journal of Peace Research*, 1, 64–91.
Hutton, C. (1999), *Linguistics and the Third Reich: Mother-tongue Fascism, Race and the Science of Language*. London: Routledge.
Kulick, D. (1992, *Language Shift and Cultural Reproduction: Self, Society and Syncretism in a Papua New Guinea Village*. Cambridge: Cambridge University Press.
Lakoff, G. and Johnson, M. (1980), *Metaphors We Live By*. Chicago: University of Chicago Press.
Milroy, J. (1992), *Language Variation and Change*. Oxford: Blackwell.
Nettles, D. and Romaine, S. (2000), *Vanishing Voices: The Extinction of the World's Languages*. Oxford: Oxford University Press.
Phillipson, R., Skutnabb-Kangas, T. and Rannut, M. (eds). (1994), *Linguistic Human Rights*. Berlin: de Gruyter.
Rivenburgh, N. (2004), 'Do we really understand the issue? Media coverage of endangered languages'. Paper delivered to the International Conference on Communication and Cultural Diversity at the Barcelona 2004 Universal Forum of Cultures, www.aiic.net/ViewPage.cfm/page1512.htm.

Other web sources

'Extinction fear for languages', CNN. Available (22 May 2003) at www.cnn.com/2003/TECH/science/05/22/extinct.language/
'Endangered languages'. Available at www.yourdictionary.com/elr/
'Agencies partner to document endangered languages', Science Blog. Available (6 May 2005) at www.scienceblog.com/cms/node/7780

'Languages more threatened than mammals', BBC Languages: Your Say. Available (28 June 2005) at www.bbc.co.uk/languages/yoursay/200506/587. shtml

Notes

1 Since my intention is to question the discourse these terms belong to, I had originally planned to put them in scare quotes whenever I was obliged to use them. In the end I decided not to, because the visual effect was so tiresome; but I hope readers will mentally supply the necessary note of caution or scepticism.

2 Humboldt was an influence on Sapir, but the 'hypothesis of linguistic relativity' is not a straightforward continuation of the same line of thought. Putting it somewhat crudely, while Sapir and Whorf would surely have agreed that language functioned among other things as a channel for the intergenerational transmission of certain ways of seeing the world, for them that was only the logical consequence of the thesis they were most interested in, namely that the structures found in a particular language will unconsciously influence the perceptions of its speakers. As inheritors (unlike Humboldt) of Saussure's doctrine that the sign was arbitrary, and of his separation between synchronic and diachronic analysis, they did not treat the structures in question as direct embodiments or reflections of the historical experience of the ancestral speech community.

3 Another example is the concept of the 'meme', a unit of ideation or meaning which is treated as the cultural analogue of Richard Dawkins's 'selfish gene'. Enthusiasts of the meme are not claiming ideas are life forms, but they are suggesting that the behaviour of ideas can most fruitfully be studied using theories and methods derived from modern genetic science.

4 The second extract's origin is likely to be more complicated, since it can be found on at least one other URL (www.un.org/works/culture/).

5 I stop short of describing Schmidt-Rohr baldly as a Nazi, because there is some disagreement about the depth of his allegiance to National Socialism; he seems to have been fundamentally a conservative rather than a fascist, and his writings on race and language were once denounced as 'Jewish effusions' by a more fanatical linguist, Edgar Glässer, who did not think them racist enough.

6 For instance, what is currently thought of as a normal and desirable way of life among British people (including many who voice anti-globalization sentiments ranging from conservative opposition to immigration and the EU to more 'progressive' worries about Third-World sweatshops and environmental degradation) would be profoundly impoverished in most people's view if it did not encompass such recent innovations as affordable international travel, the Internet and other modern communications technologies, the right to work or own property in other EU countries, imported food and (non-British) ethnic restaurants.

Index

Aboriginal languages 39, 42, 43, 45
Acadia 99–120
Act for the English Order, Habit and Language 150–1
Adams, G.Brendan 162
Adamson, Ian 162–3, 164
affect, affectivity 80, 87, 89, 92, 94
Althusser, Louis 78
Anderson, Benedict 244
anglicisation 149, 150–8, 160–1
anthropologist 3, 7
anthropology 150
anti-semitism 279
apartheid 280
Association of Academies of the Spanish Language (AALE) 249
attitude 83, 84, 88–9, 91, 93–4
authenticity 59, 64–5, 67, 68–70
authority 64–6

Bakhtin, Mikhail 171, 187, 189,
Basque Country 244, 256, 258
Belfast 157–9, 164
Belfast Agreement, The 149, 160–2, 164
Bello, Andrés 260
Bilingual Education Act of 1968 199
bilingualism 151
biology, as 'master discourse' 274, 285n.
bioprospecting 19
Blommaert, Jan 58, 169, 170–1, 175
boundaries 4, 59, 67, 73, 233–5
Boas, Franz 2
Bourdieu, Pierre 256
Britain 150, 156–7, 159, 160, 163
  British Government 149, 156, 159, 160–1, 164, 165–6
  British language 163

British North America (BNA) Act 40, 41
Britonnic 163
Britons 163
Bucholtz, Mary 57
Bunreacht na hÉireann (Constitution of Ireland) 155–6
Butler, Judith 171, 177–8, 181

Canadian Aboriginal Languages Foundation 42
Canadian Heritage Languages Institute 42
capital (cultural, symbolic) 121, 123, 125, 128, 143
Catalonia 244, 256, 258
catholicism 151, 154, 156, 158
Céitinn Seathrún (Geoffrey Keating) 151
Celtic languages 279, 280, 281
Celts 154
censuses 158, 165
centralization 217–19
centrifugal voice(s) 187–9, 192
centripetal voice(s) 187–9, 192
Cervantes Institute 243, 255, 256
Chavez, Linda 200, 202
citizenship 157, 161
codification 217
Cohen, Stanley 269, 283
colonialism 5, 8, 11, 38, 150–3, 155, 161, 166
  anti-colonialism 150, 153, 156, 166
  British 149, 150, 155
  English 149, 150, 151, 154, 164
  decolonising discourse 159, 160
  decolonization 47
  linguistic colonialism 151, 163
  post-colonialism 11
Comiti, Jean-Marie 70

complaint tradition 250
compulsory English 157
compulsory Irish 156–8
consensus 253, 257–8, 261
construction of scientific knowledge
      77–80, 82, 91–2, 97
Crowley, Tony 151, 153
Crystal, David 61
Cuervo, Rufino J. 245, 246
culture 189–190
   cultural difference 150
   cultural diversity 164, 165
   cultural ecology 150
   cultural hegemony 154, 155
   cultural heritage 2, 64
   cultural homogeneity 149, 150
   Cultural Traditions Group 164
Cumann Chluain Ard 157

Daunt, William J. 153
Davis, Thomas 153
democracy 218
Di Meglio, Alain 70
dialect 152, 162–3, 165, 216–17
dialectology 79, 80, 82, 85
diglossia 76, 81–2, 84–5, 89, 91
Dinneen, Rev. 154
discourse community 243, 256–7, 261
discrimination 228–33
diversity 4
   biodiversity 2, 14, 15–18, 31, 44, 48
   cultural diversity 164, 165
   linguistic diversity 2, 5, 149, 150,
      162, 164
   as political value 276, 283–4
   U.S. linguistic diversity 206
documentation 60, 63, 66, 67, 70, 72
Downing Street Declaration 160

ecology 62, 66, 68, 72
education 156–7, 158
elite 218, 221, 233–4
empire 10, 244, 246, 249
endangered language(s) 35, 47, 48
England, Nora 61
English
   de-Anglicization 154
   English as language of commerce,
      opportunity and power 152

English First (US) 199
English language 150, 152, 153, 154,
      156, 159, 161, 165
English Language Amendment (US)
      198
English Only 198, 250
Englishness 151
environmentalism 15, 27–32
erase/erasure 249, 258
essentialism 11, 37, 45
   essentializing discourses 57, 62, 63,
      66, 73
   essentializing languages 7
   non-essentializing discourses 57,
      73
   linguistic essentialism 37
   strategic essentialism 62
European Charter for Regional or
      Minority Languages 164
European Union 181–2
expert discourse 3
Fichte, Johann Gottlieb 153
Foundation for Endangered Languages
      61
Framework Document 160
Francoprovençal 76, 83

Gaelic
   Gaelic culture 151, 152
   Gaelic language 149, 151, 152, 153,
      154, 155, 163, 165, *see also* Irish
      language
   Gaelic League (Conradh na Gaeilge)
      153–5
   Gaelic Revival 153, *see also* Irish
      language revival
   Gaelic social order 151
   Gaels 154
   Gaeltacht 158
Galicia 244, 256, 258
Galtung, Johan & Ruge, Mari H 268
García Márquez, Gabriel 259
Gauchat, Louis 79–80, 94
genealogy 151
German Romanticism 152–3
   globalization 10–11, 24–28, 150,
      216–20, 221–6, 283–4, 285n
globalized new economy 5, 6, 10
Gramsci, Antonio 243, 257

Habermas, Jürgen 243, 253
Hans Rausing Endangered Languages
    Project 60
Hayakawa, Senator S.I. 198–9, 201
hegemony 243, 257
    English language 203–4
Heller, Monica 24–25, 169
Henry VIII 150
Herder, Johann Gottfried 153
heritage 77, 79–80, 82–3, 94–5
Hewitt, John 162
Hiberno-English 167
Hill, Jane 19, 61
Hispanismo 244, 245, 246, 249
Hispanofonía 243ff, 256, 258, 263
historiography 151
homogeneity 10
Honig, Bonnie 209–11
Human Genome Project 20
Humboldt, Wilhelm von 153, 273, 278,
    285n
Huntington, Samuel P 201
Hutton, Christopher 11, 277, 278, 279,
    282
Hyde, Douglas 154
Hyltenstam, Kenneth 173, 178–9

identity 57–9, 61, 63–5, 69, 71, 73, 82,
    84, 91, 93–4, 152, 158–9, 160–3,
    165–7, 216, 224–5, 230–1, 233
    cultural identity 150–1, 158, 163,
        164, 167
    national identity 150, 152, 153, 154,
        156, 159, 161, 163–4, 164, 169,
        176
    political identity 150, 157, 160, 161,
        164
ideologies 3, 4, 58, 62, 64, 65, 66, 67,
    69, 70, 72, 73, 171
    language 4, 8, 244, 261, 263
    bilingualism 104
    dialect 106, 111–14
    language ideological debates 169
    monolingualism 105
    standard 105, 114–16
imagined community 189, 244
imperialism 151
Indian Act 40, 41
Indigenous people 18–23, 26–32

Indigenous language(s) 6, 35, 36, 37
Indigenous rights 44
inequalities 11
interdisciplinarity 83–4
International Conference on the
    Spanish Language 247, 255,
    259
interpellation 181–2
Ireland 149, 150–8, 160, 161, 163, 166
    Irish Government 149, 155–6, 158,
        160–1, 166
    Irish language 149, 150–9, 160–1,
        165–6, *see also* Gaelic
    Irish language movement 155,
        157–8
    Irish Language Revival 158, 159–60,
        see also Gaelic Revival
    Irish Language Society 152
    Irish Republican Movement 159,
        160–2
Irvine, Judith 170
iterability 177–8

Jaffe, Alexandra 67, 72

King Juan Carlos I of Spain 258, 261
Krauss, Michael 173, 178
Kulick, Don 282

Lakoff, George & Johnson, Mark 272,
    274
language
    abolition 150
    activism 58, 59, 63
    death 150
    dominant 8
    endangerment 35, 36, 37, 39, 43, 51,
        52
    language-as-code 61, 66, 67, 70
    marginalized 8
    policy 5, 77, 81–4, 93, 95
    professionals 128, 129, 130, 131, 139,
        143,
    revitalization 39, 51
    and spirituality 45, 46
Latin 151
language ideologies 4, 8, 244, 261, 263
legitimation 58, 59, 62, 63, 64, 65, 72
linguistic

conflict 81, 92
discrimination 157
homogeneity 149, 150
market 91, 94
variability 57, 71, 72
linguists 3, 7
Llengua pròpia 'one's own language'
123–4, 134–5, 139, 148

Maguire, Gabrielle 157
Mål i mun 170, 175, 182–92
Marcellesi, Jean-Baptiste. 65, 71, 72
May, Stephen 180
metaphor 61, 66, 68, 184–6, 188–91,
272, 274–5, 281
migrant 123, 125, 135, 140–1, 224–6,
228, 232, 235
and language 210–12
and U.S. national identity 210–12
minorities 5, 6, 216, 217, 222, 228
ethnic 149
immigrants 9
indigenous 9
national 36
Mission civilisatrice 6, 247
mixed codes 64, 67, 71, 73
modernity 11, 25–6, 29
monolingualism 150, 151
moral panic 4, 269, 283
Morris, H. 154
'Mother-tongue fascism' 278
Mufwene, Salikoko 30
Mühlhäusler, Peter 68
multilingualism 187, 189, 192

nation state 3, 10, 187–8
national language 9, 155–7
National Science Foundation 59, 61
nationalism 11, 58, 59, 64, 150, 153,
155, 158, 163–4, 271, 273, 278
Spanish nationalism 122, 126, 127,
130, 134, 141–2, 144, 148
Ulster nationalism 163–4
Irish Nationalism 153, 157, 161–3,
165, 166
nationality 152–3, 155–6, 157, 161,
163–4
native speakers 121, 125, 128, 139,
140–4, 148

Nazism 11, 271, 277–81, 282–3, 285n
Nettles, Daniel & Romaine, Suzanne
270, 282
'No Child Left Behind' Act of 2002
(U.S.) 199
noble savage 27
non-governmental organizations 1, 6,
7, 23–6
Northern Ireland 149, 156–9, 160–5

Ó Bruadair, Dáibhí (David O' Bruadair)
151
Ó Conaire, Breadàn 154
Ó Cuív, Brian 152
Ó Rathaille, Aodhagáin (Egan
O'Rahilly) 151
O'Connell, Daniel 153
O'Leary, Philip 154
O'Reilly, Camille 159, 160
Oakes, Leigh 169
Ochs, Eleanor 67
"Official English" Movement (U.S.) 198
Old British 163
oral history 46
order 217–19
orientalism 281
Ottavi, Pascal 58

Parnell, Charles Stuart 153
participant constellation 126–8, 130,
139
Pearse, Patrick 153–4
performativity 171, 177
Phillipson, Robert 169, 173, 178
philology, philologist 121, 125, 128,
129, 143, 144, 239, 273, 278
polynomie, polynomic 57, 65, 67,
70–3
Pratt, Larry 200
prescriptivism 250, 261
proscriptivism 150
Protestantism 151, 156
public space 218, 22–5, 227, 228, 233
public sphere (linguistic) 243, 253ff,
257, 263–4
purism 59, 63–7
purity 4, 219–20

Quebec 38, 43, 44, 45

Race
    Race and language 271, 273, 277–83
    racial identity 154
recognition 71–73
Religion 154, 157, 218, 224, 228,
    231, 233 *see also* Catholicism;
    Protestantism
Renan, Ernest 263
resistance 64, 67, 72
revitalization projects 21
Revolution 216–17
Rights 58, 59, 60, 62, 63, 70, 71
    language rights 35, 149, 156, 159–60,
        160–4, 166
    human rights 5, 160
    civil rights 157–9, 165
Rivenburgh, Nancy 268–9, 270–1
Robinson, Philip 165
Rodriguez, Richard 202
Roman Imperial linguistic practice 151
Romand Switzerland 76, 80, 83

Sapir 2
Sapir-Whorf hypothesis 2, 273, 285n
School 7, 234–5
    school and patois 77, 82, 84–5, 89,
        91, 93–4
    homogeneous schools, Acadia and
        Nova Scotia 102, 106–7
Scotland 164
    Scots 164
    Scottish Planters 163
Sinn Féin 159
social cohesion 187, 189, 192
social Darwinism 154
social order 4
Spanish Royal Academy (RAE) 243,
    247, 249ff
Speech community 60, 65, 69, 122 123,
    125, 128, 131
Spelling 220
Spenser, Edmund 151
Spivak, Gayatri Chakravorty 62
sustainability 26–9
Sweden 169–92
    Swedish language 169–92
Swiss interactionist and
    microlinguistic model 81

symbolic dominance and linguistic
    insecurity 105

Taiap language 282
Tanton, John 199
Teilifís na Gaeilge 161
Teleman, Ulf 172, 174, 178–9, 188–9
Thomas, Daniel 152
Tocqueville, Alexis de 206–7

U.S. English 199–200
Ullans 165, *see also* (Ulster Lallans)
Ulster 163, 165
    Ulster English 162, 163, 164
    Ulster Gaelic 163
    Ulster identity 163–4
    Ulster Unionism 157, 162, 166
    Ulster-Scots 149, 162–6, 166
    Ulster-Scots Academy 165
    Ulster-Scots Language Movement
        164–5
    Ulster-Scots Language Society/Ulstèr-
        Scotch Leid Society 164–6
UNESCO 1, 6, 7, 35, 44, 47, 48, 62
unification 216
United Nations 24
unity 220–4
universalism 218, 225, 227, 236
Urla, Jacqueline 68

Valera, Juan 245, 246
variety 219, 222, 223, 229
verbal hygiene 242, 249, 250, 257, 261,
    263
vernacular language 152
Verscheuren, Jeff 58
voice 171
Voting Rights Act of 1965 (US) 198

Watts, Richard 243, 257
'We' 131, 132, 133, 134, 136, 138,
    142,
Westman, Margareta 174, 179, 188–9
Williams, Raymond 15, 18, 23–6, 32
Wolin, Sheldon 207–9
Woodbury, Anthony 69
World Acadian Congress 07
Wright, Joseph 162

Lightning Source UK Ltd.
Milton Keynes UK
02 October 2009

144414UK00001B/42/P